THE
VALLIAN TRILOGY

THE
VALLIAN TRILOGY

An Inventive Life

Part II: The Learner

ooooo

LARRY E. WAHL

2012

River Sanctuary
PUBLISHING

The Vallian Trilogy: An Inventive Life Part II: The Learner

Cover Illustrations by Larry E. Wahl
Cover Design by Jessica Moreno

Also by Larry Wahl:

> The Vallian Trilogy: An Inventive Life. Part I: The Engineer
> The Tesseract: The Path Through Optical Illusions
> The Elephant in the Room
> *Coming in 2013:*
> The Vallian Trilogy: An Inventive Life. Part III: The Zen
> Connection

Printed in the United States of America
ISBN 978-1-935914-18-1

RIVER SANCTUARY PUBLISHING
P.O Box 1561
Felton, CA 95018
www.riversanctuarypublishing.com
Dedicated to the awakening of the New Earth

To order additional copies please visit:
www.riversanctuarypublishing.com

Acknowledgements

I want to thank all participants, living and dead, who made this book—and the subsequent books—possible. Special thanks go to Maria Loeffler and Ken Habeeb for their inspiring suggestions, to Pat McCarthy and Tereza McNamee for being our cheerleaders, and to our dear friends and supporters, The Wagner family. Special thanks to Eric Wahl for allowing the reproduction of his poetry. And finally, to my editor—she knows who she is—my eternal gratitude.

LEW/LXV 2012

A nd so it is only in the embracing of our torn self, only in the acceptance that there is nothing "wrong" with feeling "torn," that one can hope for whatever healing is available and thus can become as "whole" as possible.

E. Kurtz and K. Ketchem (1992)
The Spirituality of Imperfection

Contents

Prologue

By Sharon Wahl, 2012

L arry Wahl was born Frederick George Mescher in St. Helens, Oregon on October 5, 1927 at 0415 to Ira and Gertrude Mescher—he claims this early birth time is why he is a night person. We know little about his father, except that Larry has memories of a kind, gentle, quiet man who loved to build things. But he knows much more about his mother, the first six years of which he spent with her in various locations and with men other than his kind, gentle, quiet father. We even have a picture of Gertrude.

Gertrude Pflieger ~1933

In Part I of the Vallian Trilogy, several Chapters are dedicated to his first six years, with and without father Ira, and include a stay at one of

Al Capone's brothel hotels in Chicago (mother Gertrude was supposedly one of Capone's bookkeepers). Several years followed in the desolate Portland, Oregon Italian/Jewish ghetto with hated, brutal stepfather Tony Scrano, a reject from Capone's "family." As the consequence of a severe accident, little Freddy was removed from the Scrano household, found himself first in the Beaverton Baby Home for abandoned children and then as a potentially adoptable orphan at Providence Academy in Vancouver, Washington in the company of 200 Catholic nuns—the Sisters of Providence. Larry contends that his mother would have left Tony sooner or later, taking his infant half-sister, Anna Mae; however, an unexpected and serious event involving Larry precipitated that move.

For the next 3 years, Freddy Mescher existed at Providence as the only orphan. The orphanage component of Providence had been disbanded several years earlier to become a boarding grade school for boys and girls and a high school for girls. In this environment, Larry (as Freddy) began the healing of the traumas inflicted on him in Chicago and the ghetto, found the resources to satisfy an insatiable curiosity about life and how things worked, developed some sociability, and was exposed to some wonderful, caring teachers and mother figures in the nuns. He met with his biological mother one last time through the auspices of a family friend and was then forever separated from his own kith and kin as she gently told him goodbye. At 9 he went to live with the Wahls—acquiring determinedly dysfunctional new families—and at 10 was formally adopted by Gene and Macie Wahl, after a brief, vaguely remembered encounter with his father, whom he had not seen since he was about 18 months old, the father who signed away his son to well-meaning strangers.

So in 1937, his name became Frederick Eugene Wahl, though his adopted mother never changed his birth certificate. In 1976, Larry tried to update his birth certificate, but without the signature of a mentally disturbed Macie, it ended up with yet another name: Larry Eugene Mescher. Since Larry never liked the name Frederick, soon after graduating from high school, he visited a banished uncle in San Francisco and embraced this uncle's name: Larry. Then, and now, he was/is Larry Eugene Wahl—his daughter and I had to vouch for him when he was getting a passport, verifying who he was. Social Security was another hassle.

But I digress. After his adoption—though he never really adjusted to being a member of the Wahl family—he did flourish, in a manner of speaking. He developed a gang of friends—he claims they were misfits like him—and he pursued his one goal in life: learning everything about everything!! Books were his lifeline, libraries his most revered institutions, and schools embedded in his mind the means to learn what he wanted to learn, to educate himself, even though his curriculum was seldom on the schools' agendas.

Learning was his savior. Larry's IQ was very high, but his SQ (social quotient) was not yet well developed. Lacking much in the way of strong, positive, sane male role models, Larry relied on his intellect and innate curiosity to bring him through the early traumas and later ordeals of his fragmented life. While it took a lot of learning to bring him where he is today, his accomplishments are monumental, the latest being a patent on the 4th dimension. Thus, Part II of the Vallian Trilogy is called "The Learner," and for good reason, though perhaps it should be called "The Savior." We invite you along for a perplexing, and at times, unbelievable continuing journey of the life of Frederick George Mescher, AKA Frederick Eugene Wahl, AKA Larry Eugene Mescher, AKA Larry E. Wahl, AKA Lewis X. Vallian.

Forward and Backward

This second book is written to describe the path I took to becoming a geometer, but it is not dedicated to engineers, mathematicians, geometers, or even so-called business types and computing gurus. It is dedicated to a very large group of misfits who, through their incredible suffering, confusion, and pain, have served their country and their fellow man as faithfully and honorably as any recipient of medals of war.

For these thousands of individuals, their service did not end with an honorable discharge and a chance to go home and restart their lives. For them, every year following their service was a continuing, never ending litany of misery, night sweats, and soul wrenching nightmares. (I hope the government will be wise enough, after this current "rack" of wars, to more effectively rehabilitate their veterans.) They were ordered to self-destruct: by suicide, by murder, by accident. Their histories were all soft-copy and top secret; they and their histories were buried in "black operations." There would never be anyone to take specific responsibility for what grotesque forces and black inhumanity they suffered.

The Army, Navy, Air Force, and Marines all recruited them, but when they were identified as not fitting the general requirements of a given service, these folks were routinely utilized—often without their knowledge—as a kind of experimental human clay. Military and civilian doctors, statisticians, and researchers could medicate and mold them into precise little research groups to plumb the limits of human endurance, assessing their tolerance of pain, physical and mental. These special training units could bludgeon their charges' psyches and physical resources until, depleted and helpless, they were dumped back into the workaday world. And they would re-enter this world devoid of any semblance of self-respect, with gaps covering multiple years that remained unexplained and unavailable for examination. Self-loathing and shame produced an unconscious death wish so that the terrible nightmares, sweats, and bleeding of the human spirit might end in blissful nothingness.

These, then, are the individuals to whom this book is dedicated. A majority of them are long since dead; the few remaining wish they had died. Usually they only escaped because of intensive, exhaustive therapy and/or the committed courage of a friend or lover. With this Herculean lifesaving effort, some few of us were restored and reborn reasonably sane and, thankfully, whole.

Lest the reader think that I am un-American, let me hasten to say that in the final analysis, I believe that this is the greatest nation that has ever been. It is precisely because of its many shortcomings—which will not and cannot be illuminated—that it is so great. Murder, assassination, greed, treachery, and mayhem have been around since the beginning of time. No nation can refute any of these evils present in their structures.

What makes this country so great and so indomitable is that it standardizes, generalizes, and capitalizes on every virtue and every vice with blind equanimity. It takes every honest/dishonest, practical/impractical, brilliant/harebrained idea instantly to fruition with a kind of assembly-line zeal. The code of free speech definitely means that you can—and are expected to—fool all of the people at least part of the time.

Naturally such a country, like every other in recorded history, produces victims using the very system set up to protect them from being victimized. Eggs are scrambled to make an omelet; citizens are scrambled to make political or military advancements. Means are forever justifying the ends. Just as some of the ends are tragic, so are some of the means. Thus every system, for its greater perceived good, produces a certain amount of victims and a certain amount of survivors.

I am proud to be one of such survivors. I am fully aware that anyone who is entangled in the webs of State secrecy, black operations, and paramilitary functions uneasily rides a very hungry tiger. Statistically improbable as such survival has been for a multitude of hapless citizens, I am encouraged to describe my own journey in order to sing the praises of these innocent pawns and define the soul-less treachery that gave us a derisive and collective code name: We were, and are, proudly defiant to accept being called ... "The Garbage."

Intro: The Ten Lost Years

By Sharon Wahl

One of the most endearing, but also most exasperating, qualities of Larry is his almost total inability to put his life events into any chronological order. His memories tend to be episodic rather than ordered logically on a time line. This is especially true for the 10 to 13 years between the end of high school in Vancouver, Washington and his employment at Saint Vincent's Hospital in Portland, Oregon—when he met me, and I kept the records of our life together, more or less. In retrospect, I'm not sure how good of a job I've done. My memory is also deficient, but differently deficient. While he now seems to save everything—string too short to use, pens out of ink, multiple copies of most of his writing and art—we have little documentation to lock in a specific time line for his late teens and 20s. What we have consists of a motley collection: a few pay stubs; ship "articles"; a birth notice of his first child, Penny; hospital bills from his second damaged child, Kathy; voluntary mental commitment papers; a dated article he wrote for the Vancouver newspaper; even a handwritten resume apparently done when applying for a security job at North American Aviation, which may or may not have been chronologically accurate. He also brought with him a picture of his beautiful, but misguided mother and a work permit of Tony Scrano's in which he claimed 3 dependents in 1933. In addition, we have done considerable research about the death of Sister Ursula; the fire at the lumber yard that put him in the ghetto at ~ 18 months old (these are included in the first book of this series); the Vanport, Oregon flood where he and his first wife lost their home; the year that Uncle Al (Capone) was incarcerated; a news report about the typhoon off Guam when he was sailing; a web site excerpt about the Pandora Box murder in which the mother of one of his close school friends was murdered by the father; and an article about the Battleship Oregon. We even acquired his grade reports from Providence Academy and photographs of some of his teachers at Columbia Prep (also in Book I). But in gathering this information, we found some errors in the data as reported by others. This did not help our quest!

We have tried to piece together a time line for those years and to validate his childhood memories, but so much information is just not available and what is, is subject to his unusual method of storing memories. Of course there is the total lack of a CIA paper trail. Actually he was "employed" there when it was undergoing a messy transition from the OSS (Office of Special Services) to the CIA, which further complicated his "paperwork."

Larry describes those missing years in the following flow of consciousness:

- First ship sailed on was the Marine Fox out of San Francisco; met AB's Bill and Scotty Minford; stayed in Oahu, Hawaii for two weeks

- To Guam on Marine Fox; Scotty and I went ashore, got shot at, picked up by pissed lieutenant, and taken back to landing and guard station

- Survived typhoon off Guam; to Saipan; and then to hospital aboard the Marine Fox

- Back to US; to Letterman General; cured and discharged; to Oakland during general strike in Oakland; to Red Cross and got apartment with Jess and Tom

- To Wilmington, CA to meet Ann Dempsey; met Toby and Faye Marshall

- In Wilmington met Dorothy and Lois Dixon

- To Aunt and Uncle Cecile's farm; "chicken wringing"; married Dorothy

- Moved to Long Beach, Washington for honeymoon; joined by Don Douglas

- Into cartooning with Don doing the drawing and me, the continuity (sending off to publishers); No joy

- Moved to Vancouver; worked in the Vancouver Shipyard

- To Portland; went to work for American Can Company as a line inspector
- Moved Dorothy, Don, and me to Vanport, OR; Don and I split up
- Vanport flooded; moved back to Vancouver
- Penny born; decided to sail again; to Guam on A.E. Anderson; worked at Camp One—J.H. Pomeroy Construction (CIA)
- With Dorothy moved to Sunnydale, CA, housing project in San Francisco; worked for 3 Theatres in S.F.
- Job in Oakland with General Petroleum and The Bear
- Kathy born at Bess Kaiser in Oakland with myelomeningocele; stayed till Kathy stabilized
- Got next ship out of SF, Marine Wolf; Guam again (CIA?), dream ship, strange crew
- Got ship out of Portland; P&T Navigator through canal to East Coast; three-month trip up East River to West Point; ports various
- Moved to Sunnyvale by myself; worked for post office
- Off and on, somewhere in this time period, several undocumented trips abroad for CIA
- To work for Westinghouse; there two years; did complete map of plant; many adventures; Ed Bent came up from LA to revamp the safety department, no one kept track of me, so probably some assignments for CIA
- Kathy died; had a mental breakdown; to Agnews for four months; visits from Nita; lodged in the club house with Mickey Cohen, who taught me tennis; worked on "The Agnewsette" as artist for work therapy; visited by Wes Townsend, classmate from grade school
- To LA; met Marie Redmond; job at Chicken of The Sea on Terminal Island
- Got job at North American Aviation; Salton Sea special assignment for F100 Speed Run Test
- Job at McCullough Motors; Mexican marriage to Roberta DesMartin; temporarily a bigamist; divorced Dorothy
- Atlas Sign Company; working with Richard (Dick) Bell, first black journeyman sign-painter in Los Angeles (all white) Sign Painters Union; then another sign company, Acme

- Sailed out of Wilmington on Marine Lynx; gay Bo's'n; signed on first time as MCSU (Marine Cooks and Stewards Union) when I worked food services; then didn't sail on Isthmian--C-4 from hell--anchored at pier 46, San Francisco

- Helped decommission the Marine Phoenix at Suisan Bay; black ball watch, near collision with the Hawaiian Mattson-line ship, Luraline ("GD Bell")

- To Portland; Fred Shoemaker, backdrop painting for "Most Happy Fellow"; Good Samaritan as orderly; revisited the gang; lived with Ron Kester and Red Wolfer

- Worked for Ron Spier; window decoration for Meier and Franks' department store

- Married Jan Nothiger; Steve Gann, "Old Army Headquarters" printing shop; set up studio on 3rd floor

- Sailed on Coos Bay out of North Bend to Sun Docks in L.A.

- Entered Portland State as premed; Jan traveling with Red Cross

- "Turn to page 129," quit Portland State

- Worked St. Vincent's Hospital; met Sherry at Don Carlson's New Year's party

- Divorced Jan

The memories of some of these incidents are too vague to rate more than a passing mention; others are very complete, to be discussed in subsequent chapters. We beg the reader's indulgence.

Larry offers the following act of contrition: "At some unnamed period of time, I started, stopped, and started again reading Marcel Proust. I had never read anything like it. I did not intend to write anything remotely similar. Obviously, I have done exactly that. Sincere apologies!"

A note of clarification: At the end of the first book of the Vallian Trilogy, Larry describes his attempt to join the Navy. He had been turned down at the Vancouver recruiting office due to myopia and flat feet. But, he was determined to "serve his country" so he gave a friend's address in Portland, memorized the eye chart, and stood on the outside of his feet. He got in and was sent to San Diego for boot camp. What happened there is unknown, and the next event in his memory is being in Company D Barracks 102 on the way to being discharged as a "Section 8" (emotionally and mentally unstable). While there, he complained about being mistreated by two hospital corpsmen. His complaint would have initiated a court martial on the corpsmen and kept him landlocked in Barracks 102 for an indefinite period of time until the hearing, had he not agreed to accept an honorable discharge. But something else was afoot. He signed some papers in a semi-hypnotic state, which discharged him from the Navy, but apparently enlisted him into the OSS/CIA.

On now to the rest of the story …

On Love of Ships and Sailing

2

The luck of the draw is only an illusion …
like most of life. L.E.W.

E ven when I was a small child, I knew that I wanted to sail to all
the mysterious ports in the world. Though I played with small
handheld airplane models and pretended to fly them, in my heart
I knew my "spacey" mind and slender grasp of serial time would surely
have me running out of gas or forgetting to set the altimeter properly,
resulting in the regrettably likely possibility of flying into the nearest
mountain. A recent crash of a commercial airline was noted by the FAA
as " … a controlled flight into terrain … " Sailing, with the steering and
destination of the ship the responsibility of someone else, was something
I thought I could handle. You can't get lost on a ship—you're either on
it or you're not. So, when my Navy enlistment didn't go quite the way I
planned, and an opportunity came up to sail in the Merchant Marine,
I took it.

A school acquaintance, who had escaped the draft, had sailed in the
Merchant Marine, having made two trips out of San Francisco, with
one of them being to the Orient. We were having coffee in his father's
drug store in Vancouver when he suggested that the two of us could go
to San Francisco and get a ship. Matt had been a year ahead of me in
school, and we had nothing much in common, but the desire to "get out
of Dodge." It looked like the perfect opportunity; I would have someone
with me who knew the ropes.

We took a bus, arrived in San Francisco, got a cheap hotel room, and
waited. Matt explained that I would have to go to the Coast Guard and
procure a Z number, and then go to the union and sign in there. Being in
this strange city with the noise of the trolley cars crashing up and down

Market Street, I was thoroughly confused. It didn't help to find out that things did not work quite the way Matt had explained them. The Coast Guard officer explained to me that I could get my Z number, but first I had to have a union job (berth on a ship) waiting for me. And it turned out that you could not get a union card until you had a Z number and papers. The result brought the meaning of "catch 22" clearly into focus.

The reality was that you sat for half a day, waiting in the union hall for the sailing board to go up with the ships that were in port, and then bid for the various available openings. Of course, there were a few dozen other people waiting for jobs, but most of them already had a union card and their Z number/papers. For the rest of us, it was a matter of sitting there day after day, watching the card-carriers being assigned the jobs. When the union rep, sitting in his little barred cranny, had gotten sick of seeing my face, he found jobs that nobody else seemed to want; I was shocked to hear my name called. The grizzled, cigar-smoking, short, unruly-looking Irishman wrote out a piece of paper and gave it to me to take to the Coast Guard to get my Z number. It happened so fast that I didn't realize that Matt had gone through all of this earlier, so when I showed up at the hotel, Matt seemed to be ready. He looked at my card that had the name Marine Fox at pier 35, sailing the following morning, smiled and said, "Great, we are good to go."

We took a cab to the pier, and sure enough, there she was. "She" was a 527-foot, C-4 troop ship. Nobody challenged us when we walked up the gangway to the quarterdeck and asked where the crew slept. I had purchased a "ditty bag," a small canvas bag in which to carry all the things that I was going to need on the voyage: a toothbrush, a comb, an extra pair of shoes, a change of clothing, a watch cap. We went down several ladders at the rear of the ship to a fo'c'sle (small cabin), which had bunks for three seamen. I neglected to read the printing over the rooms that had signs like 12-4, 4-8, and 8-12. These meant nothing to me, and since Matt didn't say anything, I left my gear in a nearby locker and went back on deck. Matt had disappeared, and I supposed that he was making some kind of arrangements for us. It turned out I couldn't have been more wrong.

About this time, several large busses and trucks showed up on the dock, and more than 1200 troops were ushered aboard and disappeared—in a show of organization—somewhere into the bowels of the ship. After a time, I noticed a great deal of activity. A sonorous rumbling sound started to gently vibrate the ship. Two tugs pulled along side, lines were cast down, the gangplank was pulled up to deck level, and black smoke belched from the great single stack.

I realized that I was not the least bit sure of what was supposed to be happening next. I finally figured out that a group of men were busy getting the ship ready for sea. One group was up on the foredeck casting off the lines that held us to the dock, while a similar group was performing the same duty aft. Lines were pulled in and coiled on the deck. I thought it was all very interesting, but was wondering when I would find out where I was going to work.

I heard the ship's bells; then I noticed the deep throbbing beneath my feet as the giant ship came to life. There was a gentle surge followed by an opposite reaction and then the next surge and the next. I didn't get a chance to do any more wool-gathering because the short, stout middle aged man whom I recognized as the bo's'n—he had directed the line handling an hour earlier—called out my name and ordered me to follow him.

I thought, "This is good. I guess he is going to tell me where I am going to serve."

I was a little put off by his very brusque manner, but he just grunted and kept walking. We went up the ladder to the foredeck. I was surprised to see Matt there, looking not the least bit glad to see me. The bo's'n, with a jerk of his thumb, directed us to follow him as he mounted the ladder to the officers' deck and led us into a large assembly area, which had 12 heavy, swiveling chairs, bolted around two large tables. The tables were fitted with sideboards all around. I was later to learn they were there to keep the plates and other eating utensils from sliding off the table when the ship was in a storm.

We were directed to sit on one side of a table, while three officers sat on the other. One man turned and spoke to us—not unkindly, I thought—as he introduced the bo's'n, whom we had already met, and then himself as the chief mate. The man sitting to his right was the purser, and the dark, stocky man between the two of them, the captain. I smiled brightly but then, seeing that the bo's'n had left, and the three men opposite us did not seem too cheerful, I let the smile disappear. It was clear that we had not been called in to receive medals. During what seemed like a staring contest, in which Matt and I were odds-on-favorites to lose, we just sat there, silent and meek.

Finally the purser opened a satchel and pulled out a sheaf of papers. He separated them carefully and said, "We seem to have a small problem here. This ship is at sea, and the logical thing to do would be to take both of you back to San Francisco."

I was trying to figure out what the hell I had done to get these people pissed at me. I decided that since I didn't know what to say, I would, wisely, say nothing.

The purser continued, while I noticed a sneaky smile on the mate's face. "You see, there is a little formality when a ship leaves an American port. The people who come aboard are expected to have the proper papers and a release slip with their appropriate union card."

I instantly felt better for I knew that I had my pink union card in my left pocket and, since I had just received them, my Z papers folded neatly in their leather folder, with a chain connecting the heavy folder to my belt.

But the purser continued, "The next thing that happens, or should happen, is that you come up to this deck on the appointed day and sign the Ship's Articles. The Articles are proof that you are signing on to this ship of your own accord and have not been illegally pressed into service. In addition, the Articles will tell you in what port you signed on, the general length of the voyage—legally no more than two years—and that you will be returned to your port of entry. If the ship is chartered for someplace else, then you have the right to have the ship's company pay for your air transportation back to that port. These are the rights given to you by signing the Articles … "

At this point, the man in the middle—a swarthy, fifty year old Portuguese man who, we were later informed, had been on ships since his 15th birthday—flushed angrily, rose to his feet, and, with his small, muscled index finger providing an emphasizing rap on the table, finished the purser's sentence with, " … but since you two have decided to change the rules, you are aboard my ship as stowaways. I can put you in irons, put you to work, or have you put under arrest at Hawaii, our next port of call. All of this is a royal pain in the butt for me; however, the Bo's'n has discovered that you two idiots were actually sent by the union."

He paused to take a deep breath, and, having gotten all that off his chest, he looked at me directly and said, "Larry Wahl is your name." It was a statement and not a question. He asked for and received my Z papers and looked at them carefully. "Then this is your first trip?"

I nodded dumbly.

He asked the same question of Matt, whom I found beginning to look a little happier. The captain then sat back down and said to Matt, with a disarmingly oily smile that Matt interpreted as friendly, "And you, Mr. Zapp, you have sailed before?" Matt's Z papers were produced along with his union card and discharge papers stamped with the names of two other ships.

Still in a quiet voice, Captain Esposito said, "Well, it turns out that there was just a little mistake here. We are missing a wiper for the engine room and an ordinary seaman for the deck."

Now the captain put on a more genuinely friendly face and added, "So, Mr. Zapp, as the senior member of this comedy duo, would you like to take an ordinary seaman's berth or would you like to be a wiper in the engine room?"

Matt had told me that he loved working on deck and absolutely hated even thinking about working the engine detail, especially as a lowly wiper. I found it no surprise when Matt allowed a grateful smile to twitch across his face as he quickly answered, "The deck, Sir. I'd like the ordinary's berth, Sir."

The captain gave a mirthless snort of satisfaction and started to write on the papers in front of him. He then slid the papers over to the purser, who signed them and shoved back to us, which I assumed correctly were the aforementioned Articles.

Since Matt had made it clear that the last place in the world he ever wanted to be was in the engine room, I knew for certain that that was where I was now bound. Matt tried not to look at me as he smilingly signed the papers where the first mate was pointing, but then I saw the smile immediately replaced by a look of profound hopelessness. I just wanted the ordeal to be over, but Matt looked as if he had eaten something that didn't agree with him. I watched him staring at the paper he had just signed, and then he looked up at the captain. I could see that there was something he wanted to say.

To his credit, words stuck in his throat as he took a long look at the captain who was smiling for the first time. He seemed to be inviting Matt to say something, but I could see the veins on the captain's neck visibly pulsating. The captain eased himself back into his chair and said finally, " O.K. Mr. Zapp is going to be our new wiper on the 4-8 watch, and Mr. Wahl is going to be the new 12-4 ordinary."

The captain stared quietly at Matt, making no attempt to disguise his disgust. He arose from the chair as the other two officers stood and waited until the captain had left room. The mate then signaled us to stand up and—again, not unkindly, I thought—said, "OK, you two gentleman make sure you find your bosses and your berths and don't let me see you two up here again."

This last comment was certainly not necessary. Since Matt had sailed at least two other trips, I am at a loss to understand why signing Articles had slipped his mind. He never tried to give me an explanation. He and I parted company, and to this day, I have never seen him again.

Scotty and Bill

We had been at sea several days when we were to have what was supposed to be a three-day stopover at Pearl Harbor. I was delighted with my new friends and watchmates: two brothers, sailing as able-bodied seamen, Bill and Scotty Minford. Bill was over six feet tall and so handsome that girls' necks could be heard cracking along the street when he swaggered by. Bill was long and lean, well muscled, and bright enough. He had a full head of black hair and steely blue eyes that had a slightly Asiatic turn to them. His brother, Scotty, looked as though all the good building material had already been used by his parents in constructing Bill, like he (Scotty) was made from the left over material. However, Scotty's mind was in perfect working order, and he was sharp, clever, and fun.

It was not that Scotty was ugly, far from it, but at five foot nine, he was short—certainly when compared to brother Bill—and had a face that looked like a guy you would like to have for a friend. He was quiet, even underwhelming, but had a quick and wry sense of humor that could pop out unexpectedly. Scotty was the younger brother, loose and happy whereas Bill was the older one, quick and tense. I was drawn to Scotty's easy-going manner immediately.

We became good buddies, and in short order, I was the one who decided what we were going to do when the two of us went ashore. Bill had introduced us to an American family that had moved to Hawaii and had a daughter who had gone to school with Bill on the mainland. We worked it out so we spent as much time as possible with her. But, since the period we had been told the ship would be in port was limited, we said our final goodbyes to this family; however we found out later that same day that the ship would be in port a wee mite longer.

The Reason? The ship had discharged its troops and was ready to sail, when the port captain's inspection crew discovered an electrical problem on the ship's number three generator. Because the ship carried a few thousand passengers in place of freight, it was necessary that the air-conditioning be extensive. Throughout the ship, there was a labyrinth of air-carrying vents, pipes, and chutes to force air all the way down to the deepest recesses. In a very large cabin, which included the three generating units, was a 30 by 8 foot electrical panel on a bulkhead, just aft of the engine room, which was the power center of the ship. All the lights, all the communication equipment, all the cargo wenches, and all the many powerful fans that supplied air ran through that panel. This room effectively was a metaphor of the average house's fuse box. Number three generator had thrown a bearing and needed to be taken down completely to be repaired. Though the third was only a standby generator, it had to be in operating order any time the ship went to sea.

Thus, on the fourth day in a port in which we would have been happy to spend the rest of the year, the orders were issued to test the other two generators. When time to switch them on approached, some engineer—who apparently had not learned to count—inadvertently powered up number three, instead of one or two, and proceeded to short out the hapless number three generator in a blaze of grinding sparks and a flash fire. When this was brought under control, it was clear that now a whole new generator was needed for replacement. Gloriously, this led to a two-week break while we had to remain at Pearl.

On the second week of our idyllic vacation, the plane that was carrying the replacement generator was lost somewhere over the Pacific; we got another week in port. Finally, the sailing board went up with a port and a date, which was not fictitious. At 0800 we boarded again and slipped out of Pearl for the Island of Guam. As the days had passed in port, we were joking that the Seabees had snuck in at night and permanently attached the ship to the Islands of Hawaii. All in all, our sailing schedule had been completely destroyed, and everybody on board was anxious to get on with the journey.

The first thing we saw of what passed for Guam's port at Apra—near the very end of the war—consisted of a half ruined concrete church and a two story concrete block house. These stood as a tribute to the accuracy of the 16.5 inch battleship rifles that had obliterated what had been a typically sleepy Spanish city of about 10,000. We were told that in the process of reclaiming the island, the war had left incredible devastation. All dock facilities and shore loading and support equipment had been totally destroyed. Now, a year after the original devastation, the harbor had been cleared, dredged, and made ready for the Apra Harbor Breakwater. Where all the carnage had existed, there was nothing but clear water.

Scotty and I wondered at the time why nobody else seemed inclined to shore leave, but we insisted on going ashore with the captain's skiff, which was taking a supply trip to Apra "Harbor." We were very young seamen, not seasoned hands. The bo's'n grudgingly agreed to take us along. He powered up the gig that was tied to the end of the 30-foot gangway, the distal end of which lowers to the water's edge. We both stepped smartly into the supply boat and spent a quick quarter of an hour being powered to a large, bare, concrete slab—all that passed for a berth at what remained of the docks at Apra.

We leaped ashore and looked back at the bo's'n as the boat was powered gingerly away from the "dock" on the way to some other landing. As the boat turned, the bo's'n shouted at us, "You two morons be back on this landing at 1800 hours, and no bullshit!"

Scotty and I thought the bo's'n was being a little bit snotty as we walked off the broad concrete onto a connecting dusty space covering about a city block. There was absolutely nothing on it but a dilapidated-looking tarp covering a single wooden guard post shack; a grizzled marine in fatigues leaned against the side. It was hard to tell if the marine was holding up the shack or if the shack was supporting the marine.

Scotty and I peered at the shack through the heavy stifling dust; there seemed to be absolutely no visible activity at all. The marine was reading a small mini-book, of a vintage similar to him. He looked like he was the hands-down winner of the award for the most bored human on the face of the earth. His face was unshaven, his fatigue hat was cocked over one eye, and he looked like a man who had been young a year or two ago, but had now seamlessly put on the cloak of a man twice his age. When Scotty and I approached, he looked up from his book. His facial expression was that of an infinitely patient station keeper at a train depot that had never seen a train arrive.

"Hi," I said brightly, looking toward the far end of the open space where a rough dirt road led up and over a nearby hill. "Can you tell us how to get to the nearest town?"

"Ain't none," was the laconic reply.

We couldn't quite cope with that answer and yet didn't feel like challenging his authority. Instead, tasting the hot and ever-present dust in my mouth, I asked, "Where do you get some water here?"

The marine looked a little more sorrowful—if that was possible—and, in the same bored monotone, moving nothing but his lips, replied, "Ain't none."

Finally, I asked for what all sailors want, "Where are the women?"

Again, like a sad chant, "Ain't none."

This was not acceptable at all. We had three full hours to spend in this dust bowl with nothing to keep us out of the boiling sun. Finally realizing why there had not been twenty other crew members vying for our little trip to the island, with some courage I said to nobody in particular but in the general direction of the marine, "Well, Scotty, I guess we'll just go walking up that road and see what we can find."

I cast a furtive look at the marine, but if he had heard the remark, he gave no sign of it. In fact, it seemed that a kind of sardonic smile flitted across his face as he turned his back on us. I took this as a tacit approval of our plan, as well as the understanding that it was probably illegal, which seemed to make it even more exciting. I should have seen the little cartoon blurb over his head, that said, "I'm not stopping you 'cause you're not on my list."

Distances in desert, scrub brush, or sage lands are deceiving, and so it was here. It was some time before we reached the top of the distant hill; our white tee shirts were wet with sweat. From this vantage point we could see hill after hill receding into the distance, broken only by a fringe of trees leading to a small mountain. There seemed to be a well-traveled dirt road leading up to another hill, so we proceeded.

We had been walking for about two miles when, off to the left of the road, there appeared the unmistakable wing of a Flying Fortress B-17, angled straight up to the sky. One of its two starboard engines hung down at a rakish angle, and the other was missing. As we got closer, we could see the broken remains of the rest of the plane and observed that there was either a natural—or more likely man-made—deep eighty-foot hole with an unmanned D-8 tractor on the ridge above. This huge depression held a myriad of World War II aircraft wrecks: a half dozen B-17s, F-4Us, torpedo bombers, DC-6s, a scattering of Japanese fighters, and one giant B-20. The whole scene looked for all the world like some gigantic child had tired of his day's play with these "toys" and had cast them into this deep cavity, waiting until tomorrow to play again. It took a little while, but we finally realized that the wrecks were there to provide cannibalized parts for other operating aircraft.

There was no one near this scene. The very next thought we had was to check out the aircraft. While we stood there thinking, two distant but obvious rifle shots shattered the air. I turned to Scotty and asked, "Hum, Guam. Now that the war is over, I wonder what they hunt here?" But before he could answer, we saw a jeep speeding toward us on a nearby road. The jeep, with an Army lieutenant driving, slammed to a stop. He must have been cussing from the first moment he spotted our glaring white tee shirts. With no trace of humor, he explained that though we thought the war was over, there were "left-over" Japanese still fighting and we were their targets. He drove us back to the landing, ordered us the "hell out of this jeep," and drove off.

This was my "maiden voyage" and first trip to Guam. The second trip was OK, but the third was a very different story.

The General A.E. Anderson

During the time I was waiting for a ship, I decided to get unemployment. The unemployment agency insisted on classifying me, so I said I was an artist. "Sorry," the agent said, "you have to pass a test."

Well, I didn't pass it, but I had an idea of what I needed to do to be classified as an artist. So, when I left San Francisco for my third trip to Guam, I bought a book called *Figure Drawing for All It's Worth*, by Andrew Loomis, just to have something complicated to do in expected off hours in a land that was so isolated. Camp One was at the base of Mt. Lam Lam, above Apra Harbor, and was full of some of the most detestable drunks, drifters, and hoods ever collected together. My primary job there was simply to not have my throat cut. The choice of the book was providential, and, in two months, I was drawing bodies to the faces of the girl friend pictures for many of my galley crewmates. By the time I got back to San

Francisco, I was a professional artist. I stopped by the agency, and to the representative's astonishment, I passed the test! (It is important to note that 65 years later, my wife found this very same book—it could have been mine—in a used bookstore and presented it to me at Christmas. Shocked, as I perused it, I realized that I had not studied more than a third of the book, but now understand that was enough to save my sanity during those very trying times.)

It was on the A.E. Anderson that I first (unknowingly) met my personal controller, Herman Creek (of the OSS/CIA—it was in transition at that time, and though President Truman thought he had shut down the activities of the OSS in September 1945, that did not happen). The galley crew, with whom I would be working in Guam, turned out to be agents who had been picked to keep tabs on me, namely Brownie, Smitty, Larry, Larry, and Blackie. Of course, Herman, et al, were just people I met on the troop ship, A. E. Anderson, as she plied her way across the Pacific on the way to Guam. The six of us crew members were going to Harbor Heights in Pomeroy Camp One, up in the hills, while Creek took over a bus-driving job, working in Apra for the Civil Service. It would be more than 30 years before I would be able to understand much of what actually was happening to me, and had been happening to me since I was barely eighteen years of age. But way before that, my mind was a fertile field for others intent on using my strange undifferentiated memory and psychic talents.

The ship stopped over at Pearl Harbor for two days, and we troop class "prisoners"—oops, read "passengers"—were more than glad to get off the miserable tub. There was nothing wrong with the ship except that it had a sizeable Marine crew on board working as temporary "Ships Company." These otherwise perfectly OK people were under the orders and control of the meanest, most miserable Marine sergeant I would ever know—the first of my many "Sarges." It was in those two days that the basic crew, of which I was a part, really got to know one another and blend together. I did not think it strange at the time that I did not know, and still do not know, a single one of their last names, with the exception of Creek. Of course there was no way to know whether that was his real name.

Sarge made sure that we troop class passengers—each and every one of us—understood that we were the lowest of the lowest and were not fit to ride on any ship, and definitely not on his. When we signed off the ship for a two-day layover in Hawaii, it was made clear that we would have to shift for ourselves ashore, and that we could not come back to the dock or enter the ship until it was ready to sail—not to sleep or eat. Most of us had no money—no chits were available—so one of us, I can't remember who, got us off the ship and paid for our two days and nights in Honolulu. The third day, it was back to the ship and off to Saipan. The fact that we were civilians never seemed to cross the Sarge's mind; we were treated exactly the same as the other 3000 replacement troops to be stationed on Guam, Saipan, Midway, Eniwetok, and a dozen or so other South Pacific duty tours. There were also troops destined for China, India, and Burma (CBI, as it was called).

I had already made a couple of merchant marine crew trips on C-4 troop ships, and, on those previous trips, none of us was ever specifically forbidden any part of the ship except officer passenger quarters. Our crew had been all over any deck space that was available and had been treated as passengers, no matter what rank. In fact, our bo's'n' on the second trip—who was just a little gay—assigned one young soldier to his cabin for the duration of the voyage.

But, on the Anderson, we were not allowed to lean on the rails, lean against non-operating machinery, or lean against anything else; we were limited to just the foredeck and 30 feet of the fantail. Since there were any number of troop class Marines aboard, who had little choice in the matter, the Sarge stationed them about every six feet. They were no happier with the situation than we were. Some of our civilian group were grizzled Army, Navy, and Marine retreads, old and wise, and not happy putting up with all this malarkey. So one day, inevitably, when we were ordered down from an after-housing where we could watch a movie from the back of the canvas screen, a couple of these retreads gave the Marine guard a bad time; they insisted that the guard contact the Sarge since what we were being restricted from was not on the Marine's Guard List, on the paddle he kept alongside his station. Mind you, this was a tough construction crew that had been all over the world to some of the roughest ports. They were big, mean, and ugly.

In due course, the Sarge came. He was dressed in his full regalia, with a side arm 45 and stripes all the way down his short, stubby arms. He had a barrel chest and looked as though he was older than Noah—but not nearly as nice. He listened for a few moments to the terse, angry comments of the mob and then signaled the Marine guard over. The Sarge then removed his 45, along with his duty belt, took off his jacket, and removed his shirt, leaving him in a tee shirt and pants. With meticulous care, he gave these personal articles to the very young Marine who was standing there with a look of complete wonder, fully loaded with all the Sarge's paraphernalia.

Standing there in just his pants, shoes, and tee shirt, the sergeant spit on both of his meaty paws as he glared cheerfully at the assembled throng and explained as follows: "The Official Complaint Department for the General A.E. Anderson is now open. Who will be my first customer?"

In a few seconds, it was clear he had no takers; the crowd just melted away. He was putting on his gear again and had just put on his duty belt when, almost as an afterthought, he said to the rest of us gawkers, "Troops, you perfect assholes, carry on! Carry the Fuck on!"

We carried on.

3 | Typhoon

When I had been on the bridge the day before, it looked to me as though something was happening with the ocean: the sea was making up. The color of the water was the first thing that seemed to change. It went from a deep blue to a kind of dirty green, which seemed to indicate that there was a great deal of activity on the surface but, more importantly, that the transparent blue quality was being changed by heavy movement below the surface. That this was the case became obvious as the ship's movements become more ponderous; it seemed like the ship was gingerly feeling its way through the wave forms.

I had gotten used to the 12 to 4 watch routine. Although fire drills every other day still took place about 4 PM or, in other words, at the beginning of my sleeping time, it was not too bad. The day watch on deck was really kind of easy for me, a night person, to handle. I was able to get up about 10 in the morning, go down for six leisurely cups of coffee, get an early lunch, and then report to the bridge at noon with the two able-bodied (AB) seaman who made up the watch; insurance requirements called for at least two AB's on watch at all times. One of the AB's stood at the wheel, while the other spelled him; the ordinary, which was me, stood up on the flying bridge or, at the watch commander's discretion, on the navigation bridge. It was this watch commander's habit to have the watch—called the free watch—stood on the flying bridge. On any ship, this is the bridge that forms the roof of the navigation area: the wheelhouse. It was a perfectly marvelous place to be, as far as I was concerned.

After I reported to the bridge that I was on duty and had been posted in the log as part of the entry "watch reported," I would climb the set of ladders that led to the flying bridge. It had two wings extending out port and starboard that duplicated the open wings of the navigation bridge below it, providing an almost unobstructed view of the ship's structure. Instead of the navigation and communication gear that was below me, my bridge contained only the weather-protected binnacle (repeater compass) and voice tube. But directly in the center of the bridge, about ten feet back, was the solid comforting base of the main mast. It was a large structure, stayed with crosstrees of steel and steel shrouds. At the crosstrees, the forward radar station was located about forty feet above me and above that, the connections to the radio lines, antennae, and lines for the signal flags. Just ahead of the range light and slightly below it was a station for a masthead watch, which, at 30 feet above the flying bridge, would not have been a joy to contemplate for anyone with a fear of heights as I had. I could wander a few feet behind the bulk of the mast and look into the ready box containing signal flags that, when run up on the yardarms (lines), sent visual messages in international Morse code. On this same line, the "black ball" would be hoisted when the ship was parked—not under steam. The "black ball" consisted of a folding wire contraption that would unfold underneath a heavy black material to fill it out to be ball-shaped, about two feet in diameter. It was amazing how clearly this could be seen, and at what distance, when it was observed on a ship's flag mast. I looked at the flags and, although I was interested—like many of the other mysteries of shipboard—I did not take the time to actually sort them out. It was like line-handling, which I would learn much later when the information became necessary. But up here on the bridge, where it would have done me some good and would have indicated my seriousness about sailing, I just never found the time to really develop the skills.

When the ship had a normal load, the flying bridge was 80 feet above the water, so it is not hard to understand that the view from there was spectacular. The day watches were rather boring; all I had to do was look reasonably alert. But on the midnight to 0400 watch, I was really in a world of my own. The advantage I had at night was that I was 20 feet above the navigation bridge, so I would be the first to see another ship's range light appearing from "under the water" to rise on the horizon.

Lights are anathema anyplace forward of the navigation bridge, and so there was no light on the flying bridge that could in any way reflect down into the pilothouse, obscuring the navigator's view. The only exception to this rule was a small binnacle light that, when a knob was turned, would just barely illuminate the "card" of the repeater compass. The knob would allow the light to be turned on gradually so the light level was low enough to not kill my night vision. The knob was spring-loaded so it would automatically fade back down when it was released. Since the ship had been equipped for wartime use, there was also the consideration of keeping any light from showing to a potential enemy; the metal hood on the binnacle would slip down over it if it were not manually held up.

There were handholds on either side of the binnacle, although I could not for the life of me figure out what they were for. I could not conceive of this massive ship bouncing around all that much, no matter what the seas. It was 527 feet over all and 66 feet across at its broadest point. I was not that much of a maritime engineer, but I reckoned that 27,000 tons was a hell of a heap of something.

As luck would have it, on this day the noon to 4 watch was pretty rough, and I was seeing green water clearing the fo'c'sle head. There is a metal coaming—a protective shroud—built up from the foremost deck, which is a raised area deck to begin with. With the coaming added, it means that water flowing over the coaming represents 40 feet of water above the water line at that point. When I was getting ready to go off watch that afternoon, I noticed special preparations and various lashing of deck gear. The idea that the deck watch would be busy at other than watch times did not penetrate my complacent soup, and I just assumed that there was a particularly hot and heavy poker game going on in the messroom.

On a smaller ship, I would have known what was happening, but on this ship, there were over 127 men in the crew, mostly galley help for the steward's department, which had to run three galleys. Therefore, I was surprised to discover regular cooking had been cancelled— because of the heavy seas, I later realized. As a result, I got a few odds and ends that were available for dinner from the crew mess and hit my bunk about 1800 that evening. It is a tribute to my sturdiness, to my lack of information, and ultimately to my general unconsciousness that I did not understand what was going on. I fell into a deep and untroubled sleep. I was content, and the concept of bad weather was the kind of excitement that I was looking for.

At about 1900, I became aware of a sound that I had never heard before. It took some time to figure out what it was: it was loud and it was deep. On shipboard, one rapidly becomes aware of all sorts of different sounds and after these normal sounds have been cataloged, they remain in the conscious mind for several repetitions, after which they are unheeded and just disappear into the subconscious. If there is a change in the pitch or frequency of any of these standard sounds, then the mind calls them forth and tries to figure out the significance of the particular change. At sea, the hearing of a truly new sound is extremely rare.

This sound was nothing I had ever heard before: a low growl followed by a very high vibration. I realized it seemed to be attached to the movement of the ship, but I did not really worry about it; I went back to sleep. I continued to sleep for about another two hours, pushing the new sound to the back of my mind. I didn't think too much about it even though it got a little more definite and a lot more insistent. Then, at about 2000, I was thrown completely out of my upper bunk. This surprised me because our bunks were on the starboard side of the ship—in back of the section that held the engine room—and most crew quarters had the bunks arranged bow to stern rather than port to starboard. As I tried to get to my feet, something came to my attention: In order to roll me out of my bunk, the ship needed to be changing position 45 degrees on a line passing through the center of the ship, end to end. Roll, which is side to side, is not too hard to fathom, but a 500 foot ship picking up its bow 60 feet in one wave and then changing positions so that the stern is now 60 feet up a few crunching seconds later ... this is a series of movements that is frightening to contemplate and impossible to grasp.

I hit my head hard on a stanchion as I reached for a handhold and dove to my locker as the locker doors swung open with the gear threatening to fall out. I got it secured just before everything went. Finally I indentified the noise I had been hearing: it was the ship's single propeller coming completely out of the water. The propeller is a three-bladed prop, fourteen or so feet in diameter; part of the time during this storm, it was only half submerged. At these times, it would rattle the ship like some giant bulldog worrying a small kitten.

I was now thoroughly awake and had no intention of even trying to get back to sleep. I made my way to the head where I got some idea of the ship's movement by watching the water in the toilet bowl make a complete sweep around the perimeter, occasionally splashing high enough to slosh over the edges. I gave up the idea of trying to take a shower and decided to go get something to eat—I could always eat no matter what was happening. Common sense should have told me that there would be no food, but to see the galley completely empty and the pantries offering only bread for toast and all the coffee you could drink was really strange. The large mess hall had only a half dozen people in it. The passageways had not been that full either. I had no idea where the troops were; I hadn't seen any military personnel in the areas where I was used to seeing them. It was difficult for me to realize that there were just as many people on the ship now as there had been when it sailed. In retrospect, I am sure that all of the troops had been restricted to the holds where they were bunked. As ingenuous as I was, it just did not dawn on me that at least half of the people on the ship were so seasick they did not care whether we foundered or not.

I ate a couple of pieces of toast, found a jar of peaches in the fridge, and fixed myself a large bowl. I then amused myself by taking a bite of the peaches while hanging on to the table with one hand. The seat swung from side to side, and my toast slid from one end of the long table to the other as the ship would first hit a trough, tremble, balance on it for a few seconds, and then slam down hard the opposite direction. Watching me eat the peaches sent two black messmen hurrying for the head. I finished my light dinner and, picking a book out of the reading rack, read for several hours. A half dozen people wandered in during this period, would pour themselves some coffee, sit for a short while, and then wander off. I noted that many seemed hard-eyed, breathing heavily, and very silent, but it never dawned on me that they might be scared. Since I had not sailed very much, I just assumed that every once in a while you will run into a storm, so this was a storm! It is true that I thought it seemed a little excessive, but since no one appeared to want to talk about it, I thought that they were so used to storms that it would be uncool to be too excited.

About 2330, the bo's'n came into the messroom. "Got any coffee in here, Wahl?" he asked.

"I made some in the small pot."

He disappeared into the pantry and then made his way haltingly into the messroom with a half a cup of coffee. Wearily he sat down across from me and eyed me with patent hatred. The bo's'n knew I was no seaman, and I knew he was queer. I had accidentally come upon him servicing one of the ship's soldiers in his fo'c'sle. As a result, I got some special treatment from him that I did not even have sense enough to know was the result of being paid off for my silence. He was known as a fair man and a damn good bo's'n. His personal attitudes were neither of interest to me nor a reason for antipathy toward him, but he didn't know that and assumed that I would expect favors to keep my mouth shut. Now he sat opposite me, looking like hell, and it is to my disgrace that I did not know that, among other things, he was trying to balance his needs and his life in the realization that we might all be dead in a matter of hours.

The bo's'n is a non-commissioned officer and leader of the deck crew. He is the person who has to keep the ship functioning. Only now, years later could I even attempt to guess at what a ungodly night this must have been for him: checking survival gear, trying to imagine what might give first, what things would be asked of him, and what he might or might not do in his hour of a possibly final, devastating, and deadly trial.

He viewed me dispassionately for some time, and then asked, in what I only later realized was a grim joke, "You ready to go on watch tonight?"

Thinking of all of the seasick people that I had seen, I took this question at face value and answered, somewhat in the understated fashion of a John Wayne, "You bet, 'Boats!'"

At this he threw back his head and gave a coarse, throaty laugh; it sort of died someplace in the back of his throat and left him with his mouth open and no sound coming out. He covered this strange sound with a kind of yawn, reached for his watch cap, and struggled out of the pitching room.

I realized that I had almost screwed up; here I was, showing my ignorance once again. Since no one had contacted me for several hours, and the ship's routine—with which I was just getting familiar—seemed completely strange and different, I assumed that my watch was cancelled. I was glad that the bo's'n had made a joking reference to it; otherwise I might really have been in trouble. But the ship needed me and if the ship needed me, I was going to be up to the task!

Water, Water Everywhere

I finished my last cup of coffee and went back down the three decks to my fo'c'sle. I put on a full set of foul weather gear and started for the deck. I didn't see anyone in the passageways and, as I was passing outside hatches, I noticed that they were closed and dogged down. At the very least, I had sense enough to make my way through the innards of the ship below deck in order to reach the main forward housing, areas I was not ordinarily privy to—remember, I was a stow-away so I decided to avoid the inside passage and go out on deck when it was possible.. I got lost in this unfamiliar territory for a while but finally found my way to a hatch that indicated recent use by the amount of water that was sloshing round it; this was the deck passage to the navigation bridge. I was now on the captain's deck, one deck below what I thought was my watch site in the forward housing. Signs on the door requested that it be properly dogged down, coming and going, and to use lifelines at all times. I undogged the door. It was nearly blown out of my hand as a blast of wind and water hit me, knocking the foul-weather hood off my head and immediately soaking me. The fury of the wind was unreal.

Somehow I got the hatch closed and dogged down, and then tried to figure out where I was. I finally made out, through narrowed and tearing eyes, the small metal landing that led to the set of ladders to the next deck up. I reached the navigation bridge on the port side and made out the shadowy figures of the bridge crew in the closed wheel house as I found the ladder leading to the flying bridge: my deck! I struggled up the ladder taking a step or two, then waited while the wind struggled to tear me loose. When the bow of the ship bucked up, it cut off the stream of wind so I could purchase another step or two. Eventually I made it and was surprised to see how huge and lonely that deck looked in the storm. I had never realized how large this ship was, but when I reached that flying bridge, I really knew what large was: "large" is hanging onto the binnacle and watching the entire foremain deck disappear under tons of water and seeing that ocean of water blast upwards three stories to cover me with spray.

The ship was moving in ways I did not believe it could. I uncovered the binnacle and watched the course change 10 to 15 degrees in a matter of seconds. Every twenty seconds or so, the deck would drop down under me, like an express elevator starting, and then, about three seconds later, would push up, buckling my knees. I had no idea what it must be like for the troops, especially in the forward berths, but I figured they must have been hanging on to stay in their bunks, tiered five high. What it was like in the crowded heads with all of the troops that must be sick, I didn't even want to think about.

I was truly frightened when I looked down on the port side and saw dimly that the #2 boat was torn from its davits. I knew how big and heavy this gear was and how well it was lashed down; this finally gave me the feeling of the actual force and fury of the storm, which apparently had eluded me up to this time. How long I was up there, I am not sure because I was rapidly going into shock. I began to realize that the ship was in mortal danger, that it was fighting for its life. I was so cold I was not feeling anything. It seemed to me that I actually dozed off, although I know that this could not have happened. I sat down with my head ringing even louder than all the noises of Hell that had been ringing in it. With this action, I realized that I was parked up against the flag box, twenty feet from the binnacle and behind the mast. I struggled to my feet. The fact that I was walking in a foot of water did not really dawn on me. I crawled over to the binnacle, as water poured through the scuppers; the downward and forward motion of the ship sent thousands of gallons of water pouring off the flying bridge.

I was hanging onto the binnacle (those two handles, whose purpose I now understood), when I saw a wall of water completely obscure everything forward including the kingpin housings, which were twenty feet above the foredeck. I felt the shudder as that water slammed into the main housing and felt the ship continue to dive.

It seemed like hours later that someone's hand was holding me to the starboard ladder, 40 feet away from where I had been. I looked at the hand and realized vaguely that it was mine. I also noted that 2 feet of water was trying to wash me off the flying bridge; I was choking on green salt water. As the last of the green water cleared the flying bridge, I peeled my fingers of my right hand off the rail with my left hand and crawled/limped to the binnacle again. I was bruised from head to foot and only vaguely conscious. This time I had sense enough to grab the communicator—even if they yelled at me, I was going to protest.

"Hey!" I yelled into the voice tube in a plaintive bellow. "It's getting awful wet up here!"

"Jesus Christ, man!" I heard over the communicator, "Get the hell off that bridge. That watch was secured hours ago!"

The surprise and fear were too much for me. I must have passed out or something because the next thing I became aware of was waking up tied to my bunk. During the rest of that long night I would wake to feel that sinking feeling in the pit of my stomach, as the stern of the ship would lift completely out of the water. The safety clutches would kick in, disengaging the screw, but before they could kick in, that huge screw would turn free out of water, rattling everything on the ship. Then, with a sickening thud, the ship would hit the water: thousands of tons of ship bobbing up on waves the size of large downtown buildings. The waves would then disappear, leaving the ship hanging in the air to come crashing down into the next wave.

Before this storm was over, hundreds of people would die at sea. A navy squadron would lose two destroyers that simply went into one of those waves and did not come up again. A Navy cruiser lost all of her boats, suffered heavy damage to her superstructure, and almost had her stack torn off. Dozens of small boats were lost, but we survived. I could not say that it was through anything on my part.

From *The 315th Bomb Wing Timeline*, "In either late August or early September, 1946, we were in Guam when a 150 mph typhoon struck."

At 0600 the morning after the typhoon, all hands were on deck cleaning up the debris; loose deck gear was scattered about, and the lifeboats had suffered considerable damage. We were steaming toward Saipan as we cleaned up the post-storm mess. Swabbing down fore and aft—the decks were still slopping with water—I stood up suddenly and struck my head sharply on one of the davits. It stunned me, but I did not think there was much damage.

A little later I discovered that I had the granddaddy of all headaches and could not think straight. I seemed to have strange colors swimming before my eyes and when I heard my buddies talking, it was as if they were a long, long distance away. I recognized Scotty, seemingly swimming in front of me on the deck, then heard the bo's'n telling me to report to the hospital.

The Dog

I heard myself talking, without any understanding of what I was saying, to one of the three hospital aides in the completely equipped ship's hospital; the conversation made no sense to them or to me. Soon they called the army captain, who was the ship's doctor, to check me out. Then there was complete silence, and I came to in a bed in the small dispensary room that was part of the hospital. There was a bunk below me and six more bunks in the room, but I was the only patient. I was surprised that it was now dark. I was still aching all over. A tall marine aide came in, took my temperature and pulse, and left. I did not appear to be restrained, so I slid out of the bunk, and left the infirmary. Unsteadily, I followed a short passageway and, still in a kind of daze, wandered out onto the open foredeck. I recognized that I was in "Officer's Country" but didn't care.

The dark ocean seemed lighted with fireflies and teaming with beautiful flashes of color in the froth where the wake, battered by the bow, roiled around the sides of the ship. With no apparent effort, I found myself perched on a stanchion and from there, I lurched up to the rail, where I balanced looking down at the dark waters streaming by the port side 30 feet below. I was quite fascinated by streams of iridescent, foaming algae as it glistened by. It was so beautiful. I had just decided to go down and enjoy it "up close and personal" when two pair of hands grabbed me. Their owners picked me up and bodily carried me into a locked ward and deposited me on a bunk in a locked cell. I thought about this for a while but couldn't make any sense out of the situation.

I awoke sometime later and perceived that I was a big Doberman Pincher. "Who the hell am I?" I was dimly aware that I was now in the Italian-Jewish ghetto of Portland, where I was the dog belonging to this sweet little lady who lived across the street from my mother and Tony Scrano. The old lady had two sons who I knew hated me as Tony's son and as their dog. Almost every Saturday night, the two men got drunk; when they were tired beating up on anybody else or each other, they would beat up their mother. Neither the dog, King, nor I, as King, liked them very much. One night after dog King had bit them, thus interfering with their beating the old woman, the boys fed dog King poison. I walked across the street—where I often went—and found dog King dying. I knew what they had done and watched helplessly as dog King took his last labored breaths. He seemed to say, while dying, that it was all up to me now.

And now I was King: standing on my bunk, howling and snarling as two of the hospital orderlies opened the door and approached me with a plate of food. In one leap, I had pinned one of them to the deck, as they called for reinforcements. The doctor gave me a shot. One of the marines put a stick in my mouth to stop me from biting any of them or myself. Then I was locked in. I started kicking at the locked door. An hour later, the cell door had large bows in it, and I was exhausted. I lay down on the bunk and went to sleep.

Scotty and Bill Minford came to see me after I stopped being the dog. They even brought me my clarinet, which I had shipped out with. I played a song or two for them. The marine orderlies also came and talked with me. We became friends, and I stopped trying to bite anyone and was no longer barking or howling. What seemed like many days later, I was gently but tightly bound in a stretcher and carried down the gangplank like so much laundry. The ship was in San Francisco, docked at Army Pier 5. The Marine Fox was unloaded of her troops, supplies, and crew in a great hustle and bustle. I missed leaving as an active deck hand; instead I was an errant passenger.

Saipan

I finally came back to full reality to find myself in Letterman General Hospital, near the Presidio, first in a locked room and then later, in a general ward. I now had the leisure to think about what had seemed like a very short trip to Saipan. I concluded, during those couple of weeks at Letterman, that I must have been taken off the Marine Fox while docked at Saipan because I distinctly remember seeing Saipan's outer harbor after the Navy had gotten through with it.

In the latter part of 1945, Japan made a final attempt to save the island—their last forward base—by sending thousands more Japanese troops from their now vulnerable mainland. They never made it. The Navy had cut off their retreat. None of the Emperor's troops ever saw anything but the water that became their shroud as ship after ship was destroyed. Under fire from naval big guns and bombing and strafing by naval airplanes, the area rapidly became acres of sunken ships. The scene I looked upon—a year after the Japanese catastrophe—was of hundreds of stacks, masts, and debris stretched across the shallow, jury-rigged, outside harbor of Saipan.

Among other things, the massive invasion of Saipan was meant to be a sign to the Japanese that their fate on their home islands would be just as certain and just as dismal. It had to be apparent to them that "further resistance is futile!" (Star Trek) Unhappily this didn't work out very well because the Japanese, though isolated, were dug-in, dedicated, and demented. They fought almost to the last man, and the losses on both sides were appalling.

A final ghoulish touch was the nightmarish, slow-walking suicide of ten thousand Saipan civilians—men and women with children in arms—as they dropped in small groups from the cliffs of a high plateau into a merciless bloody heap three hundred feet below. It hadn't been necessary: The Americans, in pamphlets and with bullhorns, had told them that they would be well treated. But the beleaguered Japanese military had told them that they would be raped, tortured, and murdered, and they believed their native leaders!

Sherry and I were to bear witness to those same Suicide cliffs some 50 years later.

These were some of the thoughts that kept me company as I recovered, and then I was officially released from the hospital. All I could think of was getting back to my ship where I had to find the purser to sign me off so I get my pay; I was stony-ass broke. Ah, that it would be that easy: Wrong, wrong, wrong!

In 1946, while I had been on the ship, and then in the hospital, I had lost complete contact with the so-called real world. Now it came back to me with a vengeance. The city of San Francisco was closed down for a holiday weekend. What this meant in practical terms was that transportation was minimal. I am often a slow study, and even though I was told there were no busses to the city and I would have to walk, it was OK—I enjoyed the beautiful weather. The problem was that I had missed dinner the night before, had volunteered to give a pint of blood, had missed breakfast, and was then discharged before lunch. I hit the road hungry.

I knew the ship had been moved to Oakland and planned to take the B-train over the Oakland Bay Bridge. When I got to the main station downtown, I was informed by a sign that that there were no busses running … no trains … no streetcars … no nothing! But, in those days I was fearless, so a three-mile walk across the bridge and its environs did not seem too far to hike.

San Francisco and Oakland are not far apart geographically, but they are worlds apart politically. As I figured out which way to get to the ship, I noticed that there was a distinctly unfriendly feeling in Oakland. Normally I felt at home anywhere, but now there was a pervading bad vibe every place I went. I did ask and found where the ship was berthed and had no trouble getting on board. But, strangely, there was no watch at the head of the gangway; the whole ship seemed deathly quiet. I went to the bridge to find the purser, but found no one anywhere. The first inkling that I was in big trouble began to creep over me. In the days that I had been recovering in the hospital, many things had changed, none of them good.

I at first realized that it was Labor Day weekend, and it was a Saturday. As a rule, the crew would be missing in port on a weekend but the ship would not be this empty. Still confused, I went aft to the crew quarters and found some crewmen. They were Chinese; I didn't attempt to talk to them. Two were in the Petty Officers' mess reading, and a third person was sleeping on a stack of three mattresses. I wondered if he thought he was a princess and was waiting to feel the pea.

At last, full awareness rolled over me. The ship was not in a port situation: it was dead in the water. The ship had been decommissioned and was being readied for the Suisun Bay graveyard. The officers, of course, were long gone—along with the purser and my paycheck. The following day was Sunday, and the Lykes Brother's Steam Ship Company in San Francisco—the only place I would be able to get my payoff—would not be open until the following Tuesday. It was now sixteen hours since I had had anything to eat. I was broke and in the virtually empty shipyards at four in the afternoon, and I had walked almost fifteen miles! I had only my wallet, my seaman's papers, and the clothes on my back. I had absolutely no place to go or to sleep for at least two days.

Night would be arriving soon, and the only thing I could think of was to go to the American Red Cross. They took care of disasters, and I qualified, as far as I could tell. I walked back into downtown Oakland, found a phone book, and located the Red Cross Center. It didn't even dawn on me that they too might be closed: Mercifully, this was not the case. I found the place and told my story to a lovely little old lady until I was all through and felt safely and completely in the hands of the "American (bless them all) Red (oh God, how glad I am they are here) Cross!!!"

And then, this sweet little lady explained to me that there was nothing they were set up to do for me. I was supposedly discharged because I was now mentally stable, but at that moment ... I lost it. In mounting hysteria, I reported, loudly and truthfully, that in the past I had never failed to be one of the great supporters of the Red Cross. In high school, when I went to theaters, I had always given to various charities, the USO and, of course, The American Red Cross. I described how I had missed my last meal because I was giving blood for the Red Cross, and now, when I had nowhere to turn in my hour of need, was the Red Cross going to fail me too?

By this time I was blubbering all over the poor Red Cross lady. What a pathetic clown I was. Immediately, in that quiet place, the three ladies descended on me "en masse," gave me food from their lunches, found me a warm coat, and, before I again went out onto the street, provided me with $40 cash and a chit for two weeks rent in an apartment building in downtown Oakland. I was embarrassed, given my behavior, but I could see me making it through at least the next few days.

"The House"

In downtown Oakland, near a large department store, I found the apartment address the sweet little ladies had provided me. It was a large, older building that, like many, was destined to be replaced eventually by newer multi-story apartment buildings—like the one on its left. The entrance was via a wide set of stairs at street level to a large porch on the first floor. I rang the bell, my rent chit at the ready. The door opened, and before me was a very tall, rangy-looking man in his forties, dressed in a flowing gown with beads, wearing what appeared to be a light smattering of lipstick, and standing in an indescribably feminine pose. He greeted me like a long lost friend when I told him my story, and his large gentle blue eyes laid on me a profusion of love and caring.

His name was Jess. He had the carriage of a Grande Dáme and floated rather than walked, as though he had been studying ballet from the day he was born. His long arms and graceful fingers had a life of their own. As he took me past the series of tiny apartments, he explained that, along with his partner Tom, he rented rooms on a long-or short-term basis, exclusively to veterans and their wives. He showed me one of the empty rooms; I noted that it was unusually sparse, consisting of a bed, a washbasin, and not much more. As Jess started to explain the strange architecture of the building, a young lady came flying out of one of the rooms, heading for a common bathroom. She was dressed in a flimsy underskirt—her panties and bra were covered but clearly visible.

In mock horror, Jess blocked her route, pouted prettily, and scolded her, "For heaven's sake, Vera, refrain from walking around near the windows without all your clothes on. People will think we're still in the 'old business.'"

After Vera apologized to both Jess and me, she returned to her room to don a robe and complete her journey to the bathroom. Jess explained to me, as he filled out my rent agreement, that this building he and his "business partner" had bought had formerly been a whorehouse, or—as he put it—"a known house of ill repute" and a favorite of visiting military. Occasionally, when old customers knocked on the door, they were politely but firmly sent away.

Later that day, as I was settling in—obviously a very short process—Jess introduced his partner, Tom, a working electrician. He was much older, a dumpy little man with a balding head, pleasant enough, but the two of them made a strange couple. Looking from one to the other, I would glance from gentle Jess at 6'4" to scruffy Tom who was a stretch at 5'5". They were truly an odd couple, but it was obvious they were meant for each other even though they looked like the of cartoon of "Mutt and Jeff."

In the days I lived there, I found that Jess looked out for his guests. They were mostly young women, with husbands in the military, who had come to Oakland or the great port of San Francisco to greet their husbands returning from overseas ... or to tearfully bid them good-bye as they were sent abroad. Jess was a combination of teacher, confidant, psychiatrist, and mother to these very young women who were entering a strange and exotic world from farms and homes on the East coast, in the Midwest, or South. He gave cooking classes, taught them how to set a table, and was always there when needed.

In the middle of my first week, I discovered that two of my shipmates, Bill and Scotty lived with their mother in the four-story apartment building next door. They were waiting—like I was—for the next good ship out. While Bill was the handsome one, I preferred Scotty—often described as cute—who had a wicked and well-exercised sense of humor. We had decided at our first meeting that we were going to be good friends. Their mother made "Seaman's coffee," that is to say, coffee that was made in a super-sized coffee pot and was apparently never started but simply added to. Scotty's mother was more like Scotty with her sense of humor. In a slightly gravelly voice she would say, "Good coffee is any batch that you can bend a strong spoon in."

During the second week at "the house," the whole city began to seethe. I looked but was not able to see the street; there were thousands of people jammed into it for many blocks. I was told that this spontaneous gathering was something called a "general strike."

Apparently, nobody calls such a strike, it just sort of happens. After many weeks of discontent—of what, I had no idea—thousands of people had stopped doing whatever it was they were doing and had simultaneously gathered in the downtown area. This was not a joyous group of people; it was pretty obvious they were pissed. And so, the whole city is shut down: no traffic, cops everywhere, and occasionally you hear the breaking of windows and alarms going off. Ambulances try to force their way to calls, schools are closed, and eventually federal troops are called in before it gets completely out of hand. However, I was almost totally in my head, so all this commotion was somebody else's problem.

Selfishly, the next thing I remember—after a quick, unsatisfactory visit to my folks in Vancouver, Washington—is that the three of us were aboard the Marine Wolf, happily sailing once again, compass reading 270° for Hawaii and Guam.

4 | The GD Bell

The recollection of most life experiences is volatile, often transient, and generally unreliable. But, some events by their timing, setting, or significance etch with acid permanence into memory.

During World War II, the Marine Wolf, a 496 foot, C-4 troop transport, sailed all over the world. In 1946 it had taken me on my second trip to Guam by way of the China, Burma, India (CBI) route. Both the Wolf and I now found ourselves back in our homeport, San Francisco. The Wolf was docked at Army Pier 15, several piers from the west side of the historic Ferry Building. Conveniently located on the bay and rising with great dominance at the foot of busy Market street, the Ferry Building was a constant beehive of maritime activity. Since the Wolf had finished her scheduled voyage, she was now due for survey and overhaul at Moore Dry-dock in Oakland; she needed to be at anchor, but also had to be readily available. I had never been on a ship due for lay-up so, when asked by my former watch officer, it seemed completely natural for me to agree to stand a "Black Ball Watch." The fact that I did not know what this entailed seemed irrelevant at the time. At nineteen years old, I was naïve and unfinished, both as a human being and as a budding merchant seaman.

I always walked in San Francisco, both for pleasure and to save money. Now, as I walked along the Marina, stretching my legs while I waited for the Wolf to be made ready to move, I remembered a previous hike through the Marina along the Embarcadero. Rather than proceeding in my usual westerly direction down the odd-numbered piers which reached out from Fisherman's Wharf, I had chanced to walk way east of the Ferry Building. At that time, few ships sailed from these even-numbered docks; they were mostly outfitting docks, construction areas, and company-owned truck trans-loading facilities. I had just walked past the aromatic smells of the Manning's' Coffee plant when I was stopped, riveted by a truly impressive sight! At an immense dry-dock, I found "The Pride of the Matson Steamship Lines": the beautiful 705-foot Luraline, the most popular cruise ship on the Hawaiian passenger circuit. The Luraline was far from the world's largest ocean liner, but she was a sixth again the length of the C-4 Wolf. The difference was not only in hull length, there was a much different percentage of tonnage and mass between the two ships. Generally speaking, a ship's length increases by a simple mathematical ratio, while mass and volume increase by logarithmic proportion. I had often seen the Luraline at sea: she was inspiring in her normal view, cruising majestically along the Pacific-Paradise route. But here I saw her completely out of water; her immense screws were visible next to the rudder assembly. Curves, massive and transitional, now included the bulk below the waterline, never seen at sea. Huge timbers held her safely in her mothering dock. But then, as I stood directly beneath her bow, the square middle hull sections changed and inexorably carried my vision forward to the rising and narrowing form that became her majestic bow. Stacked even higher was the forepeak deck that the Matson Line intentionally emphasized by painting the entire structure a brilliant, and distinctly visible, gloss white.

I stood just ahead of her forepeak and stared at this Giant, finding myself fascinated by the 80-foot bow plates—cutter bars meant to protect her in a collision at sea. My head was tipped so far back that I became intimidated … confused. I felt I was growing smaller. I perceived movement. I rapidly lost my sense of balance. With increasing vertigo, the entire ship seemed to be crushing down upon me …

Now, at eight bells (1600, or four in the afternoon) in early March, the Wolf's gangway was lifted after all extra stores and fuels had been discharged from the quarterdeck. She made a very sedate trip across the bay, which was still sprinkled with hide-and-seek sunshine. Her destination was a quiet, out-of-the-way inlet near Oakland. At an anchorage somewhere east of Treasure Island, semaphore bells rang and Wolf slowed to "dead slow." Most of the crew had departed at the Army pier; only the skipper, the junior third mate, two able-bodied seaman, the chief engineer, and one inexperienced ordinary seaman—namely me—were left aboard.

We sailed at this reduced speed for another twenty minutes and then stopped in a large, shallow, muddy cove. Here was a sight I never could have imagined: almost sixty ships of varying tonnage dead in the water, surging restlessly against their anchor chains. It was a chilling vision: stark grey vessels, empty of crew or spirit or life, silhouetted against a darkening sky. Hundreds of yards apart, they rode high in the water—as did the Wolf—screws and rudders visible. Large portions of their normally underwater red-painted hull sections were exposed, looking, somehow … obscene.

I stationed myself on the bridge's starboard wing in order to watch any new activity. Soon, I heard the radio crackling with obviously terminal orders. The port and starboard anchors splashed into the dark and foreboding water of the lonely inlet; the anchor chains quickly ran out.

When the rattling had finally stopped, a variety of bells and semaphore signals rang out from the bridge. I looked down from my position 60 feet above the water and observed a small pilot boat. It tooled gingerly up to our port gangway and, amid great shouting and cursing, was tied up. The gangway had been rigged to lead from the ship's welldeck down to the choppy water's edge. In this position, the gangway was a sharply angled, risky but substantial, set of stairs. The motor-launch, first elevated on one wave then lost in the trough of another, was finally buffered with shock-absorbing fenders and safely secured to the surging ladder. The bouncing boat took on the last of the luggage and boxes, along with their owners.

Listening carefully, I could hear an obvious change in the ship's noises as dozens of ventilators and fans whined to a stop. A prehistoric dinosaur could have sounded like this when it was dying.

Though I was an inexperienced ordinary, I had already learned the wisdom of not asking too many questions. In the absence of any explicitly supplied data, this evasive verbal technique made it necessary for people to have to guess whether or not one was actually stupid. Thus, with no questions asked, I had agreed to stand the "black ball watch" even though I had no idea what a black ball watch was. I figured that I could fake it. I would carefully observe everything and say nothing.

I wasn't sure what I was supposed to do next, so I crossed from the port wing into the navigation bridge that had been so full of activity only moments before. Surprised, I found that the area was completely devoid of personnel. The semaphore signal arms rested on the letters "engines done." Aimlessly, I searched other areas of the ship but finding no one, returned to the navigation bridge. With vague uneasiness, I moved again to the port wing. As I looked back and down toward the welldeck, I spotted the chief engineer. He hurried across the open welldeck, threw a heavy duffel bag over his shoulder, and started briskly down the 40-foot gangway. I watched as the big man timed the surges and nimbly dropped into the motor-launch. The operator gunned the engines and pulled away from the now completely silent Wolf. Was I alone???

There is a vast, bitterly cold, Humboldt current that comes out of Alaska. First it fans west-south-west down the Pacific coast in a giant crescent, two hundred miles wide; then it changes course to east-south-east and continues in a great arc leading almost directly through the Golden Gate into San Francisco Bay. It is seldom hot in San Francisco, even during the summer months, but in the winter, the fog and wind can be deadly cold. If one is unfortunate enough to fall into the ocean—or even the bay—at this location, the cold can kill. Previously I had observed the hospital ship, Mercy, which was sunk in a collision, having been hit broadside by the Mary Luckinbach, in the middle of San Francisco Bay. It was on a shake-down cruise and loaded with liquor and dignitaries. Later, I read that, though most survived, there were a few who didn't, even though rescue operations were carried out expeditiously. Experts identified that there are nerves at the base of the human skull that are very close to the surface of the head. When chilled deeply enough, this nerve plexus will prevent a person from voluntarily closing his or her mouth. Numbed and partially paralyzed from the cold, the unfortunate individuals will either drown immediately or perish within a few minutes from hypothermia. That image of half-frozen, drowned bodies was never very far from my consciousness.

Wind was blowing at ten knots from the northwest. It was only about 1745, yet already the air had significantly chilled. From early childhood, I had been burdened by a distinctly pathological hatred for cold weather. As a consequence, I was usually dressed in a fashion my shipmates found bizarre: red flannel underwear; an additional full suit of white thermal underwear; a pair of dress socks, covered by a pair of woolen knit knee-lengths; heavy fireman-type rubber boots; two wool shirts; a navy blue turtle-neck sweater; and topping all of this, my prize gear (obtained at a favorite store in Portland, Oregon) a "reverse lamb's wool vest, covered by its matched full-length, wool-covered, fully-lined lamb's wool coat with fleece collar." I crowned this with a ski mask and a standard watch cap. On a previous trip, a junior third had asked me dryly if I thought we were sailing to Antarctica!

It dawned on me, as I looked at the fog-obscured lights of Oakland and a distant Oakland Bay Bridge, that the temperature was no doubt going to hit the thirties, and, sure as hell, a gale was brewing. I had, however, decided that all of my watch would be carried out here, on the cozy navigation bridge. I could see the long, cold night—my ten-hour watch until dawn—spent in complete comfort, out of the weather.

Feigning saltiness, I furtively scanned the navigation bridge and adjoining chart room and then sat uneasily in the captain's chair, a huge swivel affair bolted to the deck behind and to the right of the helm. The ship's captain, who had a larger and more comfortable cabin a deck below, could use his weather cabin—located directly off the chart room—to take catnaps while still being close to any action in rough seas or delicate sailing situations. He could walk a few steps from this small bedroom and take his place in this chair—the only person on the bridge ever allowed to sit there—and supervise all activities of navigation and operation.

When the intercom suddenly rang, I almost fell out of the chair. I timidly pressed the button. It was Frank, the junior third, asking in a not-too-friendly fashion, "What the hell are you doing up there … and would you mind shagging your butt down to the mess hall?!"

I was relieved—another living, human being!

I allowed as how I would do that and rapidly made my way back down the three port ladders to the foredeck, down another ladder to the well-deck, across that, and up the ladder leading to the raised afterdeck. Above and below this deck were located the engine room, crew quarters, galley, messroom, dayroom, one equipment hold (aft the stack) and the aft housing.

I found the junior third sitting at a table in the petty officers' mess, drinking a cup of steaming coffee and eating a ham sandwich. He invited me to sit down. "Grab what you want to eat. The food's still hot."

I ate my fill, topping off a huge peanut butter and jelly sandwich with a giant piece of chocolate cake. Obviously there was residual steam pressure that would maintain the heat for hours. I made the necessary adjustment in my thinking. Instead of being on the bridge as I had previously imagined, I could tolerate standing my all-night watch in the messroom next to all the good food and a full rack of dime store novels. I did not find this new situation impossibly burdensome, but I was embarrassed that the junior third must have thought me "not too sharp" for not knowing the proper place to stand a "black ball watch." I casually settled back and tried to make myself comfortable. Frank watched me quizzically as I took off my two caps. He even smiled when I removed my coat, lamb's wool vest, and blue sweater. But he roared with laughter when a pair of earmuffs fell out of my coat pocket.

I was lulled into quiescence by a stand-by generator—felt more than heard. I was just wondering if there was a softer duty anywhere, when Frank suddenly rose and said, "O.K. Let's get on with it."

I quickly put my gear back on, curious about what we were going to do and where we were going to do it. As I followed him all the way back to the bridge, I guessed that my first hunch had been correct: I was going to stand the entire watch on the still warm navigation bridge. However, Frank continued climbing more ladders until we had reached the topmost deck: the flying bridge. There is nothing above this exposed deck except the main mast and the radar arms.

At the extreme rear of the flying bridge, just below the antennae and main range light, is a locked rack containing all of the semaphore flags and the metal clips that allow them to be attached and hauled aloft to the top of the main mast. On these flags are symbols in International Morse Code that are visually communicated to other ships and/or to shore. Single flags and combinations can indicate various conditions: "Captain's aboard" or "quarantine" or anything else to be communicated without the use of radio. Also in this locked rack was the folded device known as the "black ball." We took out the flat black shape, let it spring into its full round form, clipped it to one of the lines, and hauled it high on the yardarm above the radar mast. The ball was about a foot in diameter. Only when it was in position did I notice that all our ghostly company had similar black balls on their mastheads.

The wind had picked up to 15 knots, and white caps were forming. I was surprised to see that all the ships in the area were pointing the same direction. Being at bow anchor, they all reacted to the same strong outgoing current so there was nothing very mysterious about their behavior. Somehow though, in the gathering gloom of a fading sunset filled with extensive billowing clouds, the scene was a vast ominous panorama. In that setting, my imagination ran wild. As I scanned that strange group of ships, I saw elements of a phantom convoy—ships filled with cold and clammy cadavers—all sailing into a frozen and unspeakable hell …

I was jolted from my reverie by Frank's sharp voice ordering me to "get on with it." We secured the flag case and charged down the ladder back to the navigation bridge. I realized, at about the same time Frank did, that I did not have the slightest idea as to what it was that I was supposed "to get on with!" As we stood near the port wing, my total ignorance was obvious.

"Haven't you ever pulled this watch before?" Frank asked, not unkindly.

"No," I answered, hoping he would not think me a complete idiot.

"Well," he smiled grimly, "it's simple enough."

We trudged back down the ladders to the main foredeck and he introduced me to "The G. D. Bell!"

The ship's bell is that tool for telling time on shipboard. It is normally rung in a series starting the first half hour after 12 o'clock, 4 o'clock, and 8 o'clock, AM and PM. Since a ship functions on a twenty-four basis, sea watches are required during each minute of that time, which are maintained on a regular basis of 12 to 4, 4 to 8, and 8 to 12. The 12 to 4 watch, for example, starts at midnight and goes until four in the morning. At four, that watch is off duty until noon the same day at which time duty is resumed, continuing again until four that afternoon. Then the crewmember is off for eight hours until midnight. At that point the cycle starts over. A similar schedule is maintained on the 4 to 8 and 8 to 12 watches in both deck and engine departments whenever the ship is at sea. The main reason for this apparently confusing system is so that each man is only on duty for four hours at a time (about as long as a man is able to maintain a sharp watch) and is off for an eight-hour period. Since every watch has both a day and night component, no one will forget what sunshine looks like during a long voyage. Maintenance men, the carpenter, and some other special crew work days and sleep normally at night, but the ship's operating personnel follow the watch schedule as described.

Lights on all vessels on and forward of the bridge are forbidden since they destroy night vision for several minutes after exposure. Early in sailing history, it became necessary to develop a way of telling time that did not rely on light. The ship's bell became the answer. This ringing bell, as a clock, was as permeating and regular as the throb of the engines—persistent sounds that became audibly non-existent after a while.

In retrospect, I find it strange that though I knew exactly where the bell was located, I never did know who normally rang the damn thing.

However, the duty for which I had innocently volunteered handled the bell very differently from its usual function, and I can tell you, with certainty, who rings it during a black ball watch: It is rung by whoever is inexperienced and financially desperate enough to sign up for the duty.

In the gathering blackness, with dense drifting fog, Frank explained that he and I were the only deck personnel left; there was one wiper and one oiler in the engine room. I had never envied the engine room crew, especially when sailing the South Pacific where engine room temperatures were often in excess of 120 degrees, but I could certainly see the advantage on a night like tonight. Various scavenging circuits would keep the engine room cozy for at least another day or so, even without steam up.

Back to reality, I tuned in to Frank as he was explaining that he would keep watch on the bridge near the radiotelephone, and I got to ring the Bell! Previously I had ignored it; now I looked at the brass bell from a new and sobering angle. Innocently hooked to a heavy bracket on the outer port side entrance to the bridge deck, it now gleamed at me in brassy belligerence. It was a fairly large bell—24 inches high and 18 inches wide with a clapper the size of my hand. For a certainty, it was not a church bell but then I had never heard of anyone who had to ring a church bell while standing only a few inches away, except perhaps Quasimodo! When Frank rang it for me the first time, all the wicked pranks played on novice seaman ran through my mind. A single look at the humorless expression resident on Frank's face convinced me immediately that this was a legitimate job, ridiculous at it might seem.

Frank rang the bell in a slow measured beat for about 15 seconds, paused for about 30 seconds, rang it for a second series, paused another 30 seconds, and then, with a little bow, handed me the lanyard. The bell had not been rung for a minute or so, but my teeth were still rattling. My mind was trying to cope with the cacophony that had assaulted me. I found it totally unreal that I was supposed to spend the entire night trying to arrange my own permanent condition of deafness—as well as freezing on an exposed deck.

It was designed to be heard all over the ship, above the noisy operating sounds that are part and parcel of every large operating vessel. Until that particular moment, I admit to being completely innocent of just how high a decibel level this called for. The output might have been slightly more melodic, but in all other ways it had all the esthetic pleasure of consistently hitting oneself in the head with a mallet.

Frank excused himself with a grunt and made his way up to the cozy bridge, leaving me to the "G. D. Bell." A cold and clammy pea soup had rolled in; I heard other poor freezing souls ringing their individual bells. Buoys sang an irregular dirge, foghorns moaned, and sea gulls still aloft screeched. All sounds were muted and strangely romantic, even the other bells. But the bell I rang presented only the continuing prospect of diabolical torture for the rest of an endless and miserable night. In spite of my redundant gear, I was already cold. With savage clarity, I knew that I was irrevocably stupid!

It is said that one can get used to anything. Standing on the open deck slick with fog, I listened between bells to the ringing in my ears, louder than the actual bell sound. I thought about my shipmates, about their women, their bars and their beds, but most of all, that not a single one of them was spending the night with the "G. D. Bell!" The ship was at least four miles from any regular channel, close to tidal flats, anchored with nothing but other dead-in-the-water ships. I wondered at the insanity of maritime law: For whom does the bell ring?!!

Somehow 2:30 A.M. arrived. I was trying to decipher how many times were left to ring before sunrise. I determined, dazedly, I had only one hundred thousand forty six rings left before I died or dawn broke, whichever came first. I was hallucinatory, half dreaming of being ashore with freezing ears tucked between the breasts of a big, bosomy blond. The wind had picked up to a screaming 40 knots; white caps beat across the bay. I bounced like a wind-blown bingo ball, thrown first against the deck housing and then against the accursed bell.

With hopeless, wind-swollen eyes, I looked through the rain towards San Francisco; I thought I heard an alien sound in the banshee chorus. I imagined it would be a "taxi"—those small, white powerboats indigenous to any large harbor. They are to visiting ship personnel what the vehicular cabs are to downtown visitors. Seamen are strange and wondrous creatures. Sober, they are totally beyond prediction. With only a few drinks, they universally achieve a level of fearlessness and expanded mental and physical abilities that place them near the operational level of a standard maniac. Drink imbues them with only slightly less power than Superman. With even less motivation than that great alien, they will attempt to leap tall buildings, outrun a speeding bullet, and so on.

It was then, less with surprise than with contempt that I observed through blasts of freezing rain and fog what seemed to be a "taxi" making its way toward the Wolf. Over the wind's noise, that unexpected sound grew louder. Even in this surrealistic setting, something seemed unusual. My eyes told me visual truth, but it was incorrect … incomplete. I was trying to figure out what idiot was coming back to the Wolf and how he expected to make the gangway with mountainous waves at the ladder, when, suddenly my heart froze. In an instant I became infinitely colder: the small boat was not pitching in these high seas. It was riding steady and even!

Now I heard other sounds: unmistakable sounds of large engines, the bells, a semaphore. Magically, insistently … the sounds grew louder. Then, in a blink, the optical illusion disappeared. I was not looking at a taxi at water level, I was looking straight into the white-painted bow of the Luraline! She was about 300 yards away, aimed at the Wolf dead amidships and closing fast!

I grabbed the lanyard attached to the bell and started a loud continuous tattoo of sound, as fast and hard as humanly possible. I was crying and cursing and screaming and trembling. Only dimly did I hear the junior third's boots crashing down the ladder; I kept ringing the bell.

He bellowed with atypical hysteria at the approaching apparition, "Listen to us, damn it! Listen to us."

Frank was dressed all in black. I was thinking, "That's probably appropriate."

Fog obscured the enlarging view from time to time, but now we could plainly hear the Luraline's engines. They had not changed beat, but kept drumming, nearer and nearer.

Then there was the welcome sound of frantic semaphore bells from her bridge and the changed pitch of engines, slowing and stopping. Then more bells rang and the pounding started again, this time higher-pitched and frenzied as her screws reversed. The emergency klaxon whooped, but the distance continued to close. In an instant replay, I remembered the cruel 12-inch deep and 4-inch wide hardened cutter plates welded to the Luraline's bow when she had been in dry-dock. I could picture them cutting through our plates and decks, a warm knife slicing through tepid butter. I could hear the grinding, splintering screams of twisted steel and rent housings. I could see myself pitched down into the resulting chasm, into that awful freezing water. Like the "Mercy" victims, I saw my slack jaw frozen open, icy water pouring into lungs and stomach …

A hand grabbed my shoulder roughly. I heard Frank above the other sounds: "She's turning! She's turning!"

Indeed! Slowly, majestically, she WAS starting to turn starboard. Barely passing by our stern, her forepeak loomed above us. Even though we sat high in the water, we found ourselves on eye level with the second row of portholes below her main deck. After what seemed like an eternity, her enormous forward section passed us. We waited, doomed, for her stern to come into view, for the imminent collision. We knew it would come in seconds. She seemed close enough to touch. We could only wait for her to hit us aft and hope she would crush both of us outright: anything would be better than that awful water. We waited seconds, then minutes, but the crash never came. She had been gone for several minutes before either Frank or I saw fit to breathe.

We were both thinking: Maybe she will come back and take another run at us!

How close to Hell we had come that night we could not know for certain. We only knew the Luraline disappeared into the fog, out of our sight, heading in the apparent direction of Oakland. The incident, as far as I know, was written up by Frank as Officer of the Watch. I am sure it was put in the ship's log, but if I expected to read about it in the newspaper or find myself at a Coast Guard Board of Inquiry, I was disappointed. Nothing of the incident was ever published or discussed. Shock was so complete that I did not remember anything for days; much later, I just noted that I was ashore.

In the decades that have passed, I have forgotten who was the captain of the Wolf. I have forgotten how one gets to the lauzerette where the steering gear is located or exactly how much draft the ship had or the names of most of the crew. I have even forgotten the exact date this incident took place and whatever became of the beautiful cruise ship, the Luraline. I do not even remember Frank's last name. But, I do believe that neither Frank nor I will ever forget that cold, stormy, foggy night in San Francisco Bay.

In all the details of sailing that I have done and the details of sailing that I will do, there is one duty that I am positive I will never have any trouble remembering if I live to be a hundred or have a dozen more lives. I will never lose sight of one seaman's job, of one single important duty. I will never, ever, ever …

        forget …

    "Why you ring the 'God Damn Bell!!!'"

5 C-4's and Other Ships

Editorial Note: If you haven't already, you will soon discover that Larry, the Engineer, loves all of the intimate details of the structure and function of ships, especially the big troopships on which he sailed. A suggestion to those of you who do not share his passion: you may want to go down about 6 pages to the next section, though he hopes you won't!

Ships, Ships, Ships

Most of my sailing was done on three different C-4 troopships. The basic hull type for these ships is, a seven-hold cargo; however, all the versions I sailed on were converted to troop carriers. They were named as a series with the prefix "Marine," several dozen in all. Of the Marine series, I sailed on the Fox, the Wolf, the Lynx, and the Phoenix. In addition I sailed on a Navy troop transport ship that carried me to Guam (The General A.E. Anderson) on which I was a troop class passenger, not crew. I also sailed as mess man on the P&T Navigator for Pope and Talbot lines from the West coast to the East coast through the Panama Canal. Finally I crewed, sailing a coastwise contract, for a few months on the lumber carrier Coos Bay out of North Bend, Oregon where I was subbing for a crewman.

The C-4 troop carriers were my favorite ships. The cargo hull of the C-4 was the largest and the most common type of hull. Launched in a dozen different shipyards on both coasts and in the South, it was a workhorse, capable of being converted for many different needs. There were several major designs for these ships when used for troop transport. Those converted in the East coast shipyards were distinguished by having two troop cabin decks built over what otherwise would have been cargo holds. Those built in West coast yards contained a large section of lowered welldeck behind a higher foredeck and ended in the raised afterdeck. This afterdeck contained the engine compartment, engine officers' accommodations, crew quarters as well as the petty officers' mess and troop officers' quarters. The foredeck consisted of three bridges: ship's officers' deck, captain's deck, and the navigation deck. Atop these three "bridge" decks—so called because they allowed unencumbered transit from one side of the ship to the other—was the open top deck called the Flying Bridge. At sea I would spend half of my eight hour watches on this deck. It sported a view of the whole ship, fore and aft, although visually this is a slight exaggeration. From the foredeck, and looking past the welldeck, stood three decks of crew quarters, the ship's galley (kitchen), the mess (eating) rooms, the engine room and engine crew quarters, and a large single stack. This end portion of the ship enclosed not only the engine room, but also the boilers, machinery space, and electrical and mechanical controls for all the ship's services. Admittedly, this is a huge city: the troop officers never see the troops, and neither sees the ship's officers or crew. And the only fraternization between the troops and the crew occurs when the troops are unlucky enough to play poker with the card sharks posing as cook and messmen—all under the tutelage of the chief steward.

The only consistent love of my life, besides the wonderful lady with whom I have spent the last fifty plus years, were these ships and any other ships I could find. And if I couldn't sail on them, I painted them. What immediately distinguished the West coast C-4s from their East coast cousins was West coast's clearly visible welldeck covering half the ship's length; that welldeck contained four large cargo holds and covered hatches—unlike the East coast version whose welldeck was converted to passenger space only. In order to service these holds and attendant hatches, there were two distinctive, massive, and obvious king posts set on the well deck: steel supports three feet in diameter that rose in pairs almost to the level of the captain's bridge and supported two sets of extended booms, which were cabled with heavy steel lines attached to eight very large wenches. There were two other sets of king posts, one ahead of the forward bridge and one aft the crew and engine housing.

One might wonder why there were two different types of ships of the same general construction. The answer is that while the East coast version could accommodate almost forty percent more troop class passengers, the more flexible West coast version had four large holds that could serve as berthing for troops, or could be rigged for cargo and working gear. This arrangement insured that they could also accommodate trucks, tanks, assault landing craft, and tons of other gear and equipment. Although we often passed the East coast versions at sea, I never had the opportunity to crew on one.

Any large cargo ship is a small city. When it is in port, it is attached to the dock and becomes a small part of the host city. If it is in that port for any length of time, seaman find favorite places to eat, bars to hang out, and if they are lucky, a local romantic interest. A non-PC quote for seaman was, "A girl in every port and port in every girl." The ship, a familiar home, can always be counted on as a place to sleep and meals at no cost. Manning schedules vary from ship to ship and voyage to voyage, but there is always the sure knowledge that the ship is not welded to the dock. And one day, a black chalkboard will appear at the head of the gangway, usually on the quarterdeck, and it will bear a date and a military time for the ship's sailing departure with a notation of the next port of call.

The Marine Fox, my first ship, was not a standard cargo ship. A standard cargo ship would generally have a complement of officers and crew numbering about 30 to 40 men. As ships get smaller, various jobs are doubled up and crew sizes go down proportionately. When a cargo ship is used as a troop ship—a ship sailing on WSA (War Shipping Administration) orders—it is restricted to union crews, manning schedules, and proper safeguards in compliance with normal United States command procedures, under the auspices of the United States Coast Guard. This would apply to any American crew sailing under United States' authority. When carrying thousands of troops, a cargo ship has several special considerations. Since some of the trips would last weeks or months, not only would sleeping facilities be necessary but, of course, troops would have to be fed. On these troop ships then, the normally small part of a crew responsible for feeding the officers on a strictly cargo ship was beefed up to three or four times the normal complement in the steward's department. In this situation, the steward's department controlled about 125 men.

No matter the size or complexity of a ship, there are three and only three operational departments. The deck department takes care of all things related to handling the ship: lines, cargo, maintenance, painting, and steering. The engine department mans the engine rooms, boiler rooms, oil storage, domestic and general water supplies, and the evaporators to produce drinking water, as well as all of the ship's electrical, plumbing, generating, air conditioning, steering equipment, pumps and heating; on a small ship, many of these tasks will be handled by a single person, but on a large ship, there will be many men assigned to similar tasks.

The last of the three is the steward's department. If you think in terms of a small hotel, you will consider all of the services necessary to supply food, bedding, and all other normal necessities of life. On a C-4 carrying 1500 extra men—in addition to all of the space allocated to the feeding of the ship's officers and crew and, of course, accounting for the separation of various levels of military passengers—first, there would have to be troop officer class kitchens, supply rooms, preparation areas, dining rooms, and small bars; second, there would be similar but much smaller facilities for the non-commissioned officers; and third, the larger facilities for the general troops.

On our C-4, the same hierarchical rules applied to the ship's own crew. The ship's officer's quarters received food from the crew mess since union rules would not allow a two-pot ship, but they ate from their own pantry and in their own ward rooms. Also in the crew quarters, there was a pantry adjoining the main crew galley and a separate mess room for non-commissioned officers such as the engine room petty officers, the carpenter, machinist, quartermaster, bo's'n, helmsman, and day maintenance men. All very complex!

One of the personalities that I employ is the one I call "the reporter." The reporter is always looking in on a scene that is taking place in front of him while he himself is removed, dispassionate and unaffected personally. I have walked through my life this way, so that most of the time my view of things takes place as though the personal Larry was nowhere in sight. Sailing in the Merchant Marine gave me the opportunity to go into this very singular world, with no personal biases or attitudes toward what I was going to see, hear, smell, or feel. Each voyage I embarked on was a new book; I opened it at the beginning and kept reading until I was at the last moment of final docking. By reading each ship that I signed on, I was with it page by page from beginning to end.

Most of the ships I crewed took additional trips without me, but I never had the illusion that my being aboard was the last chapter in the ships log. Every ship has a log—actually, several. The one most people are concerned with is the "Captain's Log." This is the general story of the ship as seen from the captain's point of view, but there are others.

One of the most important logs is the Steward's: all the supplies for the ship are noted; all the products necessary for feeding, housing, and bedding are surveyed; and all of the waste products that must be removed are noted. The steward's role is the one most directly involved with the ship's morale. The steward is in control of the food!

Another important log is the Chief Engineer's where semaphore signals from the bridge are recorded, and information about the commands are sent back to the bridge indicating that the orders were followed and the time they were carried out in the engine room. There are phones, notes, and written orders as well as manifests and conditions reported to and through the various departments on board. The ship is a vast floating business complex, complete in every detail; all of this business is controlled by the captain, through the purser.

All in all, with expanded divisions, the C-4 was a very special moving city with so many people aboard including, in some cases, the U.S. military and, on one trip, 500 Japanese military prisoners being repatriated to their country. The Japanese were held under guard for the whole trip, were marched to the troop class mess for dinner, and served box meals for breakfast and lunch. They were confined to quarters in the smallest hold forward of the bridge and allowed to congregate only on the foredeck hatch. For this service and others, it was clear that a police presence was necessary. Remembering the people that I have sailed with, I find it is somewhat unnerving to realize that there is no police presence on the average cargo ship, although I had served on at least one which certainly could have used such a presence.

The military, however, takes a positive position in the matter of police services, so aboard the A.E. Anderson, we had, as a permanent member of the ship's company, a marine sergeant—who had the keys to the small brig—and two marine corporals as his staff. On any trip, he would have the right to press into service any troop class marine whom he might need to assist him in taking care of prisoners. The marines chosen for this job might be trained in military police protocol or might simply apply for the job; they were glad to take on this special assignment because they received special food and billeting considerations.

From the perspective of the 2010s, the world of my ships is pretty much a thing of the past.

1945: We in the United States had just made the world safe for Democracy, or so we thought. We had lost hundreds of thousands of our soldiers, sailors, marines, and merchant seaman in those few years before the hectic crazy last days of victory, first in Europe and then with the surrender of our then bitterest enemy: Japan. At that time, the United States had the largest merchant fleet the world has ever seen. The troop ships that I sailed aboard were licensed under many Allied and American flags, and all were controlled by what was called the War Shipping Administration. Thousands of American troops were being transported from islands in the Pacific, from England, Australia, South America, and other countries representing the Allies, and of course, there were troops who were still in former enemy territories in which they had been so recently fighting.

Besides the troops, there were millions of tons of war materials and supplies still sitting on docks and supply areas throughout the nations of the earth. There were food and medicines to be delivered to the survivors, both Allies and former enemies, where whole fundamental governance and social structures had collapsed. The Marshall Plan was put into effect at the cost of billions of dollars to reconstruct hundreds of cities that had been totally destroyed.

The largest fleet in history obviously had a purpose and that purpose was played out on an incredibly costly playing field made up of all the nations and ports in most of the known world. This was the planet and the playing field that I entered as a fledgling ordinary seaman in the year 1946. I had no idea at this tender age of 18 that I had just met the sea, the love of my life. I had entered a period in that life when a few short years of sailing experience would take me to places, to do things, and to be a tiny part of a history; it has taken me a lifetime to remember all of this.

The Coos Bay

I had been checking in at the Portland SIU (Seaman's International Union) Hiring Hall for a couple of weeks, when I heard my name called. To my surprise, it was a really weird but very desirable job, and it was an inter-costal contract. There are four types of jobs that are available to merchant seamen: international sailing contracts—which I had previously sailed; great lakes contracts—which I never had and never would take; coastal contracts; and inter-coastal contracts—which I would have been glad to take but had never been offered. The inter-coastal contracts are stranger than any of the others. As the name indicates, they never leave their country's waters. This shipping mode is rapidly disappearing because transportation of lumber and most other goods are now sent either by train or truck.

By the beginning of the 20th century, there were hundreds of contracts set up for the many lumber schooners that trekked up and down the coasts of California, Oregon, and Washington. During the time that highways were not the primary mode of transport, these graceful old-time wooden sailing craft were filled not only with lumber, but also would carry all the interstate supplies that might flow from one costal state to another. There were similar contracts on the East Coast and for Southern ports of call.

Modern lumbar schooner contracts were determined by the fact that these ships were never far from a port; as relatively small ships with small crews, their internal supply needs were not very great. As a result, the contract allowed a man to hold more than one job. Thus, it was explained to me that I would be signed on as 3rd cook, bedroom attendant (BAR), and waiter. In the Steward's Department, as in the other deck and engine departments, everyone worked long hours but were paid premium wages.

Obviously happy to get the job, I took the bus from Portland to the little coastal city of North Bend, Oregon. Just off the highway I saw the Al Pierce Lumber Yard; I knew that was my destination since I had been told that the Coos Bay was berthed there. As I walked through the mill, I was directed to a dock covered with dozens of 8-foot stacks of finished lumber. The dock extended to the busy waters of the Coos River, with mooring gear at the far end.

I had seen traditional lumber schooners, seldom more than 300 feet long with a crew of perhaps sixteen men. They were generally wooden hulls, had two or three masts, and looked pretty much like a sailing schooner should. At the end of the dock I was striding down, nothing of the sort was in sight. All I could see was a steel structure at the dock that I took to be a coffee shop since it had a stack out of which wisps of smoke were floating. As I got closer, I suddenly realized that the "coffee shop" was actually an old U.S. Navy LST (Landing Ship Tank). I had to revise my expectations and try to think in Navy terms about this ship I had signed up to sail on. The LST is constructed on the gently graceful and curving lines of a standard shoe-box. On the back of this box is a square structure that turned out to be much larger than it appeared. It was hard for me to believe that this ugly-looking thing was built to take a crew of fourteen, carry two medium tanks, and 125 men with all their equipment—originally carrying men into combat. Walking nearer, I could see that the clamshell bow, designed to allow tanks or other equipment to roll off the bow ramp and onto a beach, had been welded shut. There was a tiny bridge deck and a tracked gantry crane on the forward deck, next to a single, relatively small hatch through which lumber would be loaded into the hold. These craft were built for war, hard service, being shot at, and getting a straightforward job done.

The men who signed on to these lumber schooners were mostly retired German Matson Line officers; the crew were middle-aged men who generally worked on the ship until they died of old age. The glaring exception was Ernie Bliss, the skipper. Besides me, he was probably the youngest man aboard. I was offered this job only because a man had to spend time in the hospital; it was only supposed to last for a month. I would make a good deal of money, but with my in-built poor money habits, I thought I would be spending a lot of it before I ran out of the job. It turned out that the three positions and the short time between ports guaranteed that I would not have enough time off to spend any money. Though we were in port for six days out of a nine day round trip, the "in port" time was a killer. In the steward's department we had to be available to provide meals 24 hours a day, in or out of port!

Now, as I found the gangway onto the mid-deck, I made sure that I was going to sign on properly so there was not a repeat of my first voyage where I was legally a stowaway. The first time a crewman meets with his new ship is always a little bit intimidating. I found a guy leaning against the deck housing just past the gangway and asked where I was to sign on. He casually directed me toward a deck hatch. I walked directly across a wide passageway and into a forward office cabin on the opposite side of the ship. There, Fred, as combination First Mate, Chief Mate, and Purser, greeted me with a monstrous German accent; he was the obviously long-time, only holder of all these offices. He told me to relax, go to the galley, get something to eat if I were hungry, and just wait for sailing time since all the crew was not aboard.

In many ways a lumber schooner is a little relaxed on protocol. Generally everyone knows everyone else, and so it is a more genial working atmosphere. Since I knew I would see the galley soon enough, I just hung out at the port rail where I had come aboard. The tracked gantry was busy shifting the last load of finished lumber from the shuttling forklifts into the nearly filled hold. I watched as the deck crew worked seamlessly and efficiently, putting in the last load and securing the hatches.

As loading finished and preparations were made for sailing, I heard the sound of a taxi rushing up to the side of the ship. The driver got out of the car and was about to signal for help when three of the crew strolled down the gangway and, signaling the driver away, expertly pulled a short, thoroughly polluted crewmember out of the taxi. It took the combined efforts of all involved to get the drunken, stumbling seaman aboard and whisked down below to his fo'c'sle. Amused but confused, I asked the man watching the quarter-deck who the "pickled one" was, hoping it was not the skipper, who had yet to come aboard. I had not verbalized this concern, but the deck hand laughingly cleared it up for me anyway.

"That's our radioman. He'll be all right by the second day out."

I had serious questions about his health—and ours—if this was the guy that would be called upon to issue an SOS on a telegraph key. At the present moment, he would be hard pressed to successfully locate his butt. However, against my nature, I kept such questions to myself, the more so because nobody else seemed the least concerned. It was obvious this was a normal state for the radio operator at the beginning of a trip.

The main hatch had been dogged down and secured for sea when I got my next surprise. A cab, followed by an incredibly small, three-wheeler Vespa, swung onto the dock somewhat forward of the gangway. The front of the tiny vehicle, including the steering wheel, rotated on hinges out of the way as two shapely gals and the skipper emerged from the cramped quarters. Some kind of decision had been made between the two girls in the Vespa and the three emerging from the cab. Four of the girls, by apparent mutual consent, re-entered the cab, while the remaining one came on board arm and arm with Ernie Bliss. The Vespa was then picked up in a cargo net by the crane and lifted to the foredeck where it too was secured. The ship's heavy-duty gas engines fired up, lines were secured, gangway lifted, and we "lumbered" our way from the dock and out of North Bend to the ocean.

Besides laundry exchange, loading supplies, and clean-up work in the galley, there were meals to be prepared around the clock and served in and out of port. There were breakfast at 0700, coffee break at 1000, noon lunch, 1500 coffee break, dinner at 1900, 2200 break, midnight dinner, 0300 sandwich break—and then it started all over again, for the three days sailing and the three days in port. Two of the days we were in Los Angeles, when I might have gotten a few blocks from the ship, the steward commandeered three of us to help paint the interior of the house he was buying; he was our boss so arguing did not seem like an option. Besides, he carried an 32 automatic.

The man I was relieving had medical and legal complications, so I stayed on the job two additional months. At first I was put in the crew mess but my service was so bad that the steward changed me to the officer mess room. Even here, with fewer men to serve and more time to do it, I got in trouble: on the third day I fouled up a simple egg order for the chief mate, Fred. He was a grizzled, no nonsense German who was less than pleased with my efforts. After I had given him the wrong order for the third time, he had had enough. He rose from his chair at the head of the table, gave me a withering look from bulging eyes and a flaming face. Then, rising to his full 5 foot 4 inches of height, he gulped for air and blistered me with the following tirade: "Vuts da madder vich you, you can't spek the Ingligch?!"

Of course the problem, besides my being unable to remember simple breakfast orders, was that the man scared the hell out of me. There was a moment of terror, followed by an insane desire to laugh in his face over the murderous hash he had made of the "Ingligch langwich." I apologized profusely and promised to get it right thereafter—which I did—but then I was no longer afraid of him. We actually became friendly.

The rest of the tour became a trip from tedium to ennui as we cruised back and forth between the North Bend Al Pierce dock and the Sun docks in LA. The only break from the routine came when a terrible storm greeted us trying to berth in North Bend. The sailing characteristics of the Coos Bay were such that, at a top speed of seven knots, it normally slewed from port to starboard making the ship look like it was in need of a cane for stability. The gasoline engines gave off a sound as pleasant as a wrecking yard giving birth. When its normal annoying clatter roared into full speed, as was necessary for hours during the storm, it was terrifying.

I had seen the ship pull up to docks smartly in spite of heavy rip tides and tight quarters, but during the storm, in which we had to stay out of the bay for two full days, I got a chance to really understand in how much regard our skipper was held. The river is shallow all the way in and is guarded by fierce and jagged rocks. We really were in danger. I spent most of my time in my bunk, which was just forward of one of the two shaft alleys where the propeller had been bent on some similar trip; every third turn, I had my teeth shaken.

Ernie stayed on the tiny bridge most of the time and gradually eased us back into port when the storm finally blew itself out. It was the most exciting thing that happened while I was on the Coos Bay, but eventually there came a day when my errant relief was released from the hospital, from court, and from everything else that had troubled him, and came back to relieve me. I was as glad to see him as he was to see the Coos Bay. I got a bus schedule, got on the appropriate bus, and in due time found myself back in Portland, none the worse for wear and containing as little knowledge of the city of North Bend as I had when I first laid eyes on it.

6 | The Japanese Boys

"T he Doc" was a small intense man of about 45. He seldom smiled, but went about his business with a seriousness that let everyone know that he had been in life's battles and had survived them all. He was a heavy drinker as well as a heavy smoker, like most men in Camp One, but he never let anything interfere with his job of caring for the health of the crew of J.H. Pomeroy Company. He had been in the Navy and retired early, but still had the wanderlust so found overseas opportunities as a contract laborer. He was quickly shifted into hospital work as an HA (hospital attendant) when employers found he had excellent references as a Navy corpsman.

His drinking buddies called him Fletch (probably for Fletcher), and he had been with Pomeroy Construction on many different projects all over the world. I did not drink, but even if I had, I do not think Fletch and I would have been buddies. At that period of time, I had no friends, with the possible exception of that remarkable man, named Herman Creek, whom I had met on the A.E. Andersen troop ship that had taken over 500 workers to Guam: J. H. Pomeroy, Brown Pacific Maxim, and civil service employees. But outside of the few men I worked with as fellow waiters, I had little to do with any of the other men.

A couple of days after I arrived, a heavy-set character—Charlie something—who had served as head waiter, had completed his contract and was in the process of leaving. For the next few days, from our boss— the steward, Don Havard—I heard many insulting and mostly unnecessary comments heaped on this poor soul, even though he was leaving. I decided that I was going to do my job and steer clear of Don. As it turned out, that was not going to be possible for after I had been working a week, Don stopped me when I was cleaning up in mess hall Three and told me to come to his office. Because of that non-auspicious beginning, I was set to not like him much, so I was surprised when he offered me the job of headwaiter.

I looked at him for a long time and then said in an even tone, "Well, thank you for thinking of me but, if I take the job, I do want to get one thing straight."

"Sure," he said, smiling slightly, "Shoot!"

"My name is not Charlie, and I won't let anybody talk to me like that."

The faint smile drifted off his face to be replaced by a slight tinge of color, but he calmly answered, "As long as you do the job, you and I won't have any problems."

He turned his back on me, riffled through some papers, and came up with the correct application form. "Just fill this in, walk it up to the office, and you're on the job."

The job was easy enough. I had to take charge of the nine fellow waiters, assigning three of them to each of the three dining halls, intelligently named One, Two, and Three. I was responsible for seeing that the waiters were there on time, served the required meals, and did the proper cleanup.

These three Quonset hut dining halls were parallel to each other and were connected to the main transverse hall. On one side of The Main—as we called it—there were a series of three parallel Quonsets: the galley, the chef's office, and a storage area. The storage Quonset was locked and had screened areas for food and supplies, as well as a cold-storage walk-in. To the other side of The Main, clear of the entrances to mess halls One, Two, and Three, were freezers for ice cream and refrigerators for cold drinks and beer, as well as ice-making machines. Alongside the supply Quonset was a small office for Don, a small assembly area for the crew, and even a desk for me. Still another Quonset hut housed the "Jimmy 500" GMC engine and General Electric generator that, along with its stand-by twin unit, pumped power to a large electrical board that distributed energy for the whole camp. The Pomeroy and Brown Pacific Maxim office complex was contained in a sheltered two-story Butler-type house located up a dirt road, a hundred yards behind the mess area. That office building, the kitchen, serving halls, and the assorted 12 Quonsets scattered about below it—where we men lived and slept—depended on the 24/7 operation of the generator since we were far up in the hills on a plateau that overlooked Apra Harbor. On the Apra side, here was a sharp drop hundreds of feet to the road below, but we were not at the top; behind us, across several ravines and small hills, we could just make out the humpbacked shape of Mt. Lam Lam in the interior of the island.

I had no way of knowing at that time just how isolated I was; I had no sense of myself at all. When on shipboard as a member of the crew, there is a sense of belonging that cannot be taken away. You are a working part of the ship: you have a job, an assignment, a being-ness that gives you a sense of purpose and stability. I had nothing like that at Camp One. But, in fact, I was not physically alone: there were Smitty, Larry, another Larry, Brownie, and Blackie—the other young men who worked as waiters. We slept in the same hut 17, talked, and goofed off in the assembly room. But, I was still alone in mind and spirit.

There were a few times I remember being with Herman Creek; once I invited him to dinner at my galley. He came and he was really impressed with the food. When I asked him why he never invited me to the civil service camp, he said that their cooks were all Filipino and the only things they knew how to cook with were onions. Creek was laughing when he added, "Hell, these people would serve their friggin' vanilla ice cream with onions."

Creek was a brilliant man with a fully rounded education. Meeting him on the Andersen going to Guam, we had spent a lot of time talking about our lives. He had been an art major in college, had even sold some of his paintings, but then had changed to architecture. Sitting for hours at a time with me on the fantail of the Andersen, he would play his guitar with considerable talent and sing in a melodious baritone. He was now working in the civil service camp as a truck driver. These changes in his life seemed perfectly normal for him; I hadn't a clue as to whom he really was. When we got into philosophical discussions on the ship, Herman made it known that he had spent some time in the CBI field of operations, working for the Army as an engineer. He fascinated me with his descriptions of work on roads and bridges in that tortured area of the world. It was a place that had almost never known anything resembling peace. The natives were a people Westerners liked to use the catchall appellation of "gooks." Many who used this word were simply trying to describe indigenous people, with whom they would normally never have rubbed elbows. Depending on who was using the word, it could be a simple but crude description of the people you were working with and might simply tolerate; along the emotional continuum at its worst, it was used to describe a vicious animal, as in "The only good Jap is a dead Jap."

My experiences in the Jewish-Italian ghetto in Portland made very clear to me that goodness-evil, honesty-deceit, and all the other dichotomies were spread evenly among every ethnic and religious group. I was always disdainful of my adopted mother when she would talk of "the little black clouds," although there were very few blacks in our lily-white hometown environment. This was the case until Kaiser created the shipyards, engendering the sudden influx of thousands of workers from the East Coast and the Southern states.

In general, Creek seemed to share my feelings, and yet he had a special, deep-seated hatred for a Korean colonel with whom, it seemed, he was always crossing swords and trails. His attitude towards this man was surprisingly vehement, and several times he warned me to always hold back trust in the Korean. It seemed like a fatuous warning since I did not picture a strange Korean colonel anywhere in my immediate future.

The locals fascinated me. The island of Guam consisted of more or less pure Chamorron stock, having had racial purity for thousands of years. Then in the late 16th through the early 19th centuries, great chunks of the Pacific Island Archipelagos were discovered by Europeans looking for more land and riches to control. As is often the case, what appeared good for the Europeans was almost total disaster for the natives. However, men being men, strange combinations of mixing occurred with the result that, over time, the Spanish conquerors had turned the island of Guam and the capitol city of Agana into an almost perfect copy of a Spanish village. During this time, sailors from all parts of the world had passed through leaving their seminal signatures. It was not unusual to see a native girl whose genes might include some of the following DNA: Japanese, Chinese, French, English, Scottish, German, Dutch, and, of course Spanish, as well as her native Chamorron. When I had first started to sail, I had heard the cruel racist epithets of "mongrelization of the races." After seeing some of the natives of Guam, in particular, and the South Pacific, in general, it was my consideration that if this was mongrelization, all I could say was, "Give me your stray puppies!"

Guamanians are beautiful people. They had become Americans by virtue of the United States winning them—as in a card game—during the Spanish-American War. Because of the Spanish influence, they were a Catholic community with Spanish historical underpinnings. But also the Guamanians were Americans by virtue of modern civilian influxes. However, with the American/Japanese battles of World War II and the conquering sailors and soldiers of both warring groups, the locals lost any cultural innocence they might have retained.

The Armed Forces, and especially the Navy, had taken a real bruising from the debacle at Pearl Harbor and the losses in the South Pacific. Millions had died, and those leaders left standing—political and military—had decided that no potential enemy would ever again catch the United States flat-footed. The U.S was determined to guard its far western borders. Special local laws, protective covenants, and militarily-secure facilities guaranteed Guam's safety, but it may never become a State.

Stretching into the next century, various military codicils maintain highly sensitive locations that remain under the aegis, protection, and security of the U.S. Navy; since 1946, this has been Blue Letter Law ("leave things as they are")—like the constitution, i.e., unchangeable, permanent.

Prior to a trip back to Guam in 1992, I researched whatever sparse materials that I could find on the final retaking of Guam. During our trip, we discovered that you could go from one end of the island to the other and find virtually nothing to convince you that anyone there had ever fired a single shot in anger. Sherry and I noted that fully 30% of the island is still held by the Navy, and although we put 250 miles on a rental car, there was little left to indicate that, some fifty years previously, this had been a bastion in the war to free the South Pacific from the hold of the Japanese. But, we also found out that the Japanese are now welcome guests for the holidays. Because the high-end hotels were completely booked by Japanese tourists, we spent New Year's Eve and the next few days in a flea-bag hotel with natives camping at the end of our corridor "in order to protect us"—from what we did not know!

Guam started out as a protectorate like the rest of the Marianas Island chain, but unlike Saipan, Tinian, and Kwajalein, Guam dropped out of the covenant to which the others belonged to become a Commonwealth. If you check a world atlas you will see that Guam stands alone out of the neat box that encompasses the other islands in the archipelago.

Although Herman had just come over with me on the ship, in less than a month he seemed to have absorbed an immense amount of information about the island. There seemed always to be great depths of his wisdom in reserve, which he could sum up in just a few words. For example, his civil service camp anecdotes about their cooks' lack of dietary prowess turned out to be true. When he finally broke down and invited me for lunch, I did not order any ice cream but the fish-based concoction I did get looked like someone else had already eaten it.

One day, Herman made an arrangement with me to meet him at his camp for a drive to Inarajan that was restricted to all but the military and, therefore, illegal for me. Rear Admiral Pownal was governor of the island at that time, although it was under the titular control of local politicians and judges. This admiral, who wanted no more American bastards birthed on Guam, supported the natives. As a result, if civilians other than members of designated working crews were found in the villages, they would be discharged and shipped home at their own expense. If it were military men that had transgressed, they would have the choice of either a General Court Martial or they could sign up for a new two year hitch—to be served on Guam. Since Herman was driving the bus, I took the chance that he knew what he was doing and everything would be all right.

We picked up a busload of natives and headed across the island finally reaching Talofofo Bay; there things got a little more serious. Just before we got to a bridge, Herman told me to scrunch down on the floor where two giggling young native men sat on me. A guard greeted Herman and peered into the big yellow bus. It was a perfunctory inspection as Creek had said it would be, and we drove on to Inarajan.

As we were entering the outskirts of the city, Herman stopped while all of the natives—men, women, and children—moved to the right side of the bus. I looked to see what was so interesting. A scene that had formed a hundred yards off the road became riveted in my mind: There in the middle of the field was a native farmer with a cone hat, feeding his good-sized manhood into the water buffalo's mouth. The animal's slow fellatio with the human didn't seem uncomfortable for either of them. I was shocked to see the man casually notice the bus and wave. They waved back merrily, and then the bus drove on. But, before we had completed picking up all the natives for transport to the village, Creek blew me out of the water once again: He opened the bus doors at one of the pickup stations and greeted a smiling, missing-toothed, old lady as she boarded with, " How's your ass, Sweetheart."

Her answer came back clear and throaty, " Fine, Herman, and how's it hanging?"

I had only been in Guam for a short time and all I knew about the place was that the Catholics allegedly had reformed and conformed it. Well, forget about that fairy tale. For generations upon generations, the island has had its own paganistic and pragmatic practices. The priests had merely managed to overlay the pagan and ancient belief systems with a veneer of Catholicism; underneath were the old ways and rituals. The Guam nationals made adjustments for all of the Western and European influences they had been forced to ape. The island was full of American troops fighting, dying, and cussing—always. To the Guamanians, fuck, shit, damn, motherfucker, and all the other colorful language garnishes were simply routine English—which they took to with determined relish. I knew Herman to be a cultured human being, so this show and the man and beast performance in the field seemed to be a sophomoric stunt designed for the new boy.

It was not until almost a half century later that I came to understand what was really going on: These processes were planned down to the last detail to control not only what I saw, but what I thought I saw, what I believed, and what actions I was subsequently to perform. Herman Creek was not my friend because of a casual meeting on shipboard, and the deep friendship that seemed to follow was an illusion: Herman Creek was my first control. I was a special field agent, a carefully trained assassin, and a very unusual special CIA weapon. But, as I was to later discover, there was more to Creek's and my relationship than that.

At Talofofo Bay, when the bus stopped at the control point, the agents on the bus actually took me off. Creek parked the bus that was then taken over by another driver and continued on to Inarajan with its native cargo. Creek was now standing beside six other men, including the dreaded Korean Colonel Nu. I did not see Colonel Nu and certainly, in my catatonic state at the time, did not remember him from the Court of Inquiry held at the San Diego Naval Base.

Within a few months after I had joined the Navy at 17, I ended up as a "Section 8" due to my strange actions: I had fainting spells and times when I just "went away," not too dissimilar to what I exhibited as a young child. Since the Navy in 1945 had little tolerance for abnormal behavior, I was labeled "crazy." On one occasion after I had crumpled to the ground during marching exercises, two hospital corpsmen had bounced me off a bunk and onto a metal radiator in the infirmary—in the presence of witnesses. Since I wasn't "crazy" all the time, I complained about that treatment to the commanding officer, resulting in a Court of Inquiry. I was encouraged to take an honorable discharge, which I accepted, rather than hang around to testify when the corpsmen were brought up on charges. Little did I know that the papers I signed, under the auspices of a certain Korean colonel, were not just discharge papers, but rather I signed on to the "Special Services" (OSS).

There are few people who have more paper in their medical and psychological files than I do: these included the salient facts regarding my strange seizures and apparent narcolepsy. My life was a constant story of survival in the most trying of circumstances. My adopted parents, Macie and Gene, saw to it that I got the very best medical help that was available. But, I had nothing with which to compare myself and, as a consequence, did not know that I was, at best, a psychological basket case and, at worst, a flaming psychotic.

From the time I had officially, or maybe unofficially (no paper trail), signed with the company, Herman Creek was only one who had the power of life or death over me—even though, erroneously, Nu thought he did. The US military and paramilitary adjuncts of the alphabet soup knew far more about me than I ever imagined—I had no idea that I had been tracked from the time of my adoption. They knew, for example, the types and number of deadly situations I had been in before I reached my third birthday. The means to control me were identified, based on psychiatric evaluations and observed examples of clairvoyant abilities. As I fervently wished to be of service to my country, I was a natural pawn, given my damaged psyche and my desire for strong parental figures. My clairvoyance and other paranormal abilities brought me to the attention of Stanford Research Institute at a time when the US military was involved with attempting to surpass the alleged work in so-called "remote viewing" that was being done by the Russians. (A useful reference would be the movie, "The Men Who Stared at Goats.") These qualities made me a natural for counter-intelligence work, and the Army planned to use my services as a stealthy, almost invisible agent.

However, Colonel Nu had very different plans. He believed there were hundreds of ways, not nearly so dramatic as remote viewing, for gathering intelligence and conducting special operations. He saw my value as a semi-conscious idiot with a completely erasable mind/memory, who was fast and agile enough to make a perfect assassin. He knew, to the last incredible acre foot, the anger and potential violence that formed a reservoir of rage in me that was held back only by the thinnest of constraints.

After being escorted off the bus, I was present, but absent, as Colonel Nu and Herman Creek faced off.

Nu spoke first, "Is he still in your alleged trance state?"

Creek didn't answer, but instead walked over to me and asked, "Will you forgive me for that nasty trick?"

I answered happily that I really needed to get around more on the island.

Creek said, "Well, just sit back and enjoy the rest of the trip. We will be in Inarajan in a couple of minutes."

"Very impressive," commented Nu. "He still thinks he is on the bus with a load of natives?"

"Absolutely!"

"Colonel Creek, as you know, we have a split authorization to deal with."

Creek shifted into a casual slouch. "Yes, I understand that you want to use him as an assassin."

"Correction, Colonel, I HAVE used him as an assassin. It is important for me to run my own test, if you don't mind. I want to make sure he still follows all orders." This was said slowly for emphasis, and with a further narrowing of his eyes.

"Well, excuse me, Doctor, but I think this particular test is totally unnecessary."

"Nonetheless, it is what we are going to do. I understand that in his background there is the information that he once flew over the battleship Oregon? And, this was when he was ten? Pardon me if I find that a little difficult to understand."

Creek shifted his considerable weight and signaled for their small group to take seats at a pair of picnic tables that were set up near the water. The group, including me, moved over to the tables, but I did not sit. I was dressed in dungarees, a white tee shirt, and wore a pair of heavy tennis shoes.

When Creek spoke again it was slowly, as one might talk to a child. He made sure that he was sitting directly opposite Nu and now eyed him in an apparently casual manner. But Nu knew that the two of them, though supposedly on the same side, came literally from two different worlds.

Creek was second generation Irish; a pug face adorned his physiognomy like a map of Ireland. He had been married, fathered three children, and succeeded as a pretty good father, considering that he was gone a good deal of the time. However, his marriage had suffered, and his wife made other arrangements. He had entered the Army, fought in China with support groups for General Chennault's Flying Tigers. He had risen from field and maintenance work into photo-analysis, then to intelligence work, and finally joining the OSS working in Italy and later to the newly founded and funded CIA.

Creek did not have to pretend to be a "Good Old Boy," he just was one. He basically liked people and was effusive and outgoing. He had a beautiful baritone singing voice with deep undertones and a vocal flexibility he could force up into the tenor range, where he would sing— accompanying himself on the guitar—all the lilting Irish tunes ever written, including a couple that he had written himself. Women loved him, and he returned the favor. His method of operation was to lull people into the illusion of the simple, friendly Southerner, then turn that into a stuttering Italian, " Whatta ya mean you dona hav no bananas, Whatsamatta foyou?" A moment later he would be so Irish his brogue alone would make four-leaf clovers pop up.

In comparison, Nu was cold, calculating, and intensely cruel. His early childhood, as I was to later learn from Creek, was not that much different from my own. Nu was half Korean and half American Black, a combination that left him without a usable "footprint" in either the Korean or the American world. He was a misfit. He had been told this many times and was infuriated by such comments. The final blow was that he was disowned both by his own countrymen and his American relatives. The exception to total rejection was Herman Creek, ten years older, who had seen in the long-legged, barely-surviving, teenage waif a superior intelligence and a life track that, without intervention, could only lead one way: to the hell that Nu felt he was already a citizen of. Creek took responsibility for Nu and so directed this quiet, calculating alien to a childless American couple who adopted and took care of him. But Nu had never warmed to his new Caucasian family—again, not too different from some aspects of my own life! Nu's father was never able to communicate with the intense, inscrutable child. Nu had seen things in his native Korea that no child should have been subjected to. The experiences had left deep slashes across his personality and his character. He basically did not trust anybody.

Unfortunately, Nu persisted in the belief that Herman Creek was his only real parent and, with a totally unreasonable need for vindication, Nu had dedicated his perverse life to making Creek pay for giving him away. When he was old enough, he joined the service. His quick eyes—and a mind that matched—saw and catalogued everything that he had ever seen; this singled him out as a natural leader. He was selected for Officers' Candidate School but instead chose the intelligence service, in spite of Creek's advice to the contrary.

What Creek did not know at the time—but which he learned later when he received a posthumous letter left with Nu's will, "to be given to Herman Creek if anything happens to me"—was the secret agenda that Nu had in mind to inflict on Creek. It was Nu's intention to make Creek pay for his "superior attitude" that had allowed him to control Nu's life and, from Nu's point of view, virtually form it. Nu's ultimate goal was to make Creek subordinate to him, to eventually surpass Creek in power and control over others, and, when the time was right, to destroy Creek physically, mentally, and spiritually. Nu lived for this and he would die for it if necessary. In Nu's calculating mind, Herman Creek owed Nu a life, and that life would be Creek's own. There would be a time and there would be a place. Nu understood that when the time was perfect, he would be able to destroy not only Creek, but Creek's other "creation," Larry Wahl, that stupid, but admittedly incredible machine in which Creek had placed most of his trust and with whom he had a human relationship that Nu firmly believed should have been his.

At Talofofo Bay on Guam, Nu had set up a situation that would put Wahl in severe and completely unnecessary danger, just to prove that he could and to politically show Creek who was really in charge. The

Company had been wooed by Nu to the point that the hierarchy believed, as Nu had told them, "Creek is getting much too close to his asset and will injure the Company with his now split allegiance."

The activity Nu set up at Talofofo Bay was to prove this point. It was calculated to spread a conscious fear in Larry of being attacked by the sharks that were chummed in these waters for the shark's fins. These fins, revered for promoting sexual enhancement, were like gold in the grey markets of Asia, with much of the rest of the shark being simply discarded once the valuable dorsal fin had been cut away. Often, in senseless brutality, the wounded animals were thrown back in the bay, where their predator relatives would quickly dispatch the bleeding remains.

It was into this bay that I was sent to swim out to the wreck of the battleship Oregon, 200 yards off shore. I was directed to wait a full ten minutes and then swim back to shore through that same shark-filled bay and lagoon. Nu calculated that since he had given me a more or less conscious briefing on the "ordeal" I was about to undergo, I would be paralyzed with fear, which the sharks could sense. And even if I did not become shark bait, I would be terrified, and having barely survived, would recognize Nu as the master of my fate; he would be in charge, or so he planned.

The reason that Creek, who was invited to watch, was not really concerned was because he knew things about me that Nu could not have understood, much less coped with. When the story of my early near-death experience in the creek behind my parent's farmhouse in Goble, Oregon was shared with the Company, Creek fortuitously had left out the details of my response to the event. Water did not scare me because I was so fascinated with the water and the way that it was controlled by the magical pneumatic pump. Two more encounters with near drowning did nothing to change my basic attitude. In high school, I had taught dozens of young children to learn to swim at the Jantzen Beach Pool on an island near Portland.

When I entered the Talofofo Bay water in 1946, I was conscious enough to understand the point and the purpose of the exercise but, as Creek knew I would, I swam with the sharks aware that I was their kith and kin and would suffer no harm from those terrible jaws. The ten minutes on the protruding bow of that ancient battleship proffered no fears of the trip back. It merely logged indelibly into my consciousness the ability to recall the total event at a later date, when I would be able to use the information to a useful and self-protective purpose. And by the time that this supposedly terrifying event had occurred, I had been hypnotically involved in special training, which, of course, Creek also knew. My "basic training" may have occurred in San Diego during my mislaid Navy experience, but my real training continued on Guam, night after night!

After our jobs were done in the galley, my fellow waiters and I would sit around in the steward's assembly room and talk. I also spent time writing, drawing, and playing my clarinet (why they let me bring my clarinet to the preplanned Guam training was beyond me). After a suitable interval, I would go to my Quonset hut and to bed. When everyone was sleeping, I would get up and began my walk to Halsey Hill (the Naval Administrative site) , in a semiconscious state. I passed by the civilian guard station, where I was recognized and OK'd to continue past the lower camp, housing families, and on to the Navy compound. There I was admitted and accompanied by OSS agents to the gym, where both men and women were apparently working out. A simulated bar was set up with sawhorses and two by fours. This "bar" was to stand in for the various locations called for in the scenarios presented to me by the agent: restaurants, meeting halls, bars, etc. I was instructed to enter the room, was given rubber knives, fake ice picks, and various small caliber guns without ammunition.

In a typical routine, I was entering a bar when a man at the door would shove a gun in my ear and push me into a group that was being held hostage. Occasionally children would be present; an agent would play the part. If women were needed, either gender would be assigned to the role. These routines seemed about as sophisticated as a high school play rehearsal. The difference between the high school and our rehearsals at Halsey Hill was the presence of half a dozen people covered in white sheets who aided the physical effects of my and others interventions. A sheeted ghost (was this where the CIA term "spooks" came from?) would indicate to one of the participants that they had been shot and assist them to fall down. In order to make the actions taken seem real, I was hypnotically instructed to be blind to the "white sheets." I would be charged with disabling or killing one to four "bad guys." In my semiconscious state, it did seem real.

Some targets would be holding hostages; I would take appropriate action. Then the scenario would be stopped, and I would be put on hold while the tableau would be analyzed, following which my "records" would be cleared and another show with different conditions set up. The intent of these maneuvers was for me to kill someone, so the focus of the activity was on emotion and subtle clues—not the rudimentary physical set up. In many of the scenarios I could do nothing; in some, I was killed. The average time for a show would be a few seconds to 20 minutes—none of which I remembered until I visited Guam with Sherry in 1992 and pointed out Halsey Hill to her. When I did remember, the implanted memory had me in Rota, an island over 100 miles away by boat or airplane, but the viewing of Halsey Hill changed all that!

After about four hours, I would go back to my hut, none the wiser, and to sleep whatever time was left of the night. The Navy trained me for two months in these processes, night after night, proving in later years that they knew more about engrams than any Scientologist, but "please to call it training!" To this day, I still wake up after a few hours and have to go down stairs, often to watch television, before I can get back to sleep.

Creek took a deep drag from his cigarette, making a deliberate show of turning his head so that the smoke would not be blown in Nu's face, and asked, "So what are you planning to show me … us, today, Colonel?"

Nu let a few seconds pass, and then asked the others present to stand back by the empty bus. "There is no need for anyone but you to hear what I have to say."

When the rest of the group had moved off and gone into the remaining bus and shut the door, Nu brought forward a dossier and casually laid it on the table, shoving it slowly towards Creek.

"I'm going to bring you up to date as a courtesy. I know that you were assigned to this case a long time before I was involved and I know that you were involved with the Stanford Research Institute studies involving the so-called 'remote viewing project.' You were instrumental in pulling Wahl into this project and have read all the notes about his successes."

Here, Nu took a deep breath and continued, "You and I have had our differences over the years, and we have clashed on the proper use of this particular asset, but I must inform you that the Agency leans heavily towards my point of view. I realize that you have invested a great deal of work in this project and have had success training him to be a perfect killer—one who then knows nothing of his actions and therefore is an ideal candidate for an assassin. I know that you have been working with him on defensive programs involving reflex responses to protect him from outside pressure and attacks.

"What is now important for you to know is that I am in charge of this mission and that you will take orders from me. You will do nothing, I repeat, you will do nothing, to interfere with the rest of his training here on Guam."

Nu paused to see what kind of effect all this information had on Creek, but Creek had played poker with the best of them and nothing changed on his face.

Nu took another deep breath. "At approximately 1400 hours last Tuesday, the HA, called Doc, took the subject to the Naval Hospital at Agana and had him view two bodies. They were young Japanese officers who had served on Yamamoto's staff and had been brought up on charges—along with a small group of other Japanese prisoners—to face war crimes charges for what had been done to the natives and to captured American troops when the Japanese held the Island."

Creek interrupted, in a slow, mocking voice, "You certainly must know that I have all this information. I'm not completely out of the loop."

Nu's response was slow and even as he said, "Then I assume that you know that it was Wahl who killed them."

Creek's face registered a quickly reformed bland look, but not before Nu was able to see the flicker of incredulity that had passed across his face.

Nu continued relentlessly, "He was taken to the hospital to see his handiwork under the cover of helping Doc carry some materials to the hospital."

Nu paused and continued. "You will see from the enclosed material that the subject showed mild interest in the bodies and was left alone, with them for an hour. There were cameras taking close-up pictures of all of his responses during that hour; there was absolutely nothing in his demeanor to indicate that he had any idea who these people were or what had happened to them. The cover story was that a couple of drunken HA's had given the prisoners, who had already been condemned to death, a

Marine bayonet so they could honorably commit Suprero, the shorter of the two stabbing the other in the gut and slashing his throat; he then cut his own throat."

Now Creek was somewhat agitated: he had no information on any such events. "When the hell was all of this supposed to have happened?"

"One day earlier, at about 0400 in the morning, again at the hospital, where the two Japanese were taken after being heavily sedated. They were placed and propped into position, and Wahl was told that the two Japanese and he were in a large cave on Rota, where Wahl had been put, armed with a bayonet. He was supposed to kill the two unarmed combatants. Wahl had been told that, though they were unarmed, if they succeeded in overcoming and killing him, they would be released."

Creek remained silent, but signaled Nu to continue.

"The area was cleared and lights set up to shine on the two targets who were at opposite ends of the hospital operating room in which this travesty was arranged."

With what passed for a smile, Nu continued. "The room was then plunged into darkness, and Wahl, thinking that he was in the cave with the two Japanese, was handed the bayonet. As a sudden flare of light illuminated one of the unconscious Japanese victims, Wahl heard a voice yelling at him, 'Kill the son-of-a bitch. He has a weapon,' and then a different voice saying, 'Stick that bastard in the gut and wipe that smile off his yellow face.'

"Wahl did as he was told: He wrenched the bayonet from side to side and then cut the Japanese boy's throat, as per instruction. He stood there, drenched in blood, as one light was extinguished, and a new light was shone on the other victim. He was told to just cut his throat, which he did quickly. The lights were turned off, and Wahl went into 'rest mode,' standing there, breathing heavily and waiting for his next instructions."

Creek allowed himself to take a deep breath and swear quietly, "Jesus H. Christ, and all of this without the poor bastard having any idea … "

Nu smiled—a wicked smile—and gave Creek a mocking look. "And of course, we couldn't have done it without all the work that you had done on the ship, Stateside, and of course here on the Hill."

"Why wasn't I kept informed?" It was all that Creek could think to ask, even though he felt like a fool for giving any acknowledgment to the Korean.

"A fair question, Colonel Creek. The answer is simply that I thought that you had become much too close to 'the asset.' There was a sort of father/son thing going on that was thought to be much too … Freudian!"

This last was delivered much like the bayonet that had torn into the Japanese victim … cruel, relentless, and deliberate. It was offered with a totally unnecessary sneer.

Creek took several deep breaths, and then turned his back on the other man and said simply, "Ok, let's get on with it. What is the next 'pseudo-Chink' trick you have up your sleeve?"

Nu provided Creek with a mirthless smile, and signaled to the group in the bus to come over and join Creek and him at the table.

Much later, after I had been safely domiciled in a psychiatric hospital in Nova Scotia, Creek gave me the whole situation, blow by blow. I would not remember any of what he said, as well as the stay in Nova Scotia, until it came out, bit by screaming bit, as Sherry and I sat on our living room floor in Tigard, Oregon in the late 1970's.

7 | Toby Marshall

My Navy call-up was telegraphed to me at Long Beach, Washington; I was imbued with the sure knowledge that this was going to be a new and exciting adventure. I was at the beach alone because the folks and I had steadily grown apart and I was, in fact, living pretty much on my own. When I received my telegram, I went back to Portland and finished signing up there. Then I waited for several hours for the Navy's dedicated car on the train to leave Portland for San Diego, along with 40 other recruits.

It seemed to me—although this might easily have been the fact—that there wasn't anyone in charge, so, loving trains, I took the expense chits the Navy had given each of us and took a walk to the dining car. I noticed that there were an unusually large number of young women aboard. It didn't take me too long to become acquainted with an attractive woman named Ann Dempsey. She explained to me that she was a dancer with a USO (United Service Organizations) group that had been entertaining troops in Seattle; they were going to Los Angeles to take a ship for Hawaii.

After lunch, I went back with her to the car full of the USO personnel and sat for hours listening about her life in Wilmington and her plans as a professional dancer. I liked her immediately, so the thought that I should go back to my own car with its 40 male recruits was not too appealing. Ann and I had dinner together and laughed and talked with the other members of the troupe until I thought that maybe I should make an appearance in my own car. But when I started back toward the end of the train, I was stopped at the dining car, where I was advised the car had been made up for sleeping the serving crew and there was no passage.

Jesus, I thought, what rotten luck! If somebody was in charge and he missed me, I was going to be on report before I even got to boot camp. Well then, there was nothing to do but go back to Ann's car, happily plunk down beside her, and sleep with her head on my shoulder. The next morning, I did get back to the car and found it in complete disarray as dozens of young men tried to shit, shower, and shave all at the same time. I didn't know any of them in particular, and apparently no one had missed me, much less taken note of my first AWOL.

Before the troupe got off at Los Angeles, I obtained a home phone number from Ann and the address where she lived with her parents in Wilmington, a suburb of LA. I promised that I would visit them when I got a chance … after whatever the Navy had in store for me. I continued on to San Diego and boot camp.

After my very short stint in the "official Navy" and after I had shipped out a couple times as a merchant seaman, I went to Wilmington to see Ann. She was away with the USO; I met her parents for the first time. I got the impression that they must be very rich for there was an oil rig in their back yard, chugging away day and night. I was quickly informed that half of Wilmington had these oversized, mechanical "mosquitoes" in their back yards but the homeowners received little income from the oil; the oil companies always maintained the mineral rights—anything below the ground.

Far more interesting than the oil rig, or even Ann, were the parental Dempseys. Their neighborhood then was an enclave of middle class Whites with a large population of retirees. The Dempsey elders lived in what would have been a large, comfortable, up-scale, two-story home, except that Rose and John Dempsey were both retired schoolteachers: Rose had taught in high school, John in college. Thus their home was packed with hundreds of books, journals, manuals, and ancient tomes of every size, color, and description. The formal dining room table was loaded to the breaking point with pounds of books, and there were bookcases in every spare foot of the entire house, as far as I could make out.

John was short, both in stature and in communication, with a bald head and bifocal glasses, looking as though he had stepped right out of central casting's portrait of College-Teacher-Egg-Head. Rose was a pretty good example of the postwar "Rosie-the-Riveter" to "TV's June Cleaver," in contrast with her actual profession. A very important thing happened to me because of them: They introduced me to Toby and Faye Marshall.

When I first set eyes on Toby, it was a case of love at first sight. He was a medium-sized, confidence-exuding (emphasis on "Con") man of 50 with a loving wife and a cat that sincerely hated him. Toby and Max (the cat) shared a deeply mutual antagonism. Faye, on the other hand, got along with everybody and everything. Her garden was a thing of beauty; you had the feeling that all she had to do was throw some seeds on the ground and those seeds would kill themselves trying to be the best plants in the neighborhood. The Marshalls never had any children of their own, but from the stories that Toby told me—as we got to understand each other's characters and deficiencies—I gathered that he might have children anyplace in the known Pacific theater, including Japan, China, Burma, or India.

I once described Toby as being the kind of a man who would give you the shirt off his back as long as someone else had paid for it, but would take the shirt, pants, and shoes off of you if he happened to fancy them. I was never in awe of him because I recognized that he was just an older version of me—if I were to have the dubious good fortune of reaching his age.

Toby held the position of captain in the US Army active reserves and, since he worked for the Red Cross, had been in charge of the entire Pacific Ocean Area Civilian Service Group. He had charge of what ships were sent to which islands with goods and special services, as well as control of all the USOs in the Pacific Area. He was the man in charge of millions and millions of dollars in cigarettes, candy, coffee, clothes, and supplies—and, of course, women—in the far-flung areas of his world. For Toby, with his portable, translatable, and completely reversible moral code, this was the equivalent of putting the cat in charge of the mice. But for all of this, Toby never actually bragged about his inherent control of other people; he just did what seemed to be do-able.

I learned early on that he was a prodigious writer and that his reports, even when they were almost totally works of fiction, were never questioned by anybody. He had been a shaker and a mover, but at the time I met him, he was two years out of the service and dying to do something that would get him in the flow again. I was now a part of his life, and he was a part of mine: our fates were inextricably tied for a very real, very exciting period of time.

When I focus on someone as powerfully as I did on Toby, everything in my life seems to be on straight, steel rails. On a train, you may look to your right or to your left, but you know that the only destination you actually have is the one for which the rails were laid. In retrospect, I think that The Company probably controlled most of what happened to me in this phase of my life, but I certainly didn't know that at the time. It would be many years before I began to understand the reason for all the things that were happening in that full, rich, and more-unconscious-than-not time of my life.

What was to change Toby's life and prepare me for a strange part of my own, came in a letter from Hollywood that Toby shared with me. It was from Walter P. Skouras, a movie producer. People who waste their time finding minority groups on whom to blame the problems they have with their own unsatisfactory lives focused the most vicious and scurrilous attacks on the Jews, supposedly controlling Hollywood. Actually, there were a large number of powerful Hollywood types, thought to be Jewish, who were actually Greek. Skouras was one of those.

His pitch to Toby was that he had seen Toby's work and was impressed enough to want to offer him the assignment as writer for the proposed screen play on Greece as it was after World War II. Skouras was attempting to celebrate the bravery of the Greek underground in a story that outlined the conflict with the Russians who were exerting their influence over the Balkans, Yugoslavia, and Czechoslovakia. The focus was to be on an American falling in love with a Greek woman who was working with the Greek partisan underground to defeat the Russian Communist takeover. The hero was an officer in the OSS; however, Russia was working on taking over all the territories previously occupied by the Germans. The United States believed that this was not to their liking and tried all sorts of legal (and some illegal) ways to thwart the Soviets' global plans. The U.S. was obsessed with combating Communism.

The primary problem with the proposed story, over which Skouras had final script control, was that Toby had spent most of his time with the military in Asia, but knew little about Europe or the Mediterranean, and specifically Greece and the Balkans. Toby managed to get a contract with Skouras for time and manpower to study ancient Greek history and modern mores before attempting to write about a country he had never visited. Toby enlisted all of us as research assistants. We burned months of midnight oil trying to get the handle on a job that started with zero data. There is no way to describe the feeling of helplessness when you are trying to be an expert on a subject and a country you know nothing about.

The job was so cumbersome because we had to do tasks as simple-sounding as getting our hero into the village where he met his Greek love and have the two of them cross a village street, detailing what would be seen. What did the street itself look like; what was the architecture of the village; what type of clothing did they wear, what colors; what were the customs, local languages, and colloquialisms; how were emotions expressed, such as common facial expressions and meaningful body language; what was the prevailing environment like; what were the delicate political shadings and meanings; how had the German occupation affected the country and the people; and, most importantly, what were the deep and obvious rifts between the wealthier city folk and the poor farmers living in the hills and rocky crags?

To further our knowledge and understanding, Rose Dempsey, Toby, Faye, and I were invited to a Greek woman's home in San Pedro, where we were able to look at her trousseau and get some of her history. She had been married in a small village, much like the one we were writing about. She took us through all the hurdles that a potential Greek woman has to go through in order to get ready for her wedding.

Early in that nation's history, if a Greek woman were attractive and young enough, highly formalized business meetings took place between the potential groom's and bride's fathers. This had to do with how many sheep, goats, cows, hectors of land, etc.—as well as cash—will go along with the bride. Greek women, on the absolute value chart, ranked somewhere above sheep and below cows. Among the interesting things the bride had to do, besides being traded like pork bellies, was to shear the sheep, card the wool, dye the material, weave the clothes—which must contain a nightshirt for her husband to be—weave all the linens, blankets, and make her wedding dress. Then on the week before the wedding, she was to drape all of these clothes and woven materials out an upper window for the inspection of everyone in the village. After, and only after, all of this was done would the potential husband and his father sign off on the deal! And of course, she must be a dedicated and guaranteed virgin, a potential problem that led to the slaughter of more than one chicken.

The woman we were visiting, Mrs. Papas, learned enough about us to become very comfortable and finally shared her personal story. She had gone through the whole pre-wedding process, but was neither a happy nor compliant participant. After all the necessary business had taken place, she informed her potential husband that as soon as they were married, his father could have all the crap that she had been traded for; however, her new husband would promise his blushing bride to immediately move her to the United States. There was to be no argument about that. If he did not want to move with her, she would work out some way, legal or otherwise, to do it herself. And so they moved. As she indicated, she would rather be dead than go back.

My sense of time, being what it is, I have no idea how long we spent on the project, but I am sure it was a period of months. The contract that Toby had with the studio allowed him to give us all a small stipend, little of which any of us actually took because we were fed by Faye and felt we did minimal work compared to what Toby was doing 24/7. We were all involved with more and more rewrites and never ending revisions. The checks from Skouras were supposed to come regularly, but toward the end of the contract—however long that was—the checks came later and later, and then stopped coming at all. (Some time early on, Skouras had actually told us that the name of the movie had been decided to be "The Real Glory" and the cast had been selected with Gary Cooper as Jack Roberts, the American hero, and Linda Darnell as Penelope, the Greek heroine.)

Well before Toby's lawyers should have been contacted, we should have been studying the state of world politics instead of the movie industry, for the uncooperative Greeks, not having read the movie scenario, decided to go Communist. Everything came to a screeching halt; Skouras saw fit to walk away from the contract. We figured out that, all in all, Toby and his complete staff had worked for about 50 cents an hour. As a consequence—and for what little it was worth—we were experts on Greece. And that was the end of it. It was annoying for us, but it was a disaster for Toby. He had always been a drinker; now he fell off the wagon and under the wheels.

When he found out that the Red Cross was advertising for overseas jobs, Toby stopped drinking as heavily. He broke out his old Army uniform and wrote a letter requesting an appointment in San Francisco where the Red Cross was holding interviews the following month.

As some sort of celebration, Toby decided that he was going to take me to San Pedro to see the docks. I didn't know what he had in mind, but since he had decided that I was to be his secretary when he got his Red Cross job, he informed me we needed to get "blooded"--I had no idea what this meant. But, sure enough, two nights later on a Saturday, he went into his closet and returned with his legal Army 45, loaded the clip, shoved the weapon into its shoulder holster, and said, "Let's go."

I had never shipped out of San Pedro and I had not been keeping up with shipping news, but I think I would not have been so flippant about his arming himself if I had realized that we were going to San Pedro in the middle of one of the nation's largest seamen and longshoremen's strikes. Seamen are not the most reliable and pleasant people in general and, in times of stress, they are completely unpredictable. There was a time when San Pedro was high on the list of the world's meanest and deadliest ports, along with Port Said and Calcutta.

We started near city center and hit the bars all the way to 2nd Street and the dock area. At the third bar along the way, Toby and I had a couple of beers and watched a tiny, skinny, old black man shuffling along, casting an eager look to people willing to buy him a drink for his pitiful performance.

Toby asked me, "Do you remember a black dancer named Bill Robinson?"

I answered that I did. I had seen "Bo Jangles" Robinson in movies and once on the stage. Toby pointed to the pathetic creature shuffling around the barroom floor. "Well, that's him. When he isn't in jail for being drunk, he's here."

I had the good sense to have compassion for this wonderful performer, now ignored and disparaged.

The noise of the street seemed to increase for every block we covered, until we finally came to and made a left turn onto 2nd Street. Immediately we became aware of the dozens of people hanging out on every street corner, while the bars along the street were overflowing. There was a mean, blue aura of anger flowing from man to man as though they were connected by high-tension wires. At a bar we entered, I commented to Toby that there were very few women around, a condition that one seldom sees in seamen's bars. But, tonight there were no lovers. The exception in this particular bar was on a stage, almost slightly larger than a postage stamp, where four "cowgirls" were playing a bass, a guitar, a fiddle, and an accordion. The noise was like the buzz of hornets after their nest has been disturbed, and I got the feeling that being here was really not a hell of a good idea.

Then, from the other side of the packed floor were two voices—louder than the rest of the chaotic noise—raised in anger. Suddenly a man came flying backwards through the air and landed just to my right, banging his back hard against the bar. I didn't move, but felt my muscles tighten up for battle. The man cursed loudly, and I got ready to trip him if he changed directions. But immediately another man came through a hole in the crowd that allowed him to rush towards my new "bar mate;" it dawned on me that I might not have been properly matched had I attempted to be involved. Without looking, my "bar mate" came off the bar holding a full bottle of beer and smashed it across the head of the man rushing towards him, his original attacker. A nasty, deep gash opened up with blood and beer freely flowing from his forehead, just as two brown-clad "special officers," armed only with batons, eased the bleeding one out of the bar.

It was the first time that I noticed that there were no real city police in sight. Toby explained to me that only unarmed "specials" were allowed and that a city wagon would come along eventually to pick up the dead and dying when it was safe … whatever that meant! I smiled at Toby in appreciation for his smarts in arming himself and told him that I "got it;" now I was enjoying myself. Over the tumult, I told Toby that I wished he had brought a machine gun, instead. Somebody explained that the guys who had the run-in were brothers, which gave a whole new slant on brotherly love. When the bottle hit the guy's head, the "cowgirls" didn't miss a beat but simply had sung louder while one of them—the bass player, I think—had yelled out over the sound system, " Hit him again! He looks like he's gonna get up!"

The pièce de résistance" we sadly observed, once we were out the door, was the sorry figure of a crumpled victim propped up against a light pole, as his life's blood poured fatally from a severed jugular vein.

Toby continued to limit his drinking and, more and more, was wearing his uniform around town. When other people saw us, Toby dutifully referred to me as his personal assistant. In due time, a formal letter from the Red Cross came. Toby was happy as a clam and made arrangements for us to go to San Francisco the following week and stay at the Mark Hopkins Hotel, with expenses paid by the Red Cross. In the week before we left, through the local Red Cross, Toby had arranged a speaking tour at several Lions Clubs and visits to VA and other military hospitals; Toby insisted I be the speaker. I knew Toby was using me to show that he was important enough to have staff. I did not want to do it since there was no way I considered myself any kind of a veteran; however, this was exactly how Toby insisted on introducing me.

I did give some pretty fair speeches about the terrible way the government was treating the thousands upon thousands of war-wounded who had been hospitalized for extra weeks or months because of the continuous lack of blood supplies. At the third and last of these Lions Club assignments, as I was parading around lambasting the press for not taking the situation seriously, one reporter stood up and interrupted. He informed us that his news crew had gone to a dozen different hospitals in the LA area and were told repeatedly that they had adequate blood supply and anything else needed. This cut the ground out from under us; however, subsequent investigations documented that the reporter's information was incorrect. Obviously, the U.S. government had no intention then—as they have little incentive now—to advertise the real cost of war in the terms of the loss of limbs, eyesight, mobility, and long lasting PTSD—a condition that was called "battle fatigue" in post World War II.

Finally, the time came to leave, and Toby and I got on a plane to San Francisco. The trip was uneventful, but Toby got stares from other passengers: he had a subtle but permanent odor of alcohol about him. I could see that a disaster was coming, but didn't know specifically what it would be. Anyway, probably there would be nothing I could do about it.

Previously, Toby had told me about his transfer to a defeated Japan, where thousands of Americans were taking over the country under General Douglas Macarthur. In this period, Toby, still in charge of the USO troupes, met and fell in lust with Wee Bonnie Baker, a talented singer with a tiny musical voice doing the "boop-boop-di-doo" effects that so distinguished her. Her signature song was "I Want to be Loved by You," which reappeared when Marilyn Monroe sang it in the movie, "Some Like It Hot." Toby explained that after the USO troupe left, Bonnie Baker had stayed on in Japan, living with him. When the Red Cross didn't approve of his behavior and ordered Toby back to the States, he simply dumped her, although he swore he didn't know he had left her pregnant. I didn't believe him.

After arriving in San Francisco, the disaster came into view: I didn't know that Bonnie was currently staying at the Mark Hopkins. Toby must have noticed she was playing in one of the San Francisco theatres, but didn't bother to tell me. Only then did I realize how irresponsible a cad he was. By phone, he had set up a meeting with her in her room. What the hell he had in the back of his mind, I couldn't even begin to fathom. I was just blown away by this stupid turn of events since he had given me no clue that he intended such a meeting. He must have known that I would be appalled and would not support this action, so had quietly drunk about a fifth of whiskey to brace himself for the event, and of course I had to go with him.

At the appointed time, we left our floor and knocked on Bonny's door. She opened it and, without surprise or obvious rancor, let us in. After Toby introduced me, she took us into a parlor room and introduced us to her daughter, a small, attractive young lady of seven. I took a quick look at Toby, and to his credit, I saw him flush; it was abundantly clear that he had never seen his daughter. This pretty, but serious little girl never took her unwavering stare off Toby. I was willing him not to touch her or do anything else but to just get us the hell out of there. Toby, shiny and beribboned in his uniform, seemed, perhaps for the first time in his life, to realize he was a super-irresponsible idiot. He did manage to get us out quickly, with no argument from Bonnie. I will never forget the penetrating "lasers" that were the child's eyes burning into Toby's ruddy face.

When we got back to our room, Toby ordered snacks from the kitchen. In his warped mind he had been prepared to offer Bonnie a "reacquainting dinner," and expected that at some point I would courteously excuse myself. He found another bottle of booze, sullenly downed it, and followed with a bottle of wine from the kitchen. I reminded him that his interview was the following morning, but he waved me off, saying, "No Problem ... I'm ready."

He was SOOOOO ... NOT READY!

Our appointment was for ten the next morning, and surprisingly, Toby was up and ready to go by eight. We had breakfast at the hotel restaurant, during which Toby had only coffee; I couldn't recall what I had choked down. I felt as if I were the cruise director on the Titanic minutes before the iceberg struck.

We took a cab to the regional office. As we walked down the hall, heads turned following Toby's malodorous trail. A middle-aged woman took Toby's papers and looked him over dubiously, then excused herself and went into another office. When she returned, she asked Toby to come with her. A second woman, obviously distraught, came up to me and requested I follow her into her office. There, she explained that she had once worked with Toby, and there was no way that this drunken wreck was going overseas. That was a strong message, but it was said quietly and somewhat sorrowfully. I assured her that I understood perfectly. She asked, "What is your relationship with Toby?"

I explained, "We are good friends. I am trying my best to protect him."

"Should I tell him he is washed up, or would you rather do it?"

I told her that I was prepared to tell him, and it would be much easier coming from me.

I broke the news to Toby, who was so far out of touch with reality that he thought getting the job was a foregone conclusion. It took some time for him to realize the simple truth. I ticked off all the booze he had put away on this trip and that anyone could have followed his trail by scent alone. He called the Red Cross for verification and was given the obvious and well-known run-around. It was finally clear even to him that he was not going on the overseas trip.

Toby's answer to this rejection was to propose that he try again in a year and, just to prove how honestly committed he was, he would stop drinking—cold turkey. He had been spending like the proverbial "drunken sailor," so we did not have enough money to take the plane back. The Red Cross, as a courtesy, had picked up the hotel bill, but that was the end of that revenue source. I paid for another three days, while he did just what he said: quit drinking cold turkey. On the third day he collapsed, and I was forced to call Faye and give her the bad news. She was worried sick. She called Rose Dempsey, who couldn't drive but would be supportive.

Faye and Rose drove up to San Francisco to bring Toby home since I knew I wouldn't be able to handle him on public transportation. He was semi-conscious and only occasionally coherent; we were going to have to get him back to Wilmington and into a hospital quickly. When the two women arrived, it was plain that I was to be the designated driver: Faye was a basket case and Rose hadn't slept for 16 hours. We poured Toby into the back seat, with Faye holding him and trying to get him to stop his incoherent mumbling and to just rest. It turned out that, though Rose didn't really know how to drive, she was the original obnoxious, front-seated, "backseat" driver; she proceeded to make me crazy the entire trip.

Almost to the second that we started the trip south, one of the worst fogs of all time arrived—I took that very personally! The weather stayed in pea soup mode all through that horrendous nine-hour trip. I could only see the highway a maximum of four feet ahead; I wasn't able to go over ten miles an hour for the first three hours. Then, I was given one of the most welcome gifts ever: a Greyhound bus passing us, all honking horn and blazing lights! I immediately pulled in behind it, realizing that if anything were going to be hit, the bus would be first. However, I also noted that he was doing a safe and reasonable speed of 40 miles per hour. I lasted behind him for about ten minutes during which time Rose wailed hysterically that I was going too fast and would kill us all. I was not pleased with her behavior and thought seriously of cold-cocking her, but in the end, I wrenched the car over to the side of the road in a gravel-spewing, grinding stop. With tears in my eyes, I watched the Greyhound fade into the wall of solid white.

While I was still parked, Rose continued screaming at me until, red in the face, I opened the driver's door and asked if her demented, wailing, hysterical self would rather drive. She calmed down a little, agreed that I should keep driving, but allowed that nobody had ever talked to her like that. I didn't try to reason with her, but carefully got back on the road and continued at a ten mile per hour clip. Finally, hours later, I saw the welcome sight of a truck stop at the top of the Grapevine. I gassed the car, instead of Rose, while she made herself scarce. She came back with black coffee and a couple of doughnuts; I took them without giving her any thanks. Totally wasted, I prepared to continue our trip. At that period of time, Los Angeles was so murky that some women in Pasadena had the nylon stockings melt off their legs as they walked through the smog.

At last, as the fog was disappearing, I caught sight of the Los Angeles basin laid out like a big tank of rancid water, miles and miles of thick, visible, lung-killing muck. We descended into that sinkhole of guaranteed lung cancer. After the hideous fog-filled trip, it was simply fantastic to breath air that you could easily see through for a mile or so. Unbelievable. After I had deposited Toby and Faye, I drove Rose home. I left, and Rose and I wordlessly agreed that it never would be an option for me to be her son-in-law!

After Toby returned from the hospital with what was left of his liver and spleen, I helped Faye bring him back to some semblance of normal. He gained a few pounds of healthy weight under the care and feeding Faye gave him but, unbelievably, he was still Toby. He had bouts of DTs (delirium tremens), but never lost his calm " … and that's the way it is!"

demeanor. I had had bouts with various kinds of out-of-body experiences, but had never been around anybody with active alcoholic hallucinations. One day, as I came into the kitchen, Toby was studiously observing Max, the cat. The two seemed to be in a staring contest, and it looked as though it was going to continue to be a draw. Still staring intently at the cat sitting in front of the refrigerator, Toby asked me thoughtfully, "Larry, I'm right, aren't I? Cats hate snakes?"

I said that I thought this was probably correct.

"Well, watch this." Toby slowly approached Max and, for a change, gently, almost tenderly, tossed him towards the near wall.

Max, for his part, gave me the distinct impression that this was only one more of a series of unwelcome experiments that Toby had been inflicting upon him. Max skidded to a stop before the empty wall and turned to look over his shoulder. On Max's face was an expression that said, as clearly as a cat can, "Hey, man, what the hell is WRONG with you?" and then straightened himself out, with as much dignity as he could muster.

When Faye opened the kitchen door, Max beat a hasty retreat, slip-sliding on the waxed floor, and flew outside with a final insulted growl trailing after him. He was clearly thinking, "You Dumb Shit!"

"Did you see that?" Toby asked incredulously. "I threw the cat practically on top of that snake, and the dumb son-of-a-bitch didn't do anything!"

In more frequent rational moments, Toby was letting me help him get some notes together for a book on his life. A few days later, he called me to his bedroom. As I entered, he silenced me with a finger to his lips and then moved quietly to the slightly ajar door and flipped the bedroom lights off. Beneath the door you could see a faint sliver of light.

"Do you see them?"

I answered that I wasn't sure.

"Well there are a dozen about the size of an ant, and at first I thought they might have been termites, but I think termites hate light … " Suddenly he stiffened and, in a hoarse whisper said, "Look there. That's what they do: they just hang down from the bottom of the door and pull that door, which has to be unbelievably heavy for them, a little bit from one side to the other. I think they just want to confuse me."

I could see no reason that any outside force was needed to confuse Toby. I believe—and subsequent experiences with patients having DTs has reinforced that belief—that such patients are not lying, they actually see these things.

My life continued on its strange circumlocutions, and I moved away. Later, I got a registered letter from Toby asking me to please pay my share of the Mark Hopkins hotel bill. I wrote him a nasty letter telling him I already had paid more than my share. I told him to go to hell. Faye wrote a month later, indicating the Toby had to be hospitalized again but had been sent home for a few days before he died. He had finally succumbed to the whole litany of problems caused by his years of drinking. She said that he had been asking for me until the end.

I operate on the theory that even the worst news has a little good for someone. It is likely that the only one happy with this turn of events was Max.

8 | "The Garbage"

The submarine slipped out of San Pedro Harbor at exactly 0200 on a Tuesday in the late Fall. I did not know exactly what month it was nor, for that matter, what year. I could try to backtrack and figure it out, but it would make little difference to what happened then or how it would affect anything now.

As soon as the sub, sailing on the surface, cleared the harbor, the order was given to "dive, dive, dive!" I didn't hear this, much less comprehend it. Like a vacuum cleaner that is turned off, I didn't suck up anything, but would just sit by, unaware and unknowing, until the next time that I would be "plugged in." It was a situation that I was mostly to blame for—if blame makes any sense. In my life to this point, there was little that did. So, for me "getting there" was not half the fun, since I was locked in the code room on our American sub and was mostly oblivious to my surroundings and the mission for which I had been chosen. For Herman Creek, my control, I was just more work.

Herman Creek was talking to a very young but very dangerous child of 21. "Now, Larry, pay close attention. This is a very special operation. It is essential that you look at the uniform you are wearing: it is the uniform of a lieutenant commander. You are to be in charge of a twelve-man contingent of specialized Marines. There is a Marine sergeant in charge, but he is instructed to follow your orders. Your orders are my orders, and you will follow them to the letter. If that becomes impossible, you will do your best to complete the mission anyway. In the meantime, you will comport yourself as though you actually are a naval officer."

I listened intently to everything Creek said. In the days that followed, as we made our way to and across the Atlantic Ocean via the Panama Canal, Creek gave the Marine sergeant and his crew of twelve a general outline of the action for which we were preparing. This action had been spawned by the belief that, in the years after the Germans were defeated, the Balkans—more specifically Greece—would use their so-called "Partisan Fighters" to protect the Greek embryonic government. The partisans were willing to pay with their lives to make its people "safe for democracy."

The fly in this ointment was the Russian government and their penchant for active and sometimes vicious proselytizing for Communism. The partisans represented a small but tenacious group, thoroughly indoctrinated with Russian revolutionary tactics, never known for their subtle or gentle techniques. For centuries, the Russian people had been divided either into the very poor, often starving, peasants or the vainglorious czars who were only into producing the good life for a handful of Royalists. They were backed by the accursed Cossacks who would just as soon put a saber through illiterate peasants, as look at them.

Thus, when the trained and blooded partisans came up against the stronger, more disciplined German troops, they may have been beaten often, but never really defeated. They continued to fight with rear guard actions, sniping under night cover, and carrying on the ever-increasing harassment of the German troops. The German response was as predictable and vicious as expected; it made no distinction between men, women, and children. It was soon evident to the partisans that since it made no difference to their survival, these women and children should be actively involved in the fight; thus, the partisans became the more deadly, better-organized, and successful enemies of most everyone, including their own compromised countrymen. In the process, having little to expect from their government—which had buckled in the first place—they found the Communist Manifesto a system they could adhere to, while receiving help in supplies, fighting techniques, and esprit de corps from peoples who had fought their own weak, and mostly uncaring, royal governments for hundreds of years. The battles may have started between indigenousness Greek citizens and the encroaching Germans, but it was soon evident that the down-trodden rural farmers of outlying areas, subsisting on rocky patches of criminally poor land, had more in common with the Russians than they were ever going to have with the decrepit remains of their supposed government. It did not take too long for the various partisan bands to welcome military assistance from both the Communists and various undercover U.S. agencies. They played these two, shamelessly, and sold out or killed one or the other with equanimity.

Besides the Greeks themselves, there were neighboring groups of equally fragmented French, Slavic, Russian, Serb, and Spanish nationals, including many recruited Irish mercenaries who would have fought anyway, just for their Irish desire to fight somebody, anybody.

Into this mess were inserted Herman Creek, his Marine contingent, and Larry Wahl (aka, Lieutenant Commander Smith, for this mission).

The U.S. and its agencies, in their semi-divine wisdom, had imagined that we were fighting to protect the Greeks and all others from coming under the heel of the Communist party; this occurred at a time when the average American was being taught to look under every rock for dastardly Communists. In order to compete with the Russians, who were a hell of a lot closer to the action than we were, it was decided to hunt around "under" the underground and find the partisan band that would work with us and not shoot us in the back. The bait in this case was a new sniper rifle that could "see in the dark." It had enough power to kill at extreme ranges, while keeping the shooter's location invisible. It was fairly large and cumbersome, but tests had proven that it was deadly.

Our agents in the Greek underground had found an intriguing partisan group, rumored to be led by a beautiful but ruthless female who lusted for power. The quasi-Greek government, along with the Communists, had a reward out for her, dead or alive. Thus she and her group looked like naturals to use our latest toy. However, there had been enough bloody flies in enough sticky ointments to make the company approach this lethal lady with a backup plan. Creek was to be dispatched, with a unit of Marines and me, to check out a landing site to deliver several cases of the special weapons and to give cover and support in case anything went sour. Creek had more than a passing hunch that things could go wrong when he discovered through "back channels" that Colonel Nu might have had something to do with the assignment.

A non-descript island, among the hundreds of rocky spots with channels deep enough for a sub and isolated enough to be relatively safe, was chosen to be the site for the first, but presumably not the last tryst with the group known informally as the "Greek Witch Bitch" (so named by U.S. Marines!). Creek had spent months checking out the background of the partisan group, while trying to locate an island that just met the needs for the operation. Risking a sub in such shallow waters as were available to meet the operation's other parameters was not auspicious. It came down to three similar choices: the candidate island, named unimaginatively Island X, was chosen.

Information was sent back to the Greek Witch Bitch's group (GWB) that we would contact them and then arrive with boxes of support material on the south side of the island with a contingent of only six men, led by a naval officer. These details were emphasized to show our good faith. Of course, it had cost a few men their lives to discover that the truth was a random variable among these people, and so Creek adopted their somewhat slippery use of the truth. As a consequence, our party would be twice the size they expected, and we would meet them on the south side of the island as advertised, but the submarine and the delivery site would be on the north; a natural ravine connected the two sides. The information was withheld from the GWB that we would be arriving a day sooner, with half the troops scaling an almost vertical cliff on the windward side that would allow six of our sharp-shooters the ability to cover both landing sites, using the described special weapons. It was a grand plan and seemed to take care of all the exigencies, with a sensible and well-planned fallback position that could be taken if things went badly.

On the sixth day at sea, as we were crossing the Dardanelles, the Marine sergeant asked Creek if it was legal for Creek to give his sarge some information on "who the hell was that Navy officer who was practically never seen and what was his function?" This was a question that Creek had been waiting for. He had the wardroom cleared except for the sergeant and wrote on a piece of paper, the following:

"Your job is to make sure that Lieutenant Commander Larry Smith, who is in fact an OSS officer, stays alive. In the process, if you or your men get in any trouble, you will be able to rely on him to keep you alive … if that's possible."

Sergeant Billy Joe Bolin's answer was a quiet look on his face that said quite clearly that he was trained to do anything that was necessary to be done without the help of any "civilian." Creek just beamed one of his blinding, down-South smiles at the sarge and said simply, "Well, I would have been disappointed in you if you had said anything else, so I will offer you a contest. If, theoretically, you can show that you or your men are faster at killing the 'Commander' than he is of killing you, I will take your comment under further advisement."

Creek continued on with the conversation, and after they were through, Creek retrieved the piece of paper from the still dubious sergeant and took the sign off the wardroom door. He invited the Marine contingent, the skipper, and his exec to the wardroom at 0600 the next morning while we were still submerged.

Creek had handpicked me for this mission to prove my skills and abilities to the dubious "Company." Creek had, from the beginning, been my friend; that is, as much of a friend I was to have in this bizarre period of my life. It was my concept that I was mostly a mystery to myself, and there was no other person capable of understanding me better than this unlikely friend. Because Herman Creek was my control, he was the center of my espionage machinations. As I had learned on Guam with Colonel Nu, not everyone I was to deal with saw me as totally human. They saw me as some kind of machine, a point of view with which I was in complete agreement. It was a verdict that I could easily see in Nu, the likes of which I had met many times in my life—and in myself.

As Creek had revealed to me (in Chapter 6), Nu's history was complex and bitter. Half Korean and half American Black, he was an outcast in the country of his birth and only accepted in America after he proved himself in the intelligence service. Creek had originally mentored him, but Nu never lost his anger against Creek for not being more of a father. Thus when he first encountered Creek on a surveillance operation, they clashed, and Nu continued to carry a vendetta against Creek. He worked hard to find ways to discredit Creek. I became an easy target.

The effect of Nu's savage misuse of a valuable asset (me) on Guam was to fix firmly in Creek's mind the danger and incredible energy that Nu had built up to destroy Creek and certainly to dispatch me in the process. Nu was sure that his currency in the Company was such that there was nothing that Creek could do to change the course of history as Nu had planned it. Creek and I were given more and more dangerous missions in the belief that I would fail one of these tests. Only one failure would be necessary; only one would be tolerated.

Two days before the sub was to arrive at the chosen site, Creek arranged a demonstration of my capabilities for the 12-Marine troop contingent. Since I was still in a robotic state of semi-consciousness, my only memory of this event was from what Creek told me, the essence being that through a series of staged "battles" with me vs. one or more of the 12 Marines, I was able to identify the "enemy" and dispatch him before that Marine could draw on me. Creek told me that I had been able to convince them that I was as advertised, especially when several maneuvers were tried to confuse me but I still identified those designated as my targets, outdrew, and eliminated them individually and in groups before they had a chance to counter my actions. It had been a convincing demonstration.

I was intensely practiced in the use of small arms, and my uniform came equipped with a 45-colt sidearm in a standard enclosed holster, attached to the utility belt on my right hip. But, the one thing that Creek did not share with anyone was my second weapon, one that was my primary choice, one I had practiced with both right and left-handed draws. This weapon was a four-inch ice pick, located in an unpretentious clamshell holster on the left side of the standard marine utility belt. Encased in its holster, I had only to touch a small recessed button and the ice pick would fall into either hand.

On the first official day of the Greek operation, the sub was brought up to periscope depth, and the captain viewed the target island. He ranged his view 360 degrees and was satisfied that there was no traffic of any kind. The sub moved to south side of the island, where it surfaced and the crew rowed the rifle ammunition and other supplies, along with a $100,000 promised, to the narrow beach. This south beach was obstructed from view if one kept to the channeled ravine between the two rocky prominences. This island was right for our purposes because it was shaped like an uneven dumbbell, one side about 600 feet high and the lower about 200 feet with a deep ravine between the two sides. The rest of the Marines and I went ashore and set up a camouflaged tent. Using a raft, we took the supplies through the channel to the north side. We then returned to the south beach to make our rendezvous.

The captain brought the sub to the surface on the north side of the island, where the rest of the Marine group exited onto a small raft, rowed to the shore, and then, with climbing gear, started from the water's edge to scale the steep side of the cliff. Along with a crewmember, one of the Marines acting as helmsmen ferried the small raft the few yards back to the sub and then secured and brought ashore a case with six of the night-vision rifles. The Marine helped hook the boxes up to lines thrown down from the cliff where the other five Marines had gained the top of the ridge. They secured their positions and sent down lines for the sixth Marine to reach their location. Once the positions were secured, the sub submerged, stayed at periscope depth, and remained in radio communication with the Marines on the north side high ground.

In due time, after the exchange of light signals, a small boat came cautiously ashore. There were nine men aboard and the woman who had to be the "witch." I was generally considered a pussy addict, as well as an artist, and as she got close enough, I could see that the advertising had not been overdone. She was quite small and very dark complexioned. Her hair was raven, her body fully curved but proportional, and her eyes as dark as her hair.

She was looking us over also. Her eyes ran to the boxes, and I could see the wheels turning behind those deep penetrating eyes. She quickly brought to her side what was obviously her second in command; he took charge of the boxes while the other men made a semi-circle around us. They were all armed and looked as if they were fully adept at using their weapons; I noted that all safeties were off. She, who said her name for practical purposes was Olive, quickly gave our sarge the once over and then, and only then, spent some time looking at me. What she saw was what I projected: an order-oriented naval officer, younger than her and not too experienced. She signaled to me and introduced her next in charge as Martine, a chiseled-cheeked, slim, lithe, obviously quick-moving individual, average until you looked into his intense eyes. Her English was only fair, but the first question she asked was which box or boxes held the rifles. I saw her trade looks with Martine when I explained to her, hesitantly, that they were actually on the other side because there had been some concern that the sub might have been spotted on this side. With this information, she quickly made up her mind. Seven of her men were to remain on this side with five of our crew, while she and I, Martine and the sarge started down the passage to the other side of Island X.

As soon as we started down the ravine, however, she and Martine immediately led us left off the path and up to a small rise. Here she could see the north-landing site. In coming around the island before she landed, she had seen the shear rise of the east end of the island, but did not consider that we would have scaled it since she had noted that all the Marines were accounted for on the south shore. She broke into a run, and I struggled to keep up with her. Martine, at the same time, held back, and the sarge made an effort to stay behind him. Olive could see the boxes on the north side and was satisfied that her men could handle the slight change in plans.

As Sarge looked down to check his footing, Olive called out in Greek, "It is time. Kill the sergeant in ten seconds."

The sarge let his hand rest on his rifle, counted to six, and shot Martine in the back. He, with his innocent but universally understood drawl, was an expert in the Greek language. Though Sarge was ahead of the count, so was Martine. His fingers closed on his captured German Mauser as he spun around to shoot the sarge. As soon as the first shot rang out, Olive had unholstered her weapon and, with a wicked smile, was pointing it at me. Suddenly, Sarge's face appeared from behind a rock in front of her, and she immediately shifted the gun to cover him. In her mind, a southern Marine sergeant with his Kentucky windage was a more immediate threat than the young officer. Wrong!!!

In the meantime, almost simultaneously, volleys of shots rang out both from the opposite beach and from the peak above. In the midst of what Olive thought was her crew wiping out our Marines, it was her entire group that was being slaughtered. It didn't matter to her, she would have the murderous Marine in her sights and then would finish me off. It was to be her last mistake. She saw no movement of my right hand towards my gun holster; it was as if I were in shock, and the sarge had too much distance to make up.

She was not looking for and did not see the blur as my left hand caught the ice pick and swung it with dedicated force, driving through her gun wrist, paralyzing it. The next blow she didn't see either, for I had stepped closer as her gun slipped from her grasp and drove the needle sharp ice pick transversely through her neck, feeling the hard resistance of her cervical spine. Her eyes registered shock and surprise, while I wondered why it was taking Sarge so long to reach me. It was only then that I realized that Martine had actually turned and fired almost at the same time as the sarge, and Sarge had been hit in the left thigh. He was tying a belt around his leg as I turned back to Olive. She had fallen awkwardly backward and now lay face up, her olive complexion turning a pale grey. Somehow, she looked familiar...

As she was drawing her last breath, suddenly I knew who she was: she was Gertrude, my mother. Every memory of hunger, anger, and disappointment, and a buried insane hatred, sent a psychic shock through my body as I slipped into a complete psychotic rage. When the gunfire had stopped and the rest of our crew was racing toward our location, Sarge came limping up the hillock to find Lieutenant Commander Larry Smith on his knees, with the ice pick making thrust after thrust, driving the bloody point like a machine gun into Olive's chest, throat, and stomach. He was saying, singsong, punctuating each new blow with, "I love you, Mama! I love you, Mama! I love you, Mama!"

Sarge stood for a second trying to comprehend what he was looking at and then quickly and automatically crashed the rifle butt into the back of my head.

Nu would be very pleased.

9 | Dorothy

I've always had trouble with serial time. Events, in fact, do follow one another in a time parade, but my time, LT (Larry Time), is a parade moving around a huge circle. The beginning, the middle, or the end makes sense only to the viewer in his and her moment. At this instant, I'm trying to find the beginning of a parade led by the drum majorette, named Dorothy, nee, Dixon.

Some time after my first sailing trip, I moved to LA from Portland. I remember thinking what a strange enchanted place Los Angeles was; it was not a city, it was a megapolis made up of a thousand villages of rabbit warrens. You drifted around in this milieu with your rabbits. I ended up in the general vicinity of LA harbor. Without any apparent funds, I still managed to wander all over the place, waiting for a ship. Finally, I settled in at Compton.

After the trip with Toby to San Pedro, I fell in love with the interurban self-contained Red Cars that, at that time, connected the various far-flung parts of the city. The Red Car roamed over desert land, which seemed to be void of any life other than jack rabbits and their ilk. Armed passengers would occasionally be found on the open rear sections of the Red Car, plinking at various forms of wild life. It was a passing wonder to see great chunks of concrete in the form of bridges that went nowhere—no roads connected to them. It was warm and sultry and the special smell of mesquite permeated the air as the cars plowed across the open terrain. I sat musing in my seat in a combination tandem of two cars with the forward car carrying only three or four people.

The Choice

Dorothy and Lois Dixon were sisters only two years apart in age, but they were as different as if they were from separate families. Dorothy was

103

a slender, redheaded, freckled beauty, while Lois was a little bit chunkier and plain. They were from North Dakota, and that alone should have been enough to turn me off ... but it didn't. I met the two of them while we were all riding the Red Car; it was destined that we were going to connect. The best looking was definitely Dorothy but Lois had a nice, large frame and an interesting, intelligent face. Too bad I picked the wrong one!

As the train rocked and rolled across the unbelievably vast empty spaces that still existed in the late 40's, I could see the two girls trying to figure out which one was going to be the most interested in me. We discovered that we all lived in Compton, where I was staying in a small hotel; the Dixon girls were living together in a trailer park about a mile from Toby Marshall's house. Eventually I was invited for dinner at the girls' trailer, and before the meal was over, they had decided I would be dating Dorothy. Either one would have been OK with me. Lois indicated that she did not encroach on Dorothy's territory, and that was that. I was finishing the screenplay with Toby. As the "Greek Adventure" became, for Toby and the rest of us, a true "Greek Tragedy," things with Dorothy and me proceeded hot and heavy; at some point Lois went back home for a while. I became intent on getting into Dorothy's pants, but it turned out that this event was never going to happen until another event took place first: a formal Christian wedding.

Dorothy was working for a subsidiary of Hughes Aircraft called Sturgis Engineering, just out of Compton. This was in the period of time when Hughes was filming "The Outlaw" with Jane Russell, and Preston Sturgis was one of the directors on the shoot. Try as I might, I couldn't get Dorothy naked, so I decided two things: I would have to get a job and I would go back to Portland for a while. Unfortunately my pink sailing card drew no interest in Portland, so back to San Francisco where finally I shipped out to Guam on the A.E. Anderson, to work for J.H. Pomeroy. By this time Dorothy and I were getting along fine—I thought—except for no sex, so I capitulated and we decided that we would wait a year while I worked on Guam; then I would come back, and we would get married.

There were two things wrong with this plan. The first was that the contract was finished after only three months—Civil Service and the Navy were going to take over the camp. This would mean that we camp and culinary workers would have to decide whether to accept a completed contract and come home or stay, with our pay grade diminished to the level of the lower-paid native workers from nearby islands, including many people from the Philippines who were looking for U.S. government jobs. Even though I had been promoted to headwaiter, Pomeroy was only willing to pay half salary. This was not as attractive as unemployment pay in the States so I elected to ship back home and ask Dorothy to marry me. The long-distance romance was even pleasant, although I had no idea that I was already deep into work for the CIA. Dorothy was still working for Sturgis Engineering. The company gave us a wedding present of a beautiful pair of gimbaled, solid brass candlesticks: they must have cost a fortune. We kept them until looters stole them from our apartment in Vanport after that city's complete destruction in a flood (more about this later).

Sturgis Engineering was an interesting place: Dorothy's entire purpose as secretary/bookkeeper at the plant was to keep the place in the red. This company would be in the business of R&D (research and development) only as long as the products they produced were guaranteed to lose money. Dorothy was to document the hundreds of thousands of dollars in losses. I saw a 1/8-scale working model of a 4-6-6-4 railroad engine gathering dust in a back room, built for Howard Hughes, but not accepted by him because it didn't go fast enough. However this was good: It had cost over $60,000 to build! It joined congeries of other projects that were then legally deducted. Thus, the entire Sturgis manufacturing plan was constructed around projects doomed at birth, deliberately designed such that these unnecessarily exotic and complex product lines would never make a nickel of profit.

It was during this period of time that I was fortunate to be one of several thousand people who had lined the streets of several LA municipalities to watch the Hercules C3—the so-called "Spruce Goose"—pass by on its way from Terminal Island to Long Beach Harbor. The two immense wings traveled on two separate oversized trucks, which forced the cities it traversed to take down telephone and power lines; the total breadth of the wings was just under a football field in length, but the body, with a seven-story high tail, was what made the trip so costly.

The Ceciles

I married Dorothy at a Presbyterian Church in rural California where Dorothy had an Aunt Cecile and an Uncle Cecile. I know! But I couldn't make that up. Aunt Cecile and her husband lived on a small farm and put us up before the wedding. Their farm was close to the church in which we were to be married. Aunt Cecile was a sweet, older woman and a fantastic cook who pickled everything on earth that could be pickled and took care of the many chickens on the farm. Uncle Cecile swore better and more often than even I was used to; he intrigued me.

One Uncle Cecile story was especially worthy of note: The hen who wouldn't sit.

Uncle Cecile figured that most people he knew were sound-controlled: If your voice was loud enough to be heard across the room, you were whispering; if you could be heard in the next room, you would be just talking; and if you could be heard in the next county, you were communicating. He apparently thought these rules held true for livestock, in general, and recalcitrant chickens, in particular. So, the first night we were there, I was startled by Uncle Cecile's loud voice from the chicken yard. I came out of one of the guest rooms to see Aunt Cecile sitting in a rocker at the kitchen table. I asked her if everything was all right. She answered, "Oh yes. Cecile was just conversing with one of our hens. He thinks she is supposed to be sitting on this egg, but she doesn't think so. He has put her there about six times but she gets right back up. I'm surprised you didn't hear him yelling earlier."

I sat down beside her and turned toward the yard to better hear the chicken dialog. What followed, after a long, continuous peal of hardy cursing was thus: "There, gawddamitt, now you will sit!"

Aunt Cecile and I went through the door almost simultaneously. Uncle Cecile was standing over the inert form of the hapless hen; he had deftly wrung its neck. Then he sighed and, in a much calmer voice, said, "There, gawddamitt, now you will sit."

The "Ceciles" drove us downtown to meet the minister. We brought him back to the farm and, after a sumptuous dinner, the minister was to question my currently non-existent religious credentials. In the car coming back, Aunt Cecile was forced, as were we all, to listen to Uncle Cecile's loud and profane description of religions, governments, and anything else that crossed his mind. We in the back seat just cringed but didn't interrupt. The minister had heard it all before, but what sense was there in missing those wonderful Aunt Cecile meals. I don't remember what questions the minister asked or what lies I answered back, but apparently I passed muster, and the marriage, unfortunately, took place.

Marriage Numero Uno

We started our honeymoon trip on a roomy Greyhound bus, up the California and Oregon coasts to Newport, Oregon. At that point, however, the Greyhound turned east to Portland, and we were relegated to the equivalent of a school bus from Portland to Seaview, Washington, on the southwest Long Beach Peninsula. The previously pleasant trip became the ride from hell! We settled in the middle of the back seat of the now crowded bus with two other people, each of whom was sitting next to a window. Then to really make this the most miserable bus ride I had ever taken, at the next stop we picked up a passenger; the only seat left was next to Dorothy and me. This lady, very large everywhere but especially across the backside, plunked down as a fifth passenger (as well as a sixth) in our back seat. As miserable luck would have it, she was going one stop farther than we were. After first sitting on Dorothy's brand new hat, she so crunched me that I was halfway on Dorothy's lap for the rest of the trip. The ample woman perspired profusely and snored loudly. Mercifully, we finally arrived where we were to live: my folk's beach house.

I was happy enough for the first few weeks with Dorothy. On that bus trip from Los Angeles to Seaview, because of the bus schedule, we had a detour that provided us with a stay at a hotel in Portland for the first night (this was, fortunately, before the final, miserable leg of the trip). This was the first time that I got to make love to Dorothy; I realized that she was almost perfect, actually more than perfect.

Don Douglas joined us at the beach house after he cashed out of the Army. Dorothy cooked and generally took care of us ,and we started to work seriously at cartooning. Don would do the drawing, and I would do the story lines and the continuity. Don and I had decided the entire cartoon world was waiting for our fabulous, innovative ideas. However, the editors to whom we sent our slaved-over work were monumentally less interested than we thought possible. We lamented that all we got back were form rejection letters. But, after we sent broadsides of our material to the New York markets, we finally got an actual written comment, along the line of, "We hope that nobody, no time, under no circumstances will ever service your most desired wish. You have no right to waste our time!" We got another from a magazine whose editor must have gargled with razor blades that morning. It was very short, not sweet, and should have been written on asbestos.

The Cranberry Caper

We thought our cartooning was pretty good stuff, but we were running out of the money we had between us. Not to despair, I decided that I had better go to work; however, pickings were very slim. There was little I could find to do in that winter wonderland, where the population would be upwards of 5000 during the summer, but maybe only 600 off-season. Seaside during the winter was so incredibly dull that when the tide went out, it would be so bored it wouldn't even think about coming back in (old joke!). Finally, I found an advertisement in the paper that local farms were looking for pickers in the cranberry fields.

The well-worn bus came by to pick up interested workers at several corners on Main Street. Main was only a block away from our place, so after Dorothy packed a lunch for me, I waited on the freezing corner. When it arrived, I noted that it was full of sturdy-looking, elderly women, who answered my young smile with a symphony of tired, knowing looks. It didn't help when the one I sat with looked skyward by way of answer when I innocently asked, "These cranberries, don't they grow on some kind of a bush?"

A short cackle of laughter from the driver and the passengers was my answer, and I spent the rest of the twenty-minute journey staring at my lunch bag.

About three miles out of town, the bus came to a stop. As we got off, then and only then, did I notice that every one of the ladies was wearing some brand of rubber hip boots. Ahead of us lay a field about the size of a high school football field that was filled with very cold water on which the cranberries floated. The cranberries appeared to be wearing smug little grins on their faces that said I was six kinds of an idiot and that I should simply turn around and go back to town, hitch-hiking if I had to. Already shamed, there was no way that was going to happen, so I followed the crowd into the water. That same frigid water nipped at my butt and testicles as I knelt down with the little wooden scoops we were given and tried to capture a useful quantity of the damned berries. The old ladies didn't seem to have any problem with it, but the berries hated me. Every time I got a decent scoop full, the damn things would cling to their tenacious vines and plop back into the water. When not connected to the vines, the berries played and ducked in the water like I had remembered ducking for apples in younger, happier times.

At the end of a month that everyone tried to tell me was only six hours, the ladies went to collect their pay for the number of buckets they had filled. I heard amounts like "Thirteen dollars, Mary. Sixteen dollars, Laurie. Only nine dollars this time, Susan … "

When I staggered up to the foreman, he just looked at me with what I read as sympathy and, without comment, put $2.26 in my hand. We got back on the bus; I was let out at my stop. I could feel nothing below the level of my neck. As the bus pulled away, I realized that I had forgotten how to walk and just stood there rocking back and forth while I shuddered and shivered uncontrollably.

There was at least one fifth-class god looking out for me: Dorothy and Don were less than a block away. Something about my dead white color and wet shiny clothes sent them running to me. Each got a hold of an arm and half-dragged me back to the cabin. "I'm … a ah, (shiver, shiver) al—righ … t," (shiver, shiver). Dorothy didn't even try to understand, but stripped me to the buff as soon as we entered the cabin and plunked me into a hot bath, all the while standing behind me trying to get my shoulders out of my ears and my teeth to stop chattering like insane castanets. She and Don wrestled me, wrapped in blankets, onto the bed where the two of them took turns trying to get all the knots out of my back and some color, besides blue or white, back into my face. That was the end of my cranberry caper.

As I write this I have just realized that, besides serving up sizzling (if only Midwestern meat and potato fare) meals and trying her best to be proficient in the bedroom, after seven years and four children, Dorothy was almost a total cipher to me. I didn't know the names of her mother and father, what high school she went to, or whether she had ever seen the inside of a college. I remember talking to Don about almost an unlimited series of subjects, including his new mail membership in The Rosicrucian Order (a non-religious, mystical society). Dorothy never contributed to our conversations or asked what Don and I were doing, as she stood right beside us watching the cartooning process. Every night when we went to bed, we would have sex for an hour or so; when that was over, there was no thrill, just a final jolt of physical satisfaction. We didn't discuss the sex or anything else. I just finished, rolled over, and went to sleep. I had no idea what, if anything, it was doing for her. In retrospect, I concluded that she was happily doing what she had been taught that a North Dakota woman was required to do for her husband. Other than that, she never asked me what I thought about; what her plans or mine were for the future just never came up. I guessed that there must be a lot more to marriage than this, but we never found out. During this early period of our marriage, I was not angry with her and never had a hint as to how she felt about me. Apparently I didn't care.

As the cartooning became less and less financially rewarding, it was obvious that Don and I would have to move some other place, like Portland or Vancouver, where at least one or all of us could get real work. Don decided to go to LA to work, leaving Dorothy and me alone. We ended up in Portland. Dorothy found work in the Department of Forestry as a secretary, and I went to work at the Vancouver shipyards, where we were able to get hospitalization from Henry J. Kaiser who owned the shipyards—we were to be Kaiser patients for the next ten years, starting in Vancouver and ending in San Francisco.

The Vancouver shipyards was one of the main West coast construction sites of the 2000-ship fleet that was built for World War II, but continued on with post-war building and maintenance. Because I was kind of a veteran—with three months in the Navy—I was given a job cleaning the inside double bottoms of merchant ships that came back to the yards to be overhauled. The "veterans" crew (including me), who were assigned to this less-than-desirable work, was made up of 90% Black Americans shipped to the Portland/Vancouver area from distant "foreign" lands of the Eastern and Southern United States. To most of our traditional local citizens, these new folks looked strange and talked strange. After working an eight-hour shift in the double bottoms, my skin was the same color as the natural tones of the rest of the crew.

I discovered the effect of my altered appearance one morning after a night shift, when I took myself to a jewelry store that I had known for years. I greeted the owner heartily but was amazed by his reaction: he didn't seem to know me and exuded fear and a little loathing. I caught sight of my appearance in a nearby mirror and realized that the jeweler thought that I was one of "them." When I mentioned my father's name, he suddenly recognized me, and his attitude changed completely. I became one of the "regular people."

I wrote an article for the Columbian Newspaper on "Tolerance." It was well received, if a little long and imperious. I thought that I had "made my bones" in the reporting business until I tried to write another, lamenting the way the Black veterans were treated when they came home from the war. Wrong! It was carefully explained to me that this was not PC—not the term used in 1947—and I objected strenuously; a lot of good that did. My reporting career stalled since I was convinced the only way to write was the truth!

For a short time, I moved alone to Seattle where I worked at King Street Station, loading and unloading tons of materials from soldiers and equipment still coming back from the many countries where they had been deployed. The work was casual but paid well for what was expected.

While there, I recalled a previous time in Seattle at King Station. It was the summer of 45 after I had graduated from high school, and I was trying to decide what to do with my life. I left work one day to find a crowd of yelling, happy people. From sidewalk to sidewalk, the streets were clogged with them all over downtown Seattle. It was VE Day—Victory in Europe—and the end of that part of the war that had involved millions.

But now it was the aftermath; cleaning up was what was happening. I realized that millions of men had been, and would continue to be, coming home over many months, even years, to a brand new world. It was a world that had not planned for this sudden end—the surrender of Germany and, a year later, the bombing of Hiroshima and surrender of Japan. Many of these brave returning ex-military troops would find that they were competing with one another for fewer and fewer employment opportunities. They would also find that they were competing with both younger and older men—who had most of the jobs—and a good many of the women these troops had left behind.

Vanport

Thus, in 1947, there were still many troops returning to the few available jobs on the West Coast. While I wasn't finding anything that useful in Seattle, I got myself back to Portland to make sure I could get a good job. Shortly after returning to Portland, I was hired at Continental Can Company (CCC) as an inspector on the can line.

The CCC job paid more money than I had ever received, and I felt confident in moving a pregnant Dorothy and me into Vanport, a newly invented city on the Portland side of the Columbia River. We rented an apartment that was far larger and better equipped than the tiny place we had been living in over a small bakery in Vancouver. The new digs were large enough for Don to return to live with us so he and I could carry on with the cartooning, but this time with the artwork as a back-up job. We did find enough commercial artwork locally that Don had to work full time on these and our cartooning assignments. It was not a fat living, but it was a living … at least until the flood!

Vanport, on lowlands between Portland and Vancouver, was the second largest city in Oregon for a while. Initially there was intense prejudice against the large Black population, but also because Vanport residents were brash, inventive, and self-governing. However, the merchants in Portland could see it as a powerful new shopping market since a substantial part of Vanport's population growth would be from returning veterans with young families. Though we considered Vanport a good place for mixed-race, harmonious living, we also knew that we would be relegated as second-class citizens as far as the rest of the mostly lily-white population of Oregon was concerned.

The history of Vanport is one of those terrible tales that should not have happened … but did!

As can be seen on a contemporary map of the golf course that now occupies the location of the previous Vanport, it had been a very large "city" although it actually was a housing complex—read ghetto—for the thousands of "them"—read Black and poor White trash—manning the shipyards and other war-related occupations. I did not notice, nor did the city of Vanport notice, that we were supposed to be a ghetto. We started our own businesses and coalesced around our little city center as though we actually liked being there; in point of fact, we really did. The citizens of Vanport were bright, vibrant, proud, and active—attributes we were not expected to have. Downtown Portland was perfectly happy to put up with us as long as we did our shopping and utilized other services. As a community, we started to think for ourselves and developed a healthy ability to take care of our citizens.

Portland tried to emphasize the danger of living there due to crime and moral degradation—thought to be automatic in such a "ghetto." This was a major error: Portland had a raging gang war and its crime statistics were double, per capita, our own. Regarding the "per capita," there was never an accurate accounting of just how many people actually lived in Vanport. The numbers are estimated at between 15 and 20 thousand.

In May 1947, over 6000 of Vanport's original 9942 units remained. There were less than 1000 vacancies and these were scattered throughout the project rather than being in any closed section. Later, Harry Freeman was to fix occupancy at 5295 families containing 18700 "actual registered tenants." *(Maben, 1987: 104)*

Many of Vanport's citizens came from other parts of the country. They thought they had died and gone to heaven. They encouraged their relatives to come and live in Vanport.

Vanport had its own police, fire station, city center, churches, and even a college. What it also had was an unbelievably dangerous location. It was in a giant "bath-tub" surrounded on all sides by normally higher water, held back by dikes and highway fills. Situated in Northern Oregon by the mighty Columbia River and in a flood plain surrounded on all sides by water, it was literally guaranteed that when any major flooding hit the area, the whole assemblages of wartime Butler-type, two-story buildings were destined for a charmed, but short life. Vanport could be washed away in a matter of minutes, disappearing like a modern Camelot.

After the war in early 1946—almost two years before Dorothy and I moved there—Vanport became less popular and many were moving away. Harry Freeman, Executive Director of Vanport, established a "Veterans' Village," which attracted many returning veterans and their families. Vanport City College was founded in 1946, its main reason for existence being that there was little housing for veterans in Eugene, OR, the home of the University of Oregon. Thus, it was necessary to find a place where the vets could have both housing and easy access to a place to utilize their GI bills (Mayben, 1987:75). However in 1948, as the danger of flooding became a strong possibility, the Vanport City College administration moved all of their records, contracts, and administrative staff to downtown Portland, despite the absence of a welcoming attitude of that city. This gave the college the continuity to continue in Portland and eventually become Portland State University.

Despite rapidly rising waters on May 28, 1948, residents were continually reassured that there was no danger, and if evacuation was necessary, " … Housing Authority will give warning at the earliest moment possible" by continued siren and air horn *(Maben, 1987: 106)*.

I was not convinced of our safety from rising waters. On a Sunday morning, Memorial Day weekend, I was awakened by a slip of paper being slid under our front door. We were on the second floor in a three-bedroom apartment, with three more double-floored units surrounding a service and heating unit. The city was made up mostly of these units; ours was one of several thousand. Our address, I think, was 1304 Lake Street. The Lake address meant that we were less than two blocks from city center and two blocks from the fire station. After I read the innocuous notice, I decided to wake Dorothy, now six months pregnant, and get us the hell out of there. What the note said, in effect, was that there was no immediate danger, and that we would be given time to register our invalids, wheelchair-ridden, and old folks with a week's notice of a need to evacuate. We went to Vancouver to stay with the folks for a few days.

At 4:17 PM on May 28, 1948, a siren went off briefly before it was blown off its foundation and drowned by mountains of water as the railway dike gave way. A family friend and railroad engineer, Joe Dunnigan, was just crossing the Columbia River Railroad Bridge when he noticed the raised dike collapsing into the water, just ahead of his train. Seeing the Vanport Tower also falling into the water, he quickly reversed the engine and headed back to Vancouver. Knowing that Dorothy and I lived in Vanport, as soon as he got into Vancouver, he called the folks; Masie answered the phone and turned white. She turned to us and said, "It's gone, all of Vanport is gone! We sat there stunned; all we had was the clothing on our backs, but we—and our to-be baby—were safe. What might have happened to us is unthinkable. However, the same was not true for many of the other families, especially those who lived further up river. We lost our home and most of our belongings, but we were OK—just considerably shaken. From that mismanagement, thousands of families lost their homes and, officially, 13 individuals did not survive the disaster, though many former residents did not believe that. The official word was that the number of deaths would have been much higher had it not been for the huge number of transit buses that rushed to the area to bring Vanport "refugees" to safety. We cynical ones considered that Portland might have welcomed this "ethnic cleansing." As it was, my well-paying job in Portland was unreachable—the only interstate connection between Oregon and Washington, within many miles, was the Columbia River Bridge, which ended in flood water on the Oregon side. Fortunately a private plane was paid for by my company—but I had to stay in Portland until some reasonable transportation resumed.

After a few months of living with my folks and the emergence of a new family member named Penny, Dorothy and I departed for points south, namely San Francisco, so with any luck, I could sail again.

The Green Furniture

Dorothy was able to transfer to another position in the Bureau of Land Management in San Francisco. We immediately found a temporary home in a San Francisco Residential Hotel (of which there were many in the 1940s). We heard about low rent San Francisco housing, but also heard there was a horrendous waiting list. We went down to the main office anyway—we knew we would get "points" for having a child. The clerk explained that we would have to pay the first and last month's rent and go on a 30-day waiting list. So we decided to start buying furniture on her first payday. After we paid rent and food, we bought linens and a mattress, figuring to get the rest of the bed next payday. Surprise! Three days later came the notice that we had been assigned an apartment in the Sunnydale Housing Project, 35 blocks from downtown, near Geneva and the Mission and near Candlestick Park. We had to take possession within two days. We got some money refunded from our prepaid hotel, but all we really had with us were linens and a mattress; thank God, a stove and refrigerator as well as a table and four chairs came with the apartment. We had our pet fish, Oscar in his small bowl, and a blanket-lined grocery box for daughter, Penny. Even though, for me, this period was distinguished by killer migraine headaches that lasted two and three days, I had applied for a job at the Golden Gate Theater, and it came through. The first night we paid U-haul—or something like it—and we slept on our new mattress in the second floor front bedroom, which measured about 10 by 20 feet with a large walk-in closet. A landing led to the bathroom and a second bedroom, somewhat smaller than the first—this became Penny's room, which now included a newly arrived crib from my folks in Vancouver.

Steps leading upstairs were by the front door entrance, and to the right was the empty living room. The kitchen was behind the living room, and the only storage closet was under the stairs.

Dorothy's work allowed her a week to get settled and provided an advance in her salary so she could get kitchen and general household supplies. I was glad to work that week. I started my shift at 4 PM and ended at midnight, with the exception of live shows. There was plenty of overtime available.

In spite of our short side trip to the Long Beach Peninsula, the flood in Vanport, and Penny's birth, Dorothy was still almost a total mystery to me: North Dakota must be a very strange place. Sunnydale was such a compressed neighborhood—full of people—that your neighbors became your friends quite rapidly, but I realized later that it was just another ghetto. It provided many friends for whom this was a final destination, who never considered they could do better. I did not consider this was the case for us. Dorothy appeared to me then like so much custard, soft, yielding, and tasty, that she would do whatever I wanted. That was my first mistake; underneath was a will of iron. I distinctly remember a party with a dozen people attending, some from her work, some from mine, that turned out to be one of those very rare, perfect evenings. The evening was full of good conversation, good drinks, good food, and good cheer. This constituted my only "successful" memory of Dorothy, probably because she didn't disturb anyone, mainly me. I mistakenly thought, "Now she's got it." For whatever reason, I never felt poor—more like I refused to accept poverty even when it stared me in the face—and I always got what I wanted/needed. I had been born a mystic, which was enhanced by the experience with my grandfather's shoes: how could he be dead and they still be around?

On the first day at work, after donning my uniform, I was standing in the alcove to the left of the girl in the cashier's booth, which was off the sidewalk. It was a quiet afternoon. At the confluence of Turk, Goldengate, 7th, and Kearney, several thousand pass by in a few hours—a tremendous clog of people, cars, busses, bicycles, and streetcars. Perpetual parade. I stood watching the ticket girl buffing her nails when a tap from behind spun me around and a male voice said, "What's so funny, Mr. Wahl? I'm Mr. Weber, one of two assistant managers. I see that this is your first day and I was watching you and noticed you laughing. It was a good shaking laugh, and I just wondered what you were thinking."

Protocol has it that all movie folk working for IATSE (International Artists and Theatrical Stage Employees) union call each other by their last names. This was much different than most of the jobs I had had where you were called by first name, or maybe "Hey You," and I liked hearing "Mr. Wahl." I immediately liked the solidly built, slightly graying man. Caught in the midst of my sneaky mirth, I quickly explained our living situation. This was in passing; I didn't expect what followed.

When I wanted to go someplace in San Francisco, I "fetched" it as easily as the ships I sailed on "fetched" their ports of call. I basically believed, at some level, I was a child of the Universe and that it would take care of me—it had so far. When I had tried this philosophy out on Dorothy, she was staring at Oscar, had not had a good night's sleep on our lone mattress, and, while trying to balance the books, found it would take us more than a month to get all of the furniture we needed. Although her North Dakota mind apparently was not wired to accept this particular kind of information, I had said to her, "Dorothy, it will be fine. I'll just ask the Cosmos to provide it—just tell me what you want."

I remember a singeing stare, complete with cold, hard eyes and trembling lips as she answered, "You're crazy as a pet coon!"

Bell Telephone Hour brought major performers to the Opera House, and this broadcast series was open to everyone. It included the usual opera-goers: dowagers in real fur coats. Their place was normally in the "Diamond Horseshoe." In my jeans, tennis shoes, and black turtleneck sweater, I was subject to more than a few frowns as I plunked myself happily and comfortably in the middle of this array. It had always been so, and, I believed, it would always be so. I thought Dorothy just needed a little more time. The little more time turned out to be the actual time it would take for the ice to melt in Antarctica!

I was surprised when Mr. Weber moved directly in front of me and stared myopically into my eyes. His thumb was under his chin, as he appeared to muse deeply about something. Finally he spoke. "We have a spare bed at home, a double, but we don't have a mattress for it. But I can give you the frame, box spring, and bedstead."

I was jolted. "Gosh," I said, trying to make a good impression, "Mr. Weber, thanks for the thought, but I don't have any way to transport it."

"Not a problem," he interjected. "Where are you living?"

Now in minor shock, I gave him the address and told him it was several miles away.

He commented, "Mrs. Wabe, the other assistant manager, will be coming on duty in a half hour, and I'm off. Can you call your wife and tell her I'm coming?"

I explained that our phone wasn't installed yet, but she would be there. He turned and reentered the theater while the cashier sat looking at me through the glass enclosure, smiling doubtfully. I noted she was very pretty and had red hair, and that reminded me of Dorothy; I would have given a lot to see Dorothy's face when the bed arrived!

I closed at 11 PM, walked to Mission, and took the Mission 14 bus home. I opened the door. Dorothy was sitting at the kitchen table with a cup of coffee ready for me, which she served without a word. I sat and looked at her, and she looked at me. And the two of us studied Oscar; he ignored us both. It was some weird kind of game. Making my face as noncommittal as possible, I asked casually, "Anything new today?"

There was. We fought about it.

We discussed my philosophy several times after that incident. Our finances had improved; our bank account was set up. One morning some time later, Dorothy sat me down at the kitchen table and discussed her plans for buying living room furniture. She discussed when we would buy it, where we would buy it, and how we would pay for it. This conversation took about an hour for her to describe the dealers, stores, transport, shopping, and final delivery. And this was fine with me—this was on Wednesday. But then she grew tense. She asked for my signature on some papers and would have it set in motion by Monday. Going by the words, this was a plan, my approval appeared to be needed, and I had granted it. So we were done … not so fast, Charley! Both Oscar and I were surprised. Her eyes got that hard look, and her voice became strident: she was going to tell me a joke she knew I would not find funny. She stepped up to the base, shouldered the bat, and prepared to hit one out of the Park. She said, "Of course we could go ahead and order all of this from your Cosmic Store," as a sardonic smile crossed her face.

Everything changed! I stared at her for some time, wondering idly, "Who the Hell is this Bitch?" Keeping my voice calm, though I know my eyes were shuttered and cold, I said, "Hey, Babe, that's a great idea. Let's see, you want a davenport, a side chair, a lamp?"

"Yes!" she said defiantly. "That would be just lovely." Lovely was composed of three syllables.

"Ummm … " I said, "What color?"

"Green," she spat out.

"Done and done," I said.

I picked up the newspaper and started to read.

Thursday was very quiet. Friday I deliberately double-shifted. Saturday noon, the doorbell sounded. Dorothy answered. I was in the kitchen when I heard a little scream. I rushed into the living room to see Dorothy greeting her uncle. I could see Dorothy turn an embarrassed red—she was not ready for guests, especially a beloved uncle—her freckles looking dark as she ushered Uncle Ted through the empty living room into the kitchen. There was always coffee available, so we had coffee. Dorothy and I filled him in on what we were doing; how we were doing was obvious. Ted rapidly made himself comfortable, and shortly even Dorothy was relaxed. It was obvious to Ted that I might be in love with his niece, but I definitely was in love with Golden Gate Theater as I told him stories about my experiences there.

About 4 PM, he said, "Listen, you two, how about I take you down to Alioto's and buy you dinner?"

This was a wonderful opportunity for Dorothy to get gussied up; a neighbor would take care of Penny. The three of us got in his car and drove to the Wharf. The place was packed, though fortunately he had called ahead for a reservation, but we still had to wait at the bar. Dorothy, if not unpleasant, was not overjoyed with anything that night. When she went to the ladies' room, Ted shook my hand while saying, "Look, I get the impression you two are having a rough time. Dorothy is high-strung, always has been. She looks bright and cheery, but I always know when she's in trouble."

He was probably bellowing this for the place was so noisy you couldn't be heard six inches away. He took his hand away, and I realized he had slipped me $200. I started to refuse. He put a big hand on my shoulder; the look in his eye said very clearly, "I don't want to hear it!"

We finished a wonderful dinner, and he drove us back to the house. He told me he lived in Piedmont in a house that Dorothy had visited many times. When we were back in the kitchen, he asked, "Dorothy, do you remember that living room suite we had in the guest house?" She nodded dumbly. "Well," he continued, "I'm going to get a trailer—Marge was going to get rid of the stuff anyway—and bring it by tomorrow so you kids will have something to sit on." He laughed, gave her a hug, shook my hand, and was gone.

Penny was asleep so we just sat at the table and looked at each other. I didn't see anything in her face that indicated an iota of gratitude. She seemed to be waiting for me to say something first, so I didn't. We went to bed without another word.

Early the next morning—10 A.M. for us—I still hadn't said a word and had no idea what was going through her mind. Over the second cup of coffee, apparently she couldn't keep it in any longer. She said, "Well, I know what he is bringing—it is orange!"

I can't imagine my not answering, but I think I took one of those moments—so rare and seldom—to just stare at her.

Ted arrived at noon, we saw him pull up with an open trailer; in it were a green davenport, green chair, and a yellow floor lamp. "Uncle Ted, that's not the same furniture!"

"Yeah, it is, Honey," he answered, as I helped him bring in the davenport. "Marge reupholstered it and was going to bring it to the main house, but then got new stuff instead." Ted looked kind of puzzled; I just raised my eyebrows slightly.

We brought in the rest of the furniture: The living room appeared. Ted said he had an appointment to keep and left. I brought a kitchen chair into the living room and sat looking at the green furniture. I knew my marriage was over: I had married the wrong Dixon. This one was mean, petty, and, as she delighted in now telling me, pregnant again.

Dorothy and I stayed married—but actually lived apart—for over five more years; we came together from time to time and produced a family of four children. I was a sexual addict and the saddest kind of a useless bugger. The CIA used my services as a counter agent, and I spent many years in a deep fog, finding out other people's secrets, but operating blind to my own. With dozens of cover stories, I went through a whole plethora of jobs, always coming back to police work of some sort. I was rudderless, compass-less, and morally useless. Perhaps the only time I arose to some level of maturity was when caring for Dorothy's and my children, specifically Kathy, before I abandoned all of them.

10 | Pine Cone

The trip to France was essentially invisible to me; the trip from France was certainly sketchy but definitely not invisible. There was a constant roiling turmoil in my soul, aching fatigue in my body—no sleep—and an endless panorama of space to be covered. Over it all was a patina of sheer terror. Creek told me later that it had been a matter of necessity, and that if I hadn't done it and done it successfully, I would quite certainly be dead. Killed is a more accurate description of what my end would have been, but I was neither able to know nor to care, at that time.

In the clandestine services, all things involving human contact are subject to other people's desires, needs, and, more often than not, their greed or mere convenience. Sometimes it actually serves the purpose for which it was designed. All of this is defined as service to your country, whatever that country happens to be. It is a little like both sides on a football game being quite sure that "God is on our side." God may be too busy or disinterested to be bothered with such human self-deceit; this does not seem to dawn on either team, no matter how many games they lose. Perhaps they believe they upset that Big Umpire in the Sky in some way or just didn't pay Him enough.

Working in the service is a lot like working for promotion in a large corporation. You must fit in and do your day-to-day work, never looking overly competent, lest your supervisor become jealous. But you must be astute enough to collect enough owed favors to learn of peccadilloes and screw-ups perpetrated by the people just above you. With this information you can accumulate a secret ledger of where some of the more fragrant bodies are buried. While I was able to follow these rules while in the CIA, they didn't seem to transfer to my awake, real life—perhaps I might have stayed longer in my jobs if they had!

121

Herman Creek deposited Larry, along with properly documented papers, to the shore brig at the submarine base in Maddelena, Italy. Creek's classification and security level were high enough to discourage any questions. Under the heading of special notes, Creek indicated that the prisoner was mute, did not know sign language, and was a Section-8. Creek indicated that the prisoner was to be served regular meals, put alone in a cell with a toilet, and to be released only into Herman Creek's custody.

Creek found a quiet, middle-class tourist hotel and settled in to think about what he was going to do next. That Larry, after Greece, was a complete disaster was beyond question. By now the submarine captain's report was going through channels, and soon there would be all hell to deal with. Creek needed time to think and time to start repairs on this catastrophe. In due time, he, Creek would have to disappear. This, in itself, was relatively easy to arrange because he was high enough in the food chain that he could provide his own operational cover. Doing the same for Larry, code-named COW, was an entirely different problem.

If you were not in the Company, Colonel Nu was a formidable enemy; for Creek, Nu was a formidable enemy even if you were in the Company. Nu had a string of accomplishments to his credit: well done assassinations, covered mostly as unfortunate accidents. Nu had been Creek's superior officer in more than one project that they had worked on together—including what Creek referred to as the "Japanese Boys' Fiasco." They disagreed almost totally in their manner of handling assets, both material and human. Nu was a great believer in getting rid of assets that actually fouled up, or even appeared to have the possibility of doing so; generally he wasted little time. Creek knew that as soon as Nu got wind of the problem on the Greek Island, he would send a team to get rid of Larry immediately. This kind of removal with prejudice was always to be handled with an aura of deniability for the Company, but Creek would have to sign off on it.

In attempting to save Larry, Creek would have to pull in some heavy favors, all on the Q.T.; he would have to leave Larry's safekeeping to people he knew and could trust. They would be in minimal danger themselves, but it would only be necessary for one of Nu's men to come across Larry for Larry to have that fatal accident. As well trained as Larry was, in his present semi-hypnotic state, there was no way he would be able to assist in his own defense. There were times when he disappeared into his own black hole, and he could be in a catatonic state for days or weeks. In this state, he would eat if something were handed him and he could be led to a place to evacuate his bowels or urinate, but none of this, or anything else, was being captured in his memory web of space and time.

Now this situation came down to two possibilities for Larry: Creek could get him back to the United States, where there would be some chance of reconditioning him, or Nu would find him and he would be dispatched. In whatever way he planned to safeguard Larry, Creek would have to appear to be somewhere where he could not possibly have been involved with the process of spiriting Larry off the continent and back to the United States.

Thus, Creek set up a flight for himself and another party to Brazil, under false passports. And he arranged for two fellow agents to actually take the trip and then conveniently drop out of sight. It was well known that Creek frequented many locales in South America, so this subterfuge would work to send Nu's men on a wild goose chase long enough for Creek to find a string of safe houses to hide Larry as he shuttled him from Italy into Southern France. Once in France, Larry would be dressed as a peasant and conveyed from village to village during the busiest times of day, until Creek's associates were able to guide him aboard a French fishing vessel going to Portugal, and eventually to the American base at Rota, Spain. Nu's staff would probably waste about a week learning that the South American trip was a ruse and would then concentrate their search back on the European mainland.

It was in the small fishing village in France that Creek's plans went awry. The owner of the boat, meant to transport Larry to Portugal along the north coast, was offered more money; he turned Larry over to Nu's man. The agent, with Larry in tow, was told to bring him to a village near Tulare, where Nu would personally take charge of "debriefing" Larry.

Nu was involved in a very extensive operation, taking place about nine kilometers from Tulare. This operation—an elaborate sting—involved at least a dozen agents, besides local gendarmes. Nu had his hands full working the complex plan. He had assigned three men to a hill overlooking a wide spot in the road. They were equipped with two-way radios and spotting scopes that focused on the dusty parking area beside a large roadside farmer's market, about two kilometers to the northeast. Just a few more kilometers away, a winding country road intersected a busy highway. The plan was to drive a large rented transport van into the parking lot where it would intercept a meeting of gun traffickers. Nu's operation pitted ten of his agents and a dozen police against a dozen men located in three different cars. The suspects, who were heavily armed, would be meeting with the main gun supplier in the district. An agent in an 18-wheeler was to cut off two of the perpetrators' cars from the one they had determined was the leader's, while police would take out the leader's support group, arresting them if possible, shooting them if necessary. Larry was being held at the top of the spotter's hill, with one of the agents totally involved with keeping an eye on the questionably catatonic prisoner.

Creek located where Larry had been taken and was ready to initiate some yet undetermined action to stop what otherwise would be Larry's execution. Creek managed to "liberate" both an ill-fitting gendarme's uniform and an official car. He knew Larry was not far away, but there were way too many unknowns in the situation, so he made sure that he stayed on the outskirts of the action. As he listened in to the crackling frequencies on the car radio the French police were using to stay in touch, Creek also kept in touch with Langley. Then he noticed a blip on his portable tracker unit, centering on a nearby hill and surmised that it could be a lookout. From his vantage point, he could see the farmer's market parking lot and noted a number of cars assembling there.

As Creek was watching, a lone car separated from the group at the far end of the parking lot and headed down the main connector road. Creek put his vehicle into gear and started following at a discrete distance. He followed carefully, but suddenly lost sight of the other car and had to backtrack until he spotted a ragged road leading off the highway. A cloud of dust assured Creek that his pursued car had just taken this turn. He idled for a few moments and then drove a little way off the road, seeking a low prominence that would hide him from the car he had been trailing—when and if it came back down the road. He had the vague impression that the driver of the spotted car was Nu, but he certainly was not ready to stake his life on it. Perhaps the hilltop was Nu's command post, but Creek doubted it. If there were to be killing, and it appeared there was, Creek knew that Nu would insist on being in the middle of it. Creek had observed only one individual in the car, so he was wondering if perhaps Nu, or whoever was driving, was on the way to pick up another man or two.

At the top of the hill, Colonel Nu had brought his car to a skidding stop where a man stood in the middle of the clearing pointing an Uzi at him. Nu opened the door slowly and greeted the man by name. The guard quickly lowered the weapon and allowed Nu to pass. Nu parked near the spotting scopes and radio equipment and, with quick strides, approached the car holding Larry and his guard. He indicated with a snap of his wrist that the guard should leave the two of them alone.

"Well," said Nu as he sidled into the rear seat next to Larry, "so we meet again. This time I think it will be the last." Getting no response, he continued, "I received all the reports on your last operation and I think it is fair to say that your usefulness to the United States of America has pretty much ended."

Nu pulled a Walther PK pistol from its holster and rubbed the barrel against Larry's face. As he had expected, there was no reaction. He continued in his soft whispering voice, "How much I would like to put this gun to your head and blow your brains all over the car, but that would be both messy and unnecessary. We are going to have to arrange an accident for you. A final ... deadly accident."

As was so often the case after periods of supposed catatonia, I awoke, fully dressed and immediately aware of my surroundings. How my body came to be in this place at this time remained an unperceived memory of something that had only just happened to me—an ocean away, a second before—but was connected in my mind to the next tick of the celestial editor. For me, time was always ricocheting from the regular to the stroboscopic (Larry Time). The various agencies I worked for were cognizant of the fact that when I was active (on command), I would be super-aware—then a second could be an hour, while simultaneously an hour could pass in a second.

I was sitting, dressed in military fatigues, peering into a large spotting scope. A scene registered on my brain: I started to mentally catalog what I was seeing. I was focused on a section of the two-lane country road twisting its way a thousand yards between two large hills to my left. I tracked the scope to my right where, a hundred yards down the partially graveled road, I could see a very wide open area alongside a large farm with a fruit and vegetable stand. There were several cars parked in the commodious lot, along with two 18-wheelers and three smaller trucks. There were men, women, and children bustling about the vehicles. It appeared to be late afternoon, sunny and dry. The air was unusually still.

A voice behind me with a slight accent I knew I had heard before, but didn't quite remember when, spoke in short, flat sentences. "Keep your eyes on the farm stand but focus in on the larger truck. The one farthest away from the stand."

I did as I was told and focused in on the letters painted on the side of the truck: large block letters reading "OUI." I passed this information back to the man behind me and then slowly turned to look at him. In response, he just glared at me and ordered me to turn back to the scope. I recognized Colonel Nu, my "swimming instructor" at Talofofo Bay. I was dimly aware that he would like to see me dead, but it didn't matter because apparently I was on the job.

I kept my eyes glued to the scope as Nu continued to provide a "voice over" for the moving scene that I was observing. "There will be a convey of our cars coming, with an 18-wheeler right ahead our five cars. The first three cars will turn into the parking space and stop next to the 'OUI' truck. Several heavily armed men will get out of the three cars and attack the truck. They will fire into the sides, the cab, and the rear doors, and then re-enter their vehicles and rapidly speed away. The two cars that were following will continue on, but one of them will turn off to the road where we are. When it arrives, you will abandon the equipment, get in that car, and go back down the hill where you will be transferred to a French police car with one of our agents in it."

I listened but did not turn away from the scope, knowing that I would be in jeopardy if I did; I continued observing. Nu rustled through the bushes toward the car that he had brought to this location. I heard the engine start and saw the car began to move down the hill; at about the same time I saw the convoy heading onto the short access road going into the parking lot.

The wind, which had been dead calm, suddenly and unexpectedly roared into life. In an instant, the convoy and the traffic behind it disappeared into a fog of dust that blacked-out the entire area: cars, trucks, shops, and people. It cleared a second later to show a slow-motion disaster taking place. The company18-wheeler, meaning to pull to the right of the parked target rig ("OUI" truck), instead crashed into it. The accompanying three cars could be seen: one crashing into the fruit stand, while another side-swiped one next to it, and the third car smashed into a parked car ejecting two of its passengers and, with gathered momentum, crushed the already disabled "OUI" truck just ahead of it.

The dust blew yards of loose soil back and forth across the scene. At first I did not hear any sound, but seconds later heard the then continuing sound of multiple crashes as cars on the highway had no time to stop and smashed into one another in a long cacophony of ongoing screeching tires and multiple collisions. A large freight truck tried desperately to miss hitting an equally large petrol-laden semi, but hit it hard. The petrol truck seemed to absorb the punishment without reaction … until a second or two later it exploded into a fireball that evaporated everything in its vicinity.

The worst was yet to come. A large touring car, loaded with young men and women, screeched for many yards before it hit the destroyed freight truck, and majestically spilled its passengers, limbs akimbo like so many terrified manikins, directly into the inferno before them. The crashes continued non-stop, but I found that tears were destroying my view and I looked away. When it was over, thirty cars had become part of an instant junkyard and abattoir: wreckage of vehicles and bodies lay among the burning ruins. Nu, on his way down the hill, continued ahead. He would have to see if there was anything left of the mission he had sent these many agents on. He would not know, nor would he care, how many other innocent men, women, and children had died in this chaos.

Nu knew I was safe on the hill, and that meant that he would have to absorb his grief and anger of a moment gone bad. He would quickly make an assessment and then come back up the hill and absolve some of his pain by eliminating Larry Wahl. In the meantime, there was the agent in the other car who was guarding me. He noted the police car snaking up the hill with its lights flashing. The agent/guard stepped out to greet what he assumed to be another of Nu's agents but, as the car slewed to a stop, a hand appeared from the driver's window and fired four rounds into the agent's body, killing him instantly.

I went into an emergency self-protective stance and reached for my weapon, but didn't find even a holster. Then the driver stepped out of the car, advancing on me with a huge smile. There could be only one smiling Irish face in the world for me: it was Herman Creek's. My understanding was that, with Nu's help, he had been deported to Argentina, but here he was, in the beautiful flesh. Without comment, he stepped over his fallen victim, removed the dead agent's gun, handed it to me, and then said in a low monotone, "Well, Larry, here you are up to your usual ass in trouble."

I smiled a vague smile and stuck the weapon in the back of my belt. Herman stood beside me; I had turned away from the spotting scope to address Creek, "I thought you were banished to South America."

"Yes," stated Creek. "I am still there! So what you see is a mirage. Just like all that heavy shit down the hill. I found Nu's car and punched a hole in the gas tank. I think he'll be coming up the hill as soon as he has done whatever he can to salvage the mission, planning to personally waste you. Somehow or other he will insist on blaming you for the Mistral wind that shot the hell out of his operation. However, he'll run out of gas before he gets this far, so I think he'll come up on the blind-side of the road and pop up in front of the scope, where he expects you to be obediently sitting."

"Do I get to shoot the son-of-a-bitch?" I asked eagerly.

Creek answered slowly, "No, absolutely not! That is a pleasure I reserve for myself, but if I know him, he is going to want to prepare the speech that he has wanted to give at your funeral. I want him to continue talking, ranting, and anticipating the moment he decides to end you once and for all."

I grimaced theatrically and allowed, "Well, OK, but do I get to watch?"

"You betcha!" he said with a throaty laugh. "Just sit back at the scope, and I'll hide behind the car after I put the guard back behind the wheel; he'll look as though he is available for backup. You can keep the gun, but don't try to use it or react in any way. Just look as though you are still under and let me do the timing."

I sat back at the scope and looked at the nearby hillock that, from this position, blocked everything but the road. After a few moments, I noted Nu making his way up the hill towards me. He was visible for just a few seconds and then disappeared under the brow of a hill that shielded his continuing approach. If I had been focused on the mayhem below, he could have come up the hill, stood to one side, and shot me dead at his leisure. But I knew Herman was right, the rotten SOB was going to have to put on his little revenge act before he would think of dispatching what he considered the source of most of his grief.

Before Creek took his position twenty feet away, he put his hand on my shoulder. "By the way, how in the hell did you rig that beautiful wind? I was planning on doing a lot of dancing to get you out of this wringer, but I swear you took care of it yourself!"

I smiled, but didn't answer. I heard Creek walk back to the car, wrestling the dead body behind the wheel. I just sat there, my eyes glued to the scope. There was still an ongoing undertone of screams, cries, and the wail of sirens as more and more emergency vehicles drove towards the mess that had been a tranquil highway only a few minutes before. I reset the scope to the mangled remains of steel and bodies and sat there quietly.

Creek and my relationship was certainly not that of equals: he was my boss. Whatever else I was to him, I was still an agent under his control. From our first meeting aboard the A.E. Andersen on its way to Guam, I had worked undercover and mostly unconscious. I had, when I could remember—or was allowed to remember—learned who I was and what I had been doing. I was, to those who knew me, just an irresponsible, bright, but completely untrustworthy individual who presumably had never given a single thought to anyone's future, least of all … his own.

The work that I did would have been extremely dangerous for almost anybody else, but I had a secret weapon. It was an almost total lack of any sense of real time. Life for me was, and still is, a silly series of disparate events, with little holding them together in any kind of comprehensive grip. Yesterday was the day before this one, or years before this one, or any point in between. In any moment, I could be working on an art project, planning an engineering model, be in Guam, in Providence Academy, living with Al Capone, on the farm at Goble, or remembering something from some other lifetime. My whole life looked something like this sentence. However, in reality, it was more like:

     " … whole … something …

this … looked …

   life … like …

     My … sentence … "

with the dots being other totally disconnected lines of thought, endeavor, or memory!

Before the Navy, before Guam, and when first adopted, I would have hideous dreams full of killing and torture. One Thanksgiving, Macie got a large pinecone that had been assembled to look like some kind of turkey, but this one had its head where its ass should have been and vice-versa. It was on a wooden stand as our Thanksgiving centerpiece, with a series of words written on the base that said, "I'm a Gooney Bird … I don't want to see where I am going, I just want to see where I've been!"

A few nights later, shortly after my twelfth birthday, I had a nightmare. That Gooney Bird was now as large as an elephant, sitting in a tree with branches sturdy enough to hold it. It was just sitting there, minding its own business, when this evil-looking, dragon-like creature—twice the Gooney Bird's size—came down upon the twisted turkey. The dragon turned its huge head and, with its ugly, tooth-laden mouth open, ripped through the Gooney's head. The eyes went wide, then crossed and became defocused, while a hundred gallons of gooey green blood burst from its mangled head.

My screaming woke up the entire household.

This was not my only nightmare, but was the worst I remember. There was another involving a wide, shallow waterway: an immense wagon pulled by huge dray horses took my mother—with me in her arms—across that waterway to a lighthouse. The wagon wheels were gigantic and the dray horses—Clysdales or Morgans—thundered their way, spitting and braying through the slack waters. In this dream, there were hundreds of men with Percherons and Clysdales pulling similar wagons loaded with colossal blocks of stone. I had this dream often, and it was not until 30 years later that Sherry and I visited Newport and I understood that I was having memories of a real event: Alsea Bay during the construction of the Alsea Bay Bridge.

As I sat at the scope and watched the catastrophe below, I wondered why the nightmares now seemed to make the Goony Bird more an object of pity than an object of terror: real life held more horror than the dream state.

Suddenly Nu spoke. He was breathing heavily and simply said, "Hello."

I looked up from the scope. Nu was standing on the brow of the last hill just to the left of the scope. He had an automatic in his hand, pointed at my head. I let the scope rest and turned to directly look at him.

"I brought you up here to observe my master touch (a touch of sarcasm here?). Instead it turned out to be my downfall. At least Mr. Creek is not here to see it; most of the people who saw it are dead or crippled for life. I don't know how you did it, but I do know that you will not have another chance to cross me. You are a stupid excuse for a man, and your government has used you like a mindless puppet. You are everyman, the epitome of ignorance, and I hate you as I have hated no other, not even Creek. But now I am here, you are in my sights, and I will not miss. Goodbye, you bastard!"

He pointed his gun directly at my head, only inches away, as though he intended to wear the blood and tissue from the "blow-back" as a badge of honor. For the first time in an emergency threat, I closed my eyes. I heard the shot and immediately opened them. What I saw was Nu still standing in front of me. There was a small black dot just above the absolute middle of his forehead, from which a small coil of smoke was rising; the hatred on his face slowly morphed into a kind of amazed shock. Finally he fell stiff-legged, backwards out of my sight. His body rolled down the tall hill: seen, then hidden, then seen again, until his body stopped, sprawled awkwardly against a large rock.

I was in shock, not believing that this vicious man had ceased to exist. A blast of relief showered my soul as I realized that I was still here, but Nu was gone from my life! Miserable waste that he was, he would suffer no more.

There were plenty more of his crew around, so my troubles had only started. But for now, I arose and walked over to Creek. The two of us just stood on the hill looking down at the wreckage below and wondered if our lives would ever be remotely normal. Creek blew on the muzzle of the revolver, reminiscent of cowboy movies, and put a hand on my shoulder. "For a guy who isn't even here, I have pretty good aim, wouldn't you say?"

I couldn't think of anything to say, so I said nothing. Creek took another deep breath and signaled me to the police car, and we drove to the bottom of the hill. I took a last look at the carnage. As we moved on to the next town, Creek explained how he was going to have to get me the hell out of this country …

By the dress of the people, by the scenery and other clues, I surmised that I was somewhere else in France. Without a clue as to how I had gotten here, I was now subjected to an uncomfortable ride in the trunk of a car. There was a lot of bumping and thumping, followed by a welcome silence. The trunk opened, and a slightly built man of about 40, with a walrus mustache and vaguely European clothes, helped me out of the trunk and supported me as I shakily made my way to the edge of a warm campfire where Creek was. There were three other men whom we joined. They stopped talking as we approached; they were not introduced to me. I stood awkwardly waiting for something to happen, but nothing did.

Gradually, my vision became cloudy, and the familiar ringing started in my ears. When I blinked and looked again, there were only three of us: the man who had helped me out of the trunk of the car, Creek, and me. I was now seated on a log, just staring into the flames, which seemed to be much smaller than they had been. The face of the man with the mustache seemed to shift, become blurry, and drift out of focus. I was aware that Creek was talking to me, but once again, it did not seem to be language with which I was familiar. Finally, there was only Creek and me, but we were now in a large chateau, which was hidden in dark woods and only dimly visible in the early twilight.

Suddenly Creek was talking to me in full intelligible sentences. "Larry, you are now fully awake, feeling fine, breathing easily, and completely relaxed. We, whom you have no need to remember, will not be remembered. In fact, if you try to remember anything but my words, you will find that you have a killing headache that gets worse the harder you try."

He continued in a humorless voice. "You will be taken care of by the man who took you out of the trunk of the car, but you will not remember him either, except to know that he is your keeper. He will see that you are fed, when that is possible; he will see that you are kept warm, if that is possible; and he will see that no one interrupts your journey. He is your uncle, and you will address him that way. He is all that is going to keep you alive.

"Larry, you are deaf. You cannot hear anyone's words. You are like a brain damaged child. You are not blind, you can see, but you cannot make any sense out of anything you look at. You are simple-minded, and if you are forced to talk, you can only mumble incoherently. You will have to stay this way until I am able to talk to you again—at some undetermined time. But you have nothing to worry about: you will be taken care of!"

Creek went on talking, but his words seemed to run together and resonate—strangely echoing—the sounds bouncing as though in a large room, combined with a loud ringing. There was no way of making sense of the sounds. Gradually, I found myself becoming less and less interested in the man who was talking or of anything else that was going on around me. And then there was silence: deep, profound, vast.

What followed was a series of seemingly endless alarms, guard posts, various forms of incarceration, and a vague, subliminal fear. I was constantly cold. I would cry out at various times, and if anyone tried to talk to me, I would mumble pathetically. I slept under haystacks in wide fields; I was cold and wet. I was walking, always walking, and always trying to sleep. Uncle kept dragging me along when all I wanted to do was sleep. I climbed up mountains—shivering and miserable—and down mountains, and then walked some more. There was no day and there was no night, there was only walking, walking, walking. There would be several towns, all looking more or less alike; there would be questions of me that I would answer with mumbling or sullen silence; then there would be more walking, especially at night. I was so tired that I would sleep while walking and would find myself falling off the road, until Uncle again took me by the arm and led me on. This went on much the same for what seemed like months—as it turned out, it was. Then one day, as quickly as it had started, it ended.

I awoke in the back seat of a parked car. The car was relatively new. I tried the doors but they were locked. There was nobody in the front seat, and there was a grill separating me from it. I was now in the outskirts of a small city: it was hilly and very quiet, apparently early morning. I observed a uniformed policeman coming towards the car, but I did not recognize him except that he seemed to have a very large mustache. He walked to the car, opened the driver's door, and got in. He inserted the key and started the engine.

In a voice that sounded like he was talking to no one in particular, he asked, "Do you know who I am, Larry?"

As I started to answer, I realized that I had to begin two or three times before a voice came out that I could recognize as my own. "You are my uncle." The answer was simple and declarative.

"Good," was the soft response.

We drove a short distance until Uncle stopped the car, and another man got in, sitting beside Uncle in the front seat. The new man, also in uniform, said, "How has it gone, so far?"

Uncle reported that it had gone well and that we would be crossing the border in about twenty minutes. The new man told Uncle that he had all the papers, so we should park the car out of the way and continue on foot to Rota.

Rota, I thought, we must be on Guam … then I realized that we could not possibly be walking to Rota, since Rota was an island. Somehow this must be another Rota. A few more words were said, and I went back to sleep. When I awoke, Uncle and the other man were not in uniform, but were in peasant clothes and were taking me though a small town, built on the side of a hill with a busy port area below, bustling with activity. There were piers and a landing, with many small boats and a few large freighters.

The other man said, "I'll see you at the ship … take care."

Uncle took my hand and asked me a lot of questions about what had happened on the hill when all the cars were colliding; I answered as best I could. The answers seemed to reassure him, and he told me that we were going to "the school." He didn't tell me what school, but seemed to think that I would know when we got there.

"The school" was a two-story building very near the docks. There was a front door leading into a large room with many desks. Uncle took me around to the back of the building and told me to go up an external stairway to a room where I would find a person seated at a large desk. I was to go up to that person and give her the piece of paper I found in my pocket, then wait until Uncle came to get me.

I climbed slowly up the outside stairs and opened the door. I stepped in and saw that there were many chairs in the room; close to the door I had entered was an open area with a large desk. A substantial woman, with dark hair and dark eyes, sat behind the desk and watched me with interest as I entered and sat in the small chair in front of the desk.

"And just who in blazes let you in here?" she demanded.

In answer I reached into my pocket and passed the paper across her desk.

She looked at it, bored at first, and then came to complete attention. She looked at me with those dark eyes boring into mine. "So … " she said finally, "you are waiting for your papers?"

Knowing nothing, I said nothing. She looked at me for a long time and then reached into her desk bringing out a sheaf of pages that she pushed across the desk to me. "Read these thoroughly and be truthful!"

I took the pages and started to read them, carefully.

Suddenly, Uncle appeared beside her, just as she again reached into her desk. She startled when she become aware of his presence and began to shift the aim of the gun she now held in her hand, but was not quick enough. Uncle hit her on the head with his revolver's two-inch barrel and then, as quickly, shot her in the left temple.

He took my hand and led me down another stairway—inside the building—where we departed, in carefully determined strides, out the front door. He explained that she was supposed to give me regular exit papers, but apparently was no longer working for our side, which made it imperative that we get to the docks … quickly!

I was literally shipped out of Rota, Spain in a box and arrived, extremely wasted, in a cartage house on the East Coast near Wilmington, New Jersey.

I believe that this was my last mission for a number of reasons. I was extremely damaged by those events, but did not really know how damaged until I recovered the memories of the disaster in France some 30 years later; those memories haunt me to this day. The sight of golden sloping hills brings forth a renewed sense of despair. I had been on a number of different missions off and on through those "lost years," many of them utilizing my special psychic abilities to identify problems and to modify plans. So, why was this so much worse than the others, especially in comparison to the mission when I "killed my mother" in Greece? In retrospect, I think it was having some awareness of what was happening, but not having control over my own identity nor the ability to protect the innocents that inadvertently became involved in our event. Then, to add to the problem, Nu was the mainstream agency chief for this operation—I never did know what was supposed to come down or why, but that was not unusual. No one knew who killed him; I was the only one who had been with him who was still alive—of course, Creek was in Argentina! I was, therefore, a rogue agent and was on the "kill-on-sight" list.

How Creek extracted me alive and then arranged for my safe care and rehabilitation in a place like the mental hospital in Nova Scotia is still a mystery. Perhaps it was to protect himself since he had eliminated a dangerous enemy, but perhaps there was some degree of compassion in his character and recognition that I might not be the usual package of garbage.

When I initially recovered this memory of Nova Scotia, I perceived that I was being tortured; I was cold and terribly tired all the time. My memory of that period was garbled and piecemeal: I was playing cards with other men one moment, freezing cold the next, then catatonic, and then everything was black, and then back to playing cards again. My feelings about Creek were not very positive. But, as I write this chapter for the book, I understand that what was seen then as torture was undoubtedly 1950's psychiatric care: ice cold wraps warmed by the inhabitant to body temperature to provide calming to the terrified spirit; electric shock and insulin shock to help erase destructive memories and allay depression; and card games to socialize the lost personality back to some semblance of normality. It is gratifying to know now that Creek actually was my best friend.

11 | Larry's Kids: Penny and Kathy

There is absolutely no question that the next few pages are the toughest that I have written. When I originally wrote this section in 1981, I had been having serious medical problems and was depressed. There is no way of explaining the things that follow without commenting further on what I understood of Dorothy's character. She is the mother of the first four of my children. Of those four, only two have any degree of reality to me: one is Penny, the other Kathy. Only Penny was planned and only Penny was wanted … by me.

There is a resolute force in some people that guarantees them success because they just keep on plugging. They do not take no for an answer and they know, that in all of this horseshit, there must be a pony. If Dorothy had understood or had been able to believe me in the first few weeks of our marriage, she would have realized that we had made a mistake, and that there was no way this mistake should have been repeated through four kids, but that was Dorothy. She was not about to give up and, apparently after she learned that I was the instrument of getting her pregnant nine months and ten minutes to the moment of our first intercourse, she believed that she was stuck with me. It is interesting that she finally did get the message, and at several years too late to do very many people much good, she got off our marriage-go-round. It is a grimly humorous fact of life that doctors had told her that she would never have any children because of a tipped uterus; apparently nature didn't know that.

Penny

Penny was born in fifteen minutes on a gurney, which was being used to transport Dorothy into the delivery room. I had taken Dorothy to Bess Kaiser Hospital in Vancouver where we were living after we had been flooded out of Vanport. We had gone in a cab because we did not own a car, and when the doctor had told me that it would be eight or nine hours before the baby would be born, I decided to hitchhike the 3 miles back to town. I had reached the road, which was about a quarter of a mile from the hospital, when it dawned on me that I had forgotten my coat in the waiting room. I walked back to the hospital. When I went up to the receptionist to ask for my coat, she said, "You are Mr. Wahl, aren't you??"

I was surprised that she asked but I said, "Yes, I just came back for my coat."

"OK, but would you like to see your baby daughter?"

"NO!" I said, somewhat annoyed at how fouled up a hospital can get. "I only came back for my coat."

The receptionist was giggling by this time. "Mr. Wahl, I would be happy to give your coat back, but don't you want to see your new baby?"

I just couldn't seem to get through to this lady; all of the people in the waiting room were looking at me, smiling.

"I just left a few minutes ago, and the doctor said … "

"The doctor was wrong!" interrupted the clerk.

The first part of the message was finally starting to get through; I got my coat and went to see Dorothy and my new daughter. Dorothy was so proud of the little bundle she presented me. Penny was a beautiful baby, and I fell in love with her immediately.

"What took you so damn long?" I finally managed to joke.

I called Gene to stop by the apartment and bring some clothes and a small suitcase for Dorothy. I knew that, as cool as Dad was, he would be a pillar of strength to lean on. He never got bent out of shape over anything and knew the perfect thing to say in every occasion.

A short time later, the outside hospital door burst open and a wretched-looking man, obviously on the very edge of a coronary attack, walked to the middle of the waiting room and tried to give a speech that he had obviously spent some time rehearsing. He carried a small suitcase that had part of a pair of blue panties and half of a bra dragging on the floor.

He calmly announced, "I'm a-a-a Eugene … a-a-a Wahl … A … where do I go, I'm gonna have a baby!!"

I decided that if I just ignored this fool, maybe he would go away!

While I adored the beauty that Penny was, it wasn't until about 3 years later that I knew she had inherited her mother's persistent character. It was that persistence that made her try to find her "dear dad" some 30 years later. As it didn't work out with Dorothy, it also did not work out with Penny. She had a good stepfather and, since she probably had only spent a total of a few weeks in my presence, I did not think the disruption of two families was worth it. I told her not to come.

Kathy

I was working for the Fox chain of theaters as an assistant manager at the El Capitan on the Mission in San Francisco. I knew that Dorothy was due soon, and when she developed pains at regular intervals, she took no chance and got a cab at 3rd and Geneva in San Francisco to get to the main Kaiser Hospital in Oakland. The hospital called the theatre and told the manager to tell me that they were going to keep her, and that after I finished work, would I please call them before I came over. I thought the message was put in kind of a strange form; I had a feeling that there was something wrong. I finished my day's work in a haze.

As soon as I got off work, I took a bus downtown and called from a phone booth, while waiting for the A-train to Oakland. When I got the doctor on the line, he sounded like a man going to a hanging. He assured me that Dorothy was all right, but suggested that I prepare myself for a shock. He said that there had been problems with the baby. It is strange how things hit you. During Dorothy's pregnancy with Penny, I had delighted in feeling the baby move. I was surprised that with Kathy there had been so little movement, and Dorothy had been apprehensive during the time she was carrying this baby.

When I got to the hospital, I was ushered into the doctor's office; he asked me to take a seat. He was a middle-aged man with a grave face and watery blue eyes. He talked first of Dorothy and the difficult birth. He told me that she was all right, but that there had been problems with the baby. He said that there was a certain amount of grim good to the situation, however, because it looked as though the baby had been born dead.

Then there was the shock. Although Kathy was the result of a non-wanted pregnancy that I had practically been raped into and was, in fact, the reason that Dorothy and I had gotten back together, I felt no satisfaction in the fact that the baby was gone.

Then the doctor corrected my impression. "You see, the baby is still alive, but she has spina bifida and a myelomeningocele. What this means is that the spinal cord comes through a neurological defect in the vertebrae (spina bifida) and appears as a small out pouching (myelomeningocele) on the surface of the back at the lower level of the spine. Unfortunately that delicate tissue was pierced with the forceps in the process of the difficult birth. Because of this defect, there was a problem with the hips and the legs (paralysis). The birth was similar to a breech birth; it was a very rough delivery for the baby. As a result, she will die in a few hours from infection, which has direct access to the spinal cord."

The doctor then opened a drawer in his desk and removed a sheet of paper. "Mr. Wahl," he said as he pushed the paper over to me gently, "this a death certificate. If you will sign it, we will simply indicate that the child was stillborn, and you will be saved the agony of your wife even having to see the child."

"What does she know?" I asked with tears streaming down my face. "What does Dorothy know?"

"She knows that there is a problem, but we decided to let you explain the situation. We thought that it would be easier that way."

I signed the death certificate and went up on the floor to see Dorothy. I hugged her immediately, and we did not say a word. I just held her, and the two of us rocked together in our confusion and grief. Finally she gently pushed me away, so that she could look into my eyes. She asked, "How is our daughter?"

I told Dorothy about my meeting with the doctor. She said that she realized that they were trying to make it easier on her, but that she really wanted to see the baby. I told her that the doctors would not let her because the baby was in intensive care. I told her that she would be dead in a few hours, and that we should just think of her as being born dead.

A day later they asked me to pick up Dorothy. Dorothy was feeling much better, but when I talked to her, as she was getting ready to leave, she had some rather surprising news. "Kathy" Dorothy announced, "is still alive!"

"What?" I asked incredulously. "She's still alive? For Christ's sake, I signed a death certificate! They said she wouldn't last the night."

Dorothy explained that the doctor had told her that somehow the injured opening to the spinal cord had crusted over, and Kathy had not developed any symptoms of infection; she had been transferred to the nursery. I asked Dorothy if she had seen her.

"No, they really didn't encourage me."

When I go berserk, there is a feeling that comes over me: a heat builds in my head and rolls down my body until my feet tingle. I felt like that now. I told Dorothy to go ahead and get ready to leave; I would see the doctor and meet her at the emergency entrance. I went to the doctor's office; he was waiting for me. I believe he realized when he saw me that he was not dealing with a totally rational man. He told me that in the nursery they were treating the baby properly, and that she was taking formula well. The myelomeningocele protrusion was being protected by a "doughnut" that made sure there was no pressure from it touching on the bed. He said that she was going to die in any case, and that we should just leave the baby there and let them take care of it. I asked through clenched teeth where the baby was and was directed to the nursery.

When I got to the nursery, I had no trouble finding Kathy: she was in the hall, on the visitors' side of the glass window! I looked down at the sweet person that looked up at me. There were golden ringlets of hair surrounding that Dresden face. It could have been the face of Larry Wahl: There were deep blue eyes, wise and patient beyond her days. At the end of the crib was the notation: Baby Wahl.

I pulled back the blankets and saw the helpless little legs, tucked as though for all the world she was a little practitioner of Yoga. The feet were turned in, folded on themselves. If the legs could have been straightened, the child would have been destined to walk on the sides of her ankles. When I touched the feet, they were cold, and the places that I touched left little blanched spots that took a while to pink up. And then I saw, lying next to her, a large brown object: the doughnut! I went into total rage. It was not all right that my own mother may have tried to kill me with a knitting needle, and it was not all right to kill the innocent when the world was full of assholes that really needed killing. But here was Baby Wahl, and they had put her out in the hall like garbage to be collected. Someone who thought it was their duty to hasten her death had removed the life-protecting doughnut, which had been the only pitiful thing that they could do for her. I reached under the baby and turned her over. I almost passed out. The myelomeningocele was like something out of a nightmare. The baby was so small, and this thing was so huge. It was red and swollen, and looked even worse because it had been so compressed. Red veins and grey dura (tissue covering the spinal cord) vibrated with every breath and pulsated with every heartbeat. It was as if this grotesque growth lived a life of its own, threatening to destroy what was my child. A nurse happened to come by at this time; she told me that I should not be touching the baby. I told her to call an ambulance, the doctor, and the police if she liked, because I was taking my baby home, and I would kill the first person that got in my way.

The doctor appeared on the scene and took in the situation. What the doctor saw was a young man holding a newborn baby in his arms and leaning against the glass wall that shielded thirty other little babies who were going to live, who were wanted, who were valuable, who were whole. He tried to explain to me that what had been done was for our benefit. This got him nowhere. A couple of husky-looking orderlies appeared, but the doctor waived them off.

"What is it that you plan to do with the baby? Who will take care of it? Do you know how to care for it?"

I yelled at the doctor, "I will put her out on the front porch and will sandpaper the area until it bleeds, just like you have been taking care of her!"

"What do you want from me?" he asked quietly.

"I want my wife and I want my baby and I want an ambulance and I want to get the hell out of this god damn butcher shop."

Still huddled against the wall, I was holding Kathy tightly and cooing to her when Dorothy was wheeled to where I was standing; a dozen nurses and orderlies stood by. She looked at me like she had never seen me before, and I am sure that she saw some things she had never expected to see. As the doctor ushered us to the emergency exit one floor below, she was wheeled beside me. There was no conversation; all talk had stopped. I noticed two deputies standing by the door. When we approached, they simply held the doors open for us and helped Dorothy into the ambulance. We all sat in the front seat. I gave the baby to Dorothy to hold; she looked like a Madonna as the ambulance made its careful, quiet way from Oakland to San Francisco, and then, Kathy was home.

Adrenalin had supported Dorothy and me through the hospital experience. There was no thought of what was going to happen next: it became a matter of putting one foot in front of the other and just keep moving. We had already put a crib in Penny's room and had collected quite a set of clothes for the baby. The house was completely ready for a baby, but it was not ready for a patient. I was so unhappy with the doctors that I would not even consider calling them. I did realize that when I had signed her out of the hospital, everything that was going to happen from then on was my responsibility.

In the days that followed, Dorothy and I got a chance to really understand what kind of process we had signed up for. Every time Kathy messed her diapers, the area of the myelomeningocele became completely soiled. A baby performs this operation a good many times a day. The mass of the myelomeningocele was so delicate-looking and so transparent that it was scary as hell every time I had to touch it, especially since I knew that it was the actual spinal cord just covered with a layer of the meninges—a layer of connective tissue that extended from the spinal cord to the brain. I would not let Dorothy do anything with the baby's back; I insisted on doing the cleaning each and every time by myself. I knew that I had signed Kathy out of the hospital AMA—against medical advice—and what I had taken upon myself to do could be the proximate cause of her death.

In the beginning, what I did each time the area was soiled was wash it with a dilute hydrogen peroxide solution and apply a bandage to the area. This usually was such a scary business that I would finish the sessions of cleaning, sweating from the strain and the fear. But we soon learned that taking care of this baby on the basis of bandaging her each time was thoroughly impractical from a time standpoint, but more importantly, the cost of bandages was keeping us broke.

Over the next few weeks, Dorothy and I worked out a system, which turned out to be very effective. We were so unhappy with having to disturb the tender area of the myelomeningocele, which we knew could be torn just once and that could be death for Kathy. Yet we knew that the area had to be kept clean. We ended up using a huge double boiler. We placed large quantities of four-inch bandages into the double boiler, and then dumped in Vaseline from a pharmaceutical supply that came in two-quart containers. We would cook the bandages in the Vaseline for over two hours. One night a week, we would take about three hours, and wearing masks and using forceps and scissors that had been thoroughly sterilized, we would put together Vaseline-impregnated packs. These were collected in half-pint sterilized jars, which would hold seven of the packs each. With any luck, the packs would last for a day.

After the area around the rectum was thoroughly cleaned with the peroxide, the Vaseline-impregnated gauze protecting the myelomeningo-cele would be replaced with a clean Vaseline gauze pack. Careful attention was given to completely sealing off the area around the anus. This was done in such a way that, when Kathy had a bowel movement, the area of the myelomeningocele would be shielded from the feces by at least three layers of bandages. With this system, the baby could be cleaned several times a day without unduly handling the myelomeningocele and with little danger of contamination. At night, the bandages could be checked—and changed if needed—and Kathy put to bed. In the morning, all of the bandages would be removed and the entire area inspected and cleaned of any material that had seeped through. The system worked so well that there was only one time when the myelomeningocele was anything but squeaky clean.

The major conceptual problem we had was that we did not really know what a myelomeningocele was, even though the doctor had tried to explain it to two very stressed parents. It was an obvious growth, and you could see through it in the early weeks, so that the form of the uncovered spinal cord could be made out. It was also plain that some of the grey material plastered on the inside of the myelomeningocele were spinal tracts and nerves, and it was clear that these were the nerves—the wiring—that connected Kathy's feet, legs, sexual organs, and the like to the motor and sensation areas in the brain. That the anatomy (and physiology) of what we were looking at was the reason for her paralysis would have been clear to anyone who knew that wires pulled out of an electrical junction box would create disruptions in the systems to which they had been connected. What troubled us, however, from the standpoint of care, was the nature of the covering we were looking at. This thin transparent plastic-like covering was obviously not composed of the same material as the skin on either side of it, nor above and below it. Was it, therefore, a protective material—which seemed obvious—or was it part of the problem and something that we needed to get rid of. It may seem like a small point, but the philosophy upon which I have operated, or tried to operate, is that the first thing that is necessary in a battle is to learn the nature of the enemy. We had not received any medical instruction, but were visited weekly by a nurse from the Phelan Institute that had received a large grant to assist families such as ours. I'm not sure who sent her because she just appeared one day, and there was no cost to us.

We had been thoroughly turned off by the nature of the initial care Kathy had received at Kaiser. We concluded that this was one of those areas in which we gave it our best shot and we either helped or killed the person, but at any rate, we would know we had done something, that we had not just stood by helplessly. I have thought back over the years and tried to think of the number of people whom I have "saved," at least in a medical sense. The number runs to at least three dozen that I can think of off-hand, so the need to intervene is something that, it seems to me, I was born with. Both Dorothy and I came to realize early on that we might do something that was absolutely wrong and kill Kathy outright. But we had spent hours discussing it and we had tried to cover all aspects, with the nurse's instructions. The one thing that came out of the experience was the realization that no one was to blame, and that it was a learning experience. We agreed that no guarantees had been asked for and none had been given: it was simply the way that it was.

I have never understood Dorothy. It is likely that since I was in the middle of my "programming," there was no way that I was likely to understand Dorothy or anyone else. But in this one aspect of our marriage, Kathy stands out as a beacon. There was never any question about what we were going to do; there was never any discussion about the necessity of it; there was never any problem about taking the endless responsibility of it; and there was never any fear of the outcome.

During this time, Dorothy was working for M.S.T.S, the military shipping branch of the U.S. Government. It was a good job, and she made relatively good money, especially for a woman in the 1950s. The only job that I could get was working at the theatres. I loved the work, but it did not pay a living wage and therefore my financial contribution to the family was very limited. Prior to Kathy's birth, I had stayed away from home for long periods of time and had had a liaison with one of the girls who worked at the theatre. But there were other things going on in my life that no one else knew anything about, and I knew even less.

It was many years later that I was to learn, from totally independent sources, the nature of the clandestine events that were taking place in the Bay Area at the time, especially the military interest in the private lives of the politicians. A great amount of OSS/CIA resources and tax dollars were allocated to setting up data bases on each congressman, senator, and local dog-catcher who would, at some future date, have anything to do with voting on military appropriations. I did not know then that the San Francisco Bay Area was the center for these high jinks: think SRI in Menlo Park! I considered myself a completely non-political animal; I am not even sure that I would have been particularly shocked if I had known, at a conscious level, what was going on. I wouldn't have wanted to be sitting right in the middle of it, but that is the way that things go.

The nature of the information that I received and the jobs that I was sent on for the Company necessitated a wife who was trained to do as she was told, so I considered, upon later reflection, that Dorothy may have been picked by the Company to be the kind of a dupe—as they would view it—that would put up with almost any kind of bullshit without balking. She also seemed to lack any kind of viable thought or concentrative process. Unfortunately, I had little concept of her as a person. It seemed to me then, and in retrospect, that I was more conscious in the classical sense—even when doped and hypnotized—than Dorothy was when she was fully awake. There was a quality about her: She would risk any pain, go to any lengths, and bear any problems to support her man.

One can find a martyr's life interesting, but it is hard as hell living with one, especially when you are a real stinker. The one thing that you can count on is that you are always going to be right about only one thing: you are always in the wrong! It is nothing that the your partner has to say to you, it is simply that she is always going through life with a big sign that says, "You have the divine right: go ahead and kick me."

It becomes relatively unimportant whether this is a good idea, or whether you really want to, but it is a hell of a challenge to an animal as perverse as a human being to be told, over and over, "Go ahead and be as big an asshole as you can possibly be; there is nothing you can do that will make me stop loving you." There is, in each of us, a desire to find out where the limits are. There is then almost nothing that can happen to a marriage, or unreasonable facsimile thereof, given an unconscious sadist and a willing masochist. I believe there was this quality of masochism in Dorothy since the constancy she had with me would not have been warranted for any human being, and especially not for me. There was only one exception, and that exception was the care of Kathy. Kathy was the first and the only job that I had done from beginning to end, or at least to the point where there was nothing else that I could do for her.

After the first few months had gone by, and we had the bandaging and all of the other Kathy-care things taken care of, there was still time to try to train Penny; I was even managing to give Dorothy something that was passing for love. We had reached the conclusion that the myelomeningocele was clearly shrinking. The nature of the covering changed little by little: the transparent quality receded and in its place there was a kind of opaque grey overlay. The material looked a little bit like scar tissue, but what was the most surprising was that it was a hard horny-like cover and it took fewer bandages to protect it. We had started out having to overlap two four-inch bandages to cover the more than seven inches of the length of the "blister." In about three months, it had diminished until one bandage would cover it, and at the end of five months, we had stopped dressing it altogether. It now was the size of a large thumb, was no longer transparent, and was hard as a rock. There was no danger of accidentally re-rupturing it; we were able to put Kathy on her back without the doughnut for limited periods of time.

She was a beautiful baby and a joy to be around. Her eyes were old and wise, and anyone who saw her was struck by the resemblance between Kathy and me. She ate well almost from the beginning and did not have any serious problems other than the mass that nature had presented her with in the beginning. I had seen some babies with the same difficulties with their feet (clubbed feet) who apparently had not had the myelomeningocele problem. I knew of the process of straightening the feet with special braces and surgery so that the legs could operate in a normal fashion. I was of course aware that she was still paralyzed from the lumbar area down, but during the exercises that we had faithfully performed on her, we had noted a small response in both motor and sensory nerves: limited motion and reaction to pain and pressure stimulation. So it was that on the six-month anniversary of her birth, we took her into the San Francisco Kaiser clinic.

It is in my nature generally, and was further trained into me by the CIA, to be perfectly reasonable about something up to the point when I was to act. This was not a hard thing to train into me; it was natural. I had steeled myself to give no outward sign as to how I felt about something so that people were completely unconcerned about what I was going to do next. When the threshold considerations were met internally, I would act: suddenly, decisively, and often mortally, with no external warning whatsoever.

It was in this spirit that we took Kathy to the clinic for a check up. I was willing to forgive and forget what they had to done to her—or more to the point, the things not done for her—if they would take care of her now. What was needed was for them to get on the ball and fix her feet.

I was feeling mild and bland, but just below the surface were my negative feelings about hospitals/clinics in general and fool doctors in particular. We had made an appointment in the general clinic and apparently her file had been brought in. This file contained only general and minimal information of the birth trauma; this was all that was known to the doctor who was assigned to us, until he came into the room to examine Kathy. His consternation was palpable, and he was clearly confused. I smiled as he looked at the pitifully thin file—a single sheet—that he was holding in his hand, and at the cooing, happy baby that was lying on the examining table. The folded legs and the obvious lack of movement told him that the child and the file matched … sort of.

With perfect reasonableness, I said, "So, we have brought her in to have her feet straightened and braces fitted for her legs."

In all fairness to the doctor, it was serious data to throw at him all at once. He was completely out of touch with the situation since Kathy had had no follow-up clinic care. The doctors had initially handled the affair with incredible stupidity; they didn't seem about to improve their batting average this time.

What the doctor said, with a flushed face and through clenched teeth, was, "Damn it, man! We can't fit this child with braces. She is going to die and there is nothing anyone can do about it."

My mind went into overdrive. I needed to kill this fool. At first I thought I would simply Karate chop him in the neck where he stood. Then I got inventive and considered picking him up bodily and throwing him through the frosted glass window into the corridor. I could, of course, slowly choke him to death.

I began explaining to him loudly, "I can die crossing the street; she can die tomorrow, but today she is going to get some help! You had not even taken footprints or weighed her after birth—the myelomeningocele was the size of my fist; we worked our butts off getting it to the size of our thumb."

All of this was said in a "whisper" that could be heard a block away. My comments brought in a senior surgeon who was visiting. First he calmed me down, and then gave Kathy her first complete physical. The two doctors exchanged looks; the senior man, Martin Jones, told me the rest of the story. He told me what we had not been told by the birthing doctors: she also has hydrocephalus—excessive fluid in the brain—that will eventually render her brain nonfunctional. He explained how cerebral-spinal fluid that has no exit strategy would gradually build up pressure causing the brain to herniate downward and negatively affect the vital structures in the brainstem. End result: coma followed by death.

Why hadn't I seen the subtle changes in her head size that were not the result of normal growth? Probably because we were so focused on managing the myelomeningocele to prevent death from that problem.

Dr. Jones told us about an innovative surgery for hydrocephalus. The operation consisted of putting a shunt in the ventricle of the brain and running it into the back of the throat, thus allowing the excess fluid to be drained via the gastrointestinal system. The only problem was that any cold or throat infection would have ready access into the brain. To date the surgery had had little success and was no longer being done, pending more research. However, he would consider performing the surgery on Kathy as long as we fully understood the risk: only 50% got off the table, and of those who did, none had survived past one year. We enthusiastically agreed, any treatment was better than certain death.

I finally did understand that the doctors, from the beginning, had been trying to help Dorothy and me. I knew that they had watched dozens of marriages break up as the parents tried to care for disabled children. The doctors knew what guilt parents had, and if there were other children in the family (like Penny), the awful price those children had to pay in loss of parental love and attention because of having a damaged sibling.

New Year's Eve Nightmare

After that trip with Kathy to Kaiser San Francisco when I was given the full extent of Kathy's injuries, I thought that I had taken in this new information with a kind of grim acceptance. It turned out this was total illusion: I was destroyed! My Company training taught me to never flinch in the presence of terror, but rather to fall apart later when it was relatively safe. I was fairly sure that this was the case, but somehow in the back of my mind was this nightmare of Kathy's head growing larger and larger while her brain grew smaller and smaller. But, those were God's grisly jokes.

I had quit working the theaters and was now taking the A train across the bridge to Oakland where I worked as a warehouseman at a General Petroleum Plant. The work paid a great deal more, but the round little

Caesar—we called him "The Bear"—that ran the place made damn sure our crew of eight worked every second of every minute of every hour we were on the grounds. I loved the work, and Dorothy and I were as happy as two people can be—given that these are people who know absolutely nothing real about each other except that they share one healthy baby and one that is a congenital disaster.

The doctors were working on setting up the newly reorganized surgical procedure for which Kathy was to be the thirteenth case in a process that had mostly been a pathetic failure. As it turned out, Kathy's operation was the only true success, and the reason the operation was not abandoned. It was a close decision as the plan had been pretty much scrapped before Kathy and I burst on the scene.

Time moved on, and as the time for the operation approached, I found myself winding up. Nothing was helped by a new worker on the job, Joe Baca, who bitched continually, avoided the work, and was generally mean. One day, in a spirit of helpfulness, I approached him and tried to explain to him why the guys were giving him such a bad time. I was quite calm as I stared at him and his pair of silver glasses. I reached out to touch him on the shoulder, smiling. What happened next was probably predictable, but I had not expected it: he shoved me back hard. I looked at him, standing in front of me, and was shocked by the miraculously strange thing that was happening to his face. As I was observing him with detachment, his glasses separated into shards and the frames were bent. It took a second or two for me to realize that I had hit him. I immediately apologized and told him that I would pay for the glasses and a visit to a doctor if that was necessary, but cautioned him that I was highly trained in the martial arts and that hitting me in anger was a very poor choice of activities. He walked away, and The Bear fired him an hour later. The Bear then stuck his face in front of me and asked, as he peered over his glasses, "Well, do you want to hit me?!"

A few days later on the job, two detectives sent for me. Actually they simply asked me to come with them. I assumed that it was in relation to an accident to which I had been a witness, so I didn't think there were any serious problems. When I entered the district attorney's office, the first thing I saw was Mr. Baca, sitting on a bench and glaring at me: this was not about the accident! So, I would tell my story to the DA, and that should be the end of it ... wrong!

The district attorney listened closely, and now had both Baca and me in the room together. There was a slight commotion in the anteroom. I was happily surprised to see The Bear and two of the guys from the plant with him; they had come to back me up. The DA looked a little disappointed, but asked me a question I have never forgotten—most important, have never forgotten what the proper legal answer is. He asked me if I was afraid of Baca. I looked at him in shocked surprise and answered instantly, "Of course not!"

The DA responded. "Well, Mr. Wahl, I am sure that what we are looking at is a clear case of assault, two to ten years, which is proven out of your own mouth … "

About this time, I began to understand a little more criminal law.

Now turning to Baca and his attorney, the DA added, "However, Mr. Baca, if you wish to proceed with this criminal complaint, with the witnesses Mr. Wahl has, I believe he could successfully counter-sue you for false arrest. So I would recommend that you both go on about your normal activities and forget this incident."

When we got outside, The Bear took my arm, spun me around, and asked with a grin, "So, tough guy, who are you not afraid of now?"

I laughed involuntarily, took a defensive pose, and said, "If some sixty pound, three foot, alcoholic guy in an iron lung attacks me, I will swear on a stack of Bibles that I am scared to death!"

We went back to work, and The Bear cheerfully docked our pay for the time off the job.

A month later, Kathy had her operation and survived, but it was going to be many months before we would know if it were successful. I was running bank-full and was primed for a fully catalogued, frothy, pre-fabricated catastrophe!!

It was New Year's Eve and an hour before quitting time, we were all assembled in the main office. The Bear gave each of us a fifth of Vodka and a fifteen-pound frozen turkey. We laughed and joked around for a while and then left for our homes.

I didn't want to go home, so stopped at my favorite restaurant and asked them to hold the turkey for me. The manager and I were friends; he did so willingly. I continued working on the vodka until, finally, I had arrived at the place I had been looking for all this time: I was in hell, but it wasn't too bad. I can remember hollering, and screaming, and breaking furniture, and saying, "My baby's going to be an idiot," and being thrown bodily out of the restaurant. Then there was a long spell of wandering around the midnight streets of an Oakland suburb. I was arrested for public drunkenness, all the time talking about Kathy.

I was taken to the station house, told to go directly home, and released. A lot more time passed, and another group of uniformed policemen wrestled me into a paddy wagon. Again, by the time I reached the station, I appeared completely sober and was once again released. The next thing I remember is hammering on a store window, being arrested, and taken to a hospital where I was tied to a gurney in full leather restraints. I slipped these as though they were made of stretchy rubber and was wandering out into the streets again.

This time I was very, very tired and found myself slow-dancing on a raised wall next to a cement stairway leading to a basement (memories arose of the Jewish store and the "accident" that solved a lot of problems when I was six). If the fall didn't kill me, I could go to the hospital and at least get a little rest. No, wait … I already had that chance. Again Oakland city police wrestled me off the wall and booked me into the drunk tank. Ten minutes after the cell door clanked shut, I was fully awake and sober. But, it was four long, cold hours standing with a puking, stinking crowd of drunks on New Year's morning until I was released and given a chance to call Dorothy to come and pick me up. She didn't sound surprised at all. She drove me back to our Sunnydale home, and I finally got to go to sleep. I don't think Dorothy and I ever discussed the evening, then or later.

The next time I was scheduled at G.P., I stopped by the restaurant after work. The manager saw me coming and disappeared into the kitchen. I came in and sat down. He hurried over with my turkey, gave it to me, and without a smile, informed me that I was barred from ever coming back into his restaurant in my lifetime. I took the turkey and left. Dorothy and I had a New Year's turkey dinner a few days later.

As life would have it, shortly after Kathy's operation, I happened to be having coffee in the bus station when I spotted a woman with dead eyes and the weight of the world on her shoulders. I never did anything like this, but for some reason I went over and sat next to her, commenting that she looked like she had had a tough day; did she want to talk about it?

"You won't understand," she said.

"Try me," I responded.

In a few short sentences, she explained her burden: a hydrocephalic child. In one sentence, I shared my experience, and we hugged. I never saw her again, but we had become members of a very elite group.

Kathy got her brain operation, her feet fixed, and her leg braces. She lived another two years—mainly with Dorothy's rigorous care—before she succumbed to the viral effects of a common cold. And I succumbed to a suicide attempt, spending some quiet time in a mental institution—Agnews State. But I do know that my insistence on Kathy receiving this operation paved the way for more and different operations that eventually provided long lives for many such afflicted children. Because of her, they continued to research new procedures.

Ten years later and with a different wife, I again produced another defective child: Eric was tentatively diagnosed with Autism when he was about 2 years old. With my history, it was clear that I was not going to let Eric be farmed out, despite the avid recommendation of Sherry's two nurse aunties. He was my responsibility, and I was required to grow enough to survive him, but one thing was also absolutely true: I wanted no more children. My egotistical irresponsibility had been the cause for at least a dozen children being brought into this world, while I was not even marginally there for a single one of them. Eric was to be my punishment for these dozen other lives I caused to begin.

It had been a time at Westinghouse where everything connected with work was going as well as it possibly could, but there was something else on the horizon: the inevitability of Kathy's death. I did not know just how hard the news was going to hit me, but when it did, it came in two sections. The first section was the information itself that she was dead. There was almost a blessing in this, since the quality of life she had to look forward to would be problematic at best. The second section came at the funeral. In spite of the fact that I had not seen Dorothy for almost a year and was certainly not missing her, the funeral itself was a terrible jolt.

Relatives, including Lois, came with friends. Good food was served, and it was more like a birthday party than a funeral. I was numb from the neck ... both ways. It was very strange, and I was even more surprised when Dorothy insisted that I stay the night; that night resulted in another pregnancy and confirmed my vow never to see her again.

12 | RCU

I have tried to figure out where my religious, or rather spiritual, education began. Certainly the nuns at Providence Academy did what they could but in my childhood, the most significant event occurred when I realized my grandfather's shoes and tools existed long after he did. Even the experiences of sitting in the fabulous chapel that said grandfather helped design and built was not the beginning—I was already "there" by that time. No, it turns out that my initiation into spirituality occurred nowhere in this lifetime. Down at the beach with Don Douglas, when he was perusing the literature he received by mail from a mysterious place in California called the Fraternitatis Rosae Crucis, he would often ask me about arcane and profound subjects. I would give him my best answers, and he would tell me the material was saying just that.

Finally he showed me a pamphlet called the Mastery of Life and the "monographs" that he was reading; that became my first contact with the Rosicrucian Order. These lessons consisted of the writings from and about the world's most brilliant savants and masters, many occurring well before the advent of Christ. I found that I had studied most of this material someplace even if I could not remember where or when. I made a note of the place in San Jose that was the center of the organization and planned on visiting it sometime in the future.

Another spiritual entity, I had encountered Scientology, without knowing it, while reading multiple books on science-fiction in high school. Here I ran into numerous stories by an author I was unaware had any connection with a religious group, but was to become Scientology's—originally Dianetic's—developer, spiritual leader, and general Poo Bah. Ron Hubbard had written literally dozens of novels, and his were like so many at the time: veiled incursions into the "human" condition, set on foreign planets and worlds where the social structures and all too human defects, which could not even be brought up on our planet, could be examined and sometimes even solved—on the planet "Scintilla."

The Universe, in its infinite wisdom, had seen fit to attach me to so many con men in so short a time that I was forced to develop a sense of right or wrong to keep me only scraping my knees and banging my shins, never falling off a terminal cliff. In the practice of business, which is often a cover for robbery or even extortion, I learned to always, but always, leave a back door open for escape when the wolf packs or the deadly ambush of the cunning coyotes were immanent.

I have ears so sharp that I can sit in a coffee shop and monitor at least three full conversations going on around me without leaving any signature that I am there. Thus, if I am interested in a particular talk that is going on, I will tune in. I have used this training by the CIA much of my life, and it has saved me from demise more than once. The animal model for my behavior, probably taken from my early days in Goble, was the no-nonsense bear. The bear will bear a lot of weight, strain, and aggravation, but when he has had enough, he will let you know, clearly, without any opportunity to miss his meaning or intent—usually by tearing off an arm!

I had this model with me from the earliest years, but what I did not understand was that this beast was a cultural symbol for many Indian tribes throughout the millennia. In their cultural underpinnings, the bear was one side of a coin: the other was the coyote, seen as under-handed, sneaky, duplicitous, and wily. I got a full explanation of this dichotomy on a train wending its way to Portland, Oregon from Seattle, Washington.

On the East Coast, the transfer of Indian property—usually useless for any other purpose—was developed into gambling casinos, set up with state investment advantages, and made many tribal members instant millionaires. The rationale was that there would be hundreds of jobs provided for otherwise indigent Indians. The process was a little slower getting to the West Coast, but it got there; unfortunately it got there, giving time enough for all the con men in the world to get a seat at the table.

The train was rolling slowly over poorly maintained tracks, and I had moved from the child-noisy car to the vestibule (the boarding space between cars) with the welcome noise of the tracks and engine sounds. It took a moment to realize that I had company: a businessman on a telephone on the other side of the vestibule talking, with great sincerity and great concern, to an unknown (to me) someone. The ambient noise was loud enough for the man, who turned out to be an Indian, to convince him that he could not be overheard. Wrong! I busied myself looking out the open half-door window with my back to the man, but listening to every word of the one-way conversation. It appeared that there was a deal in the offing that involved millions of dollars for the tribe, and it was apparently "going south."

The conversation went on for some time as the Indian business-man's voice became more and more hysterical. Finally there was a note of resignation as the sound of his voice kind of drained away, and he sighed. After listening to the other person talking for some time, the Indian summed up the conversation with the following comment, which emblazoned itself on my mind ... "I guess I thought he was a bear, but instead he was a coyote!"

Symbolically, the bear and coyote are simple opposites: good and bad.

When I received my first monographs from the Rosicrucian Order, but before I saw the Park itself, I received a sense of continuity of modes, methods, and persona down through the centuries: Hippocrates, Pythagoras, Sophocles, etc. The original Imperator, H. Spencer Lewis, had died 15 years earlier and his son, Ralph, now ran the entire operation from a one square block, containing an Egyptian museum and operat-ing Planetarium—connected to the National Seismic Net for detecting Earthquakes. The planetarium was the first one established west of the Mississippi, engineered and built by H. Spencer Lewis himself. Gathered around a large garden area were an auditorium and science building, where an impressive list of inventors, scientists, and researchers from all over the world would convene for classes for three weeks during the summer. When I was there, I had the pleasure of meeting Theremin and his machine that produced other-worldly sounds and was the very first basic Moog synthesizer, the beginning of all electronic music.

Not to be known only for cutting edge science, mechanics, engineer-ing, and history, the grounds supported a large temple modeled after the Temple of Memphis on the exterior, with an interior that was a ¾ size Temple of Karnack, complete with a moon that moved across the artificial night sky. Multiple mystic ceremonies, initiations, convocations, and worldly events—including weddings—were held there. It turned out that Scotty and Bill Minford's mother was an officer in the Order—head of the Council of Solace.

In the early days—the 1920s—the organization had its own postal code, sending arcane lessons all over the world, and was incorporated, which leadership was to be passed down through the male progeny. The corporation had large amounts of money coming in and going out through membership dues and mystical paraphernalia. The corporation was given a tax-exempt status. It had a lot of political power and made a lot of money for the city of San Jose, which bent over backwards to give the organization special privileges. At one time, you would not be ticketed for a minor traffic violation if you explained that you were a Rosicrucian. But, money being what it is, relatives being what they are, and with concupiscence running amuck, since Ralph Lewis had no male heir—heavens no, it couldn't go to his sister!—a young prodigy was selected to be the next in line and, when Ralph died, was appointed Imperator. Unfortunately, this young man was not of the mystical persuasion, and his next step was to go to South America with several millions of the Order's funds. Later on, the French Grand Master assumed leadership as the new Imperator, and the headquarters moved to France, though the Park continued to offer classes and mystical services.

Rose Croix University

Every summer, Rosicrucians came together for three weeks from all over the world to renew their spirituality and take classes offered by experts in many fields: mysticism, science, art, literature, music, and the arcane. During my three weeks at RCU, I was in unsuppressed amazement at the caliber and qualifications of the people, foreign and domestic, that I met.

Also during that three week session, I signed up for a music class, a writing class, and drama class. In the drama class we presented Cyrano de Bergerac, Our Town, and The Doll House. We also did a spoof called "Mistakes in Action," which exposed the various mystical happenings that were supposed to take place, such as finding your soul mate—I was too disingenuous to think I would find mine! A trophy of an eight inch lollypop was awarded to the worst character in each skit, which then was ceremoniously given, with great glee, from the last recipient to the next.

Dr. Talley

In a pick-up ballgame at the Park, I saw one student try to stop a thrown ball with only the fourth finger of his left hand. The finger took on a blanched shade and protruded from the hand at a 90 degree angle, obviously either broken or dislocated. Dr. Talley, to whom I had yet to be introduced, walked over to the injured man, took his hand, mumbled some words, and gently stroked the injury. The potential patient immediately recovered symmetry and went back to the game, apparently as whole as before. I made a decision, then and there, to seek out Dr. Talley to deal with my own aches and pains.

Later I did contact him, went to his clinic location where, after providing a medical history, was exposed to a series of colored lights with soft music playing in the background. Then Dr. Talley explained that the emotional body and the memory of pain and unconsciousness, though appearing to be intertwined, are actually completely independent of one another.

By my manner and response to his comments, he inferred that I disagreed. He said, "I understand that you believe in proof. I'm prepared to provide it, if you will be part of an experiment." He went on to explain that he had been working with nitrous oxide. I agreed to be part of his research.

He put a mask on me and told me to clear my mind, think of nothing, and count from ten backwards. At about seven, I lost all interest in counting. I lost all interest in everything. I just didn't feel too good. Then I felt a little worse and then I felt even worse and then I felt definitely lousy. In the midst of this activity, I remember trying to figure out what was bothering me, but nothing came up. Next I felt distinctly panicked, generally fearful, hurt, and confused. The more I tried to be conscious, the rising despair more than doubled. Finally, I descended into pure, unrelenting agony. It was minutes—it seemed years—and then I progressed again with no thought up through the stages, until I was at the point I had been when I entered his office. And then I was mildly amused—at nothing—and a little more amused—at nothing—and even more amused—at nothing. Gradually I broke into a giggle, at least in my mind, struggling to suppress laughter, and then by gradual steps into full blown hysteria, and woke with surprise on Dr. Talley's table.

"And so," he said, "you can stop punishing yourself emotionally since I've proven to you that those emotions are purely chemical and have no reality in worldly experience."

I was elected class vice president, hung out with the president, and found Barbara Ream, even though she was not my soul mate. The whole Rosicrucian experience was a bright spot in an otherwise dismal existence.

When Barbara moved to San Francisco, I followed her and moved in with her in a very strange apartment building. Thus began my serial adulteries.

The Clay Building

I was working at the El Capitan in San Francisco where Barbara first caught sight of me; she left her address and phone number. Since I was walking everywhere in SF, I walked to her place near Golden Gate Park that was, to my surprise, a mansion. The building was no place I imagined her living, but I got my heart out of my throat, walked up a pile of stairs, rang the bell, and a man, older than God, answered the door. He was friendly, in a creepy sort of way, and when I asked for Barbara, he said, "Oh yes. She's in the basement."

I thought she must be a servant. Basement, in my mind, brings up galleries of pictures—this place did not fit any of them. Everywhere I passed was made up of soft mahogany trim, with parquet floors and walls. In the old days in England, you would find servants in garrets, basements, sheds, or horse stables, but in this neighborhood, they were all parked in the very tip-top. I knocked on door #6, indicated as Barbara's. Though it was called the basement, the parquet floors, wainscoting, and picture rails were all in evidence. In several apartments that I later visited—friends of Barbara's—there was no limit on the amount of travertine and other types of expensive marble. In its original state, Barbara's domicile was no basement.

Barbara greeted me with her same low key, diffident attitude that I had gotten to know at RCU, and had a kind of smirk as she stood looking at my Orphan Annie eyes. I was about to ask her, "What the hell is this place?" when there was a knock at the door. A masterfully assembled redhead with startling green eyes, from apartment # 1 down the hall, had seen me come in. I now understood: the ancient gnome, who had obviously more money than he knew what to do with, owned this place, all five stories. The house had contained everything any house needed, except pretty young girls. He solved that problem, beautifully, I thought, by butchering this manse into dozens of little apartments. As far as I could tell, though very old, his eyes were in excellent condition.

Kathleen, whom I just now met, was not in the apartment for five minutes before her boyfriend arrived and made completely clear that he knew Kathleen in every way except platonic. There were house rules, but they didn't seem to prevent a constant seepage of testosterone-packed males into the edifice—like bulldogs over barbed wire fences!

Again, Barbara had amazed me with her ability to immediately fit into any environment. Under the circumstances, it became obvious that we would live there together, illegally; she was having a ball as she always did confounding and confusing me. From that moment on, she was San Francisco: kept me amused and disturbed. This was especially so when she told me she was modeling. She was 5 foot 3 with dark, short hair, kind of greenish eyes, glasses, a tad lumpy, and although she had all of the equipment, would have been an also-ran pitted against Kathleen or any other of the apartment dwellers. I didn't say anything, but my dismay at her being any kind of a model was obvious.

She said, "I'll take you to the Clay Building tomorrow, and you'll see for yourself."

The Clay Building turned out to be a stupendous, screaming wonder—literally screaming—pre Haight-Ashbury in every way. This was, gasp, in the financial district, but seemed an anomaly since the people I passed had green hair, purple hair, whatever. There was some kind of frou-frou bar on every corner, including across from the Clay building. I think it was about ten stories high and obviously constructed as an office building, but you smelled it and you heard it long before you entered. There was a cacophony of multiple pianos, clarinets, saxophones, and from many vents, the odor of cooking food. As we entered and passed by a bank of elevators, Barbara indicated that we were taking the stairs to the fourth floor.

"What's wrong with the elevator?"

"She," said with bitter disdain, "shut it down!"

"Who is 'She?'"

"Don't have time," Barbara answered, and we kept climbing.

We entered a hallway on the 4th floor, walked down a few doors. She entered one without knocking, and there he was, in all his glory: an old man sitting at an easel. Barbara stripped off her clothing and sat down on the model's chair, assuming a predetermined pose. I tried to place myself behind the artist to see what he had done, but his movements discouraged me. As I stood by, I realized that, to them, I wasn't even there. I was pissed. Leaving, I thought, "And I didn't know there were that many dirty old men in San Francisco!"

A few offices away, there was an open door. I peered in. There was another modeling stand upon which sat what appeared at first to be a very elegant woman. Then a figure stepped from behind the easel. He had an open black smock over a beautifully tailored shirt, a baseball cap turned backwards, and everything in the room had a quiet panache about it, including him. When he saw me, I started to turn and leave, but a fluid baritone voice said, "It's all right, you can come in. Are you an artist?"

"No, I'm a writer," I lied.

The model made a kind of screeching noise. "Shit!" she said, "Why the fuck don't you sell tickets?"

The thirty-something artist stepped away from the easel and, looking directly at me, smiled, "Isn't she just a sweet talker," followed by, "Sweetheart, if you want this portrait ever finished, shut your mouth and take the pose."

He introduced himself as Tony Bratta, and I offered my name. He asked if I lived in the building; I indicated that I was visiting Barbara Ream.

"Oh, yes. Barb. I've worked with her. She's now posing for The Master!"

My anger returned. "The Master … ?"

"Oh, yeah. He's a big man from New York. That's Alex: Alexander King."

There was a rustle as his model stepped off the stand, grabbed coat and purse, and headed for the door.

"Same time next week, Sweetheart," he called out after her, but we only heard high heels clicking rapidly down the hall. "Ain't she a piece of work," he said fondly.

I screwed up my face and answered wryly, "There's obviously real rapport there!"

I noticed that he had covered the painting before I had time to see it. Then he looked at his watch, took off his smock, put on a blue blazer, and asked, "Got time for a cup of coffee? Great little place right in the building on 2."

Down we went.

Tony was a dark, handsome Italian. As we passed various doors and people in the hall, he was warmly greeted. When we got to the coffee shop—originally an office—there was a working bakery and steaming hot coffee. Tony gave me his history which included being a chef in an upscale, downtown restaurant. He explained that, as an artist, he was starving, so had decided to get into the culinary arts.

"Alex King, on the other hand, hasn't figured it out yet. He claims to be a writer, but no one has seen anything he's done. He is very good with the brush. He makes Barb kind-of glow," here he stopped and looked at me, "but I guess you would know, she ain't that special—no insult intended."

"None taken," I answered. "Well, if you're a major chef, what the heck are you bothering with that miserable little snot on the stand?"

He laughed joyously. "She's hot for my body and thinks she's going to get it. I couldn't get rid of her any other way, so I said I'd do her portrait for seven grand. Turns out, where she comes from that's chump change, so she's going to pay it. But the rules are she can't see it until it's finished, so we'll see."

I had seen several pieces of his work in the studio—that he was an accomplished portraitist was beyond question, but I still didn't get the dynamics. When I said, "Well, I draw, but I'm no artist. But even for ten grand, I wouldn't put up with her."

He laughed so loudly the other six patrons involuntarily looked at us. Smiling broadly, he said, "Larry, you are in a very unique position. I think you are a pretty good painter and very good at whatever you do, but what you don't understand—apparently Barb hasn't explained it to you—is that as soon as you enter the front door this building, you have entered Oz. I can't leave, I'd lose my rent controlled space.

"Maybe a little later, I'll take you up to 10 where my attorney resides, a guy meaner than a shark, but much more discriminating about who he eats. He's kept my balls out of the fryer when I've been in trouble, which is often, and I know I'm going to need him with 'cuddly Caroline.'"

Tony mused a moment, took several sips of coffee, and allowed as how he didn't have the time to climb the friggin stairs right now.

"Why would you have to climb the stairs?" I asked, innocently.

Tony gave a mirthless grunt and said, "I'll set up an appointment later this week, if you're still around … "

If you're still around hung there like a bad smell. Did he know that Barbara and I had been lunching on suspicion and dining on distrust?

Sure enough, when I left with Barbara, we got in a wingding about her posing for Alex King. She wanted to know why I didn't stick around while he worked—was I ashamed of her? I managed to answer that query with the right negative answer, but since she was still glaring at me, I added—wrongly—"Well, shit, the truth is Tony could do a portrait faster and better than that dirty old man."

Oh boy!! It was a warm Fall day in San Francisco, but it was cold where I was. For the next week, when I went with her—I really went without her—she did her posing, and I wandered about the building happily. Near one of what were to be my last days, Tony caught me as I was going by and said, "Ralph is available. I'll call and tell him you are coming."

When I got to the elevator bank, I was disappointed but not surprised to see an out-of-order sign. I noted someone had scrawled beneath the sign: "Open Christmas, 1980" and in an even smaller note under that: "True, only if you believe in the Easter Bunny and Santa Claus." I thought the joke was funny, but it lost some of its cachet as I labored up ten flights. I knocked on 1020, and the door swung open. A life-sized owl sat behind a desk, with ears—you couldn't see—and huge eyes—you could; Groucho Marx's glasses, a droopy mustache, and a cigar hanging from his mouth.

"Larry?" he asked.

"Yes."

He motioned me to a seat. "They say a picture is worth a thousand words. In my business, a file is worth a thousand lawsuits." Here he pulled out a four inch stack of legal papers. "I am in the unique position of representing a group of SF citizens, 'the greatest collection of clowns, fairies, and dingbats ever collected since Barnum and Bailey went out of business,' and I have a job for life." Here he giggled.

"Tony wanted me to compress this file for you into a semblance of sanity, which, in this building, as you have no doubt discovered, is technically, practically, and legally impossible. San Francisco has, what they laughingly call, a renter's rights' law—which says current residents cannot be evicted and their rents cannot be increased, but if a person leaves, all's fair! There may be something like it on some other planet, but it is unique.

"The avant guarde former owner of this building died, and his square, conservative children decided to sell it. There was plenty of interest in a building of this size in the financial district, until the local buyers discovered who a fifth of the residents were and what they did for a (?) living. They dropped the price three times—ridiculously low—and advertised it for sale in New York, Chicago, and LA. Finally they found a pathetic old lady in New York who read the advertisement as: twelve story building (which was true), in good shape (which was true), immediately available—how could she go wrong? She snapped it up. I didn't realize at first that I not only had a new client, but a long-lasting, busy career.

"Our bons mots were civil enough in the beginning, then got a little tense, and finally I was dealing with a whole battery of other attorneys that would have done good duty for the San Francisco 49ers backfield, ends, and line. I am now the resident guru on San Francisco tenancy law, eviction, squatter's rights, immanent domain, and so on. She has owned this building for a year and a half, has numerous suits against the city and me, and has one fifth paid occupancy, which won't get much better. After she stopped playing nice, she threatens to tear off the roof, regularly decommissions the elevators, tries to cut off the water and electricity, and is generally, what we call in the trade, a dissatisfied client."

By this time I was choking with laughter. I began to understand the pickle this poor New York soul was in, how much money she had thrown good after bad. I suggested to the attorney, laughingly, "I've got a simple solution. She should hire a hit man!" (I wasn't volunteering for the job!)

Smiling broadly, he answered, "That wouldn't work. I've got a half dozen of my own goons living here."

On my last day at the Clay building, I wandered off across the street to a bar named "The Pink Pussycat." Now if I thought the building was strange, this was Dungeons and Dragons, many years before they existed. It was noisy, but instead of happy, it was hysterical. There were drinks I had never heard of and various hues of hair color on the patrons that even Tony couldn't capture. There were pretty girls and ugly girls, and some pretty ugly. I wasn't a "suit," I was just dressed casually, but in that crowd I stuck out. A thing, half my size, half my age, a recent kindergarten graduate, slid up to me, tapped me on the shoulder, and looked soulfully into my eyes. She had on a red blouse, fifteen strings of beads, spiky black hair with lips to match, a pug nose, and dark circles painted around her eyes. Her major missing accessory was a late model broom. She said something I didn't understand, probably asking for my sign. I responded, "I beg your pardon?"

She glared at me for a second, then spit out at me, "You bourgeois, subversive lackey." And floated away.

The coup de grace of my departure from Barbara's hearth was when she suggested a ménage à trois. I was game and indicated that I would have a go at her neighbor first. That was not all right! I was out of there on the next bus … to anywhere!

Turn the 40 Heads …

Alexander King had not published anything in the late 40s when I had momentarily met him. But in the early 1960s, we saw him on The Tonight Show with Jack Parr and it reminded me that I had once met him. After, seeing him on TV, we did buy his books: *Mine Enemy Grows Older* (1958) and *May This House Be Safe From Tigers* (1959). While his life reminded me somewhat of the people that Truman Capote wrote about, the books were very interesting, although rambling, with lots of humorous anecdotes.

The cautionary tale that saved me from many an art director's manipulation—actually saved me from art directors, period—and became my mantra for many of life's situations was the following story he wrote in Chapter 18 of *May This House Be Safe from Tigers*—not word for word, but as abstracted by me.

King had a sincere and everlasting disdain for phonies and counted himself as chief among them. As a clever dope addict, he managed to exalt himself on Monday, excoriate himself on Tuesday, and check into drug rehab on Thursday. Through all of this, he drew and painted, was an excellent cartoonist, and made sufficient money illustrating books, which illustrations he had complete control over.

In more than seven pages of Chapter 18, King expounds on his feelings about advertising, especially after his attempt to become an artist for the trades. He had always made enough money to keep him in the lifestyle he preferred, but lately, being an avid magazine reader, he had become familiar with commercial advertising and had gotten a picture of how much money is involved in producing the attendant art work. This results in his proposing a new avenue of finance for himself, and in this mental place, he runs into a man named Mr. Dekker who is a junior executive at a Park Avenue advertising firm.

So, he is called to Mr. Dekker's office for an interview. Passing through the building lobby, he briefly encounters a gnarled factotum—named Chrisholm—complete with dealer's light-shade and celluloid wrist protectors. In the office, Dekker gives King an apocryphal view of an advertising lay-out of 40 or more couples dancing on the open deck of a luxury cruiser, and inquires if King is up to the job. Of course he is, but 40 of anything is a lot—the individual's character and personality exposition is inherent; joy and complete freedom is the message. All and all it would be a difficult job, and only a tour de force would accomplish it.

After three weeks of blood, sweat, and tears, King finishes the master drawing. Again, encountering Chrisholm, he is immediately ushered into Dekker's office. Dekker oo's and ahh's and pronounces it marvelous and states it is "perfect"! King describes his joy as unbounded. Then there is a slight delay. Dekker steps closer to the painting on an easel and says, "Ah, there's just one little thing I would like you to do for me. Would you turn the 40 heads just a little bit to the left … ?"

King expresses his takeover by the Furies, the Banshees, and Beelzebub, with phrases like son of a bitch, etc., etc., culminating in his tearing the painting to pieces and stalking out where he dumps the remains of his masterpiece in the nearest trash basket. Chrisholm rises and blocks King's exit, admonished him. Pulling a scrap of the painting from the wastebasket, Chrisholm points out, "You are very young and very foolish and you just made a terrible mistake."

King answers, "I know. It was coming here."

Showing a shard of the painting to King, Chrisholm points to what is obviously a woman's arm, and says, "All you had to do was draw a hairy arm, obviously male, in place of her arm."

King, barely able to speak, croaks, "Why in hell would I do that?"

"Because," responds Chrisholm, "it would be a mistake you could easily fix, and Dekker could have caught this terrible problem, pointed it out to you, and earned his salary: everyone would be happy!"

It was about 14 years later, and unfortunately several art directors—or the reasonable facsimile thereof—before I read that book and really, really got the message. Ron Spear, Fred Schumacher, and a seemingly endless list of other sharpies, con men, bamboozlers, and assorted rats would now no longer be needed for Larry E. Wahl, Frederick George Mesher, Lewis X. Vallian, etc. to be a student and learn their ways of the world.

Whenever in any situation requiring the approval of some higher up, we always remember to leave a hairy arm.

13 | Westinghouse

I arrived at Westinghouse in Sunnyvale, California after a period of time that was only marginally remembered and with experiences definitely forgettable. To this day I still get the "wim-wams" whenever I hear the term Nova Scotia. It was cold, it was miserable, and it was necessary—I recognized this many years later. But fun, it was not!

So, after a couple of voyages on troop ships as deck or galley crew, a marriage and two children, a pleasant time working in the San Francisco theaters, and an awful job at General Petroleum in Oakland, I found myself—separated from wife and children—in Sunnyvale, attending Rose Croix University in San Jose and applying for work at the Westinghouse plant as a security patrolman. It would be fascinating to be working in a place loaded with machine shops and in contact with engineering disciplines of all types.

In 1951, Sunnyvale (population 20,000) had only one of the few "Safety Departments" in the United States. The reason for this concatenation of police and fire departments was to conserve the amount of taxes that would be necessary to support two separate departments in smaller cities. It was a good idea, in the short run, but would prove to be a prelude to disaster as later happened at the neighboring Libby-McNeil & Libby plant in Sunnyvale.

Anyone who has ever been a policeman or fireman knows instinctively that they go together like oil and water. Both are accustomed to hazardous situations and understand that a certain amount of exposure to danger is a necessary part of the job. However, unlike firemen, policemen have the additional responsibility of absolutely controlling the environment and the activities in dangerous situations, and have the possibility of legally and intentionally harming its citizens: the power of arrest is unique and has no similar operation in a fire department. It is true that firemen may prohibit you from entering a burning building and thus may restrict your movements, but they cannot bring you up on charges without police involvement. The exception is arson investigators who do have the power of arrest in conjunction with local district attorneys.

Joshua Hendy to Westinghouse

The Joshua Hendy Iron Works had more than a hundred-year history; it had been established in San Francisco in the 1880's and was moved, after the 1906 earthquake, to Sunnyvale, bringing along the valuable experience of its foundry workers. Much later, to become Westinghouse, the Joshua Hendy plant's main contribution was the production of small, heavy-duty steel rail cars for carrying coal and other materials on the small gauge rail systems that existed in the thousands of miles of mines that dotted the whole state of California. For a number of years, Hendy's business was a going concern, contributing to the tremendous expansion of investment capital and labor in Northern California. Years ahead of its time, the foundry formed the backbone of a local industry that grew in into a general manufacturing center for all manner of heavy-duty machines, mining, and fabricating equipment. Because of this, the 65 acres of original land created the need for what were the largest all-wooden buildings in the early 1900's.

For The Love of California

The entire state of California was land rich with huge vistas of fertile, rolling farmland perfectly suited to growing a huge array of fruits and vegetables, along with the infant wine industry. San Diego, San Luis Obispo, San Bonito, San Jose, Santa Clara, San Francisco, and other less well-known towns formed a chain of Catholic missions, starting in Mexico to provide the first great "trail to highway" of the Alameda and the El Camino Real. This chain of trails took root, and cities for farming, mining, transport, education, and trade emerged. And in the growing and prospering cities of San Francisco, Oakland, Los Angeles, and San Diego, there were active ports for lumber and general cargo. But it was the huge Santa Clara Valley that stood out for me, with its thousands of acres of unbelievably rich and productive soil. Spanish-speaking natives, in a State that had once been a viable part of Mexico, farmed many of these land grants.

This was so before I arrived, and it continued until the advent of the computer revolution. I was able, while a local resident, to see vast fields of California produce: plums, apples, peaches, figs, filberts, lettuce, oranges, tomatoes, pears, cherries, strawberries, olives, avocados, and artichokes. In those days one could stand on any hill in the Santa Clara county and see rolling fields of verdant green stretching as far as the eye could see on all points of the compass. I would wake up in the morning and "breathe in" my breakfast!

My Westinghouse

Before Westinghouse acquired the plant, it had been equipped with a huge gear-hobbs facility that could handle double helix ship gears, twenty feet in diameter. Joshua Hendy had been planning on making and placing the gears into the engines of thousands of ships for worldwide distribution. It was a government contract thought to be immune from downsizing. The truth was that procurement contracts assigned by the United States could be—and were—withdrawn at any time.

After the destruction of the San Francisco plant and Hendy's move to Sunnyvale, the plant would need to protect its expensive equipment and specialized workers; thus the entire plant had to be provided with a 3.5 million dollar—then state-of-the art—automatic sprinkler fire system for all of the huge wooden buildings. In debt from that upgrading, the company found itself in dire straights when military contracts expired. The expected increase in ships to be sailing under American flags went from thousands to hundreds; foreign governments latched onto these ships, replacing American union crews, manning schedules, and maintenance with foreign flags. Countries whose merchant fleets had numbered in the dozens were, almost overnight, swollen to hundreds, having been purchased at bargain-basement prices. The seaman's unions had two or three thousand fewer jobs per day than at the heyday of the War Shipping Administration, and a million seamen found themselves permanently beached.

Joshua Hendy was now millions of dollars in debt with very few important government or civilian projects on board and not enough purchasing power to blow its nose. And so it was that Westinghouse seized the opportunity and, with a sledgehammer's degree of grace, bought the entire 65-acre location for 3 million—not even the cost of the original sprinkler system. This serendipitous coup included millions of dollars of high-end machines, casting, electrical, and switchgears, along with huge ovens for heat-treating the completed gears, and all the rest of the necessary paraphernalia.

The Roving Patrolman

At this time, with a seriously impaired memory, I had vague suspicions—but could not prove—that I was a member of the CIA, and had been from the time I had arrived in San Diego to begin my brief Navy career. Since I had this government "experience," I found that the job advertised by Westinghouse for a man with police, fire, and government service, seemed to fit my intuitive skill set. In short order, I applied at the Westinghouse Safety Department with glowing recommendations from my last (completely bogus) job, complete with top security clearances, and had only to wait the two weeks it would take the FBI to check out my references.

Since I had never had problems before, I was less than surprised when all my papers came back stamped: "approved." I received purchase orders for my uniforms—Navy blue whipcord, the same as the Sunnyvale Safety Department—Sam Brown Utility Belt, Eisenhower jacket, leather police motorcycle-type jacket for cold nights, baton, and identification and special police badges from the Sunnyvale police chief. We were required to purchase our own firearms, and I selected a five-inch, Colt 41 DA caliber revolver. I acquired a clamshell holster that was a show-off piece of equipment, but I didn't get any sass from anyone when I showed up wearing it.

The 41 caliber revolver took 38 caliber rounds and, in general, was only good for close up protection, doing the same amount of damage you would do by simply throwing the weapon at an adversary. On the utility belt hung two extra cartridge pouches, a ring for the heavy baton, handcuffs, and a place for a can of debilitating spray. As I recall, the spray was a relatively new item for police forces at the time. There were no radios available, and communications with the office were done by phone from numerous workstations about the huge plant.

So, with a little help from my subterranean friends in the Company, one warm summer evening, I found myself carrying a large ring filled with keys to every door in the Westinghouse plant. I was working my favorite midnight shift, walking various patrols through a half dozen of the largest buildings ever built. However I was not yet aware that I was now a member of one of the most ridiculous security forces ever thrown together, but … that came later.

I resorted to mocking-up a job for myself as a roving patrolman. With this self-inflicted responsibility, I found enough unlocked "secure areas" and flaming infractions of both safety and common sense, to give the shift lieutenant the conclusion that I was not there just to find a good place to hide and perchance to dream. In fact, I developed a deep affection for the plant; it was very special.

A gleaming, red, Ford combination fire truck, a utility truck, and two patrol vehicles were parked in the garage next to the control office. However, there was absolutely no patrolman on duty after the day shift who even knew how to start the damn fire truck or drive it safely, much less use any of the multiple pieces of equipment, tools, hoses, pumps, and the intake and output port connections on it. Strangely this didn't seem to worry anyone in the office.

After Westinghouse took over, the Navy immediately placed an order for gears that kept the highly skilled hobbs and foundry crews in business for years. The foundry also received an ongoing contract for 47-KVA transformers, units so large that special rail cars had to be built to carry them. They were the size of an average kitchen but several tons heavier. And there was a contract for steam-driven turbine power plants that would call for castings and baffle plates also weighing many tons.

All of this stuff made the place unique, perilous, and a total wonder to anyone interested in large-scale manufacturing, foundry, and machine work. The beauty was that every aspect of engineering equipment, from electrical motors you could hold in the palm of your hand to giant 30-foot cross sections of wind tunnels and double-helical gears, was present in this machinery-rich "Disneyland." Last, but not least, a Navy contract arrived for a duel mount, 40 mm, anti-aircraft, rapid fire Mark IV gun, complete with a totally enclosed turret. A department was assigned to build turbine blades and ship propellers for the newest submarines, which included the nuclear fleet. When I remarked on the size and sophistication of the Sunnyvale plant, one of the production managers pointed out my ignorance by telling me that the whole of our plant would fit six or seven times in some of the East Coast plants. Still, it impressed the hell out of me.

When Westinghouse received a contract from the Navy to supply shipyards on both coasts with large marine helical gears—double-faced and 20 feet in diameter—there had to be many auditors to keep track of the amount of money that was being spent. This was still in the period of NOY (Navy Overseas Yards) contracts based on the manufacturers' cost-plus-ten percent—the golden rule for profit. The cost-plus system simply meant that the more the company spent, the more it made. It was of course a license to steal from Uncle Sugar if a good manager had any comprehension of numbers.

The "gear hobbs" section of the building held the gear cutters that were loaded with hardened-steel, circular, blank sections fresh from the foundry. Here the double-helical gear's 8-inch long and 2-inch wide teeth were patiently cut into 20-foot blanks, hour after hour, finally yielding two 8-inch mutually-opposed, angle cuts on their milled surfaces, ready for the ovens. The hobbs' building was heated to exactly 72 degrees Fahrenheit, day and night, while the humidity was held at 72 percent. No hospital nursery was more concerned about its "children."

During my time at Westinghouse, Buildings 31, 41, and 51 were touted to be the largest all-wooden buildings in the world; I don't know if this was true, but they were certainly in the running. Each had a trolley crane that rode on railroad tracks, 40 feet up, along an 80-foot width to the buildings' maximum length of 300 feet. The peak of the roofs were at 125 feet and could only be reached by a series of outside ladders and landings at each end of the buildings. Presumably these were there for fearless fire fighters to climb up, dragging an inch and a half line to spray water on the roofs, should the building catch fire. Due to my unfortunate childhood, I was left with a phobic fear of heights. Realizing this was not a good condition for a firefighter to have, about a month into my employment, I risked climbing to the top of Building 31. It was not too bad; the stairway and the landing seemed well constructed and adequately maintained. I was proud of myself for doing this, but had little illusion that this bravado served to reinforce any of my credentials as a real fireman: I felt much more secure as a policeman. The gun at my side seemed like a credible part of my uniform, and in this place, it served as the closest thing I had to a partner. I remember having real living partners, but the pickings from this motley crew left more than a little to be desired.

The Copper Wire Caper

My off-the-job hobby at this time was breaking up as many marriages as I could and mindlessly parting young women from their principles and their pants. Pathetically, it was just that: a hobby. I came across this hobby while working for the CIA where lechery was my payment of choice and, when left to my own devices, was my personal license to be as big an asshole as I could possibly manage. Believe me, I am not bragging; there are enough screwed up, lost, and confused people to supply any mangy wolf—like me—with vast opportunities to louse up lives. Unfortunately this stable of gullible women included a lovely and innocent real woman who didn't deserve the rough time I gave her or the summary kiss-off when I left.

For the first few weeks, as I was getting my feet under me, I was trying to figure out what the security force here was all about. Besides the fire/policemen, there was a heavy quota of FBI "suits." They were necessary because half of the plant was military, and the hundreds of workers there on the three shifts included, in percentages, as many crooks as would be found in any normal population. These folks came up with some pretty fascinating projects for ripping off Westinghouse. One that sticks out in my mind is the "Copper Wire Caper."

Copper wiring, for electrical equipment and for the transformer shops, was a hot product and a continuous offering for theft. The plant had a Main Entrance (Gate One) and Gate Two, with its parking lot where most of the workers arrived and left at the end of their shifts. Gate One, at the Hendy Avenue entrance, was well guarded, but the Gate Two location was also a frequently used service and supply entrance; it was a better bet for skullduggery. Sunnyvale's weather is ideal but it does rain, and Gate Two became a muddy quagmire when it did. One unlucky day—at least for one electrician—it was pouring rain. The electrician, a rotund-appearing, red-cheeked man in his 50's, was dressed in large overalls and an even larger raincoat covering his ample form. As a service truck finished its inspection and pulled away from Gate Two, the electrician had just walked past the guard shack and was almost safely off plant property when he, choking back a groan, slipped and fell down in a helpless rolling motion. He thrashed about in the mud for a moment before his heavy raincoat burst open, completely exposing the fact that he had wrapped a couple of hundred feet of heavy copper wire around his body and tied it securely so that he could walk a pace that would be normal for a man of considerable heft. Well, not that securely! The wire unwound rapidly, trapping him helplessly in a scene that looked like a Daffy Duck cartoon, while other employees laughed and pointed unhelpfully. The guard picked up the shack's phone, alerting the office, and with the help of a couple of workers, proceeded to disentangle the miscreant from his ill-gotten gains. As I was completing my patrol, I noted that he was actually quite a thin dude.

I had my own embarrassing events. In the middle of the night shift—again in the copper supply area—I climbed to the 2nd floor supply loft, where I thought I had heard a suspicious movement. I crept stealthily up the stairs to where I was able to see the sky through an open skylight and, when I still heard the apparent stumbling about, I called out in my best authoritative tone, "Ok, come on out and let me see your hands!"

There was more shuffling about, and I realized that whoever this was, he was probably flirting with a federal beef since most of the copper wire was government supply and supervised by the FBI who, I believed, had little sense of humor.

Finally, concerned, I withdrew my weapon while simultaneously spotting my flashlight around, and still nothing happened. Now I was hugely concerned! We had no radios, and I was in a really dead part of the plant. I did what I did only twice at Westinghouse: I drew my weapon. It happens that in the quiet of a moonless night there is no sound quite as loud, or as guaranteed to get your full attention, as the sound of a revolver being cocked. Suddenly there was a furious flurry right in front of my eyes. I took the stance, locked the gun and the flashlight straight ahead, and put a half-pound pull on the trigger ... as an immense owl careened in front of me and, with a massive effort, went straight up and through the opening in the roof! It was a tribute to my deep undercover training that it was not necessary for me to go back to my locker and get a change of shorts.

Disappearing Lathes

It also turned out that I had misjudged the FBI's sense of humor. A few weeks later, at our shift patrol assignment, the lieutenant informed us that the FBI had told the security office that something funny was going on in Dead-Stores Supply #3. A janitor had reported that one of the many small lathes stored there seemed to be losing parts on a regular basis. Dead-Stores Supply is a section of one of the buildings that is used to store working equipment temporarily not needed for ongoing work. These are inventoried, and when they are needed again, put back into service in whatever far-flung area of the plant they are to be used.

If you are going to steal from a company that is using a great deal of federal government equipment, you should make sure that the piece of equipment that you are coveting does not have a U.S. seal on it! If the equipment belongs to Westinghouse, they may not notice the theft or may not think it worth worrying about or may just mark it off as the cost of doing business. If, on the other hand, it belongs to Uncle Sam and the FBI hears about it, they will spend a fortune more than the damn thing is worth to put you in jail for a few years.

The lathe in question was relatively new, in good condition, 48+ inches in length, and in the back row of a section of small lathes. At that time, each lathe cost in the neighborhood of four thousand dollars—about two months salary of the idiot who was trying to steal it. Upon inspection, it was discovered that the thief had purloined the faceplate, a dead center, and a tool rest. One of the FBI men came in and asked our department to put a patrolman from each shift undercover as a janitor to check on the comings and goings around the machine, but they were to do nothing.

As the motor and gears for the targeted machine evaporated over a period of weeks while the janitor-guards played hide and go seek with the thief, one inevitable day they saw him; it took another week to find out exactly who he was and in what department he worked. Once this had been determined, we were sure that the Feds would pounce, but instead they told us to forget about it. We were surprised. A couple of months went by, then one day as I was going off shift, there was a flurry of activity, and three Feds informed our department that they were now ready to arrest the man; they would not do this at the plant. While we had all but forgotten about him, they had staked out the man's home and had watched him as he had taken the smaller parts in handible packages and, with the help of a couple of guys on graveyard shift, had picked up the larger parts, which included the long drive screw, the base, and the foundation supports. Over the weeks nothing had happened to discourage them, so they had become bolder and bolder.

One Sunday, the miscreants were having a potluck luncheon, celebrating their mutual victory: the lathe—now set up and operational. A carload of FBI agents complete with a fork-lift and a pick-up truck, swooped down on the party and, with the help of the local police, nabbed the entire group, families and all. The FBI agents lived on this spectacular success for weeks, since most of the things that went on at the plant were deadly boring.

The Lunch Bucket Pinch

Away from the plant, we fireman/policemen had no particular authority. But we could and did make arrests that were directly involved with plant security. Thus, one day near the end of my shift, I left the plant at Gate 2 and walked along the outside of the fence-line, ending up on the long street that led to the offices and Main Gate. I was in full stride, about a quarter mile from the office, when two men passed a lunch bucket over the fence to two men on my side. The guys on the street side saw me first and stopped dead in their tracks.

After you have worked in a place as large and varied as Westinghouse, one worker begins to look just like any other, so it is likely that the two men inside the plant fence could have walked back into the nearest building and the two outside could just have walked away. I wouldn't have been able to identify the two insiders and had no authority over the other two. There was a moment of stunned silence, and I looked at the guys inside the plant—who must have believed I could identify them—and I said in an authoritative but kind of mellow voice, "Ok, boys, you're nicked." I gestured to include the two on the sidewalk outside as well; as far as they knew, I was a fully designated cop. I had heard the expression "nicked" used in a British police film and thought it sounded just right for the occasion. I waved the quiet group towards the main office and, where the fence ended, joined them and ushered them pointedly up to the service desk. I took the lunch pail, handed it to the sergeant in charge, and said, "These four gentlemen want to show you what they have in the lunch pail."

I gave a mock salute and left, my shift being over. I wondered what happened after that, but didn't worry about it too much as messages seldom got through from one shift to the next, or from one shift to its own members, for that matter! I had to imagine what a horse's ass I would have been if the pail contained only a half-eaten apple and a banana peel.

The "Safety" Department?

The plant was so large and so varied in the different types of articles manufactured that several large buildings in the plant were used for temporary storage. This made my walking tour truly fascinating for, after two days off, I came back to work to find a new building sitting in the middle of a path that I had been taking. The whole plant was in the process of becoming something else; division of work in the plant was complex and always changing due to the influx of military projects.

In one case, I found a huge hole in the ground of one building that was filled with enough concrete to build a good-sized apartment foundation; I wondered what was going to be put in that hole. A week or so later, machinery started to arise, and what looked like a circular steel dance floor, gradually appeared. After that was in place, a two-story super-structure was added, and the whole contraption began to look like what it actually was: a 50-foot in diameter, vertical boring mill. The mill was put in place, hooked up, and started constructing shell sections for a wind tunnel that was going in on a mountain top, somewhere east of us.

We were also building the parts of a telescope. I don't believe we did any of the lenses for the thing, but we did put together the skeleton of the framework that was to hold the lenses. The major part of the framework was a "T" shaped, horizontally-constructed tube, with a counter-weight balanced on the other side. The framework had dozens of adjustment points that would automatically respond to wind and thermal variations, and had a star-pointer system that would keep the whole contraption absolutely locked to a specific location. This assembly was laid gently into a specially machined sleeve that carried the entire weight of the assembly on bearings of compressed air, released continuously through very small channels cut into the sleeve. I was told that the assembly was so well balanced that a fly's weight would start it revolving. Of course I never felt like testing it, and I imagine that after it was hooked up, no fly would be able to move it since the regulating equipment would be in full effect. I found wonders upon wonders in every department in the entire plant … with one exception: the Safety Department I had just joined!

The department was run by a little, wizened police/fire chief; fortunately I only encountered him once on the job. With an alcoholic for a chief, it soon became clear that the whole department had problems. There was never any real leadership. There were the FBI agents who worked with our department, but most kept their own counsel, and enough of these FBI folks to take care of the obvious employee theft of any government-owned material and to monitor any subversive elements in the work force. But the obvious safety, fire, and ordinum of the plant were left to us, a severely dysfunctional family.

The patrol, with or without clocks, was routine, something any half-wit could manage. I distinctly remember walking down building 41—which at various intersections melded with building 43—and seeing the guard who was walking along his route parallel to my own. During a couple of our 20-feet-apart, side by side patrols, I waved at him, made faces, and whistled, but he proceeded straight ahead in a kind of somnambulant state, for all purposes sleep-waking; he apparently didn't have any idea I was there. The object of the patrols was supposed to be safety protection, but it was clear to me that, in this condition, he wouldn't have spotted a fire if it were his own pants. Good patrolman!!!

As time went on, I found more and more reasons to realize that the entire department was potentially criminally liable, as were all our officers, up to and through our supposed leader. There was no mistaking the fact that the plant was easily one of the most dangerous places in Santa Clara County. Besides all of the obvious dangers involved with the high voltage devices made there, there was tripping, crushing, and cutting machinery without end, and oil. And there was a locked shed where pounds of Union Carbide—a black, granular material, the primary ingredient in acetylene gas for welding—was mixed with water, generating acetylene that traveled through multiple pipes for all the welding services throughout the plant.

But, of course, we had that fire engine: that bright red, shiny, Ford Combo. It was an engine, which meant that it had high-pressure pumps, a tank holding 3000 gallons of water, and carried 1½-inch direct lines and 9-inch draft lines. The pumps could be connected to a 3½-inch line, but it would take three men to hold the hose, as well as an engineer on the truck to monitor the water pressure. It is often necessary for the hose to go around corners, thereby bending it; the wrong increase of pressure could straighten it out with dire consequences for the three men holding it. If the nozzle man were to lose his grip, the loose, flaying around nozzle could easily incur severe injury.

There were a million + gallon, pear-shaped, high-rise water tank near the main offices and two, 1 million gallon open reservoirs (ponds). These two reservoirs had small shacks near by; each held a GMC diesel engine connected to the 9-inch intakes that would then output 120 pounds pressure to the main supply lines serving all the thousands of sprinklers in all the buildings throughout the plant.

The only problem was that nobody, on any shift, had ever driven the wonderful red wagon to, or participated in, an actual fire. All we knew about fighting fires or water pressure we learned from the "telegraph" in our office. It was state of the art and was connected to every building's 9-inch multiple input risers. These risers reported any significant drop in water pressure by tapping out a code on the telegraph in the office. I can still hear their signal: a bell sound … ding, ding, ding (3); a short pause then ding, ding, ding, ding, ding (5); another longer pause and then ding, ding (2). This signaled that a riser had lost at least ten pounds of pressure per square inch at its associated sprinklers in buildings 35 and riser 2. Before we tried to do anything, we would wait two minutes; if the alarm repeated we would go to the location. If nothing happened in those two minutes, we would listen for the signal telling us that deep well reservoir 1 or 2 had started up, pushing the pressure back up. At this point, the GMC pumps would turn off and the system would reset.

In all fairness, we were trained to check the system at the risers. We would drive out in the pick-up, open a small valve on the output side of the riser that would lower the pressure, and the telegraph would pick up the pressure drop and signal in to the office. This we did regularly. It always checked out: we heard the pump starting and stopping, and so we were sure the system was operating. Yeah sure! Of course, the pressure never dropped system-wide as would happen in a real fire. The pumps that turned on at the reservoirs would only fire up for a few seconds and then turn off again as the ten pounds pressure was restored, immediately shutting down the occasionally cycling engines. Everything was checking out … so we thought!

Things happened that were to change my whole attitude—toward the plant, toward my job, and toward myself.

I was in the process of mapping the entire plant, which got me off any general patrols and gave me free run of the plant. On this particular day, I was walking along the corner of the plant next to a relatively new housing area. I came upon a shack that was on a part of the plant that was almost devoid of structures except for an acre system of pipes connected to each other and to the shack; the shack contained Union Carbide. As I was coming around the front of the Carbide shack, I was shocked to see that the door was open and a tall maintenance man was standing on the concrete slab ahead of the open door. I yelled out to him, "Freeze!"

I swear that is what I called out. Perhaps he thought I was getting ready to shoot him. At any rate he did "freeze" in place, as I quickly came up to him and my worst fears were proven. The man was wearing "hob-nailed" leather shoes; they actually had nails sticking out, driving into the ground. I asked him to start backing off the slab … slowly, and when he was clear, I shook his hand and explained my concern. The small shack held a lead-lined tub, half filled with what looked like water, and extra bags of black, highly explosive Union Carbide. I pointed to a sign printed in large letters: "Extreme Danger! No metal to metal contact." He still looked like he had no clue so I pointed out the concrete he had been standing on. Trying to get my heart to settle down, I continued, "If you had made a single spark in that environment … " Here I turned him around to face the first three blocks of the houses off Mary Avenue and said, "you and I and all these homes, not to mention half of the plant, would disappear in one horrendous blast."

My hob-nailed friend moved quickly away to do whatever his next job was, and I, still surveying the hundred or so houses near the plant grounds, slowly and carefully closed the door and reset the lock.

The Turtle

Dozens of other incidents took place, the listing of which would create another good-sized book. It is sufficient to declare that I was scared out of my wits most of the time. My tolerance for bull is relatively small, and so many of the continuing "screw-ups" made me bitter and resentful. One of the ways that I got back at the department was to draw cartoons of the particularly gratuitous idiocy. Part of my pay came from the government when Westinghouse was contracted to build a super-secret, double-barreled, rapid-fire, five-inch cannon for aerial protection. I wrote at least a dozen reports on outside doors that refused to lock properly, especially the drafting building, as well as the building where the innards of the gun were being constructed. I was never given an answer as to why these conditions were allowed to continue in such a supposedly tightly guarded area. Even the men working on this artillery became dubious.

Later there was construction on the fence-line directly across from a main entrance door, providing, for two weeks, direct access to these buildings from outside the plant. Since it seemed that no one cared, I drew a cartoon showing a long-range view of a hundred small ships. In this drawing one of the ships was labeled the "Westinghouse Super-Secret-Weapon," while the rest were described as the repair and support ships. It had some effect, and in due time I was called into the security chief's office and dressed down for my offense. Properly chastised, I listened to the man until he was completely through and then showed him copies of the dozen reports I had written. When he still defended his security principles, I showed him pictures I had taken of the "turtle," on my off-duty time.

"What turtle are you talking about?" he demanded.

In answer I produced the Polaroid picture taken through the south gate near the foundry. There, in plain sight, was a huge "turtle," uncovered and free to be viewed by anyone passing the plant. The turtle had a curved back, took up 30 by 40 feet of space, was 30 feet high, obviously constructed of steel, and with two side-by-side, curved, cut out channels for the gun barrels it was to hold.

"I have racked my mind for weeks," I said penitently, "and cannot think of anything this could possibly look like except a gun turret ... or a very large, top secret turtle." It was, in fact, a Mark 4, dual, 5-inch, rapid-fire, auto-loading Gatling gun, fully armored and covered by a standard navy turret: my "turtle."

The Phil

It is obviously not necessary to reiterate that I had a big mouth and was a royal pain-in-the-ass, but in my defense, I will say that I was not the biggest mouth or the worst pain. One day we were treated to a new recruit. There was something very wrong with him; he seemed to be totally oblivious to us or to what we did. He was just another patrolman, but when he sat at the "long table" in the office where we all passed some hours of our shifts, the first thing he did was to take a seat at the head of the table, which "everyone knew" was the seat for the "Indian." The Indian was one of our crew who took no guff from anyone. He was over six feet tall, built like a small sauna, with arms like trees; he had little sense of humor.

The new man came into the room as if he had been working there all his life, and as the Indian was about to take his favorite seat, the newcomer—whom I will call Phil—slid the chair out, placed himself in it, and caused the Indian to make an awkward crabbing movement in order to avoid sitting on Phil's lap. The Indian stood there looking at Phil in stupefied anger, but Phil appeared to be deep into the newspaper he had unfolded as soon as he sat. He looked like he had lived in that chair forever. Finally, not knowing what to say and having no script for dealing with this kind of fool, the Indian just moved over and sat down on another chair. He continued to glower at Phil, but Phil appeared to not notice.

The very next night in the middle of the shift, those of us in the office were amazed to hear the fire truck starting up. The automatic doors opened, and there was Phil in the driver's seat, roaring out into the night without any crew. We got up as one and watched as he drove down the road toward building 51 and then out of sight. He didn't seem to follow any rules, including those that we took for granted.

I have, so far, been describing the fire vehicle as a truck. Technically this is incorrect: the Ford combo was an engine. While you might think any truck should have an engine, engine in this case is the proper description of a fire vehicle equipped with complete pumping capacity. Our engine was filled with three thousand gallons of water and carried several different sizes of hoses and nozzles. It included lengths of heavy four-inch draft lines used to pump water from lakes or reservoirs, needed when fire hydrants were not available.

In all fire services, based on their truck equipment, the stations are described as Engine Companies, Ladder Companies, and Hook and Ladder Companies. The latter are the huge trucks using two drivers, one at the front and one at the back; this truck is generally articulated in order to get its extreme length around corners. Many other Companies are ordered to specifically take care of salvage, medical emergencies, etc. The one common element in all these vehicles is that they are very large, very heavy, and very hard to drive. The fire vehicles don't drive like, don't steer like, and damn well don't stop like any passenger car; these are not your father's Willy's. As a result of the foregoing, if you hear a heavy fire truck start, within seconds you will know whether the driver is competent to drive it or not. Turning corners with these vehicles, like driving commercial buses, is a critical skill. Phil's mastery of the essentials of driving a fire truck was obvious.

Later one night on patrol as I was passing building 11—the one holding the "secret weapon"—I saw the fire truck parked there. I went through the unlocked door to find Phil sitting in the lunchroom assigned to the engineers and mechanics that were working on the gun. He looked up at me disinterestedly and nodded. Phil was chewing on candy from one of the many dispensing machines in the room. That he was driving the engine without an order or permission from the head office never seemed to be something that anyone, including our shift lieutenant, saw fit to ask him, so I didn't see any reason why I should. I had seen so much nonsense at this location that it never even dawned on me to question his behavior.

About 40 years later, I met the chief engineer for the Mark 4 gun project. He suggested, with some heat, that I was one of the guards who broke into the candy machine. I tried vainly to explain that I was not in the habit of finding things before other people lost them, but he did not look reassured. It was when he told me that he had often seen me on the fire truck—which, of course, I had never been on—that I realized he was talking about Phil. I asked him why he didn't report the machines being broken into.

All he said was, "But who the hell was I going to tell? … Besides the gun operation was about to die." The former gun boss went on in a more friendly way, "We were trying to make the loading automatic and continuous, but this was way before super-fast integrated circuits, and we had only fast switching equipment. Not fast enough, though, and the Navy pulled the plug."

Apparently I looked a lot like Phil, and Phil looked like a whole lot of trouble. Phil coming in while the gun was still being worked on and Phil leaving, apparently just before the Navy contract was pulled, gave me wonder: Was there some connection? Phil didn't look like Navy, but then of course, he didn't look or act like a guard either.

In any case, the department clopped along like a spavined old war-horse until one day in Spring of 1952, notices appeared that a state officer of some kind was coming to the plant to finally train and test us in firefighting equipment and technique. At last, after many months, I was to find out what you actually do with a fire truck.

With a full milk carton and a paring knife, anybody can prove the physics of "hydraulic head pressure." The experiment involves punching a hole near the top, another hole further down, then another, with the last hole near the bottom of the carton. The top hole will dribble out the milk; the next will shoot it out farther, and so on, to the bottom hole where there will be a substantial stream: the height of the fluid is the determining factor. Thus, a reservoir held in place by a dam will be constructed in an inverted V-form so that the base will look nothing like the top surface, which is 10 to 20 times smaller than the base.

Because of the complications of fighting fires from ground level to many-storied modern buildings, the amount of pressure needed to get the water "uphill" is a major engineering problem. This was the main reason that, if I were asked to take 1½-inch lumen hose (a garden hose is about half an inch) up to a 125 foot level—125 pound pressure per inch is standard for this hose line—it would stop pumping water at somewhere less than half the distance to the top. The head pressure of the pump would be neutralized by the same weight of the water in the hose. In other words, the pump has to be set to produce pressure greater than the height of the building and then enough more to make an effective stream. Every increasing inch of rising hose calls for addition pressure at the pump.

I will not pretend that I had the remotest idea of the technicalities involved in maintaining proper pump controls at the engine in any given situation. What I do know is that I would absolutely refuse to take a fire hose up those winding outside stairs of Westinghouse's tallest buildings with any single member of our night shift at the controls of the pump. I had nightmares of trying to do this particular job with any one of the incompetents I worked with. Even at only 40 feet, the hose, straightening instantly under too high a pressure, would fly me through the air like a big fat bird.

At some point I realized that we supposedly had been instructed in the correct use of carbon tetrachloride—small canister fire extinguishers—only to later learn they should never be used in confined spaces: with relatively short exposure they would cook your liver. In short, the place scared the hell out of me. This was before fire instruction, of which I had previously received less than 15 minutes.

The equipment at the plant I did trust, which seemed in working order, was the obvious plentitude—in volume—of the water to service the entire plant from the plant's own supplies, without any reliance on Sunnyvale's water system. Two open ponds/reservoirs—I was told—contained a million and a half gallons of water each. Each pond's water was drafted automatically through its own attached pump station and then to the main lines feeding hundreds of standpipes, supplying the entire network of sprinklers. We felt confident in this system because we actually tested it every shift and the alarms responded accordingly. A reasonable conclusion. Dead-ass wrong! Backing this pond system was the half-million gallon tower soaring above the height of the other buildings, located near the entrance. I had thought the 150-foot tower would take over when the ponds became depleted, but I was wrong: the ponds were on a different system and were kept full by the Sunnyvale Municipal Water System.

One fateful day, as advertised, Ed Bent from Southern California appeared on the scene and for the next two weeks taught or tried to teach us "Firefighting for Idiots." For the first two days, the night shift didn't see anything of him. He spent one day each with days and evenings; on third day we got him. Our night workers were properly introduced to "Mr. Ford"—the little engine that could. When anyone but Phil passed it, we wondered what all those wonderful gimcracks were for. The Ford combo was always scrupulously cleaned—we assumed by somebody else because, other than Phil, we never touched it.

We rotated through the shifts for the rest of this two-week period. This was, at least for our shift, a full-time demonstration in daylight of all the characteristics and abilities of the combo and the tasks it could perform. It was my belief—though I had no proof—that Bent had probably scheduled between three and six days for this training, but it turned out differently.

With six of us aboard the truck, plus Ed, we drove to the number two pond where Ed had us withdraw eight-foot sections of draft line from the truck. These are thin-walled, four inch in diameter lines to be pushed into a nearby water source; here it was the pond. The engine was then fired up creating suction from the source to the truck. Next we pulled the 3½-inch folded canvas hose line from the truck. To my knowledge, this line had not been used since the truck arrived. Bent had spent some time with one person from the day crew, showing him how to operate the knobs and levers for controlling output. With the hub end of the hose connected to one of the output lines, a ¼-inch, solid brass nozzle—all 18 pounds worth—was attached; three men were assigned to that hose. It was strung out in the field alongside the northwest corner of the plant. This field was separated from the main plant by a fence but was wide enough to perform this operation. Phil, for obviously reasons, was selected as the nozzle man. I was picked as the center man, and one of the day crew was behind me. We gathered that there was enough pressure that three men were required to ground and control this hose. If the nozzle man wanted to go to the right, the last man would go to the left, and I would pivot. Apparently there were enough great forces at work to shove a large volume of water through a 3½-inch line, which would exit as a powerful stream of water forced through that ¼-inch nozzle—incidentally, a loose nozzle could beat a man to death. I personally was thrilled to think that I was going to be at least partially in control of this torrent.

All three of us braced ourselves as Phil prepared to open the valve. We heard the pump roar into action; five seconds went by, and then it unexpectedly died. In those five seconds, only air blasted through the line, but under pressure. When the pressure hit the nozzle, supposedly screwed into the hose, the nozzle separated from the hose and described a parabolic arc of more than 30 feet. For Phil, the effect was immediate and apparently terrifying: while the nozzle was cruising through the air, Phil was cruising over to the fence line. Actually cruising wouldn't describe it: it was a full-speed, panic sprint.

As we heard the pump go silent, we heard Ed's voice ringing out, "Jesus-H-Christ!"

I was standing closest to what was left of the end of the naked hose—still quivering in my hand—as a large dollop of water parted from the end and made a puddle at my feet. Ed, still cursing, grabbed the hose from the remaining two of us and looked with bewilderment at the stump. In the meantime, having no job, I looked over to see Phil disentangling himself from the fence.

Ed carried the hose to the errant nozzle. The retainer ring, which should have been part of the hose, was firmly coupled with the nozzle. I have seldom seen such a look of amazement on a man's face as was visible on Ed Bent's. Phil, in the meantime, with all eyes on him, had slowly walked to and disappeared behind the truck; I'm sure that Phil would have traded any broken bones for that long walk back. At point of service, he did the unthinkable: he ran and left his buddies behind. I believe he left the plant at that moment—never saw him again! His combo-riding days at Westinghouse were over. I felt kind of sad for him.

Ed didn't even look for him, but brought the hose coupler and its attached nozzle over and called us to observe it. In all our talks, he had proven to be soft-spoken, direct, and pleasant and had used no foul language, except what we had just heard; now he was red-faced, trying hard to control himself. He held up the pernicious piece of equipment that had failed: a heavy piece of brass with an equally heavy handle and control lever. The nozzle had come from an equipment bin on the truck. The part it was screwed into was a 3-inch male-threaded retainer ring that belonged with the hose—it was supposed to be an integral part of the hose.

"Guys," he said sullenly, "this has got to be the worst goddamn screw-up I've ever seen. Somebody should go to jail for this fuck-up."

The end of the hose had been retrieved; he put this close to the errant hose-coupler to which the nozzle had been attached. "When this hose was manufactured, there was to be a female coupler at both ends, one for connection to the truck, the other for a connection of various nozzles. On this end, when the coupler is attached to the hose, a special metal ring is installed that fits snugly between the inside of the hose and outside of its coupler. It is then heated to a high temperature and the metal expands, clamping the hose to the coupler. Obviously, this was not done: the 100 pounds of air pressure blew it apart. I can think of a hundred situations in which this screw-up could have cost lives. This sure-as-hell was not the lesson I intended to teach today, but it is sobering one for all of us. You can believe someone will be flayed for this piece of BS."

I found myself thinking this must be the worst day in Ed's teaching career. As it turned out, I was wrong. There was a more horrendous and unbelievable screw-up ahead, which that expression doesn't begin to cover.

The Fish

Since we tested those 9-inch standpipes and pulled water from the supply side by running the equivalent of a garden hose for two minutes, we were always rewarded by the sounds of the pumps kicking in. After this, the pressure would bounce back up to 125 pounds per square inch and the pump would dutifully shut off. This is the one piece of equipment that we trusted. And so, it was on the following day that Ed Bent drove the truck to Building 51, got off, and walked to one of the standpipes. There he pulled open a large locked outlet valve, 6 inches in diameter. Now instead of about 50 gallons of water being drained from the system, 150 gallons flowed into the street. This would be the effect of 15 or 20 building sprinklers going off in approximately two minutes; a large fire would normally use at least that much water. The main gauge immediately dropped to 60 pounds and we could hear the nearest open draft pool pump, the GMC 500, roar into action. Absolutely correct. What followed a few seconds later was not.

The GMC 500 HP diesel engine roared for five seconds, then gave a sickly gasp and died. Cursing, Ed quickly closed the valve, ordered us all back onto the engine, and we drove back to the pump house to find a loud siren blowing and smoke pouring from the exhaust pipes. Ed found a phone and called the police department to ignore the clanging bells and to send a couple of hydraulic engineers down to Pump House One. We had gotten off the truck and were standing around, bewildered. Eventually two engineers appeared with their toolboxes and started to check out the pumps. The pumps were fine, but something was definitely fouled at the underwater intake. One of the engineers was fully flummoxed and so jumped in the pond, which was only three feet deep, and fished around in the water with his hands. He wrestled with an obvious obstruction for a minute or two and finally lifted up the entire body of a thrashing, three-foot, unhappy catfish, throwing it on the ground. He pointed to the thrashing fish and said in a gravelly voice, "I think this one's cousin is in the pump!"

And so it was.

Preparations were immediately made to drain both open reservoirs and put Sunnyvale City Water on alert; we would need their services for back-up.

A couple of days later, while the ponds were being drained and inspected—it took at least two days—we were assigned to do other things, including collecting about 50 pounds of milled scraps containing large amounts of magnesium for a demonstration of how to fight these dangerous fires. An inch and a half line connected to the fire truck's pump was operated by a nozzle man and, as we stood in a group more than 50 feet away (the nozzle man as well), a stream of water was directed toward the pile of metal which was burning sullenly. An immediate explosion: a bright white flash and the entire pile was fiercely burning. Pieces of burning magnesium scraps were thrown 30 feet in all directions. We gasped and jumped back a foot or two as Ed called out, "What don't you do in a magnesium fire?"

Immediately we responded with variations of "No water!" "Don't spray water!" "Don't use water!" "NO Water!"

We had time to think of how many drill presses, lathes, and other machines were made, in part, of magnesium. Ed went on to explain that during the war, when thermite bombs with magnesium were dropped on enemy cities, a stick that landed on a roof would burn through several floors to the basement. The only fire retardant useable is sand. Even then, since the magnesium contained its own oxygen, while the sand would protect surrounding territory, the magnesium itself would burn until it was all consumed. Imagining any of this stuff in contact with a human body would lead to seeing a horror show … and often did.

I had a couple days off and when I came back on duty—afternoon watch—and walked out to where we had been, I got to see a completely empty pool/reservoir. Grinding away from the scene, in low gear, were three fully loaded trucks—four cubic yard capacity each—containing the former fishy inhabitants of the two open water pools. One wonders where the Adam and Eve fish came from? We had many fishermen among our employees, but apparently they didn't know the fish were in residence. In the end, this was made well: the ponds were refilled, the pumps were repaired, a better filter system was introduced, and special inhibiting agents added to the water.

The problem was now solved, yet in the midst of sleep, I would see 15 or 20 sprinklers being called into service to extinguish a minor fire. In this nightmare, the 15 sprinklers gagged and stopped, and the rest did not turn on as the fire increased in volume and ferocity from one area to the next. Oxygen would start to pour into the vast open areas, and windows would implode as a hundred different materials, including magnesium, roared into fury. Next went the building itself, and since water was called for, and the entire system had none, all 65 acres of the plant grew into one giant fireball and eventually burned to the ground. In my dream, I would find myself rapidly walking out of Gate 2, leaving the plant to shift for itself. Each time I had this nightmare, I would feel an unfathomable cowardice sweep over me and knew exactly how Phil felt as he clung to the fence.

I believe that part of the reason for my trip to the mental hospital, Agnews—in addition to Kathy—was that I never before conceived of walking away from a job in the middle of a catastrophe, but I would have walked away from this one. During the months of finishing the drafting maps of all fire and safety services and equipment, I knew that our "safety department" was one sorry, nonfunctional joke.

When I finished the map—all 16 pages, with notes and adden-dums—that located all the fire extinguishers, stretchers, and fire exits that were blocked, I felt the need to add a cover page full of unwise and scathing remarks. This I topped off with a drawing of our police chief, sleeping behind his desk—or perhaps drunk—with his feet up on the desk and a brace of his pearl-handled six-shooters lying alongside his cobwebbed-encrusted feet. I rolled the document into a container and left it on the desk of the security chief.

I knew that sooner or later, most likely sooner, I would be through at Westinghouse, given my attitude. But I had one last job to do. In the middle of a cold, moonless night, I went to the bottom of the high-rise water tower, knowing I intended to climb up to touch the 150-foot range light and then come back down again. Because I suffer from a paralyzing acrophobia, evaluating the safety stairs as I had done on the buildings was not an adequate test of my supremacy over that fear. The ladder to the top of the water tower was a simple caged series of steel steps that I slowly climbed in the dark. My concern was that if I reached the range light, I would freeze there, my hands locked on it, and in the morning, a full scale, fully-viewed rescue would be necessary!

Things went well until I reached the upside-down turnip that was the tower, at which point the ladder ended. Concentric rings formed hand and/or footholds necessary to arrive at the top. By this time, after having firmly grasped the range light base, it dawned on me that I did not know if I had come in a straight line off the main ladder or had moved in a circular fashion, left or right; I wasn't paying attention. I wasn't about to turn around to look down to find the ladder. I had forgotten that the tower was round and as I backed down feeling for the easily locatable rings, if I missed the ladder, I would plunge the 150 feet to the ground. At that time, I would have settled for any situation EXCEPT being stuck there, including falling 150 feet. Since I am writing this, it must be obvious to the reader that I found the ladder. I went off duty and walked home; I quit a short time later.

14 | Agnews State Hospital

I had finished mapping the Westinghouse plant and had written the scurrilous note condemning the police chief; I knew I wasn't destined to be there much longer. This was also during my womanizing time, when I was supposedly in love with Nita and planning somehow to include her more permanently in my life. Then the military intervened and sent her husband home on spousal leave. Suddenly he became a reality to me, and the full stupidity of my arrangement with Nita weighed heavily on my conscience—what there was of it—especially when sitting in the restaurant in which she was waitressing. When her husband sat down next to me and asked if he could talk to his wife, I lost it. I broke up the place and was taken to a near-by hospital, where I attempted to slit my wrist. Thus, I was committed involuntarily.

When I arrived at Agnews State Hospital in April of 1953, it was obvious that I was not in the best shape emotionally or mentally. After a month or two of rest and lack of contact with Dorothy, I was partially mended. However, the military was not quite through with me. It turned out that Mickey Cohen was also there. I was in the wards, but Mickey was in what was called "The Clubhouse." Apparently he had convinced the powers that be that he was not only a stone-cold killer, but a mental case as well. After good behavior and several humiliating sessions with the "therapy board," I was allowed to move to The Clubhouse.

The Clubhouse was a large house on the grounds, but removed from the wards and the main offices. It was the equivalent of a halfway house. It had only an attendant: no guards, no locked rooms, no fences, no alarms. There was a bed check made against a master list, but other than that, we enjoyed much freedom. There were patients who had "home privileges" and could go home for weekends, and there were some—notably those who had received prefrontal lobotomies—who could go anywhere with help.

These poor souls, in particular, would display various modes of antisocial, or at least inappropriate, behavior including playing with themselves. They would sometimes wander off alone; the San Jose police knew to check for their hospital ID's and would bring them back to the wards.

I tried to make my transition as smooth as I could and I had developed a couple of friendships, both in the wards and in the Clubhouse. Mickey Cohen was brought right from jail to Agnews. His girlfriend—a brassy blonde looking as though she had come directly from Central Casting—would bring a picnic lunch and a blanket. They would have a leisurely time on the luxuriant grass, kept that way by inmates who had yard duties. Since I looked reasonably sane, it was not long before Mickey and I became friends. (Ironic, isn't it that I had spent some of my very early years with his ilk!)

Agnews was an equal nut provider, and one day at an assembly (sounds like high school), a former patient—now a congressman—came to talk to us. I thought this man had fantastic courage; he would have lasted about three days in office had his mental history been known (remember Vice Presidential candidate Thomas Eagelton?).

It is important to understand that this was a time when California had the best school system and one of the most advanced health care services in the nation. The state has fallen on hard times since, but in those days, the mental health care was outstanding. Mickey, of course, was working the system, and the feds were still trying to get information out of him; he was leveraging that information into special treatment.

It turned out that Mickey was an inveterate tennis fan, and though not very good, was still good enough to give me lessons. He had a wicked serve; I never did beat him. I was familiar with his past as a lone killer, and knew of his association with "Lucky" Luciano, who, Mickey knew, was meaner than Mickey. Mickey's total score of people he had killed was in the neighborhood of a couple dozen but, to me and with me, he was a pleasant uncle. Of course we must not forget my early association with another pleasant, but notorious uncle.

The staff had refused Dorothy's attempts to visit me, figuring quite logically—though not totally accurately—that a call from her had been what had set me off in the first place. Westinghouse was still paying my salary, but there was little question in my mind that when I went back to collect my last paycheck, that would be the end of my fireman/police career. After three days spent in a straight-jacket in the violent ward, I had converted back to a rational being—or at least a rational-appearing being—and started working my way out of the place. Life, or the Navy, or the CIA, or whoever had other ideas was still pulling my strings.

While I was on the general wards, when they found out I was an artist as well as a policeman, my occupational therapy became drawing cartoons for the onsite newsletter, the Agnewsette. One day, one of the "inmates"— an established alcoholic and a highly rated chess player—allowed as he was going to have to get out of Agnews to get sober since he was receiving more booze in this place than he had ever gotten when he was out on the street! We got to discussing our individual situations. After I had shared the nature of my Westinghouse job with him, he asked if I knew a drunk who bragged about his heavy drinking while carrying two loaded, pearl-handled revolvers into bars in Sunnyvale and San Jose—when he was police chief at Westinghouse? He had been a previous resident of Agnews.

One of the first things patrolmen at Westinghouse had talked about was their drunken police chief. That was just hearsay, but now I had the date he had come in, the number of days he had been committed, and thus enough stuff to give me a hell of a lot of leverage. I figured I was going to need it if I was going to get references for another job. Having tapped into the active grapevine, I learned about another ex-Agnews' patient who had gone berserk at work—again at Westinghouse—had been cornered in one of the offices, and thrown a typewriter through a window trying to escape. I had worked with this guy, night after night, and knew that he was a nut, but didn't know that he had (like me!) the history to prove it.

I had written a letter to North American Aviation and had received a date for a job interview on their police force. I figured, correctly as it turned out, that I would be able to go to the Westinghouse chief of security when I was released and secure a perfect reference. The typewriter story was just an extra dollop in case the security man had any doubts about the amount of information I could give to the FBI.

One day, to my complete surprise, Wesley Townsend, with whom I had gone to grade school, arrived at the Clubhouse to visit me. Wes was a sergeant in Army Intelligence and a photographic analyst. He explained that he had been in Korea and had taken pictures of American troops who had been over-run, had their arms tied behind their backs with wire, shot neatly in the head, and rolled into a roadside ditch. He showed me the pictures in case I didn't believe him … but I did. He also explained that he was into hypnosis, which I thought was a strange comment to lay on me considering the place I was currently residing. But later, it all went together. I got around to wondering how in the hell he had found me after all the years that had passed; then my friendship with Mickey Cohen began to make sense. I did know that I had often been used for covert Intel and had more than once been on loan to various services.

In a life I could barely understand and the strange places where I sometimes found myself, I "knew" that I was the artist, sitting at the corner of an outside French restaurant, hearing a half-dozen conversations going on around me, and relaying the pertinent information to a control. The nightmares never stopped, and I guess that I just thought that I was demented. How I had passed on information about Mickey Cohen, I was unsure—or maybe it was the other way around. At any rate, by the summer of 1953, I was on my way out and on to a cherry job at North American Aviation. And Mickey was on his way back to jail, where eventually he was killed. Sorry, Mickey!

After I left Agnews—having been protected from Dorothy's interference while there—I spent my last few day at Westinghouse before I packed up my trailer and headed for LA and the new job. Nita—deserving better treatment from me—had visited me regularly at Agnews. She apparently had made the decision to stay with me, which I neither understood nor appreciated. She had the idea that our relationship was more than it was: for her it probably was. I believe that she did sense that we were not going to be a couple, but still she followed me to the trailer as I walked home. I was cold and indifferent, trying to disabuse her of the idea of an "us." Nonetheless, we made passionate love, after which she lay there looking through me. She put on her clothes and said, with the saddest voice I had ever heard, "Larry, you are a strange piece of work."

We never saw each other again. No one, since or before, has had a lower opinion of me than I had of myself.

Larry at the Door

About three days after I was released from Agnews, Dorothy called and insisted that I see her to make arrangements for her new pregnancy.

I told her I would come visit, and we could talk about it. I felt completely trapped. She was finally going to get her way, yet at some level, I knew she wasn't. I took the trip to San Francisco and carried my gun with me, fully loaded. When I knocked on the door, I expected Dorothy to say something cutting or sarcastic. Had this happened, my intention was to empty the revolver into her body, then wait for the police. Instead she smiled gently, undoubtedly reacting to whatever madman's face I was wearing. We talked quietly, and she suggested we go to a movie. I'd never seen her so solicitous. Before we left, she said softly, "Why don't you leave the gun in the closet?"

I did. After the movie, we talked and I left, retrieving the gun, and went back to finish up work at Westinghouse.

15 | North American Aviation

What easily seems like a hundred years ago, I presented myself at the employment office of North American Aviation in Los Angeles. It was an employment office that looked like a thousand other company offices in the United States—all over the world, for that matter. I was like a hundred thousand other employees entering into the service of some kind of business, manufacturing, or sales establishment.

The facts were a little simpler. We were officially Los Angeles deputy sheriffs whose real authority came from the natural interface we had with the Department of Defense, the local L.A. police, the State of California, and most importantly, the special authority of the Federal Bureau of Investigation. More than a few times on the job, I had the duty of arresting a worker in the plant who had lied on his employment records. Even if it was a little white lie, the fact that he or she had seen fit to lie to the United States of America for a job in a secret and very sensitive part of our American defense scheme was unacceptable. This responsibility for honesty was more than enough to have the FBI and yours truly, escort a worker immediately off the premises. (On everyone of these trips, I was aware it should have been me!)

If all of this seems harsh, it is important to remember that at this time we were in the middle of the Korean War, and one of our country's more serious disagreements with the Soviet Union. North American was on the cutting edge of fighter aircraft construction and was known for its own unbelievable technology. People familiar with the mighty North American Aviation knew about it from the treasured and honored list of warplanes, both fighters and bombers that had helped win World War II. Many a pilot had fond and/or terrible memories of the many aluminum wonders that had left North American (NA) plants: the P-41, often thought of as the most beautiful aircraft ever designed by man, and the two engine bomber B-25, famous for flying off an aircraft carrier when the bombers first attacked Tokyo in World War II.

The preceding was just some of the history of the company. When I was there, the pièce de résistance was the production of the F-86 Saber, and, before I left, the development of the F-100 Super Saber that would hold the world's record for supersonic speed in level flight. The North American main plant took up the entire south side of the Los Angeles International Airport complex.

Along with all the other employees of this famous plant, the FBI checked me out; some time later I was to hear from my first grade teacher that even she had been contacted. Of course this was a joke in a celestial vein since my former abode, before checking in with NA, had been that three-month stay at Agnews State Mental Hospital. If the FBI had received a true and accurate report, including my stay at the funny farm, I could never have received clearance for security work at North American, but of course I did—talk about a little white lie!! As far as the alphabet soup (CIA) was concerned, I was stable enough to operate as an agent and grounded enough to slip in and out of a life that was essentially a complex fabric of cover stories. In trying to go back and pick up some of the pieces, I realized that I couldn't remember a time when I lasted on a job longer than two years. I was so out of touch with the rest of the world that I did not consider this unusual—nowadays, this wouldn't be that unusual. I was just ahead of the curve!

After maneuvering the security chief at Westinghouse into a no-win situation, I was able to encourage him to provide me with a sterling job review after my release from Agnew's (using information I received from fellow inmates). I moved back to the Los Angeles area with my ancient Buick and the trailer I had been living in for three years. There were about an equal number of people in Sunnyvale—and Westinghouse—glad to see me go, as there were people saddened. As to personal responsibility and job savvy, I was still totally ignorant. I was prone to undermining authority, skipping the hard jobs, and shirking responsibility—at Westinghouse, as long as they let me do what I wanted to, I was an acceptable worker. My dad, Gene, attempted to be a role model and tried to teach me to take the responsibility of completing a job and taking pride in it. It was long after he had died that I finally realized what a sterling man he was, and just how much of a hand he had in giving me, eventually, a sense of proportion, not to mention some common sense.

During the two-week wait for the security check, I was virtually broke and when I stopped in Long Beach, I met—at a swimming pool, apparently by accident—a pretty-enough young woman who seemed to be looking for me. I had no way of knowing what I was going to do for those two weeks, but my new friend, Marie Redmond, took care of that. She allowed me to park my trailer next to her house, invited me to live with her and her daughter, and got me a job at the Chicken of The Sea tuna fish processing plant on Terminal Island—where I ate nothing but the finest tuna fish from off the processing line. All of this followed the first night of screwing Marie on the couch and advanced from there to her bed for the rest of my stay. Marie's intervention made my two weeks before I started work as a Los Angeles County Sheriff virtually painless.

For the Love of Aircraft

I came by my love of aircraft at an early age, starting at the Hamilton brothel in Chicago, where, among the dozens of toys available, was my favorite: a "sit on and ride" version of the Pan American Clipper. But one of the earliest memories I have of being in an actual aircraft was the chartered plane that flew my mother, Gertrude, a couple of agents, and me from Chicago to Portland, under auspices of the FBI. Afterwards, when we were living in the Portland ghetto with "stepfather" Tony Scrano, she was gone a lot; I now surmise that was because she was, as one of the bookkeepers for Al Capone, possibly given special treatment for testifying against her former boss. But back on the airplane, I was seated in my mother's lap in the Stinson airplane, which represented the latest in "passenger" aircraft at the time. You would board this—what seemed like a huge plane—from a side-door and enter directly into the fuselage where you would be seated in single seats bolted to the floor on either side of the plane.

We landed in a farmer's field where the farmer, in order to make a little extra money, had established a landing site on his land. It was a fresh, bright morning, and the eight of us sat under the branches of a huge tree. The pilot did not seem to be around, so I assumed that he had been taken to the large house, half a block away, where he was fed and did whatever pilots did in those days. The farmer's wife and daughters came out of the big house with milk and heaping plates of sandwiches, berries, and other stuff; we passengers ate under the cool, leafy tree. There are no further details of the trip, as it was a flight without a destination, as far as my memory was concerned.

Airplanes were fully explained in many of the Big-Little Books I had access to when I was an orphan at Providence Academy. Later, adoptive father, Gene, got me small airplane models, as well as a toy aviator's helmet, complete with goggles—I took a lot of grief from the other students for them. I habitually stuffed one of the models in my coat pocket and "flew" from home to school after I had been "Wahl-i-fide." I was always reading aircraft magazines and riding my bicycle to Pearson Air Park, where I could watch the soldiers marching on guard duty and the military and civilian aircraft taking off and landing. Gene was extremely sensitive to my flight obsession and encouraged that interest. I suspected that he might have wished to have been in the Air Force instead of driving an ambulance in the First World War.

At any rate, my love for airplanes never subsided and in watching the dozens of movies and newsreels after Pearl Harbor, I became familiar with the North American B-25s that bombed the Japanese homeland from the carrier "Shangri-la" and, what many believe to be the most perfect fighter ever built, the North American P-51 Mustang. In addition there were the stocky and determined P-40s used by General Chennault in China. I built balsawood versions of the beautiful and complex twin-boom P-38 with its two Allison in-line engines and of many other English and American stand-out fighters and bombers of World War II. I was never to actually fly any aircraft, a fact that stands me in good stead with countless others who might have ceased to exist if I had ever been issued a pilot's license. Eye problems—myopia and astigmatism—and uncontrollable mind-wondering through various discontinuous ages would surely have had me flying, full throttle, into the first mountain I encountered.

There was always a seemingly invisible hand that appeared to be directing my path, a system that made sure I was never to see "the Man Behind the Curtain." I was so enamored with new my job that it was almost impossible for me to fail: I had a job for which I would have easily paid the company. In the middle of the first year at North American, I was picked as one of two patrolmen to patrol and protect the engineers and their equipment at the Salton Sea ground-tracking and-timing stations for the F-100 speed-run test. But, I am getting ahead of myself.

Back at North American

I got my deputy LA sheriff's dark blue uniform, badge, a standard police issue 38 revolver, Sam Brown accessory belt, handcuffs, baton, reload packs, and identification papers. I set out to learn as much about the aircraft industry as I had earlier been able to learn about general manufacturing, as well as electrical, heavy machinery, and foundry work—at Westinghouse. Because North American was a place that worked in the aviation field, it was not as diverse as Westinghouse. I met the chief of police, was given the indoctrination tour, special FBI identification and keys, and shown the location of the top security burn boxes where tons of waste documents and blueprints were collected and burned under strict security every day.

About a week into my new job, a group of us "new troops" were introduced to a couple of smaller fire engines and an ambulance. We were told that in an emergency we would be called upon to drive these vehicles. We were given extensive examples of why we should treat them as special and were to change all our normal driving habits (slow down!) to fit their particular idiosyncrasies. In effect, we were supposed to be able to drive these vehicles—technically attached to the Fire Department—in a manner that got them where they were supposed to go, doing what it was they were supposed to do, and all of this without turning them over and/or killing ourselves or others. One recruit, who apparently didn't realize that the combination truck and engine he was driving was not exactly like his last ride—presumably a bicycle—was making a mandatory turn, when the trainer beside him suddenly had to wrestle the steering wheel away as the novitiate attempted to make a right turn. The vehicle didn't care for this maneuver and signaled its displeasure by riding the corner with only one front and two rear wheels still in contact with the tarmac. This recruit's career lasted till the end of that first day. During our few days of indoctrination, I read all the material and understood that the described small fire vehicle was a 3000 gallon "engine," which meant that it was complete with high-pressure pumps and weighed in excess of twelve tons; unlike the unlucky recruit, my common sense told me that it didn't adapt to "wheelies." We were then introduced to the Main Fire Station and saw monster fire rigs most of us would have had trouble getting into gear.

Next stop was the firing range. Unable to read instructions, one recruit had come with his revolver, but forgot to bring his ammunition. I was a little ticked off when the sergeant asked me if I had brought more than six rounds. I admitted I had, and for some strange reason—I thought—the Sarge had me fire fourteen rounds at two different targets, took the total, divided by two, and gave us both passing grades; that galled that hell out me. I made a mental note not to have this dim-witted recruit patrolman as a partner or backup.

Finally we spent a day touring the main facility. There, in the huge assembly building, were fifteen F-86s in varying stages of construction. Those farthest away appeared to be merely angular pieces of metal almost totally hidden in the round, rolling fixtures that were used to transport them from their present condition to the final and 15th position in which they were complete, except for preliminary military acceptance, fueling, and test flight—finally to be accepted, numbered, signed-off, and transported. These F-86 jet aircraft were amazingly small, but they were one of several models that were the backbone of the military. As far as I know, they were never used on aircraft carriers; I didn't learned why this was so. The Navy was known—e.g. notorious—for never wanting anything the rest of the military used unless Navy-modified; in all fairness, Navy planes had to be able to handle the extreme forces of launching and recovery.

At the time I started at North American, there was a model change to produce the F-86-D. This D was a completely different airframe and bore little resemblance to its older but smaller brother. I got a chance to see this bird on the firing range. It was blocked into the semblance of level flight, targeted to 1000 yards, and all I can say is WOW! Two of these aircraft—fully fueled, armed, and ready to fly—were on standby at the airport under U. S. Military Joint Defense American and Canadian Dew Line Authority. If World War III were to start, I would be one of the first to know.

Sergeant Blaine

Three months went by, and I was given about a dozen different stations or patrols at the airport. Each patrol had a three-digit number, which was also the number of any entrance or exit gate involved. It turned out that the training program was such that if you wished advancement (which I didn't), you would be given patrols farther and farther away from the main plant.

In due time, I discovered that incompetence is a disease that no large or small company can avoid. This disease can even happen to sergeants. Sergeant Blaine was a short, bull-necked man who had been with the company since its inception. He had once been in charge of security, but was an old Chicago police retread and had realized, without anyone telling him, that as the company got larger and the product more complicated, he was out of his depth. Thus, he helped younger men take on the job of learning training for high level security. He willingly locked himself into the equivalent of top sergeant, while training men who would increasingly become his superiors.

I realize that he, like many dupes before him, thought that I had "the stuff," as he described it. For at least a year and a half, he put his money on what he thought was a good bet, i.e., me! I seemed to be a good bet because I loved the job, got myself everywhere in the plant, and seldom needed instruction. Blaine ended up liking me all the more after I handled a "crime" in which he was unknowingly involved.

It happened one night when I was in a guard shack out on the tarmac, a mile from the main plant—almost to Sepulveda Boulevard—where a new series F-100 Y was parked half in and half out of a small hanger. It was there for some kind of engine test but, since I was on the graveyard shift, no one was supposed to be working during this time at this remote location. I was looking out towards the field where a huge C-130 was just taking off from the Military Air Transport Facility a hundred yards from my location, when, in my peripheral vision, I sensed something wrong close at hand. I whirled about in time to see that the fire sprinklers just started to spray in the F-100 Y hanger. I reached for the phone and got the dispatcher's immediate reply: "Control Center."

"This is patrolman Wahl, on 117. The sprinklers have activated in the hanger to the right and rear of this station."

The line immediately went dead, and in less than six seconds, there was the sound of sirens from the main plant. Right behind them was P-2, Sergeant Blaine's hopped up Ford coupe. As I continued to monitor the hanger, the deluge stopped as rapidly as it had started. I tried to call back, but Control Center answered with a brief announcement: "Busy!"

So I shut up and waited while three huge trucks and a couple of cars pulled up in front of me. All attention was centered on the hanger, which, I was pleased to see, was still belching water down the tarmac. I had no orders to leave my shack, and since there was a whole army of bodies there, I stayed put. At last, all of the trucks drove off, and Blaine and the Lieutenant of the Watch came over and complimented me on my fast response: It had beaten the mechanical/electronic alarm by several seconds. I watched as Blaine and the lieutenant drove off in what I had thought was the P-2 and I was once again alone.

I had two days off. When I returned to the plant, there was a special notice on the bulletin board that P-2 was missing and presumed stolen; this rang a bell. Apparently Sgt. Blaine had gone back to the main plant in the lieutenant's P-6 and, in all the fuss and the report writing, forgot about P-2. And there it was, parked next to Station 117, kind of off by itself. It had been parked in the only space left open by the big fire rigs, which put it almost directly behind the guard shack.

I picked up the phone to the Control Center, but when I heard the CC operator come on the line, I thought, " … let's wait a minute," and I said, "Sorry, ignore the call," and hung up.

When I was off duty, I normally went directly home after leaving my watch report in the little box on the inside of the locked shack, but this time I hot-footed it back to the patrol office and caught the Sarge before he had a chance to depart. He looked at me quizzically. I explained, "A couple of young kids were driving up and down the tarmac in a police vehicle, and I thought at first they were field personnel—you know how crazy those wannabe airmen are. I guess they were just hot-roding around for kicks. Apparently they dumped Patrol-2 behind the 117 shack."

I said this all in one breath and waited patiently while Blaine pondered this bogus report. I couldn't understand Blaine making this kind of a gaff, but later I realized that the airplane, half in and half out of the single hanger at this location, was the first plane equipped with the new JP 57 engine, which we had already lost—once before. Blaine looked at me for a long time, during which time I could watch the gears grinding.

"Do you want me to write it up?" I suggested, finally.

Blaine let just the smallest trace of a smile wander over his pumpkin face and then said, more or less matter-of-factly, "No, Patrolman Wahl, I'll take care of it … "

And as I turned away, I heard the faintest sound of "Thanks."

Expanded North American

It seemed unlikely that LA Municipal Airport was ever going to deed any of its land to North American, so NA, of necessity, had to move many of its operations to far-flung facilities. Some of these included sites in Crenshaw, the Edwards Air Force Base, Compton, Culver City, East Ridge, and Apple Valley. As attrition, promotion, and advancement changed the Police and Security Division, opportunities for new officers became available; it clear that I was on a promotion track. Though not anxious to leave the main plant, I found myself increasingly on outside facility patrols given to men who met the requirements for handling themselves without supervision.

I remember, in particular, being the relief graveyard shift patrolman at the Crenshaw Facility. Here the patrolman would clock into the facility at the beginning of the unmanned midnight shift and literally have the run of the entire plant. At any hour, a sergeant might check in, but other than that, the Crenshaw facility would be empty except for the one patrolman. I loved the midnight shift there. Crenshaw was one of the sites where a variety of sub-assemblies were brought together and included a large research and development lab. And Crenshaw was the main production facility for the honeycombed, but very transparent, plastic laminates that made up the canopies for the cockpits and smaller plastic-based components. Especially interesting to me was the design and engineering lab where full-sized and ¾ sized models of the hydraulic, electrical, and mechanical sub-systems were designed and built.

Since it was a roving patrol with few patrol clock-check locations—some of which would report back to the CC—there was more than enough time for me to spend studying the complete layout of the very complex hydraulic systems of the F-86. Crenshaw was responsible not only for the general assembly of such systems, but had to develop operation manuals on how the things were put together on the airplane. There were various traveling displays describing the assemblage and operation of sub-units at the main plant.

Other facilities were similarly set up, some working two shifts and some operating all three. Edwards Air Force Base was involved with pre-flight and flight control and communication systems, but was one of the few facilities that I did not get to. Patrolmen there were much more organized and supervised since much of its work was super-secret; the whole operation was a good deal tighter. I was not particularly intrigued with the idea of working in a closely supervised place that, in the Mohave Desert, was a good distance from civilization. Available housing was in on-base facilities or motels and included a generous per diem.

Airplanes That Fly and Those That Don't!!!

A tremendous amount of engineering, machining, pounding, drilling, scraping, and milling, as well as thousands of pages of documents, plans, drawings, and models go into a modern fighter. The avowed purpose of all of these machinations is to create machines that fly: to lift one or more living human beings into the air, assist them to complete their mission, and to bring them back alive. While this is the avowed purpose, it is contradicted by the fact that there are always dedicated forces on the other side that hope to defeat these goals; but occasionally, defeating the machines' purposes might be innocent or inadvertent. An example of the latter is when the crew themselves are the problem. A couple of cases come to mind.

On certain field patrol days, I would stop by the pilots' lounge that was available through a special gate. Military and/or company test pilots would enter this four-story building, which looked like a house on stilts. The only reason that I could see for it being raised on this stilt-like structure would be to give the pilots or their wives, who might have passes, the ability to watch their husbands taking off and landing. This pilots' lounge had a homier, living-room quality than the average antiseptic ready room.

Generally, testing airplanes of any sort is a high-stress, high-danger job, but like everything else at the NA, most of these planes were coming off the line and were tested to specs laid out for the original prototype aircraft. By the time the bugs were all exorcised, and the line was belching them out by the hundreds, all that was left were military acceptance flights. These were about as routine as these things ever get, which may account for the civilian audiences. Generally this was limited to close family, but often included children.

When I passed the lounge and keyed the guard clock at the base, I did not enter the lounge during the day when the pilots or their families might be present. However, when I got the same patrol at night, I would often go through the facility. In the actual "Pilots Only" area, I noted a large blackboard with printed white lines separating the various flights in standard order, with space alongside for the pilot to check in and a place for the plane number and the date. During some consecutive flights, I had clocked in and had seen a late-model convertible with a gorgeous thirty-something blonde and three equally adorable children. The woman acknowledged me. I learned her husband's name and that he was one of the Army acceptance pilots.

There were many military pilots who had flown fighters of various types, including the ones that we were building, and it was always interesting to see the difference between the way they made take-offs as compared to the company pilots. The company pilots would roll down three-fourths of the field before lifting and retracting the landing gear; in contrast, the military pilots would take-off, using the minimum amount of field to get airborne, with the gear retracting almost before they had lost contact with the tarmac. George Welch was one of these hot-rod military pilots who got great joy out of hanging the brand new F-86s and F-100s on a hook and going as close to straight up as their high-powered F-45 GE engines could take them.

In between patrols, I would look for George's name penciled in chalk on the duty-board. The pilots would test two or three aircraft and, after the flights were completed, they would sit in on a thorough discussion of the particular flight with the company engineers and the accepting military brass. After their day's work was done, pilots would erase their names, making way for the next pilot to sign in for their assigned aircraft.

This one night, I returned to my shift after the day of George Welch's scheduled flight, climbed the stairs to the lounge, and looked into the "Pilots Only" area. There I saw the partially erased remnants of George's name. This was normal after the pilot had flown his full complement of aircraft, but the last number of the plane that he was flying was marked as an F-100, a plane scheduled in the middle his working day. Later, as the news spread through the entire plant, I learned that his F-100 had gone down minutes after take-off.

That was bad enough, but what was worse was the description of the short-lived flight: the plane's engine had suddenly flamed out and, with no place to go, the plane had dropped at high speed with a full load of hi-test aviation fuel through the front door of a very popular ice cream shop during a fully attended birthday party. The children who were not killed would have the memory of that hellish scene burned into their memories forever. In a marvelous example of afterthought, the company put in a rule that henceforth all test flights, regardless of pilot affiliation, would take a full trip down the runway before they became airborne. From then on I did not see the convertible with the pretty lady and children. The 38A patrol dropped off my list of favorites.

After this example of unnecessary death and mayhem, came one even more pointless. Aircraft, after being completed, were released from the plant to field control. As released aircraft, they were moved about the field to various locations, where their radar, sights, and instrumentation were evaluated, and engine run-ups performed. Finally, the planes would have their inertial navigation gimbals centered for the first time. They would be lined-up on a carefully marked position containing the "compass rose"—a large compass painted on the ground with precise north, south, east, and west locations. Airplanes are situated on it in such a way that all three of their internal gyros are locked to those universal latitude and longitude—celestial—coordinates. After this last important activity, the airplanes would then get final documentation and identification decals and would be parked, like so many brides, waiting for a destination.

There was a group of "field jockeys" that had the valued job of steering the planes along the field to these locations. These people were pilot wannabes who thought they were a little bit hotter and a little bit better than the rest of the plant employees. However, one of them, as it turned out, was unsure of his own job description; he had been on the job long enough to know that most of the planes were fueled and ready to go, with the explosives—installed and operational—necessary to eject the pilot out of the aircraft.

Leaving an airplane under an emergency situation is never a pleasant maneuver, but it is absolutely necessary to have a means for exiting an aircraft that might be out of control. This is accomplished with two sticks of dynamite attached firmly to the pilot's seat assembly, and includes a parachute and tracks for punching out—the term for leaving the plane under those circumstances. First, the endangered pilot has to blow the canopy and then lift two bright red covering handles from connections on either side of the seat ejection package. Before he does this, he pulls down his face-shield against the blast of air he will receive and finally, he will simultaneously pull the handles on both sides of the ejection unit. He will be blown, with the complete assembly, at tremendous speed—straight up and out. After a brief time delay to let the pilot clear the aircraft, an automatic device in the seat rack will trigger and deploy the attached parachute.

The plane-jockey was trained to know and comprehend all of this information about the plane he was moving; he had been instructed to keep his hands the hell off this equipment. The rules said that the jockeys were never to close the canopy while they were in the aircraft. Obviously they could not see the field for many feet around them and had to rely on the tow-craft driver's sense of direction.

You would think that "piloting" this wonderful killing machine would be thrill enough … well, in this one case you would be wrong. For reasons never to be discerned, as the towed plane rolled to a stop, the jockey released the safeties and pulled the eject levers. He had already belted himself to the seat assembly, so was destined to go where it went. Where it went occurred with a tremendous blast of sound and smoke as the assembly blasted off into the air thirty feet up and came to rest with a resounding thud twenty yards behind the aircraft. Everyone in sight was shocked to see the would-be-pilot describe a full flight parabola and crash heavily into the tarmac. It was, of course, his first and last flight: he was dead on arrival. The device is not made for getting someone out of a plane when parked; there was never time for the parachute to open. I did not look for his name—but would not have found it in any case—erased on the flight board in the pilot's lounge … but he sure as hell was dead. And for whatever it's worth … he did fly!

The Gooney-Bird

At about 0950 one morning while I was on the tarmac side of the plant guarding our clutch of F-86's, this monster came to visit. It was an astounding sight to behold. It was long, wide, and had wings that measured nearly the length of a football field. It landed on a long stretch of the main runway and rolled to a stop only forty yards from me. Field personnel ran out to set chocks against the multiple wheel assemblies, and I smiled in spite of myself as I looked at the obviously drooping wings. The specifications call for the wings to go from this negative dihedral to about four feet from horizontal in flight. With four engines on each wing, it is easy to see why there needs to be a long outrigger wheel extending close to the near end of each wing. Any variation in landing could cause one of the wings to drag on the tarmac with a guaranteed disastrous result.

So there it was, in all its glory, parked near the middle of the plant. A couple of service trucks, obviously not in emergency mode, drove out to the plane and planted a couple of theodolites (special laser lights that indicate balance, like a carpenter's "level") ahead of the aircraft. Nothing else of note seemed to be happening so I continued on my patrol. Three hours or so later when I arrived at where the plane was parked, I could see that the crew was back aboard. An engineer told me that the theodolites had been set up to check on the horizontal position of the wings relative to one another; the plane had passed the test, had been released, and was now ready to take-off.

There was no way I was going to miss seeing this "Gooney Bird" taking off, so I stretched my time between stations as the plane went through its clearances. Finally all eight engines were revved up and all inspection ports closed. The plane had final clearance orders from the tower across the field and started to move forward. It moved majestically down the long smooth runway, got up to speed, but just when its wheels should have left the ground, it lurched suddenly and unexpectedly to the right like some beautiful prima ballerina suddenly staggering in the middle of a pas de deux. The auxiliary starboard wing-wheel was still in momentary contact with the field as the plane made the most awkward looking take-off in its history with a thundering roar as all eight engines strained at maximum output to get airborne. It fought a moment, finally righted itself, and got some altitude. Alarms rang all over the field, and I could hear fire trucks from the main station come alive and roll into position on the runway.

It was obvious to everyone that something deadly and absolutely unexpected had happened to the beautiful monster. The whole aircraft shuddered through a weird series of near-acrobatics until, under some semblance of control, it made a wide circle and came back for an emergency landing. The plane had no more than come to a safe stop when the pilot debarked and ran towards the engineer's office. I saw his face as he blasted past me: it was obvious he was not a happy man! I moved on down the field, completed my patrol, and went home at the end of my shift, not seeing the plane again.

The next day after sign-in, I was talking to my counterpart who told me the whole unbelievable story. Setting up for the theodolite was a long boring routine, during which the ground crew opened and inspected various service ports on the aircraft. During one of these inspections, a mechanic who had been trading practical jokes with another mechanic—absent from duty this particular day—took his absent colleague's tool chest and sealed it in one of the under-wing inspection ports. He pulled this stunt at a time he thought the theodolite would pick out that the right wing was dipping much lower than the left.

His major mistake was that the theodolite test had already been done and had been signed off before he installed the small but heavy tool chest in the wing. Without going into all the mechanics, a tool chest that weighed 20 actual pounds, when placed 40 feet off the centerline of the aircraft, would lever into 40 times 20 pounds and, upon take-off, would unexpectedly present the pilot with an airplane severely out of balance. For all practical purposes, instead of a nominal take-off with a just checked plane, the pilot would be trying to take off with a starboard engine out of service. This was so much so that, without his steel nerves and instantaneous reflexes, the right wing would have dragged, spun the plane about the field, and exploded into a thunder ball of fire, debris, and death.

The mechanic who had left for vacation—and had not missed his tool chest—and the idiot mechanic who pulled the stunt were immediately fired. To say the Air Force was not happy was a masterpiece of understatement!

The Patrols

As I settled into a routine that covered various patrols in all parts of the plant, the job was an education and sheer joy for someone who loved airplanes of any kind as much as I did. The main thing about the various schedules was that they involved a product—the completed aircraft—but all of this daily activity was routinely confused by an equally confused cadre of workers. Some of these people were funny and some tragic; some were sinister and some dangerous. But their behaviors were always unexpected. I had been blooded by my previous years at Westinghouse so I had learned to expect the unexpected.

The main North American facilities consisted of two large general areas, separated by internal gates. The entire perimeter was fenced at all outside points. Immense assembly and sub-assembly areas, with offices, control points, and separate departments such as the police department, fire department, engineering and technical offices, and supply areas existed on the Imperial Highway side. Aviation Boulevard on the north and Sepulveda Boulevard on the south completed the entire acreage that made up both the Los Angeles Airport and all of the property belonging to N.A. Along the Imperial Highway were the various flight facilities located on the runway side, with the L.A. airport parallel to the Imperial highway from Aviation to Sepulveda, including the longest runway for all the landings and take-offs.

I will list the actual different patrols with fictitious names. However, as they involved me, I will tell you what I remember, without trying to be very accurate as to actual days and times. This is true simply because I do not have that good a sense of linear time.

Wahl-Patrol 184/ Field location 5:45 PM Tues. Intercepted and stopped transport of F-86 #328: Violation 157-c / George Maloney badge 731/ Cited: For moving aircraft against written orders forbidding field movement of manned aircraft after twilight.

I ordered the man driving the tractor that was towing the plane to stop and ordered the field-mechanic, sitting in the cockpit, out of the aircraft; the tractor driver stood alongside his vehicle. The "mechanic-pilot" was not happy and came out of the plane, clearly with a full head of steam. I was writing up a violation slip when he faced me and said, "Dammit, man. It's still light, and we were supposed to get this last plane to hanger six."

In answer, I looked around towards the recently set sun and asked, "What part of twilight do you fail to understand?"

"Sir!" he responded in a manner that indicated he thought of me every possible way except as a sir, "This is an aircraft building facility, and we are trying to get airplanes built and in the air as soon as possible, and you and your 'tribe' are making a damn hard job more and more difficult!"

I stopped writing and just looked at him steadily, while the tractor driver disinterestedly chewed gum. The tractor driver was in no jeopardy; the mechanic had authority over him.

"I see," I said, with easy sarcasm. "You think of yourself as a hero working for Justice, The American Way, Victory, and the Security of the United States?"

"Yeah, " he said, "Sir. I damn well do!"

Changing the subject, I asked, already knowing that this was a closed shop, "and you work for the company and are a member of the union?"

"Yeah," he answered tersely.

"Well, you might be interested in knowing that your own union set up the aircraft transport rules for its union members, as a matter of safety. As far as the company is concerned you can drag this damn plane around, far into the night, endangering you and anything or anybody else you might crash this $86,000 aircraft into."

Here I flipped the violation book shut and said, "I'll tell you what, Sport. Get back in and drive the damn plane across the field, into L.A. International, if you like. I'll let you go and kill yourself and screw up your union's bargaining agreements, if you think that's what you want to do." Then I took a long pause and softly said, "What the hell, screw your union. The company needs more heroes like you!"

I turned and walked away, but not before I noted the tractor driver had set blocks ahead of the plane's landing gear and was disconnecting the tow bar.

Wahl-Patrol 86/Paint Locker location, Deluge riser F-7 7:12 PM Tues. Found Gate Lock #1285 Open: 5:22 PM/Secured this hour.

"Secured this hour," but not before I opened the door to this 50 by 50 foot storage area and looked at the hundreds of drums of paint and paint products. I noted, especially, the three-inch diameter, heavy duty standpipes that could flood this building with 20,000 gallons of water in about two minutes. So, that's what a deluge facility means!

Dreaded Traffic Control

Wahl-Patrol 113/Traffic Control Aviation Blvd. and Imperial- 4:12 PM Fri. 4-6 Assisting LAPD police sergeant Stuart Fielding/Secured 6:00 PM-routine patrol.

These Traffic Control Patrols were not my favorite because they actually took time and energy, not to mention that some crazy L.A. driver could kill you. At North American, some 22,000 people entered—or left—Gate 4 each and every shift, raced to the parking area, and headed for home. Although the largest, we were not the only plant feeding traffic to Highway 1 and points north, south, and east. The intersection at Aviation Blvd and Imperial Highway was my post. The company provided us with brightly colored bandoleers, white gloves, a whistle on a lanyard, and a wish for us not to use our accrued hospitalization benefits. Luck was necessary.

LAPD Sergeant Stuart Fielding and I held forth in the middle of the huge and complex intersection for about an hour, after which, as traffic slowed down, Fielding would get on his motorcycle and go somewhere else. We seldom got to talk except when there was an incident such as a drunk driver, an accident, or an altercation. There were only a few of these, but Sergeant Fielding and I got to know and respect each other's moves as we spent a couple of weeks on this patrol. Mostly it was a couple of hours of boredom followed by a few seconds of controlled terror.

On our first patrol together, Sergeant Fielding looked me up and down, kind of disinterestedly, and asked, "How ya doin' fellow?"

I had the feeling he was not that interested but answered evenly, "Pretty good so far. How about you?"

He answered my question in a kind of multi-paused monotone: "Ya know ... well, pretty well ... ya know, kinda OK ... By the way, how many times have you been on this patrol?"

I didn't mean to be a smart-ass, but I was uncomfortable and it just came out, "You mean, counting today?"

"Yeah ... " he answered, eyes narrowing while he chewed absent-mindedly on the half cheroot (cigar) he was not smoking.

I noticed that when his eyes narrowed and his bushy mustache quivered, he looked a little like Yosemite Sam in blue. "One day?" I answered causally.

"Well, it's simple enough," he commented, glaring at me with the look he was often to give recalcitrant drivers.

"Is that why they sent a sergeant to do it?" I regretted the remark the second I said it.

In answer, he paused for a long half minute before he growled at me, "Are we gonna get off on the right foot or the left foot, Sonny?"

"It's just a question, Sarge ... " Immediately I amended, "What are we supposed to do, Sergeant?"

"Well, as I said, it's simple enough, Sonny. I'm in traffic every day. I'm a good sergeant: I know my work. But you ... you are a County Mounty, if you don't take exception—a kind of rent-a-cop, and not under my control."

"Oh, yes I am!" I answered with great fervor, realizing that if I was going to have to handle hostile traffic, I really did not want to take on the LAPD as well.

"What makes you say that?" he queried.

"I'm in your territory and I haven't a clue. Just what the hell am I supposed to do here?"

"Well, as I said, it's pretty simple, Sonny. You get out there in the middle of the intersection, check on the lights, and try to work with them. Unless you intend to shoot somebody, the most important tool you have is that stupid whistle."

I looked down, unbelieving, at the silver whistle hung about my neck and extending down my chest.

"This thing?"

"Yo," he answered, growling. "That thing! It can easily save your ass!" He went on to explain that "The Whistle" was the standard way to "talk" to the criminally stupid—otherwise known as the driving public.

"Most of the time they can't hear you any other way. You set up a few simple movements that tell them where you want them to go and back it up with the whistle. If you blow on it lightly, it kind of purrs but loud enough to hear even in traffic. If you blow a little harder, it means that you are annoyed, and they are doing something you don't like."

"OK." I responded penitently, "Got it, Sarge … Sergeant!" I noticed that his steely blue eyes never left mine.

Then the sergeant let the trace of an almost happy smile glimmer across his heavily weathered face. "And, by the way, don't forget to dance … "

I gave him—he who was four inches shorter than me, but close to the same 200 pounds—a doubtful look but, wisely, said nothing.

"And by the way," he repeated happily, "Don't you be afraid to dance … they love it!"

I had trouble with the basic concept but kept an open mind.

"But if they are really pissing you off or not paying attention, you really let them have it with the whistle; this will generally result in a hell of a screech of breaks while these idiots try to figure out who you are yelling at."

"OK. Got it, Sarge!" This time I tried it without the more formal "Sergeant."

By now, the good and wise sergeant had my full attention, so he continued in a softer voice. "At this point you look directly at the moron who is either moving when he shouldn't be or isn't moving when he should be. You give him a look that says, 'I'd just as soon throw your sorry ass in the can as look at you!' This usually gets the right results. If that doesn't work, you stop traffic in all directions, and your partner, hearing that 'whistle comment' will stop all traffic in his control.

"You will then walk right up to the car and glare at the guy until he lowers his window, and you will gaze at him as if he were not worthy of even looking at a motor vehicle, and say, in a voice you would use in dealing with a retarded five year old, exactly what the hell you want him personally to do to stay off your shit-list."

"OK," I said.

"So now I will give you your first and hopefully last lesson, Sonny. Take your time and watch me for a minute or two—take your time, but not too damn much, I'm out there by myself!"

Here he wadded out into the middle of the traffic and, after blowing the whistle for attention, started working with the lights. As much as he weighed, he moved every bit as well as me—probably even better—and sure enough, he did dance! When he wanted a lane of traffic to move fast, he pushed his foot out as if kicking a football to tell the traffic to get their collective feet off the brakes and hit the gas.

As he explained later, there would be a certain number of people who would not get the message, even if you explained it to them in Braille, complete with semaphore flags. He said to just wait until they get out of the way, no matter what kind of stupid driving they were doing. I had asked if he gave them tickets, and he just shook his head sadly, indicating that I was three kinds of a fool.

He asked, "How fast did you say you could run, Sonny?"

"Not as fast as a car!" I replied, knowing this was the right answer.

"Right, Sonny, and that's why I ride this patrol on a motorcycle instead of a patrol car. If they really don't give a damn and are deliberately trying to kill me, they can see I have a cycle and a radio; I can take off and get their license and I'll call for back up—their Ass will be Grass. Mostly you can stop traffic in all directions at will, but you don't want to do it too often or too long."

I waited a few seconds, blew the whistle, and waded into traffic. Sarge was right, we did both dance, and I even did a kick or two. The two hours went by pretty rapidly.

On the same patrol over the next four days, I got better and better and I was glad that nothing too untoward happened ... until, of course, it did! The most significant accident that happened while I was there unfortunately involved my sergeant friend, Fielding.

The near disaster occurred a day or two before my last job with the good Sarge. It was near the end of the shift, the traffic had slowed to a trickle, and we were ready to let the lights do the rest of the work by themselves. The sergeant had walked back to his motorcycle and was radioing in. I could hear the radio traffic with its terse police jargon as the traffic lights indicated green for traffic going south and west. I heard the motorcycle engine roar into life as Sarge checked the traffic for clearance to his east. I was legally crossing with the light on my way back to the plant, when a little old lady ran the light, swerving at the last second to avoid hitting me.

Sarge, unfortunately, was just revving up and not expecting the senior citizen with the oversized Austin Healy to be driving directly into his path. He must have imagined that I was watching the traffic, but in my attempt to avoid the grandé dáme, I had to jump out of the way, and the whistle was not in my mouth. I grabbed for it and blew like crazy, but it was already too late. She slammed on her brakes, and Sarge T-boned the solid vehicle with a resounding crash. Sarge flew over the handlebars and, at a slow speed, arc'd majestically through the window on her passenger side—fortunately empty—and was immediately deposited into her lap.

I ran over and quickly moved the bike off the street and onto the sidewalk as a crowd began to assemble. I rushed up to the open car, and there was Sarge, just righting himself and carefully getting off the lady. She was staring straight ahead in frozen panic. Sarge was somewhat dazed; his face was first white and then gradually grew to a purplish-red. He looked at me helplessly as he wiped broken cigar bits from his mouth and face. He took several deep breaths and, more quickly than I might have imagined he could move, extracted himself from the front seat of the car and stood panting, just looking at the lady.

For the lady's sake rather than the sergeant's, I quickly attended to her. I talked softly to her and ascertained that she was all right—under the circumstances; it was hard to figure who, of the two of them, was the most consternated. Sarge had a limp for a moment or two, but straightened himself out and checked that the lady was all right. I noted that the guard from an adjacent parking lot had already called CCC. In the distance, approaching sirens could be heard.

Convinced that he was not injured, Sarge got a statement from me that he wrote down in a shaky hand, and then we cleared traffic. When we were back on the corner, we just looked at each other without a word for a moment or two, then two traffic units pulled up. I heard a traffic officer call out, "Do you need an ambulance, Sarge?"

"Not for me," he answered too quickly, "but make damn sure you get one for the old broa-ah—I mean sweet old lady—and don't charge her with anything. Pick up my bike that she hit"—I noticed no mention of his parabolic flight—"and Wahl and I will clean up the intersection so you can clear the call."

As things settled down, I just kept staring at the sergeant, trying my best to not let even a suggestion of a smile wander across my face. I am a smart-ass, and unfortunately there isn't much I can do about it, so I found myself saying, "Wow, she was a pretty good looking old girl, not too good a driver, but pretty good looking … did you get a chance to give her a quick kiss since the two of you were so close?"

The tormented man looked for a moment as though he was going to bend a baton over my head but then a broad, relaxed grin took over. He stood there smiling idiotically, while rocking back and forth with mirthless humor, and simply asked, "Are you cop wannabes required to write reports?"

"Yes, Sir!" I answered militarily, almost, but not quite, adding a salute.

Sarge looked at me in mock anger, but drove his point home with a stubby finger poking my chest for emphasis, "You write this little scene up so somebody sees it, and it gets back to me, you, my "mountie" are a dead-man!!" He got into a waiting patrol unit and took off.

I was off on other patrols and didn't see the sergeant for several months. He had a long memory and he knew, even if I didn't, that there would be a day of reckoning. And there was, months later.

The Strike

The plant and the unions had been at each other's throats in useless negotiations for a couple of weeks when the unions officially went out on strike, and the plant closed down. A strike is a very nasty and a very dangerous thing, not to be taken lightly. There are a certain number of uncontrolled idiots who will do anything to give their former employers hard and—more often than not—legal trouble. When I turned up for shift one morning, and the thirty of us were lined up for inspection, we were given outside gate protection duty; I didn't find that strange. All of us on outside gates were to be on the street. These are public streets, and, in effect, we were given general police powers either on or off the actual site. This was still O.K. and not surprising: what followed was.

Each of us had personal lockers at the plant, and when we reported for line-up and patrol assignments, we wore our Sam Browne utility belts consisting of our weapons, handcuffs, spray, reloads, and batons. However, the next order startled us: we were told to shed our utility belts and lock our weapons in our lockers. There was a collective murmur. Unless you have carried a "hog's leg" 38 on your hip for many years and felt its comforting weight, you have no idea of how naked you feel in nothing but a uniform and a badge. You also feel as though you are listing a little to one side.

I drew patrol 117 where I had spent many a night inside the gate, on the field, or in a guard station, but today 117 was to be stood on the street side, better than a mile and a half from my former traffic patrol at Imperial and Aviation; it was a long walk. I took my lunch with me and stood outside the gate. Every few minutes, cars would drive by on the otherwise deserted street, and somebody would throw garbage, mostly tin cans or fruit. There was much taunting and name-calling, but nothing I felt I couldn't handle. Our lack of weapons, under the circumstances, was a little off-putting, but most annoying was the fact that we had no direct communication with anyone.

I realized that I was given this very isolated post because somebody thought I was up to it, but my thrill at this show of responsibility was suddenly dampened when a car that had passed me several times, screeched to a halt a few feet away and three nasty-looking customers emerged and walked toward me. "Whoops!" I thought. "Let's see: how long has it been since I've been in a fracture ward?"

The biggest guy was about my size. I checked: he didn't appear to be armed. The second was also unarmed, but was swearing and abusive. The third was a short, pimply-faced little bastard but he was carrying a regulation baseball bat. I leaned back against the fence and carefully watched the one doing the talking. He apparently was the ringleader, but I had dealt with mob mentality before. It is real simple, hard to do, but simple: plan to get hurt, accept it, deal with it, but work out a response. I spoke to them in civil terms while they told me what kind of a fag, asshole, and moron I was.

I made my plan: I was going to kick the big one in the nuts; quickly and smoothly karate-chop the loud mouth in the throat; but most importantly, I was going to get the bat and bash out the teeth of the weapon-carrying bugger with his own bat. He didn't talk, but what he did was spit on my uniform. A big gob hit me on the left shoulder; I dodged just as he was aiming for my face. I looked at the goo, wiped it off, and got ready to boogie.

In a controlled and soft voice, I asked him, "Hey, that was real cute. What do you do for an encore?"

Whoever was going to make the first move would be my first target. But everyone suddenly froze in position as a black and white pulled up just behind the miscreants' car. Two uniformed LAPD officers—pretty good-sized—stepped out from the unit's front seat and approached our little group, ready for anything. They were wearing police-issued 38's and looked like they would welcome the opportunity to use them. I relaxed. Then I became alert again, as the back-seat door of the patrol car opened and out stepped my former traffic mate, Sergeant Fielding. He was cradling a wicked-looking, twelve-gauge shotgun.

The bad guys visibly shrunk as Sarge walked up and, directly facing me, asked politely,

"Officer, are you having any trouble with these gentlemen that you would like LAPD to help you with?"

In answer, I walked over to the skinny guy, took the bat, made a couple of pretend swings with it, and pointedly handed it back to the creep.

"No, Sarge. The boys and I were just having a little discussion on the chances of who would win the pennant this year." I was looking serious, with just the slightest trace of a smile.

Sarge smiled back and said to the assembled, "Well, OK, you boys might get back in your car and find some other place to play 'cause the man here is busy. We'll be around for a while, so don't let us find you here again. Understood?"

The rowdies quickly agreed and got back in their car and drove off. The other two officers got back in the front seat of the cruiser and waited for the sergeant.

He just stood there looking at me, and finally said, "I imagine you here, naked and all, were fairly glad to see us."

"Absolutely," I answered.

"We got to get together and do traffic again, when things are a little more settled."

"Absolutely," I agreed. "Absolutely 'gooood duty' and a hell of a lot safer than this patrol!"

Sarge laughed as he turned away and after closing the door, still cradling his shotgun, said through the window, "Well, Sonny, you all have a good day now … ya hyear!" And they drove away. The rest of the patrol was routine.

North American Aviation was a job I could have made a career of—if they didn't try to bump me up into management—however, my messed-up relationships were to get the better of me and mess up yet another job. But before I leave my dissertation on this very significant place, one last anecdote stands out in my mind.

Not Even on the Road

I was caught in a speed trap in Inglewood, along with a whole raft of other speeders. When I went to court, remembering (of course) to wear my uniform, I chose to be the classic fool-in-court: I represented myself. Looking sternly at the officer who had written the citation, I drew myself up to my full height and said in a loud, clear voice, "Your honor, first of all, I would like to categorically deny everything the officer has said …"

At this point "hizoner" raised his voice to a mocking falsetto and almost leaped off his high pulpit as he bellowed, "OOOOOoooo … cat-a-gore-ically!" Then in a more normal voice, still dripping with sarcasm, he retorted, "you were not even on the highway?"

The court roared with laughter. What I had failed to realize was that I had drawn the Supreme Court Jester of Judges, but though humorous, he was to be taken seriously. I reserved the honor of class idiot for myself. Even though the charges were dismissed, I never forgot the point … in the case of any accident, you are, at the very least, responsible for "being on the road!!"

16 | The Tijuana Jail

Egotistically I was not that surprised when I was picked out of our 120 man police force to go with engineering to provide police services for the proposed F-100 speed run trials at the Salton Sea in the California desert. After make-up one morning, the duty sergeant called me over and handed me a piece of paper describing duty with the engineering group in charge of the ground station's speed analyzing equipment, cameras, company vehicles, and several tons of electronic gear. The notice indicated a guard—Ernie Bloomberg—and me (unnamed) were to be the police force. Promptly the next morning, I met Ernie, a tall, tan 30-year old North American cop who had been on similar assignments. Arrangements were made for him to drive his own car on necessary patrols while I was to alternate between his car and P2 (the company patrol car). He would get per diem for the use of his car and all of our expenses were to be handled by "chits."

We left in the two cars with uniform changes and light travel cases with personal supplies, following the route of the 54-4 engineering staff (eight people--mostly senior engineers) two days later. The engineers were billeted at Indio in a relatively posh hotel, while Ernie and I stayed at the Niland motel, not known for even a modicum of luxury; the plumbing worked … sort of!

Niland is a dusty spot in the road at the south end of the Salton Sea, near Calpatria. It is a major stop for truckers, having the only decent restaurant for over 50 miles on Highway 111. More to the point, Niland was a division station for the Southern Pacific railway freight line, which for many miles ran just inland of Hwy 111. The crews of these trains often stopped at Niland for change of crews or rest/meal breaks. When I had ridden regular passenger trains, I had never seen train employees carrying weapons, but for these freight trains, the crews were expected to carry and know how to use silver-plated sidearms. Niland was also one of the district headquarters for the U.S. border patrol.

As indicated earlier and subsequently made obvious, Los Angeles—indeed most of California—was little known terrain to me, so I did weird things with geography. If I wanted to get anyplace, including work at North American, I simply turned left or right off Rosecrans onto either north or south Highway 1, also known as The El Camino Real, and for all my stay in LA, I veered little from this path. It is notable that I still rarely veer far from El Camino in my current living area, when driving by myself. The special detail, however, took me far out of my comfort zone. On "my" map, Hwy 1 went all the way to Tijuana, passing through the Salton Sea on the way. This basic mistaken perception in relation to the Salton Sea moved the sea to the general vicinity of the ocean and eliminated dozens of cities, several counties, and the Sea itself.

I have often been described as a brilliant human being, but one who is also obviously incompetent, if not downright stupid, in earthly matters, so here I am at 84, trying to figure out where this Salton Sea detail actually was. The least bit of interest on my part would have clarified for me that a great deal of the California coast from Crescent City to San Ysidro is canted at a 45 degree angle, west to east—where was my geometry when I needed it! But in my geographically challenged mind, I had US Hwy 10, which went due east across California to Arizona, as parallel to Hwy 1 going southeast to Tijuana Mexico.

When Ernie and I were ensconced in our motel room, fortunately next to the restaurant, Ernie wasn't, but I was, surprised by the fact that the very active, very loud bar sported over 30 people, all carrying sidearms, including us. There was quite a sartorial distinctiveness among the variously colored attire: brown uniforms of the border patrol, the "blue-jean" bib-overhauls of the train workers, the khaki-green of the highway patrol, and us in blue serge; throw in a couple of county-mounties (sheriffs) and one could very easily imagine oneself in the early wild-wild West! There weren't any dancing girls, but there were a couple of cute waitresses.

When I took the job, knowing I would see parts of California I had never seen before—not counting my short stay in San Diego—I didn't realize that for the three assigned weeks, I would, to all practical intents, be in Mexico: Niland is about 36 desert miles from the border. The Imperial

Valley is an immense farm existing only by virtue of the All American Canal, which directs water from the Colorado River to what otherwise would be parched fields. The farms exist because of two major resources: water and migrant help. For every white man in this area, there are 300 Mexicans, and this is probably vastly underestimated.

After the first night, Ernie and I saw little of each other because we were working 13 hour shifts. While one man had one of the cars on site or on patrol, the other was sleeping, eating, gassing the other vehicle, and preparing to take it on site—while the first man would take his time off. I generally spent more time in P2. The result of Ernie and my distant relationship was that I made friends with the ubiquitous highway patrol and other officers, as well as the motel and restaurant staff.

The Competition

The F-100 aircraft is berthed at Edwards Air Force Base. It takes off from there, flies about 100 miles to the Bertram area, a railroad division station. At Bertram, the NA engineers built the setup for measuring the speed of the new planes, starting with two fires at each end of a three-kilometer strip of sand, a "race course" creating smoke stations. Located about a mile from the smoke stations are telephone poles with several lateral markers one-foot apart up the pole. The pilot is to pass through the smoke and will be photographed by Polaroid cameras behind each pole that will record the plane's speed as it passes by. The pilot is looking for heavy smoke about a mile from the three kilometer "race course"; when he see the smoke, he knows this is roughly the entrance to the course. He immediately throttles up to full speed (Mach 1), blowing through the smoke, and pursuing a straight line only 20 feet above the ground just past the high telephone poles off his left wing. He maintains this straight line for the six seconds it takes to reach the end of the course. If he has done it perfectly, he will have maintained 20 (+- 3) feet for the six seconds it took him to get through the course, without varying his side motion more than three feet from one pole to the next. At the second, most important, smoke station, the plane has to abruptly climb to a much higher altitude to miss the Chocolate Mountains. It then returns to Edward's Air force Base.

FIA (Federation Internationalé Aeronautica) is the only legal determiner of speed records. We ran our top speed about the second time we ran the 3 kilometer course, but the FIA "referee" was on contract to

Douglass and located at Edward's Air Force Base, so would not validate our speed. Done with the course, done with the record, done with the FIA man, Douglass was supposed to leave the course and FIA man to us, but they knew we had run out of an appropriate temperature: lower temperatures required relatively higher speeds because of heavy vibration. Douglass got all the press and held the record. FIA regulations indicated a three kilometer course record had to be exceeded by three percent of speed, but a fifteen kilometer course could be run by a mileage increase just over the baffle speed (at exactly the speed of sound there is a heavy vibration that makes it impossible to break the barrier). With the now lower temperature, the NA engineers chose the mileage option.

So, I was getting ready to go home, especially after watching six big trucks and a 100+ people from Douglass leaving the site gloating and chortling. But, two days went by and our chief engineer came to the timing station where I was on duty and said, "Larry, I want you to be on the lookout for a farmer who may ask you what the hell you are doing on his property. We are moving the north smoke and camera station 12 kilometers north."

And we did that to get the fifteen kilometer distance. That last week I was giving North American Control in Los Angeles verbal temperature reports every half hour throughout the day. The temperature finally climbed up a few degrees; we ran the plane. Of course we beat the record. Back at NA, Charlie and I mused over some absentee farmer coming upon a vacant telephone pole, sunk in concrete, with lots of communication wires hanging around and wooden slats a foot apart running up the pole. We figured he wouldn't have a clue.

The Tijuana Fiasco

Since we worked 13-hour shifts, we were given sleep time to recover: 13 on and 13 off. I thought Tijuana was close by—remember, I thought the Salton Sea was next to the Pacific Ocean—so I gassed up Ernie's car, which was in my possession at that time, and headed south. I arrived at El Centro—again thinking I was on the coast. I asked an attendant at a service station how far to Mexico, and he said, "Can you spit? Mexicali is just south of us."

I said I wanted to go to Tijuana so he directed me to Hwy 98 at Calexico, which rambles along the border changing its number several times until you get to the border crossing at San Ysidro. I set out for a short trip with his written directions in hand. Surprise! It was about 180 miles. I was wearing summer tans and had left gun and badge at the motel.

When I arrived at Tijuana, I had a ravenous thirst. The first and only place I stopped was called "The Long Bar." Because I had to buy gas, I had only $4.00 left in cash and my $64 paycheck from NA. Even though seeing the "ALTO" (stop in Spanish) signs, it did not dawn on me that I had left the world of legal Latin nomenclature and of concepts like prima-facia evidence, nolo contendere, and writ of habeas corpus.

Meanwhile, back in the bar, Stupid (me) was trying to get the bartender to cash my North American check, which he made abundantly clear was not about to happen. In a purple funk, I headed out the swinging door, giving it a significant kick on the way. I emerged directly into the arms of two special police: "Pardon me, Signor. You must come with us."

"What the hell," I thought. "I'm a policeman. Surely they have reciprocity." In bitter late understanding, I should have realized my four American dollars would have got me sprung, but Oh No, on to the central police station we went! There I went before an amiable police lieutenant who checked out my ID cards and became very conciliatory while he told me that because I was a fellow officer, he would just have to adjust some papers while I stayed for "a few moments" in a holding cell.

Three hours later I was removed, handcuffed, leg-chained, and attached to a long chain connected to fifteen other upstanding Mexican citizens. We were herded into a 6 by 6 truck, now guarded by obvious federal police with wicked-looking weapons and no sense of humor. We drove some 15 miles through rocky, trail-like roads to finally arrive in what appeared to be the Mexican equivalent of nowhere. In this nowhere stood a large adobe barracks with a few shacks around and twenty or so armed guards. As far as I could make out, this structure was rectangular with one door set next to a barred window. Was this was the infamous Tijuana Jail?

Everyone around me spoke Spanish, period. No one around me spoke Latin. We fifteen "dangerous felons" were now lined up in a single row, standing for what seemed like hours as nighttime snuck up on the scene. Powerful lights went on, and the Comandante, a rotund man about 5 feet in all directions, strode up to us with an assistant who read from—what I assumed—was a charge sheet. "Pedro Feliz, bla, bla, bal, bla ... Jose Comendez, bla, bla, bla ... " until they reached the middle of the line, "Lorry Woohl, bla, bla, bla ... " As each man's name was called, his shackles were removed and he was escorted with intense care to the door, which was opened from the inside. He entered, and the door closed again. This went on until "then there were none."

I'd been trained by the CIA to quickly scan 360 degrees when in a new situation. If you know what you are doing, you can rapidly gain a tremendous amount of information, whereas, the untrained might take much longer to absorb and assemble useful data. At some level, far, far down, I was fearful. At this point in my incarceration, however, I had not been separated from my wallet with my NA identification, California driver's license, and, of course, my four American dollar bills. This seemed unusual. As mentioned before, my uniform pants were an undistinguishable tan and, for some reason, I was wearing a semi-transparent yellow shirt, no coat, no sweater—heavier clothing having being left in the car parked in the middle of downtown Tijuana. In my right rear pocket sat the NA payroll check, certainly one of the most important I was ever to receive. My watch was still with me so I noted that I had passed through the jail entrance at 9 PM after arriving at The Long Bar at 5.

To my immediate right was a tin latrine, one toilet, an open box containing an overhead shower, and, further in, a spigot that was attached to a coil of hose. Looking to my left, I saw a small built-in room that apparently had access to the one window I had seen from the outside. Sixty feet back was a concrete wall and, in between, moving nervously to and fro, were about 120 Mexicans. I could discern no other American as I kept my eyes down and my mouth shut. Most of my fellow prisoners were substantially smaller than me and, gathering by their clothes, represented a gamut of citizens ranging from the unfortunate to the wily to the depraved to the hopeless. I had no idea precisely what I had been charged with or, much more importantly, what my sentence was. There was one exception to the normally smaller-sized population; that exception was about 6 foot 2, sturdier built than I was, heavily muscled, and wearing nothing other than breech-cloth, i.e., a diaper. I noticed that wherever he went, people moved away like water moves away from oil. I also noticed that he entered and exited through a small door connected to the built-in room, which was approximately 10 by 12 feet. In addition to this room's window to the outside and door to the inside of the jail, there was a barred service opening facing into the prison proper. There was one other door, midway along the left wall, which opened to something else; I was pretty sure it was not freedom. The structure I was in, therefore, was roughly a 60-foot square box with a 40-foot ceiling, completely surrounded by a narrow catwalk that had two Federales, armed with shotguns, casually sauntering around its perimeter. Obviously they had an outside source of exit/entrance that I couldn't see. From time to time, I would see certain individuals wander over to the barred service opening where there would be some sort of exchange; they would come away with cigarettes or a drink or a small package of something. Over in the far right corner were piles of blankets, and since I saw nothing resembling a bed, I assumed correctly that we slept on the concrete floor. There was a constant drone of Spanish, generally subdued but occasionally broken by a few hints of hostility, and through it all, the quick, reliable understanding that once the outside door had closed, this prison, like any other, was run by the inmates. I was now about six hours into my thirteen of sleep time, sure of only one thing: Ernie's car was in downtown Tijuana, I was in the Tijuana jail, and no one back in Niland knew where I was!

I found a place on the floor to sit, as most of the others had, and noted that, amid all the conversation, certain alliances were being arranged. This resulted in dozens of clumps of people, clustering in several personal groups to isolate themselves. I felt very much alone until I heard a voice next to me say in English, "Hello. You are Americano?"

I was startled since it was the first English I had heard since the lieutenant. "Yes," I answered. My "bunkmate" turned out to be Pedro Feliz, and I recognized him immediately as a con man and street hustler. Satisfied that he wasn't going to cut my throat during the night, I spoke openly with him, including about my job and technical data on the F-100. When he translated the 654 miles per hour into kilometers, his eyes opened wide and he said, "Muy ràpido!"

I assured him that all this was true and finally got around to explaining how I was about to become his associate. His eyes had lighted up when I mentioned the check in my right hip pocket. "Sí, sí, sí, and you couldn't get this cashed?"

"No," I answered.

He gave me a wily look and asked how much? I told him 64 dollars, and added, "American."

His smile broadened as if he had just seen the Virgin Mary. "Oh Ho, no problema! We fix tomorrow."

Considering the problems I'd had so far, "No problema" was exactly what I was looking for.

He looked at me cannily and asked, "Do you trust me?"

I looked into his soft brown eyes for a long time and then wordlessly reached into my pocket and handed him the check. The first thing he did was excuse himself, go up to the man in the breechcloth, and say a few words to him. Then he came back, gathered up our gear, and moved us to another location, closer to the outside door and the door of what turned out to be a room for conjugal visits. Pedro explained to me that Mexican sentences were indeterminate: anything over a year and a half went to Federal Prison and anything less, and he did mean anything, was dumped in this Tijuana jail or other municipal jails.

I cursed the fact that I was wearing that stupid transparent shirt because a number of fellow prisoners did not hide the fact that they found me "muy attractive." The next morning, while in line for thick oatmeal, one of my admirers ran a safety razor blade, held flat, along my arm. I turned slowly to face him and gave him a look that said, "You may cut me, but you ain't going to fuck me!" He left me alone. However, this incident brought me to the attention of what was obviously the sergeant-at-arms—the big guy in the diaper. He came up to me, stared at the proposed inamorato, and then carefully looked me over. By now, everyone in the place knew I was "the rich gringo." I saw many eyes comparing my physique to his … Mexicans are betting folk, and I could see the wheels going around. If I was not sure before, I was sure now—I HAD TO GET OUT OF THIS PLACE!

Breakfast started at 6 A.M. with alarms going off and lights going on. Four more guards appeared on the galleries, looking anxiously for targets. The mystery door, which I had no idea where it lead, was now opened, and Guido, as I named him, ushered us into another compound of equal dimensions, but with a single spigot for water. While we were here, our original compound was being "bathed," the water flowing into a large central drain; this turned out to be the height of hygiene in this place. It was September and hot. The difference between where we had been and where we were now was that while the walls were still 40 feet high, there was no roof. From through a wide passageway, we could see another identical area, also with no roof. Then magic happened: roughly a third of the 120 prisoners, including Pedro and me, were returned to the original, now bacteria-free, cell. About another third stayed in the roofless area, and the final third, apparently the damned, ended up in the last compound—this one was 60 by 60 feet of pure misery.

Guido stood guard in our area, while the second group had to get permission to come in and use the latrine and toilet. The damned, who seemed to know whom they were, never entered either of the other locations, but stayed all day under a blistering sun—over 105 degrees. If they were fed, I didn't see it. A small 12-foot round trench was their toilet.

Thus our day consisted of the dividing of the original group into threes. I was now into my 13-hour NA work shift. Pedro had regaled me with stories of tourists and other visitors who returned to their cars to find engines, wheels, and just about anything else gone. I don't remember ever praying for a car before, but I did now. Pedro indicated to me that we were to go to the service window where all business was transacted—apparently you couldn't bank at the bar, but you could at the jail, with transactions occurring through the service desk, out the back window, and to "whomever it might concern." Pedro told me to knock on the outside door, give the guard three pieces of paper, and I would be released. I had expected Pedro to walk with me, but he stopped at the door and gave me the most appealing puppy-dog look I have ever seen from a human. I looked at the guard, turned, pointed to Pedro, and made a gesture of pulling him out of the jail. The guard looked at me for a moment, looked at one of the pieces of paper, wrote on it, signaled Pedro to come, and we both left.

I don't remember how we got back downtown, but the first thing I did was check the car—amazingly, it was OK, even the gas hadn't been drained. Next, we took the papers to the bank and the bank gave me about $32; I gave Pedro $5—he actually kissed my hand, but as we came down the steps to the street, it was obvious we were about to part. I looked at him, knowing he would soon be back in the Tijuana jail, but I didn't plan to see Mexico again this lifetime.

I got into the car, drove to the border, and then realized it was harder to get out than to get in—much more fuss and feathers—but I had adequate ID. Upon reaching California, I stopped the car, got out, and kissed the ground; I'd heard that expression for years and never believed anybody did it. When I finally got back to Niland, I took a quick shower, put on the rest of my uniform—sans see-through yellow shirt—raced out to the site, and stopped at the restaurant to get a thermos of coffee. Only six hours late, I relieved Ernie, presenting him with an intact car. I was ready to give a full explanation, but he didn't seem to need one; he just took his car and left. Later in my shift, it dawned on me that though the people in the restaurant looked at me, no one but Mary said anything; the normal complement of gun-toting folks were not present at that time. When my shift ended, I drove P2 back to Niland, went directly to bed, and slept the sleep of the righteous, though I was not one of them.

When I came into the restaurant for my breakfast, a little after noon, the place was loaded. There were even more police than usual: the state patrol was there, the county sheriffs were there, the train crews were there, and the fourteen border patrol officers—including a sergeant I'd given such a bad time about the Mexican illegals sitting in open cattle semis for hours while the border patrol guys ate lunch and drank beer—were there. The place was bouncing, but as I entered the door, a weird silence fell. I even heard the jukebox die. When a roomful of people goes silent, all grinning idiotically, something is wrong! I made a lot of noise sitting at the counter, but Mary didn't come immediately. Finally a chair squeaked and the border patrol sergeant sidled up alongside me.

"Hey, Larry. How the hell are you?" he boomed out in his Texas voice. I didn't say anything, but just looked straight ahead. He was going to have his fun, and God knows he deserved it.

He continued in a silky voice, "I understand you were a special guest of honor of the Mexican government."

Now the whole place erupted in laughter, and someone put a nickel in the jukebox, playing Herb Alpert's "Tijuana Jail." I got up from my chair, turned a full 360 degrees, saluting each group as I turned, shook Sarge's hand, and sat down again. He waited for just the right moment and then asked me, "What do you think of our visitors out in the cattle truck?"

"They think," I said slowly, "they think they are in an air conditioned limousine drinking coke and beer!" Another round of applause and then I got to eat my breakfast.

17 | Killing Robertazcar

As I mentioned in a previous chapter, Nita sought me out after I was out of Agnews and expected me to be with her; all I had to do was ask and she would have gone anywhere I wanted. I had already screwed up one marriage and some potentially good relationships, as well as disrupted the lives of a number of perfectly good women—except they did not seem to have the good sense to know what a rotten choice I was for a mate. At this point in time it was a mystery to me why I did all this destructive behavior: much later I was to understand the effect of my early life and CIA influences. It was, however, even harder to understand why none these women seemed to see through me until it was much too late to undo the emotional damage.

Not being one to leave well enough alone, on roving patrol through the main North American plant, I happened to stop in at the cafeteria, and there was Roberta! I cannot say that she was a ravishing beauty, but she was sexy-looking and had a delicious sense of humor. It was lust at first look. Our first date took place the week before I was slated to go to the Salton Sea for the F-100 speed run test. Like the Irish leprechaun, when I am not near the girl that I love, I love the girl I am near. It was inevitable that I would make another meaningless conquest (Mary) during the month that I was down on the desert. When I got back, Roberta and I immediately became an item. I met her family: mother, drunken father, and overweight, thoroughly bewildered teen-age brother. I fit in well with this group of losers and even developed some fatherly feelings for the 14-year old brother.

I did not have any idea who this woman was, but I was destined to find out. It seemed that there were far more things I did not know about her than I did know; among the most important was that she had a daughter from a former marriage. The child's name was Becky, she was four years old, and she was a little doll. Somehow or other, the next thing that I knew, Roberta and I were in Tijuana getting married by a justice of the peace—my second ill-conceived trip to that Mexican oasis.

Back at the plant, things were going along routinely and smoothly, but unexpectedly Roberta became very ill. When we went to the doctor, I learned that she was four months into a failed pregnancy. At the hospital, they removed the dead fetus, cleared up her immediate problems, and she was able to go back to work. It turned out that this woman I had married made friends instantly and bedded them just as fast. The old joke applies: "My wife only screws her friends and doesn't have any enemies, except me!" Thumbnail description of Roberta … and, of course … me!

I had married my female "doppelganger," and for the first time in my life I got to see how easily someone like Roberta, or me for that matter, could screw-up. Life became a virtual hell. I found myself trying to help her dysfunctional family, trying to keep her brother out of the gangs, getting baby sitters for Becky, and generally starting to look like the rest of the "trailer trash" I lived with.

At first, it didn't affect the job, but gradually an incipient stomach ulcer—I later named it Roberta—created bouts of pain that finally sent me to the hospital. During this stay, I was in such bad mental shape that in order to get any sleep, they kept me drugged. I kept trying to get them to cut down on the drugs, but before I could complain, they dropped me into unconsciousness again, and again. During this time, Roberta visited me regularly. I thought that was a good sign until I was discharged and discovered that she had left me a note and was now living with my former, good-looking young hospital mate and had moved into his upscale, double trailer.

It was a period of time in which I was in such terrible emotional condition that I actually went to this guy's trailer and begged (literally on bended knee) for her to come back. She did and then things got really bad! Her father was admitted to the hospital for drying out, and Roberta quit (was fired?) from North American. She went to work for Martini Brothers' Landscaping, a block down the street from our trailer park. In a short time, she was bringing home x-rated material from her employer. We were having no sex at all, and then she announced that she was pregnant and was leaving, taking the car we were buying from the Martini brothers. She tried to intimate that it was our child since she was calling it Larry, but one of the brothers' names was also Larry, and

I didn't believe that she was going to be the second woman in history to have an immaculate conception.

Finally, the security chief at North American had had enough, especially since one of the lieutenants had written me up for being inattentive at a high security guard on the field. It was only two days later that I was on a bicycle patrol, winding in and out of a group of F-86s parked near the Compass Rose. By this time I was getting about three hours of sleep a night and, as I came alongside one of the F-86's on the tarmac, I seemed to believe that its left wing was missing. I drove the bike at full speed right into the trailing edge, driving my nasal bone farther into my skull. The lights of the plant had blended in with the plane's wing, making it invisible—at least that is what my pre-suicidal mind perceived. I did not try to plead this lame excuse since no one had ever seen a plane at field-test-ready condition without a left wing! Bleeding profusely, I was rushed to the hospital where I was kept for two weeks to check for any internal bleeding, brain damage, or infection.

I went back to work, but was called into the chief's office where he made it clear that I was definitely not pulling my weight and had better straighten out pretty fast. It was certainly not the high point of my life. A week later I went back to the hospital with another bleeding ulcer; when I was released, I found that my presence at North American was no longer needed. The chief had arranged my discharge under the heading of personal decision, without prejudice, although God knows he had plenty of reason for prejudice. In spite of being fired, the chief had not revoked my top security clearance and had given me a good enough recommendation that I eventually found a job at McCullough Motors—only after I spent a month or so being a apprentice sign painter.

After I had worked a few months at McCullough, I discovered that Roberta also worked there. She was attached to the cafeteria and drove a self-propelled food cart to distant parts of the plant. One day, with me driving a forklift and her on the food cart, we came across each other—as it turned out, not a good state of affairs.

When killing people is your job, as it was mine for the years I actively worked for the Company, it was never about killing. Of course, this would be a fine point for the fourteen or so people who ceased to exist because of definitive actions on my part. This is not killing or even man (or woman) slaughter. It is none of these because, while working with the Company in the furtherance of the "Mission," the "Job," the "Operation," you are only following legal orders. It calls for a special kind of compartmental-ization, or magic, to accomplish these fine distinctions. When you are blowing holes in another person's body or ripping his throat open with the simple slice of a sharp knife, any pre-consideration is neither allowed nor needed. The "innocent" guard you are creeping up on does not and, if you do your job right, will not know who you are: he is there, and so are you. You strike and you KILL him. Actually you "off him" or "eliminate the target" or "light him up" or "neutralize him" or any of a dozen other Company metaphors. This double-think is necessary since this person is the enemy. You have a license to kill, and it is your duty to do any or all of the foregoing, without any legal consequences. At least that is the theory. However the trigger of a weapon is the most unforgiving lever in the world. Once it has been pulled, there is no way to change its mind: it is done. Whatever the consequences that may follow, you are within the law of the position you hold. The worst thing that can happen is that you are killed. If that happens, the best or worst outcome is that you are going to become one of the ubiquitous stars on an otherwise blank wall at Bethesda.

Trained to kill and allowed and encouraged to do so, these skills stay with you for the rest of your life. In my case, the most deadly of these training skills has taken the better part of four decades to calm down to the point where I am not a danger to the general public or myself. There are exceptions, of course. These are points at which you find yourself ready, willing, and able to kill … read "MURDER"! There is no Company, no Uncle Sam, and, consequently, no silver or any other star. You are not legal, you are not protected, and you will not be rewarded. In the best possible case, you will be dead yourself or imprisoned for a considerable number of years.

In the wake of your disastrous action, you will, as in my case, have produced grotesque and non-erasable memories for innocent children who know their mother was suddenly destroyed. This almost happened two times in my life, and as you might by now imagine, one of these cases concerned Roberta.

Keep in mind this scenario: Roberta, four months pregnant with someone else's baby, has left the trailer, informing me over her shoulder that the car I rely on to get to work, has been signed over to her, and that she is taking it, along with Becky, to drive over to the Martini Brothers and leave me for good. I am certainly not unhappy with her going, but the car is damn well going to stay. I get to her just as she is getting into the car, pull her out, and throw her on the ground.

"You little bitch, get your whoring ass out of here and leave the car. You are this close to being dead!"

She left and walked the two blocks to her job and her new lover, Larry Martini.

That would have been the end of it, but a week later I got a letter from a lawyer ordering me to return the car. I took the keys out of the car and walked down to the Bro's shop with a gun in my pocket and murder in my eyes. When the brothers saw me, they carefully moved away from the counter but their eyes never left me. When I asked them where she was, they told me instantly that she was in the big trailer in the back. I walked straight there, opened the door, and found her sitting on a couch. We both just stared at each other. I couldn't believe she thought her married "friend"—who was screwing her instead of his wife—was going to get killed to protect her, and at that moment, I could see in her eyes that she got it.

Roberta just glared at me as I shouted at her that we were done and that she was a pitiful example of anything resembling a woman, much less a mother. I told her I just wanted her, her kids, her friends, her troubles, and her idiot family the hell out of my life. There was no fear in her eyes, just white-hot hatred, and she was daring me to pull the trigger on the revolver we both knew was in my pocket. I thought about it: amazingly, I thought! I actually considered the consequences, then turned and left. The brothers were waiting, but I just looked past them as I walked back to my trailer camp.

Back at McCullough, I was driving the heavy-duty forklift, when Roberta appeared in the self-propelled lunch cart. A thousand ideas went through my mind, none of them good. Her path was going to cross mine out here—a far removed area of the plant where there were no witnesses. I could see myself stepping on the gas, raising the forks, and pinning her into the wreckage, broken and finally out of my life … for real! She glared at me and kept on driving. I gently put on the brakes and let her pass, not three feet away.

But, I knew I still HAD to kill something. I was going to give the car back and had made preparations to buy another one. I had filled her gas tank with sugar, so in the long run it didn't make any difference, but I knew I had to kill something, even if it meant the end of my job.

I went out to the parking lot at the end of the shift, took the lug wrench out of the trunk, and proceeded to beat the already doomed car into a cracked, bent, windowless hulk: all the gear on the engine block was beaten off, the battery was cracked, and two tires were flat. I called her attorney on the phone and told him to come with a wrecker and take the car. Amazingly, while this operation took the better part of a half hour, and dozens of people had come out to their cars, nobody tried to stop me, and when I went to work the next day, nobody said a word!

18 | Dick Bell

Roberta and I were definitely and negatively apart; however we had not yet formally divorced. As my lawyer had explained to me, when Dorothy decided to file the final papers, which I had been under the delusion she already had, it would have the effect of ending my legal California marriage to Dorothy and would automatically end my illegal Mexican marriage to Roberta. As is apparent, I was an unknowing bigamist for several months. Those vows with Roberta were never worth a damn anyway.

My next job was located close to where I lived in a trailer camp on Rosecrans Avenue, in north Hawthorne. I had rented that space just after the trailer lost its brakes—fortunately, outside of a trailer park.

At Ajax Sign Company, I was interviewed by the boss, Mervin Thrash, a round, surly-looking, gruff piece of work who seemed to be happiest when he was chewing out someone. I was surprised to find that the complete crew consisted of two people: a union journeyman, Dick Bell and a master sign painter, Jimmy Norton. Norton was a sixty-something, occasional drunk, who could draw a surgically perfect line only when he was half-potted. I had the feeling that this new job was not likely to improve my ulcer.

Being a drunk was hardly unusual among master sign-painters. By way of explanation for this ongoing state, the sign-painters swore that the liquor was necessary to counteract the effects of the deadly paint fumes! In the old days, they would carry their tools with them and go from town to town doing their sign painting, tinkering work (literally working with metal and solder), and whatever hole-digging, electrical rigging, or half a dozen other trades that were needed. These, and many more, were the jobs that any man could do who claimed to be or actually was a journeyman or master craftsman. At this time, they had added to their multiple accomplishments: forming and blowing glass tubing and adding the illuminating "noble" gases such as neon and argon. In a field that sign-painters are masters of dozens of different spheres, I honor every one of these stalwart men. The same is not true for all of their employers, and Mervin Thrash was to be one I learned to hate. An unlikely thing about Ajax Sign Company was that Thrash had hired a twenty year old Black man as a journeyman sign-painter. I had no idea how rare a creature he was; as he explained to me much later, he was the ONLY Black sign-painter in an all-White union in the entire Los Angeles area. I shook hands when I met him and noted the surprise on his face. I have never had time for all that "nigger, wop, chink, spick" BS, in spite of the attempted training by my adopted family and the generally bleached population of Vancouver, Washington.

I considered myself some kind of real man, and so I climbed into the powerful Mack utility truck, with its oversized bed and built-in small derrick, without too much concern. With Dick Bell at the wheel, we drove silently to my first job; I was mentally bulking my muscles. As a sign-painter "apprentice," I was to learn all about digging holes since there always were holes to be dug. There were little ones and big ones, as well as ridiculously huge ones to support those 20 by 30 foot sign boards, as much as 20 feet off the ground.

With enough lumber on the truck to build a house and some serious 4 by 4 by 8 foot long, creosoted posts, I was anxious to arrive at the site. I figured additional crew would join us there. But, when we arrived at the empty lot that was our destination, I found that the crew was already there: we were it … Dick and I.

With what passed for a matter-of-fact look and with just the trace of a derisive smile, Dick asked me, "You were a warehouseman on a previous job?"

"Yes," I answered succinctly and with some pride.

"OK, let's get on with it. Dig a post hole wide enough for a 4 by 4, right here," he said, pointing to a particular spot and handing me a really serious looking 5 foot wrecking bar—it had enough heft that I figured it could remove a man's head in one swipe.

"OK," I said nonchalantly, as I picked up the heavy-duty wrecking bar and poised myself to drive it a foot or so into the ground. I grasped at about the middle of its length and brought it down with all my strength. Severe shock went through my body as the hardened steel bar rang church bell-like, lazily sending up a couple of atoms of chips from the surface of the cement-like ground. When both the steel bar and I had stopped ringing, I looked up in disbelief at the now definitely smiling Dick Bell. Shaken, I asked pitifully, "How many holes?"

"Only six," he answered, obviously imagining a scenario in which I quickly left the area by a cab or bus.

I made more pitiful attempts to seriously challenge the surface: no joy! After about ten minutes, a chuckling Dick Bell walked over to the truck, opened a cavity in its side, and brought forth a very large posthole auger. He brought it over to where I had made my ridiculously tiny hole in the dirt, and the two of us rigged a tripod, commencing with some really serious drilling.

"Works a little better wouldn't you say?"

"Just a little," I answered, smiling in spite of myself. "Just a little."

It was 6:30 in the morning when we had arrived, and by 6:00 that evening, we had planted the six posts 4 feet deep in what turned out to be the hardest ground I had ever encountered in my entire life. I was sunburned and ached from head to foot, but I was, by God, a genuine "Sign-Painter's Helper"!

We went back to the shop, closed the gate, and I drove home, where I fell into bed and did not rise until 5:00 the following morning.

At about 6:00, I greeted Dick, we drove back to the site and finished the sign deck and backboard, and then took another trip back to the shop where we loaded the 4 by 6 foot pieces of tin plate, which had previously been framed, primed, shellacked, and painted. We finished the job, again by 6:00 that night. When we got in an hour later, the boss was waiting for us impatiently and, after checking the empty truck, he glared first at Dick and then at me. I was expecting a "well done," but what we got was, "What the hell took you so long?"

As the stout little man turned to leave, Dick winked at me and gave me a high five.

When the three of us were in the shop, we were working on much smaller signs; they were the bread and butter of the trade. Often we would be doing repaints: signs that already had their wooden frames with the tin plates, but were variously weather-faded. It was explained to me that they would have to be lightly sanded, shellacked, and then let dry before Jimmy Norton would be able to paint on them. This was because the old paint was capable of "bleeding through" the new painting, and red was an especially fugitive color that would always leak through, without proper preparation. Cheap workshops would occasionally bid low for a job and not do the extra step of shellacking. The results were always a bleeding through, ruining the sign at some time after it had been sold.

Except for our menacing employer, I enjoyed the job, although I was not the best worker to come down the pike. There is a lot that goes on in a sign shop, and Jimmy, even though he didn't particularly care for me—or anyone else if it came to that—would give me occasional lessons in the trade. On one day when he had a large Masonite board he had sprayed with a thick red paint, he called me in to watch him do some of his beautiful free hand art and lettering. He dipped his brush in some stinky material that was kind of grey in color and drew the letters and design without a sign of the tremor that usually was evident when he was not actually working on a sign. It was a slow day, and since the boss was gone, I got to watch as he let the painting dry. Then I went back to my work on a couple of frames.

When he called me in again, to my surprise, he had sprayed the whole sign white. The white had completely covered the painting I had just seen him do. Confused, I just looked at him. He gave me one of his infrequent smiles, smoked a cigarette, waited a few more minutes, then got a hose, put the sign on an easel, and sprayed water over the whole thing. The stinky stuff with which he had painted the sign slid off cleanly, leaving perfect red lettering and art copy, as he had first drawn it. I was fascinated with the "paint" that had washed off. Norton smiled and explained that it was guano (bat poop) that was universally the perfect consistency for oil painting and will resist any other oil-based paint. But as soon as water hits it, it washes off cleanly and leaves nothing but the crisp base color.

I've often wondered who and why somebody figured out this amazing process, unintuitive as it is. Think about it!

As the days turned into weeks, Dick and I grew closer. He had a wicked sense of humor and appreciated me thoroughly. The only problem we seemed to have was when he told me that he was a practicing Catholic, at which point I asked him what the hell the Catholic Church had ever done for him. He smiled, but told me that it really didn't matter what church you went to, as long as you were able to have your own personal connection to the Lord; he had a very definite moral compass. I learned that he was very married; he was such a champion of marriage. He was constantly trying to get me to go back to Roberta: that was so not going to happen! Still, on most things we agreed, and we worked hand-in-glove on every project.

I have had a history of constantly getting myself into trouble backing the "novel" idea that all men are created equal. I realized that this was not universally accepted, and I had been in a fight or two with various "red necks": loud words mostly but on one occasion a knock down dragged-out battle. But even though Dick was a good-looking, beautifully muscled specimen of manhood, most of the people we ran into did not see past the coal-black color of his skin. Time and again, as we pulled up to a job, the owner or manager would come out and walk up to me to discuss the job. I took inordinate pleasure in telling them I was only the helper; Dick was the journeyman. I made a point of emphasizing the man in journeyman. What usually followed was a confused pause in the conversation, as I could see the white customer changing mental gears and then finally addressing Dick directly.

In a short time, it became clearer just how tough the work environment was for a black man in the L.A. area. One day the boss called us into the office and gave us a job request in the Bellflower area. Mervin Thrash knew better than to send us on that job, since the various cities and municipalities all had contracts with their local, city, and township unions; there were harsh legal consequences for straying from your own area. But Mervin stared at us, daring us to say anything. We didn't, but Dick looked unusually nervous. We drove into Bellflower and came upon a full block covered by a car dealership. I was driving because Dick was insistent that I drive even though he knew the area better; he didn't want to be seen driving a company truck in Bellflower. As we approached the Buick dealership's entrance to its used car lot, I asked where I should park.

Dick spoke like a man with a heavy rope already around his neck. "Keep driving!"

We were about in the middle of the complex, when I asked again where we were going. Dick answered in that same choked voice, "Keep driving!"

We were headed towards the middle of the service area, and I could see a road leading back onto the highway, perpendicular to the one we had entered. Dick silently pointed towards that open gate and again said quietly, but firmly, "Keep Driving!"

Now, I could see why. Out of the repair garage and out of the show-room, a dozen men were running fast towards our moving truck. The ones from the showroom, mostly in suits, were glaring, but more importantly, the crew from the repair garage were all armed with everything from wrenches to hammers to baseball bats. There was just a second when I allowed myself to imagine they were going to invite us to a ball game, but with more speed than usual, I just kept driving, wrenching a wicked square corner onto the highway. I kept on going.

After a few minutes, when no one seemed to be following us, I looked over at Dick, slowed to a legal speed, and said, "I have the feeling that was not a legitimate job!"

Dick smiled grimly, "You think?"

After that near catastrophe, which Thrash seemed to take in remark-ably good humor, we were called to repaint a sign on the sloped roof of the Christian School and Bookshop Center in Hawthorne. We were making measurements from the top of our medium ladder, when a lovely middle-aged lady came from the store and, ignoring Dick, asked me if I could have the "boy" move the truck a little forward because the manager was coming in with a life-sized store dummy. I sweetly went through the process of explaining that I would ask the boss. I did so, and Dick smilingly gestured me to do it.

The lady, appearing terminally confused, went back into the store as a Chevy station wagon pulled in behind the truck. A nicely dressed businessman got out of the station wagon and, again talking only to me, introduced himself as Reverend Lindsey. He took a long time looking at Dick, and I could feel the hair on the back of my neck bristling. The reverend, old enough to know better, got a weird smile on his face, as he opened the station wagon's back gate and turned to me. And then instead, with look of child-like glee, addressed Dick.

"Boy! Do you know what I've got in here?" as he pointed to the large crate resting in the back of the wagon.

I thought, "No, no, that nice looking, reasonably intelligent, Christian is not going to say what I think he is … no, he just can't."

But, sure as shit, he did!

"Well, boy, I've got a body in here!"

I was mad, crushed, unbelieving, and nonplussed.

Dick was just smiling, making those teeth as bright and shiny as he could. For just a second, he opened his eyes wider, but then relaxed and, coldly but politely, answered, "Well, sir, that really doesn't bother me too much; you see I worked my way through college as part time helper in a mortuary."

A half hour later, I was still fuming, while Dick was making it worse by putting on his idiotic black "Step-n-fetchit" pose and saying, "Why sho nuff, masta suh, I gwanna go on don and fetch da parsnips don at de shed, masta, suh! I sho don wanna be lookin round no ded folks!"

I laughed in spite of myself and then, thinking that this was a good time for it, asked him how in the hell he had got this obviously dangerous job in the first place—with this kind of bullshit being pretty regular. Dick got very serious and answered thoughtfully, saying that Mervin Thrash was a member of the Hawthorne Better Business Bureau, an incumbent for local office, and who projected a sympathetic attitude about minorities and the down-trodden. This was why he had hired Dick. It hadn't mattered to Dick that he was required to work hours longer than anyone else for the same money and, while employed by Thrash, would never be given the position of master sign painter. However, feeling grateful, Dick had naively asked his employer to his home for dinner. Dick said he would never forget the look on the man's face. It was clear that he was "busy" that night, and that he would always be "busy," and the whole wretched situation had just hung there like a bad smell.

Thrash couldn't fire him; it wouldn't look good. But he also discovered the white sign painter's unions could still black-ball him from many jobs as punishment for hiring a "nigger." Thus, ever since that uncomfortable dinner invitation, Thrash had loaded Dick up with nasty jobs and additional long hours, as well as projecting a growing antagonism. Dick was costing him money from lost jobs—Thrash wanted to get rid of Dick, but not tarnish his liberal reputation. Now it made sense to me: those pointless and dangerous out-of-territory jobs, where we obviously could get seriously hurt.

But, another illegal job Thrash sent us on, bit him instead of just us. It was to be a large sign on an undeveloped corner lot in Redondo Beach: a 10 by 20 footer, with a 4-foot rise. The third day on the job, we spotted a Redondo policeman who slowly drove by and took a good look at our truck, then passed on. He stayed away until the exact moment when we had finished the job and were loading our tools; then the police officer stopped, got out of his car, and came over to us with a citation book in hand.

Dick said, under his breath, "Don't take this opportunity to be my helper or we'll both be in the slammer. You're the boss."

"Got it," I said, as I walked over to meet the officer.

"You and your boy have a city license for this sign?"

He obviously knew we didn't. He looked at me, then at Dick, then back at me, and said, "Well, these little mistakes in location will happen. My brother owns a sign company, so how about I just put his name as the contracting company, and you and your boy drive off. Please be sure to tell Mr. Thrash that it was nice not doing business with him. Next time, though, I might not be nearly so generous. Now the two of you scoot, and I would recommend that your boy not be anywhere near here when I double back in a half hour."

We didn't waste any time in following his suggestion, and Dick looked happier than I had seen him in weeks. He did, however, pretend to be terribly concerned that Thrash had put in $300 on that job and had only come away with a warning ticket to show for it. Dick and I kept a low profile for the next few days.

Thrash still wasn't through, and I realized that he hated me as much for my obvious friendship with Dick, as anything else, and so, once again we were given a job that, although in our territory, was nearly impossible. How little he thought of either of us was made clear about a week later. The general sheets on which we did most of our sign work were 16 gauge green-coated plates set on their long edges on a loading platform that was just the right height to be able transfer them, one by one, directly to the truck bed when parked alongside. There was only about a foot of clearance between truck and dock. Dick and I were sorting through about thirty of these 4-foot by 6-foot razor sharp-edged sheets weighing nearly 25 pounds apiece. Our process for doing the sorting was not the smartest thing that either of us had done. We separated out about half of the 30 sheets by leaning them toward our bodies, holding them with only the pressure of our knees. We must have realized simultaneously that our stack was unstable, but had no time to signal the other to step out of the way, and neither of us was willing to jump away and let the other take the full weight. There was a millisecond in which the weight of the fifteen slanting sheets surpassed the weight of our two bodies: our stack launched us into space.

I regained consciousness under the truck, shook my head, and counted to make sure all my body parts were still there. I didn't seem to be surprised to be under the truck, though I couldn't remember why I was there. I started wiggling my way out. From there, breathing deeply, I was able to see Dick near the front of the truck, scrabbling along on the ground, trying to get up on his knees and then sinking down again. I thought, "I'll be damned. I didn't know Dick had epilepsy."

We were the only ones on duty at the time: old Jimmy was on an outside repainting job, and the boss was at a meeting. As we finally got our wind back, we helped each other stagger to the loading dock and, one by one, we replaced the fallen sheets; Thrash returned just about then. He looked at the two of us and realized that some sort of accident had taken place: We were bruised and dirty, bleeding from scratches, and more than slightly incoherent. Neither of us was making too much sense, but he finally figured out what had happened. One of the things that he had was accident insurance. However, he really didn't want to file an insurance claim or have us medically examined, so he gave the two of us the day off, and that was that.

The next challenging job happened shortly thereafter.

A company in Hawthorne was changing its name from the impossible moniker of "The National Cash Register Company" to a simpler NCR. The sign had 36 individual letters including spaces. The sign lettering was constructed of 6 inch high individual 16-gauge metal capital letters, screwed into a long 16-gauge steel base (actually a trough), 4 inches high, 2 inches deep, and 14 feet long. The whole sign had been assembled to be installed in a cement and brick niche just made for it.

The problem in removing the sign was that it was twelve feet up, and the gauge of the lettering was just heavy enough to keep the individual letters connected to the base. Their form would maintain as long as they were without any strain and as long as no attempt was made to pull them away from the long, thin base that would have no stability once it was removed from the niche to which it was attached. Once the letters were installed, they were never meant to be taken down in one piece, but that was what Thrash insisted he wanted. I had never seen Dick confused before, but it was clear that there was no way our truck crane—certainly capable of handling the weight—could possibly get the letters and base down without them turning into a roller-coaster of bending, mangled metal. The whole ménage would have been a mass of wet spaghetti.

Dick realized that our friendship was likely to cost him his job, and I decided at the same time that I had had all the shit from this little Hitler that I was going to take. I asked Dick to drive us to a coffee shop, and he looked at me like I was crazy. "Hey man," I said, "Trust me, I think I know exactly how to handle this job."

Dick looked at me for a long time and then waived me to the truck, and we went for coffee. I asked Dick how much he imagined each of the letters weighed; he said about a half a pound. With paper and pencil, I took this figure and multiplied it by the number of letters and asked what the size of the screws were, since we had both seen them clearly.

"They are ¼-inch by ¾-inch, self-tapping metal screws," Dick answered.

I did some figuring and noted that the entire sign weighed in at about 125 pounds, letters and trough.

Dick said, hopelessly, "It's going to be like trying to keep a 14 foot worm straight, while moving it to the truck."

"OK, listen to this. The whole shebang weighs 125 pounds, and there are 26 letters. If you divide 26 letters into 125 pounds, you get less than 5 pounds per letter. I tested the amount of strain to pull one of the letters off its position on the base, and each letter would take over 40 pounds of pull to rip it loose. Now some of the letters have open tops, like the I, Y, and L. On all the rest of them, we can get a light rope through the top loops; the base's entire weight is less than 20 pounds per loop."

Dick still looked dubious, but I continued, "All we have to do is get the crane to put a couple of 2 by 4's horizontally over the top of the sign and loop the length of rope—of which we have plenty—around the 2 by 4's and around each of the letters until we reach the end. We will then unscrew the bolts holding the sign in place and haul the whole damn thing down in one try, without bending or tearing off a single letter; the base will come along for the ride!"

Our impossible job completed, we drove back to the shop less than an hour later. The complete sign, with 2 by 4s and ropes attached was sitting on the truck; we arrived feeling victorious! As we drove into the yard, "little Hitler" was waiting to meet us. Thrash must have imagined one or the other of us in a sling hauled to the top of the sign—presumably me—while the other guided the arm and the truck down the line of letters, unscrewing them one by one. If it didn't kill one of us, the job would have taken hours. My fatal mistake was giving away the secret by leaving the ropes in place.

Dick and I got out of the truck, and Thrash came over and looked at the complete sign. He glared at the two of us and asked, "Who the hell is responsible for this shit?"

I saw that Dick was set to say something argumentative, but I beat him to it. "I did," I said.

"Who the hell told you to do that?" he sneered.

"Nobody, it just did the job."

"Who told you were supposed to make any decisions around here?"

"Hey, MAN! Every once in a while I can have a good idea. Have you ever had a good idea or made a mistake?"

"Yeah," he growled, "I hired you!"

"Well that was cute, but I'll tell you what. I have better idea: How about you take this job and shove it up your ass. I quit." I grabbed my gear and left.

I don't know how much longer Dick lasted at that shop, probably not long. But unfortunately I lost track of him as my life continued to rocket along.

I took on one more sign job before I realized I had other things I needed to do. This one was a real sign company, with six times the working space, good working conditions, and a staff of sixteen. They routinely did signs that Thrash never could have handled. They had a full time glass blower, three service trucks, and plenty of work. When I applied, the boss asked me where I had worked before. When I told him with Mervin Thrash, my new boss laughed while saying, "Well then, you sure as hell know how to work! You're hired."

The boss and his art director did their own designing, while all I had to do was drive a truck to potential customers, bringing shop estimates, and the like. My second week there, I was walking by the office and saw the drawings for an immense, very complicated sign. It was for a hardware store front.

This sign was to be 20 feet long and 10 feet high, designed to fit perfectly into a recessed space, 6 inches deep. It was to be full of neon flashing animation and all manner of mechanical movement with complex wiring. Ordinarily the base—heavy gauge, heavy-duty sheet-metal—is drawn in architecturally flat drawings so that all of the dimensions can be explicitly measured and drawn to scale. In an additional drawing, three scale flat views may then be projected and sketched into one that looks more like a realistic three-quarter camera view of the completed sign, with all the whistles and bells. The prospective will be altered in that view, so naturally it will look larger at one end than it does at the other. Specific dimensions should never be included in this latter drawing. The three-quarter view, while giving an impression of the completed sign, may allow errors if measured dimensions are entered: whereby hangs a tale!

As I was waiting in the office for assignments, I was scrutinizing this large three-quarter view drawing. I saw that major dimensions had been drawn in on the larger side of the drawing, which could result in variations—mistakes—that are easy to make but hard to see. This can render the drawing less accurate; measurement accuracy is what the flat drawings are for. On the three-quarter drawing, I noted that there was a disparity in the overall height written on the larger side on offset angles showing from there to the smaller side. Adding up the figures as written would make the sign 20 feet, 2 ½ inches high, more than it should be. The sign was supposed to fit into a niche in the wall with proper clearances, much like the one we had dismantled at National Cash Register, but there the similarity ended. Not using the customer signed-off engineering drawings, but using the three-quarter view instead was a rookie mistake.

About this time, the boss came in and informed me that my job was carrying materials from one place to another; he didn't appreciate me looking at things that were none of my business. If it hadn't been for Thrash, I would have argued with him and showed him where the overall height of the sign was in jeopardy. Instead, I apologized and left.

That sign kept the whole staff busy and had been the reason that extra help, including me, had been hired. The completed sign was finally done, down to the last relay and switch boxes, paint, animation, and a couple of hundred feet of neon tubing. I waited for the two big aerial trucks with their gantries to leave for the site. The third truck was loaded with the sign, and everyone but me was ready for the installation: I didn't go. It took no imagination at all, though I wasn't within ten miles of the place, to visualize that magnificent piece of work hooked to the gantries and lifted slowly into place. Then and only then, with a blinding flash of shocked realization, would everyone involved know that that 20 foot, 2 1/2 inch high sign was not going to fit into that 20 foot space.

I was there when the whole parade made its defeated way back—with the sign. No funeral parade has ever had a group of people more crestfallen and embarrassed. I could almost see the lawyers trying to figure out whom they were going to hang first. When the boss came back, red-faced and apoplectic, the first thing he did was go into the office and ripped the three-quarter drawing into a thousand pieces. He caught me looking at him, and I decided, without any prompting, that I had spent my last days working for him, or for any other sign company.

After my short stints as an apprentice sign painter—I think this latest job lasted all of one or two months—I got a job at McCullough Motors as a forklift driver, to give me some time to figure out what I was going to do next. While Dick Bell, as well as the crew at McCullough's shipping department, brought me a little lightness and humor, I was pretty depressed with my life in general and myself in particular. As it turned out, Dorothy was to decide what would happen to me and where I would end up.

19 | Ending Two Marriages

Dorothy and I had started divorce proceedings several years earlier, and all that was necessary was for her to sign the final papers; I assumed she had. But then, after what seemed a long time later, I received a letter asking me for alimony. In this letter she informed me that we were still legally married in the State of California, which made my Mexican marriage to Roberta a significant problem. I remember going to work—I was at McCullough Motors at that time—and telling the other guys about my ongoing troubles, and the fact that I was now a bona fide bigamist.

One of the clowns I worked with asked me if I had an attorney. I said, "Of course, I had to!"

I wondered why everyone was looking at me so snidely when he asked me the next "question?"

"And, what is her name?"

Everyone, including me, broke up.

It was not nearly so funny when two detectives arrived at work and put me under arrest for "failure to provide." Much to my surprise, the guys at work got together and raised my bail, and I made arrangements to go to San Francisco to answer the charges. I had spent only one night in the Los Angeles jail, but after getting bail, I took the train to San Francisco where two detectives—playing good cop/bad cop—almost got me to take a swing at them when they accused me of not having a bail bond. I am lousy at keeping track of papers, but that day I managed to hang on to two things: my bail bond receipt and, more importantly, my temper!

When I got to the hearing, I discovered that Dorothy had dropped the charges. There was certainly no reason for her to do so, but it became evident that, even after all that had happened, she still wasn't willing to let go. We ended up in her bed, but for once she didn't let me complete. The old joke was that every time I put my pants on the bedpost, she

251

became pregnant. It was no joke to me. However, that was her last hur-rah. I informed her that the child support I was going to give her went to pay the bail when she had me arrested, and that was the last she was going to get from me.

I went back to L.A. and paid off the money the McCullough gang had put together. It seemed clear to me that it was time to move on, and so I did: I moved to Portland Oregon. San Francisco and Dorothy were no longer a choice. An uncle of my original family had died and left several thousand dollars to my half-sister, Anna Mae, and me, conditional upon my real mother being legally dead. I had identified her belongings in a suitcase that had accompanied a woman found dead in the Woman's Park in downtown Portland several years earlier, but the seven years required for her to be declared legally dead had not yet passed. I needed the money, so I got an attorney, but it was still several years until I had the money in my pocket. The court dealings had all been in Portland, so I just stayed there and started working at being an artist.

I approached this job as I did most, with full attention and many opportunities, but I needed a full time job and a place to live. The place I found to live was off NW 23rd Street in Portland and the hospital I would later sign on as an orderly—after some devastating, but educational experiences in the fields of art and design—was only three blocks away, and so I found my work, my living, my drinking, my friends, and even my new wife, all within a few blocks of one another.

20 | The Lincoln Theatre

I didn't start working at the hospital or painting wall murals right after I got to Portland. Instead I applied for work by answering an ad as a graphics designer. The business was located in an old part of Portland near what is now the City Cultural Center. I met with the owner, Fred Shoemacher, who worked out of the old Lincoln Theatre running an outfit called Allied Productions.

In the old days, the Lincoln Theatre had been a very successful opera house. The building had also featured several attached shops, including a bakery and a meat market. It was all one huge complex where, later, the floats for the famous Portland Rose Parade were stored. Surprisingly, it occurred to me that the bakery portion was, in 1929 or so, where the Italian ladies kept me from starving.

Now, the main part of the theatre, with all its seats and flooring ripped down to the concrete base, was vast and empty. However, from the proscenium to the back of the large theater building, all of the stage—which included lines, controls, electrical banks, curtains, and fife rails—was as completely equipped as it was when it first opened as a very modern, fully functioning theatrical unit. There was even a set of right and left audience boxes still located just to the sides of what had been the orchestra pit.

Until I was hired, the entire office staff was Fred Shoemacher and a secretary, both of whom worked in the front offices that were still heated and generally in the same state they had been when it was an operating theatre. Another larger office had tables, bins, and drawers for show railings, stanchions, and electrical boxes used in hotel and business shows, and also 4 foot tubes containing building floor plans of the 10th floor of Meier and Franks department store where the business shows were held.

253

This room held the stock used by Allied Productions for booth and display work, and was where a third employee, a retired certified stagehand, hung out. He was yet another Sarge in my life. I had plenty of time to figure out that I was the new recruit in this army.

I was young and not too smart: to the interview, as a proof of what I could do, I had brought a twelve-inch, hip-moving model of "Elvis" holding a guitar and standing in front of a microphone. The body moved sinuously and the tears would roll down Elvis' cheeks when a button was pushed in the support base. After I was hired, Elvis resided in one of the two windows flanking the front door. These windows had held pictures of up-coming theatrical productions but were now used for advertising the services provided.

My lack of sophistication became apparent when wages were discussed. With my approval—I am ashamed to say—I agreed to a two-tiered pay arrangement: half the designer's pay when I "helped" Sarge in the main theatre, and a higher scale only when working on official "art projects." It did not take too long for me to realize that I was in fact a cheap flunky for Sarge, and that the opportunity to do anything creative was going to happen damn seldom. When working as official lackey, I would be doing menial and mostly make-work for Sarge. He hated me and went out of his way to show that he was the man with multiple years in stagecraft. I was less than nothing. I would have quit after a month but then I found out why I was really there.

When a big show came to Portland, we would need all bodies available as well as some of Sarge's International Theatrical Stage Employee (IATSE) Union cronies to fill in because we supplied curtains, booths, electrical sub-circuits, and traveling displays for the various trade shows. The IATSE had a very powerful union with very rigid protection for its members; therefore, I got all the shitty jobs. But, I was learning the trade, and as long as I could see that I was continuing to learn, it was worth it. I put up with the cold in the main theatre where we would often open the outside doors in the winter to let the "heat" in. God, that concrete was cold!

I learned that during the biggest local show, which was the Portland Rose Festival Parade, Shoemacher had the contract for dozens of the good-sized pull trailers that formed the foundation for many of the floats; at least eight of the floats would be on the main theatre floor at any one time. Dozens of artists would be working on the mechanics, wire frames, and structural components, while many variously aged volunteers placed the flowers that were featured on the floats. Besides all the activity and the people, I loved working these shows because heavy-duty gas heaters warmed-up the place! I liked to believe this was to keep the flowers from freezing.

Sarge managed to make a fool of me at least three times a day, and our hatred grew. I hadn't realized that Fred was complicit in this as well. Fred loathed real talent and knew that I had some. He also knew that his wife had more in her little finger than he had in his whole body. She owned and taught in a very successful dance studio and had more money accidentally than Fred made on purpose. (Many years later, wife Sherry took ballet lessons from Mrs. Shoemacher at Portland State University.)

I had just about given up on Fred when he came out to the cold auditorium and invited me to his office. He poured me some coffee and said that I was going to start receiving my top pay; he had, at last, a job that called for my talents; my resume indicated—tweaking the truth a lot—that I had worked on shows before and had had an operating studio of my own. We went out to a truck, and Fred and Sarge, while smiling conspiratorially, packed plants, pots, screens, holders, and fishnets onto the truck. I should have been suspicious when I noted that Sarge was doing the heavy lifting and Fred was emphasizing, repeatedly, that this was going to be my big chance.

When we reached our destination, the three of us quickly unloaded all the supplies and equipment. Only after our arrival at the site was I told that the large hall was to be decorated in an underwater scheme. Before I had a chance to organize my thoughts, Fred made a series of what I could only consider brilliant suggestions as to the location and the arrangement of the stuff we had brought. He would stop, look at me seriously, and ask, "What do you think, would this look good here … and then maybe we could put this there, and maybe that would work … what do you think, Larry?"

In every case I had to agree that what Fred suggested was brilliant. It became apparent that I was present only to observe how clever he was. If there was any doubt about my conclusion, the dopey smile on Sarge's face erased any consideration to the contrary. After Fred had made five or six masterful decisions, I stepped back and just did as I was told, but

I turned off completely and did not give any sign that I was disturbed in the slightest. I complimented the two of them and opined that wasn't it wonderful that there was not a single thing on the truck that had not been used in the display, and "my, how wonderfully fast it had all gone together!"

The trip back to the shop was very quiet, and the two of them looked like a bad kid had spoiled their birthday party. Up until this time, I thought Sarge was my problem, but at this point, I started working on the time and the place to get even with Fred Shoemacher.

Several days went by, and Sarge became more and more surly, until finally, one day he just couldn't take it anymore. He growled at me, "Wahl, don't you even realize that Fred and I made a fool out of you? We got together and spent several days putting that whole show thing together just to watch you freak out."

"Yeah, Sarge," I answered lazily, "I realized. Didn't work too well did it? But if you personally like to waste time and money, it's all right with me."

I knew that he would not tell Fred, fearing that he, Sarge, would get the blame for their performance not having the required effect. I also realized that I was not going to stay there for much longer. But before I was able to make my escape, we got a trade show featuring male models on a catwalk that called for a light operator to go to an older downtown hotel and operate a small Klieg light. I would be required to operate a following spot (the light moves with the model) for the Men's International Clothing Buyers' Show. Spotting was generally a tedious and thankless stage job, but there were no union people available; Fred had to give me the higher salary rate to work the union show. I am sure that he was glad to get me out of his sight for a while, and the sentiment was heartily returned.

I had been running the spot for about twenty minutes in one of several test performances using the runway when there was a brouhaha and I was ordered to "kill the light." The commotion occurred because the small but powerful Klieg light was shining through the well-built young men's clothing to their underwear, showing one of the models clearly wearing only a jock strap. This would have been a disaster as the unexpected transparency would have rendered the expensive and supposedly highlighted clothes invisible! An incident like this would make an audience laugh, no matter how hard they might try not to; it would destroy whatever mood was being attempted. The unusual spot lighting conditions would ensure the advertising of x-rated underwear instead of the high priced duds they wanted their worldwide buyers to concentrate on.

During the two-day job I was to stand by until needed, so after turning off the light, I just curled up in my little booth and took a nap. After catching some Z's, I grew bored. I decided to mill around with the show people and actually volunteered to do some work. There was a large local crew, as well as the advertiser's own; there was no way of knowing I was not one of their hires. It was clear that they were not going to use the light, so when not helping someone, I just sat there and watched the whole show, as well as the company's discussions of how good a show it would have been. In the process I was able to watch all the sales' routines and absorbed both printed and spoken copy that was used in the process of running an international company program, preparing its domestic as well as overseas agencies for a major Spring clothing presentation. The usually professional and eloquent speaker completely lost his temper the next afternoon when the show ended. Seeing how thoughtless some of the participants were because many had left the very expensive brochures and sales materials on the tables before going back to their states and countries.

After the production closed, packed up, and left the hotel, I unplugged the light, wrote a note saying the Klieg light was Allied Productions equipment to be picked up the following day, and left it there for Sarge. Driving to pick up the equipment on the next morning, Fred and Sarge would suppose I had been working the light almost two full days. I—for some strange reason— had not called the office to tell them I was available almost from the beginning of the first day, but instead I stayed warm and comfortable for the full day and a half. I left the show, but only after eating a ton of the project crew's lunches, smiling, and conversing knowingly—a bona fide stage hand. When everyone else had gone, I contentedly made my way home. I couldn't get the warm smile off my face: I had gotten even and was ready to quit!

But again, Allied got busy and I stayed on, only now I insisted on always being paid my top salary—with the implied threat that otherwise

I would contact the union. I got it, but was still thinking about quitting when a most amazing thing happened. Fred again called me to his office, only this time a penitent-appearing but sullen Sarge was there. Also there was a tall well-dressed man in his 50s who was in the act of signing a contract for a job I assumed to be another local show. I was never more wrong. As I sat listening, they were finalizing the contract arrangements for a third party's salary and working conditions. I could only imagine that I was going to be the fool once more. Instead, bewilderingly, Fred introduced me as the company Art Director ... Art Director?! He told me that I would be assisting the professional scenic designer who would be painting all of the sets, flats, and incidental art for a new stage production of "Most Happy Fellow." How Allied Productions had got this contract I could not begin to understand.

I kept waiting for the guaranteed, nasty punch line, but it never came. The following day, I was again called into the office and introduced to a small, wiry man in his late sixties or early seventies, clad in bib overalls. He shook my hand and looked me over carefully. After what seemed like way too many minutes of observation, he apparently made a decision and gestured me to follow him to the bowels of the theatre.

The first thing he did, with me in tow, was walk up on the stage and examine all of the fife rails, still loaded with a multitude of lines leading up to the overhead catwalks. I had never looked at them, possibly because I thought nobody was ever going to use them again. On the three catwalks, fifty feet above the stage, were various spools, pipe brackets, pulleys, and sand bags. There were also batteries of spot, flood, and variously colored gelatin lights, still fully wired and cabled across and down stage-right and into a large, electrical board near the controls for raising and lowering the curtains.

The Lincoln Theatre had suddenly become a living actuality. It was clear that there had been, in some long time past, actual professional shows working on this stage. I realized that, without this opportunity, I easily could have left the job without ever being aware of anything that was not in the auditorium proper. Sarge brought in a desk and two chairs; this was one of the few times he came within conversational distance of the old man.

Samuel was an accomplished artist, whose real name I am ashamed to admit I have forgotten. For purposes of this narrative, I will call him Samuel Mortenson. Mr. Mortenson immediately sat down in a chair in front of the desk and started to fill several pages of legal-sized paper with lists of materials. He continued his task working with only a fiercely bright stage light. After beckoning me to sit on the other chair close to him, he started talking to me. I was petrified, totally in awe of him! Something was really going to happen, and I had not a clue how I was qualified to help. Mr. Mortenson told me that Fred had informed him that I was well qualified to help; this must have been more a prayer than a definite statement. I just concentrated on the wonderful fact that Sarge didn't seem inclined, or better yet, permitted to come near the old man … and I was.

Mr. Mortenson soon told me to address him as Sam instead. He informed me then, that he was going to need the materials for a palette; I knew what a palette was, didn't I?! He said that Fred had told him I had sold many paintings in the Portland area, something I had no idea that Fred believed even though that misconstrued information was in my padded resume. Now, when I'm ready to fall on my ass, Fred believes me!!

A palette to me would be a kidney-shaped, tablet-sized, thin, flat piece of wood or plastic, with a hole in it to accommodate an artist's thumb. This would allow him to set up his paints on the palette, held in his non-painting hand, where paint from tubes would be mixed in small dabs. When I answered Sam's question about palettes with this description, it seemed to me that I saw a rueful smile play over his craggy face. He turned back towards the sheets he was working on. After a while, he ripped off and handed me a three-page list of materials for *his* palette.

The largest painting I had done to that time was 14 by 16 inches! My mind numbed, as I read the following partial list:

1. Palette: Order four 4 by 8-foot sheets of exterior grade, ¾-inch plywood.

2. Two dozen 12-inch aluminum pie plates, and a dozen oblong 4 by 6 inch baking trays.

3. A heavy-duty saber saw.

4. Sixty pounds of flaked glue.

5. Thirty 1-quart cans of a complete assortment of dry paint pigments.

6. Assorted house painter's brushes, the smallest were to be several dozen 2-inch sash brushes with a half dozen 14-inch "mop" brushes.

7. A dozen 10 quart plastic buckets, as well as two 10-gallon mixing buckets.

8. A rag service.

9. A 40 foot by 5 foot wide trestle bridge, capable of being "flown."

10. A portable 6 ton hoist, and

11. Twelve pounds of painter's "blue snap chalk" along with 100 yards of high-test twine. This was augmented by dozens of auxiliary tools and objects.

I immediately took the list to Fred, who pulled several sheets out of a drawer and gave me a block of blank purchase orders printed with the company logo. As I remained standing there, and seeing that I was just standing there, Fred said to me, "Well Larry, don't just stand there, go get the man's stuff," and added what I thought was an almost pitiful … "please … and make sure that you sign for everything. You have full authorization."

I left quickly, lest he change his mind. "Larry, the Official Purchasing Agent/Art Director" had been born. I had vowed to never work with an art director, and now I was one!

Returning back after several of my trips of ordering materials, I would see Sam standing in the orchestra pit, waving his arms about for all the world like an orchestra leader, observing an invisible—to me—area somewhere in the deepest recesses of the stage. It suddenly dawned on me what all this stuff was about. Along with all the other flats, Sam was single-handedly going to paint a dozen canvas flats of various sizes as well as a canvas backdrop 40 feet high by 60 feet across.

I was told that some of the equipment, including this immense piece of heavy-duty canvas, would be delivered through the backstage loading door, but the office would handle the billing. I believed that I had more than enough work to keep me out of mischief for a while, so this arrange-ment was fine. I had no idea what a roll of canvas that large would even look like, much less weigh! This canvas would be the backdrop for a play I had never seen. I did thank God for my having performed in a couple of high school plays, giving me some idea of what stagecraft was, but what an introduction to Professional Stagecraft 501! Although I could barely get my mind around all that was happening and all that was going to happen, I fully believed that, with some admittedly amateur help, Sam fully intended to paint the completed scenery sets—to be delivered somewhere—for an actual stage performance of "Most Happy Fella."

Right here I am going to take a necessary break while I give you some idea of what I learned about what Sarge did as a stagehand. To take care of our needs, Sarge drove the forklift with one of the parade-float carts behind, carrying the huge roll of canvas, which drooped over on both sides of the cart. He drove this up on the stage from the loading door, and carefully arranged it such that it was midway back of what would be the individual pieces of canvas flats on which interior room scenics would be painted. Sarge, in his glory, allowed me to watch and help him as he untied the large bundle that was the backdrop. We went over to the pin rails (fife rails) and brought down a set of clamps attached to the main lines, plus divisional lines (ropes) that would set the top margin of the backdrop about every four or five feet across the loft location, so it is absolutely horizontal. At the pin rail, the rope was run out until most of it was coiled on the stage. This end of the rope turned out to be the "byte of the line," while the clamps and other attachments would be at the other end. Just as is the case of elevators, counter-weights were necessary—as in heavy bags of sand—and are needed when the scenery was to be flown (lifted). This means that at various places, heavy pieces of wings (side flats) were attached to various lines, anchored to tracks on the upper ceiling and led down to the pin rail. From the pin rail, they could be lifted above the audience sight line or lowered to the stage, as needed.

For the first time, instead of being completely ignorant, I got a chance to see what Sarge had actually done for a living. My appreciation for his skill, if not his personality, shot off the charts. Because of his work on the stage, I was made aware of all the intricacies of "The Stage": from the ancient Greek, Aristophanes, to the present time. The amount of heavy equipment that was flying high above the stage was mind-boggling. In lofts overhead were hundreds of rope and steel cables rising up to the vaulted ceiling 40 feet higher than the rest of the theatre proper. Hanging from this upper ceiling were wall-to-wall tracks, complete with all manner of blocks and sheaves. Between some of these ran parallel tracks holding heavy-duty lighting fixtures and hundreds of special hooks and receptacles for "flying" pieces of scenery. That Sarge knew all of these lines, where they originated, and exactly to what they were attached made me think of him in nautical terms: an old time clipper able-bodied-seaman, working the sails. Like these men, Sarge had to know many different trades, tools, methods, and procedures.

In all the time I had worked with (under?) him, I had never seen him required to produce anywhere near as much work in a year as he produced in the process of getting the stage wired and rigged for a complete set of scenery. He had nothing to do with me because the only thing that Sam needed from him was his basic skills and safety knowledge. Sarge did this setup work quietly and efficiently—even though the years that he had been out of all the active stage work had allowed him to add many pounds to his already short, stout frame. Now, when we passed each other, he looked at me levelly and with as much grace as he could muster. It was clear to him that I did know something and had the ear of the master, so he was not about to mess with me.

I attended to everything Sam could possibly want, and I was loathe to let him go to the bathroom by himself, lest I miss any of the processes and tricks by which he did this miracle. He would start talking almost non-stop in the middle of the process and tell me everything that he was doing as he was did it. He treated me like a legitimate apprentice!

The trestle—a 40-foot horizontal ladder—on which the rolling palette was lifted was done the same way the backdrop was lifted, except on different lines attached at the pin rail to a belaying pin. All lines were identified with tags describing function and position. The flying trestle was constructed to easily hold the 4 x 8 foot palette, which could then be rolled from one end of the stage to the other and set at any height wanted. This palette was essentially the 4 by 8 foot surface of ¾ inch plywood with holes cut in it to receive the pie pans for mixing and holding the paints. This palette was also wired into an electric plate for melting the flaked glue, which was then added to the water-based paint to make the paint stick to the canvas. All of the outlets on the palette were connected to the stage by a long electrical cable. I was so in tune with Sam that, after a short time, when he asked for some strange piece of equipment I had never seen, I would have it in his hand almost before he asked for it.

One day, down on the main floor, he brought in some prepared colors and told me to mix a 10-gallon container full of a light hue of fawn-colored paint while he was taking part of the day off. I thought myself as a pretty good colorist, but I had never had to figure out how to mix this much of anything. I started out with the base-color of white, to which I figured there would have to be some green and some red to get into the tertiary grayed-brown that will result. As long as I was pouring white, everything was fine, but as soon as I started to add the red, the result was actually a sickening pink. This was a hell of a long way from fawn, so I tried to balance it with a little blue. Wrong! I suddenly realized that I had a 10-gallon bucket full of a paint color that Sam had assuredly not requested. I continued blindly adding colors until I was left with 20 gallons of a perhaps interesting, but non-ordered, purplish-tinted mistake! I was heartsick. There was absolutely nothing I could do about it, and I wasn't about to try any more creative mixing. I considered that my tenure as "Purchasing Agent/Art Director" would be coming to a premature but emphatic end.

I am sure I was sweating and breathing like a man caught in the grip of a heart attack, when suddenly Sam appeared behind me, looking at the mess I had made. My face must have told him everything, but all he said was, "Well … that was not exactly what I had in mind."

This undoubtedly would qualify as one of the grandest applications of understatement ever heard. But, finally as he stood there looking at the unwanted color I alone had created, he sighed and then, seeming to have made a decision, took one of the buckets and walked up on the stage, signaling me to bring the other.

I had had visions of him taking me to the bathroom sink and drowning me in 20 gallons of purple paint. Instead he took one of the six inch "mops" and started laying on the paint in huge graceful arcs on the up-to-now pristine backdrop. After a couple of hours, he had covered the entire canvas with most of the paint, but put one of the 10 gallon buckets aside, loaded with the accursed purple paint, which he divided into two smaller cans. Into one of these, he introduced a small amount of mixed dark brown and to the other, a couple of cups of titanium white.

With no signs of malice or hard feelings, he sent me up on the trestle bridge. The bridge had been rigged to be flown by use of full controls on the trestle so that I could operate them to place me anywhere. I was now holding one end of a long line of white-chalked twine. At the other end, standing on the stage next to the backdrop, Sam held the snap-line container, loaded with a light blue chalk and directed me to raise the trestle to its full up-and-left position. While at this extreme upper left position, he had me anchor my end of the line into the canvas with a sharp-pointed u-bend pin. Down on the stage, he pulled the twine tight and then snapped it with his finger, leaving a diagonal light blue line cleanly across the canvas, leading from the top left to the lower right where he was standing.

He did this again and again, deftly ordering me where to pin my end, as he sighted the desired line. He held the other end himself, having me move down 10 feet at a time. When finished, there was a grid of lines farther apart at my end and closer together at his. When we had finished this part of the job, he sent me off to get another list of materials, a round trip that was going to take at least two hours to complete.

I left, but left with many questions as to what would he be doing with the rest of the purple paint—all he had was a monotone purple backdrop. Purple was not a color that could be used for the turn-of-the-century, dark brown wainscoting and dark-hued wooden panels. Almost all of the interiors for the various rooms in the sets were in the old mansion, which was the location of most of the scenes.

I came back loaded with supplies, stopped at the main office with the bills and receipts, and noticed that both Sarge and Fred were beaming with approval. I raced back to the auditorium, entering from the back, and stopped in my tracks: there, overpowering the otherwise empty stage, was a symmetrical set of gently sloping hills, loaded with purple grapevines, fading off into the distance. The grapes, loaded on the vines, looked for the entire world like you could go up and pick them! I never knew, never asked, and Sam never told me what it was that he originally wanted the fawn-colored paint for. This incident gives new meaning to the concept of making lemonade …

On day when I was up on the stage, I noted Sam painting three colors in a single stroke on the flats at the back of the stage. I was looking at the colors and knew what they were supposed to represent, but to me it just didn't look like the wainscoting he was attempting to define. He must have sensed my presence for, without looking around, he said, "I can see you're not too impressed. Try viewing it farther back; the orchestra pit will be fine."

I was chagrined that I was so dumb, but what he knew—and I

didn't—was that there was a marvelous lesson to be learned, which was to later have a profound effect on my mural painting. From the middle of the stage to the orchestra pit was only about 15 feet, but at just that distance, the separated fragments of the three-tone brushstrokes blended perfectly into the back wall of the interior of a spacious Victorian library. The inlaid wood parquet woodwork was so instantly real I expected to see termites. It was just a miracle!! I hadn't said a word, but Sam turned around and gave me this shit-eating grin that spoke volumes. The master had amazed the rookie once again.

On the day when the eighteen-wheeler pulled up behind the stage and started loading all the flats, furniture, and assembled pieces for the play, there came a moment when I am sure that all of us felt as if we had lost a member of the family. It became very quiet. But, not long afterwards, Sarge and I started to eye one another again with suspicion and distrust.

After that wonderful job was completed, I attempted to do a lettering job for a restaurant nearby; I was prepared to use a set of die-cut letters that were readily available. It turned out that the owner wanted a different kind of letters, but lettering was not my forte. I did the one thing that you should never do with any customer: remain out of touch and hope they just … go away. Sarge was on me in a second, and Fred joined in. Because they knew I had some experience as a sign painter, they kept hounding me to take care of the job. This was a hell of a downturn in the career as a set designer I had just completed with flying colors.

All of the reasons for me to get out of there were back in effect. I was miserable, and nothing looked like it was going to change. Just when I was ready to quit, Fred called me in and laid out a set of blueprints for Meier and Franks' downtown Portland store; there were three different scales of drawings for the south side of the complete block-sized, thirteen-story building. Fred let me study it for a while, then he pulled out a sketchpad and asked me to draw a very simple sketch of a Christmas tree. He had a gleam in his eye that made me think we were going to do a reprise on the scenery job that he previously had set up to put me in my place. Instead, he began to ask me very specific questions about the amount of wattage that would be necessary to supply a thousand strings of lights. I looked at him in total dismay. He continued, and I slowly understood that he was describing a Christmas tree outline made out of at least a thousand commercial strings of outside lights that would hang from the top floor of Meier and Franks to the heavy canopies that extended from the mezzanine floor out over the street!

When I had the basic idea of what he was planning, I asked about the crew. He said he thought that we could do it. We, in this case, would be Sarge and me hanging the lights. I immediately came up with fifteen reasons why this could not be done, but Fred just ordered me to do the sketch showing "The Tree" superimposed on the side of the building.

I finally admitted that I could do this—at top salary, and Fred made it clear that I would be doing the rigging. I am sure that Sarge knew that I had a height phobia, and there was no way in hell that I was going to be swinging out 300 feet over the street. Nonetheless, I took all of the blueprints home, drew a projected view of the stupid, impossible tree in 1/8 inch scale on the M&F building blueprints, and took it to Fred the next day. He seemed like a kid with a new toy.

It would have taken a full ream of paper for me to outline all the reasons why this piece of idiocy could not be accomplished in any of our combined lifetimes. However, Fred, in what I thought was an amazing turn of events, called Meier and Franks, asked for the Display Department, and got the head man, Mr. George Haynes. Fred signaled me to sit down and put the phone on loud-speaker. When Haynes answered, Fred disclosed his idea for the Christmas tree and asked for an appointment, assuring him that Fred's chief designer—who, I could only guess, was still me—had looked over the project and found it feasible.

There are many times in my life when I have found some project daunting, but this was about twenty clicks beyond impossible: definitely, absolutely, obviously, financially, and legally! Taking just the legal ramifications, the idea of a non-experienced rigger operating over city sidewalks was absurd. There would have to be licenses, permits, insurance, and special dispensations . . . from the Pope. The building's structure was a box within a box. Banks of elevators were part of an outside shell that contained separate stairwells, and these stairwells faced the outside of the building. Once you were in areas away from the stairwells, there were no windows anywhere. The building's exterior was all beautiful stonework that nobody in their right mind would let anyone carve into. Everything, including the power cables, would have to be set in the stairwells—a raving fire hazard, as well as shock danger—and only a gantry on the roof could possibly handle the working load, presumably with me hanging out over the street in all my glory!

Everywhere I looked, I could see that this whole project was some kind of debacle I wanted no part of, not to mention the idea of seeing what would be left of me after a 13-story drop to the street below. I was convinced that George Haynes, presumably being sane, would do something like hang up the phone. I was amazed to hear him come on the line and, in a few moments, agree to a meeting at 4:15 the next afternoon.

Fred looked at me with a maniacal gleam of triumph in his eyes, while I rolled mine. But I agreed that I would go with him to the meeting and show and explain our plan. My God, what a plan!

I figured that it would be impossible to do the job for less than $60,000, for crew alone, plus several thousand dollars for the lights, plus $10,000 for crane and motorized baskets. I agreed to give it a brave try. I got busy trying to make the drawings look like they were not the output of a severely demented mind. I don't remember sleeping too well that night; I kept wondering what the hell was the matter with George Haynes. He just had to know there was no way in hell this was doable even if M&F could come up with the bucks. I gathered all the pitiful stuff I had available, minus the work projections, time studies, feasibility reports, safety outlines, salaries, expenses, insurance, etc. etc. And then before I knew it, it was time to go with Fred to meet with Haynes.

We rode silently in the elevator to the offices on the 12th floor and then took stairs to the 13th where the display, print, and advertising crews worked. Haynes met us in the anteroom and invited us into his office, where I took a seat. Fred and Haynes, who had worked together many times, shook hands genially; then Fred introduced me. I wished sincerely that I could either die or just disappear. Fred reached for the pitiful plans that I had drawn of this God-forsaken, hormonally unbalanced Yule tree. In the process, as Fred reached down for the plans, I looked up just in time to see Haynes give me a sly wink, while gently touching the side of his nose. I recognized this as the quick, subtle sign one hustler gives another—kind of fraternal signal. I found myself beginning to relax a little.

While Fred was getting the material ready, Haynes abruptly interrupted, indicating that Fred should sit down again, and said, "By the way, Fred, maybe you can answer some questions I have had covering the years that we have been working together."

Since I had been at Allied Productions, I could think of three Meier and Franks' shows for which we had supplied materials and crew.

Fred looked seriously confused. "Why sure, George. I hope that everything we have done for you has been completely satisfactory." This was said with a great deal of sincerity.

"Oh yes, your work has been just fine, and we have always been happy with you. It helps that you have mostly been low bidder, and from time to time, I have wondered how you managed so well."

All of the conversation was spoken with the casual air of two friends who have worked together often and well.

George Haynes continued, "The thing is … " and here Haynes reached for a whole series of papers clipped together and instantly at hand. "Let's see, you bought Allied Productions from Allied Arts, just down the street. Right?"

"Right," Fred said, with the look of a man who feels a little tremor underneath his feet … nothing to worry about … but a little bit of a tremor.

"Well," continued Haynes, "if I'm not wrong, you bought the old Lincoln Theatre from Mickey McCafferty for about a million five, along with all the fixtures, bunting … and," here he looked at another sheet, "40 wheeled carts used as parade bases for floats, 200 pound racks of velour, posts, drapes, 12 junction and power distribution wagons, a large nearby supply location, and several hundred feet of connecting heavy duty wire, plugs, and … "

Fred looked as though the tremor had become a substantial, but small, say in the vicinity of 4.1 Richter scale, event. I watched as the blood drained from Fred's face, but he didn't feel like interrupting, and I certainly didn't want him to.

After a few more "after-shocks," Haynes stopped talking and looked amusedly at Fred, who seemed to have shrunken in his seat until he looked like a small boy, waiting for his punishment.

Haynes was now smiling genially at Fred, as he reached into his desk drawer—like Felix the Cat's bag—and withdrew a couple of pieces of legal-looking paper.

"Let's see. This is a bill of sale and a promissory note from Mickey McCafferty assigning all of the aforementioned to the Meier and Franks' corporation in lieu of a debt and as collateral on a loan from said Meier and Franks, due and payable upon demand."

Fred now looked as though he was in the full 9.3 San Francisco 1906 event! He made a kind of gurgling sound as Haynes continued, " I don't see anything that says Mickey ever paid off this note and I think that means that all of the equipment we have been renting from you, including the theatre itself, belongs to us!"

As if the damage were not already done, Haynes reached into his drawer one more time, and drew out another piece of legal paper. He read it to himself once and then continued, "Right after you paid Mickey, presumably so he could pay us, Mickey went on a buying spree and, among other things, bought himself the brand new Ryan seaplane—it would be Irish wouldn't it?—he used to move to Alaska."

I don't think that either Fred or I actually remember leaving the building, I only knew that, finally and for good, "The Great Christmas Tree Caper" was history. I don't think I actually resigned from Allied Productions, but I do know that this was the last time I ever saw Fred, or Sarge, or Allied Productions.

21 | Ron Spear

The Portland Art Museum was an unlikely place to find my next boss: this happened on a trip to the museum where a Jackson Pollack exhibit was being shown. Since I was now doing a great deal of painting, I believed I was thoroughly involved in art or ART or "artie fartie" … whatever. At any rate I had a higher opinion of myself than was warranted (my general condition). Over my up-to-now lifetime, there have been times when I have found myself rolling along in the middle of my strength, and this seemed to be one of those.

I had been in the museum for a couple of hours when I came upon a lady dressed in all black. I could tell by her posture and manner that she was old; I was a very young 28 years old, with the common sense of the average 12 year old. The old lady and I were alone in the gallery where some of the more intriguing Pollacks were located. I thought, "What a wonderful opportunity to share some of my extensive art knowledge with this little lady … sort of make her day." It was a serious, serious mistake! Always look first at the person you are addressing so that you have some idea with whom you are dealing. As it turned out, I sort of slid in behind her and softly asked, "What does it say to you, ma'am?"

The moment she spun around to face me, and the moment the words were out of my mouth, I realized I had made one of those boo-boos that are destined to affect you the rest of your life. Her black eyes were like onyx in her pallid face—a bony, wizened face that was totally overwhelmed by those intelligent eyes. Her speech was machine-gun-like, delivered with the ease of one practiced in more than one art and superior at expressing herself at all times.

"What do you mean, young man? Analytically, chronologically, experientially, psychologically, mechanically, constructively, philosophically, organizationally, or some other modality?"

I had just made a complete moron out of myself with the organizer and partial owner of the exhibition! I knew exactly how Napoleon felt at Waterloo. I must have looked totally crestfallen, so taking pity on me, she continued in a friendlier vein and gave me some of the details on the exhibition, then let me quietly slink away.

I felt like I was gasping for air and needed to be somewhere else, so I went to the front of the building and sat on the concrete balustrade and practiced deep breathing. I had been sitting there for some time when I realized that I had company. A middle-aged man approached me and, looking somewhat bemused, said, "I couldn't help overhearing that conversation you were having."

"Oh God!" I thought. There was a witness to my stupidity.

But he was not laughing at me and continued, "I gather that you are an artist."

"Not in her caliber," I replied, though that information seemed superfluous.

The man introduced himself as Ron Spear. "I am looking for an artist. I can't pay much, but there is a good opportunity for advancement."

We made our way to a coffee shop and talked some more. When he got to the part where he described doing some special display work for Meier and Franks, I really tuned in. It seemed that he was going on a field trip to Eastern Oregon where he would be bringing back Madrona trees and Manzanita bushes. We made arrangements to meet the next day at his assistant's house; we would take her truck for the day, bring the materials back, and construct some "Sugar-Plum" trees. I had no idea what they were—something to do with Christmas?—but I needed a job and the pay was much better than nothing.

At eight o'clock the next morning, I showed up ready to go to work and met Alice, the assistant, who owned a large boarding house. She claimed she was not the world's greatest cook, so she let her boarders provide their own food. Alice was not exactly homely but she was not exactly not. She was a hard worker who had the misfortune of occasionally having a "thing" for the worst of her tenants. She ended up taking care of them instead of taking care of her own family: her three daughters. The kids were pretty much brought up by the eldest girl, who was smart, cute, and bright enough to dodge the lodgers, although as I found out later, from her, there were many close calls. I am not so sure the younger girls totally escaped, but the whole group kind of crippled through.

Ron, Alice, and I drove past Mt. Hood into Indian country, which was mostly desert, but there were vast open lands for grazing cattle. We pulled off the main highway onto a dirt road and started cutting swatches of Manzanita, which is a plant native to the mountainous desert. Ron knew that we were trespassing but didn't seem to worry about it. We took a different path back, passing by a creek that was surrounded by large Madrona trees. We cut down a couple of the smaller trees and pitched them in the back of the truck, then headed for Portland. At Alice's, we unloaded the trees and bushes. Ron told me to come back in the morning to help trim and paint the materials.

I arrived the next morning, dressed in newly bought overhauls; Alice was already stripping many branches from the smaller Manzanita's and trimming the ends to a sharp point. When Ron arrived, he began working with a half dozen of the Madrona's bigger and straighter limbs, drilling holes in them so as to receive the Manzanita branches. The whole thing looked pretty awkward but after assembly and gluing, Ron expertly trimmed the branches that resulted in a 3-foot high, 18 inch wide "sugar-plum tree." When a dozen were finished, Alice fired up a compressor and sprayed the trees with a heavy green paint; after sparkles and various colors of bright glint were tossed on them, they were allowed to dry. They looked, for all the world, as if they had been grown in the middle of Santa's workshop!

I was pleasantly surprised that my new boss had all this talent. He didn't seem to have a care in the world and looked as though he couldn't have been happier doing what he was doing for a living. A few days later, we delivered the sugarplums to Meier and Franks' display department, where they were gratefully received. Ron picked up new orders for Maidenhair fern. We were now going to Sweet Home, Oregon to pick them.

The difference in working conditions between Ron Spear and Fred Shoemacher was so startling that I knew I was right where I belonged and I was going to learn a whole lot more about the display business from this man. I was making good money, loved what I was doing, and felt appreciated for the first time in a long while. In Sweet Home, near a riverbank, we selected Maidenhair fern and batches of obviously coarse weeds; this confused me. However, by this time I realized that Ron could do almost anything with anything so the weeds did not concern me, though I was hard-pressed to figure out exactly how he was going to transform them.

The so-called weed, which turned out to be a "fairy-splendor," was called Queen Ann's Lace. It looked interesting, but didn't give me any idea of what it could be with a little of Ron's attention. It was a tough weed and, though it was attractive and delicate-looking, it was all fibrous and wiry. However, with a layer of glue and a swatch of blown flocking material, it became a thing of beauty and wonder. Again the job was interesting and the customer ecstatic.

The professional manner in which Ron handled the customers was simple and honest. In short, they had no problems with him at all. One of the best jobs we had was for the grand opening of Seattle's Bon Marche department store. The display work was extensive, and the contract included purchase, delivery, and installation of a Cigar Store Indian; however, we were on a short schedule because the store opening had been moved up. The "Indian" was to be full size; we were given a month to get it made and delivered. In the three months that I had worked for Ron, I never saw him fazed by an order. Thus, I was less than surprised to be in a pickup with Ron and Alice on our way to Ridgefield, Washington, a small town a few miles north of Vancouver. There, just off the highway, we pulled into a store where we were introduced to a large Indian, named Chief Lalooska. He was a master carver, painter, and maker of totem poles, and certainly capable of producing one of his kind in the fashion of the cigar-store wooden Indian—the kind that were placed in front of stores in the Old West.

Chief Lalooska showed us around the shop. It contained many of his masterful carvings, including a 1/8th-inch scale model wagon built to be an exact replica of the old Prairie Schooners that took the early settlers across Middle America and into the new West. Pulling the detailed wagon were six horses, fully carved and straining at their yokes. Ron suggested Alice and I continue to look around while he and the chief went into a small office to discuss the creation of the Indian carving for the Bon Marche.

After our visit to Chief Lalooska, we made several trips to Seattle to deliver displays and bunting, and finally, on time, delivered the Indian. While he charged the Bon Marche $1200, he indicated that he paid

Chief Lalooska $800—the profit of $400 was to be divided between the three of us. Ron was unusually quiet on our way back from that trip, but seemed happy enough.

There were more jobs, less spectacular, but I was learning the trade. Ron introduced me to a whole world of display professionals and got me jobs when our work was slack. One day he came to my basement apartment and saw the mechanical Elvis Presley that gyrated and cried as he played his guitar. Ron was properly impressed and asked if I were an engineer. I told him that I knew how to make things work, when I wanted to. He gave me this strange smile and said, "I think I may have an interesting job for you."

The next week, Ron came by and laconically told me to get in the car. We drove to a house in southwest Portland where a man gave Ron a fairly good-sized package. We took back to my apartment, and there he unwrapped it. It was a case carefully welded out of extruded aluminum, with 12 by 16 inch plastic sides, open to receive two transparent plastic pieces carrying colored advertising for Rainier Beer. Ron pressed a small button on the case; one of the picture surfaces released, and I was looking into the innards of the device. It had a beautifully balanced base attached to a hidden interior power take-off on insulated bearings. There were two tiny lamps inside, one for each of the advertising logos. But that was all. There was an electrical plug-in card attached to the base, but there didn't seem to be a motor to turn the sign. After careful investigation, I looked up at Ron with a quizzical expression.

Ron smiled, "Tell me what you see."

I described, "This is beautifully balanced and obviously is meant to turn, but there is no motor. On the internal shaft, there are two rotating channels that I imagine are for the power take-offs to run the motor as well as positive and negative contacts."

"Precisely how the thing works, but there is a problem," said Ron. "It needs a very small motor, but frankly I can't find the right one to do the job. What I do know is that the motor obviously has to move its own mass as well as that of the case and display plates."

"Why didn't whoever constructed the case find a motor?" I asked.

Ron gave me a look that I had never seen before. He didn't answer for a while and then, looking distressed, finally mumbled, "The outfit that did the case didn't offer to do anything else."

It was a strange moment. As he turned to leave, I said, "I'll look into it." But right there, for the first time I sensed he had lied to me.

Ron nodded and left.

"Looking into it" involved going to an electrician's supply store and being brought up to speed on small motors: they were used for all sorts of applications. The first question I was asked was "How many pounds pressure do you need?"

I knew about pounds pressure … like nothing, so I just looked at the store manager, blankly.

He gestured for the use of one of my fingers. "Hold your finger stiff while I apply a twisting pressure. Do you feel it takes this much force?" Here he twisted my proffered finger with a medium amount of torque.

"No, way less," I offered helpfully.

"Well that was about six inch-pounds of torque. If it was a whole lot less than that it would be about two inch-pounds torque." Still holding my finger, he exerted much less pressure.

"Yeah," I said, "that's just about it."

"Well, we ain't into multiple horsepower, so there are a whole flock of miniature motors that will meet your needs. Tell me, is this some kind of turning display unit?"

"Exactly," I answered.

He went to the back of the store and came out with three different motors, all small enough to fit in the palm of my hand.

"Now," he continued, "this is where it gets complicated."

My heart sank. If it was too complicated, I was in deep water.

He saw my consternation and quickly continued, "If this thing moves and is in the two inch-pounds range, this motor—or this other one—will work and not burn out if over-loaded."

"What is going to overload it?"

"Being stopped for a period of time—if it is an induction motor."

Again my heart sank: I could see any number of situations in which a display sign's movement could be blocked. A picture of a devastating fire due to over-heating flooded my mind.

"But," he continued, "these two we have in stock are hysteresis synchronous motors and have permanent magnets in them. They will take being stopped for days without damage and then will take off like champs as soon as the blockage is removed."

"Wow," I said, "You're great! I'll take the two of them and be on my way."

He gave me the package and then added, "Of course you'll have to deal with the pressure on the transfer gear."

"Yeah," I said with emphasis, as though this problem was well known to me.

I paid the man, took my goodies, and went home with a light heart ... and so it is with fools who happily plan on draining the moat, just before they meet the alligators that infest that water.

The next few days went by, and I got a chance to make up a circuit board to connect the specially built commutators. These connectors had special fingers that engaged the two turning channels electrically and were connected to the base for energizing the two fixed miniature lamps. It became obvious to me that there was no room for the motor to fit independently on or in the base, but would have to be included inside as part of the rotating sign. There was no particular reason for this. It could be argued that since you had to have a base you might as well put a motor in it. As I was to learn in the devilish "Art Of Widget Making," engineers are always tempted to make something difficult for any innovators trying to imitate.

So, having to place the motor inside meant I also had to develop "fingers" of my own to trace around the positive and negative electrically-connected, stationary channels, essentially part of the base. The built-in, light-power pick-up took up half the space around the circumference of the two channels, leaving me to make and connect a pick-up for energizing current to the remaining available half of the stationary channels. To this equation, the slight but additional weight of the motor and mount had to be a negative force on the inch-pounds pressure, but more importantly this operation would inevitably add resistance. The coefficient of friction would be high enough to use up most of the 2-inch-pounds force the motor provided. I didn't realize at first how critical this step was going to be.

I wondered for the first time—but just slightly—that maybe some of these problems should have been given a little more weight by Ron. He had done so much perfectly, it became difficult to think of him in any other terms. The next week I tried every combination of pick-ups I could, but they all added enough weight and resistance to stop the motor. I changed to the more powerful of the two motors, but with the same result. Now, I just looked at the inside of the case and at the problem. I realized that even if there were some way of solving this, I would still come "a cropper" of the rules of electrical safety. This seal of approval from the government agency on all electrical equipment would call for some kind of circuit breaker or fuse: still more weight!

What I do in these situations is to build a "Wahl's wall" that stops me from thinking about the problem in any way. I just put it on the shelf or, more accurately, put it in my "mental Mixmaster" and turn it on. After a certain period of time, I turn off the Mixmaster, and what is left is the answer.

During my self-imposed absence from this problem, I had occasion to go to a formal party. With my thick neck in shirt and tie, I almost always look and feel like I am going to a hanging in which I am the "hangee." To manage this dilemma, I found, in a men's store, a set of very thin, very elastic, and very strong end-pointed wires called "collar anchors." These would go in the front of your dress shirt as you secured the top button: the sharp ends would be pushed into the finished corners of the shirt collar, holding them down. With this tool, and a simple clip-on tie, I could manage to look halfway respectable without feeling like I was choking to death.

When I finally opened the mental Mixmaster, there was my answer—the "collar anchor" straightened out to become wire-like! I checked collar pin with an electrical tester and it conducted electricity very well. I figured out how to connect two pieces of the wire directly to the circuit board and set the wire, with only a slight amount of pressure, against the curved commutators channels. The "collar anchors" worked perfectly. I closed the case, plugged it in, and away it went. I blocked it off for two hours and watched it like a good movie; nothing heated up and nothing broke. I called Alice when I realized that I didn't have a daytime phone number for Ron. I also wanted to share with him the fact that we didn't need a fuse. I knew this because one time, with the power still on, I accidentally produced a short circuit: there was a flash, and the wire simply vanished. It had vaporized. There was no way that anybody would ever find a better or simpler circuit breaker. Fantastic!

Ron was paying me $200 a week, so I was salaried. It didn't dawn on me that this could end at any time. With the string of successes we had going, I saw no reason to be concerned. When I first met Alice, I assumed she had a similar arrangement with Ron, but that she did some of the bookkeeping, something I was not very much interested in and was even less successful with. When I called her asking for Ron's number because "I had some wonderful news," I got a very strange response. Her voice was harder than seemed necessary, clipped and pressured. She finally agreed to call him for me and have him get in touch.

I never thought of her as being my boss in any way, so I was a little miffed. Alice had a certain sexual attraction, but was hardly my idea of a fem fatale; I had a passing thought as to whether Ron had ever slept with her. On the job all of us dressed like farmers or loggers, so I had never even thought of her as naked. I should have realized that this in itself was strange since I can generally strip the garments from any female with a single look and almost always do—I'm an artist, remember! I knew she owned a house and had three young daughters, but Alice was more of a mystery than I realized.

Not much time had passed before I got a return call from Ron with a quick approval for a meeting at my apartment the following afternoon, when he returned from Seattle. About five the next evening, Ron showed up. I was so proud of myself, I was practically bursting. I showed him the sign: I held it in a multitude of positions while it merrily ran on. He seemed impressed, especially when I took the cover off and showed him what I had done. He reminded me that that the beer company was set to order 2000 units to start with. Obviously everything had been done to insure the product was ready to go, and only the manufacturing approval was needed. I assumed that somewhere down the line Ron would be incorporating his business, if he had not already done so, and I would be looking at a job for life as an engineer! I was surprised that Ron looked amazingly cool and perhaps a little sad. But after a thoughtful moment, he said slowly and rather ponderously, "I'll take the unit with me now, run it by the manufacturer, and finalize the deal. I'll get back to you and we can go together to Olympia, just you and me."

He left, and I tried to be joyous, but something was off key. I had been to Rainier and there was a deal ... but ...

Two days later he called and told me he was bringing back the unit. I expected this, as it had been the test model and the only one that I had ever seen. However, when he unwrapped it, I saw that only one of the advertising plates was on it.

"Jesus, Ron," I gulped, looking at his sad face, "what happened to the display?"

"I accidentally broke it, so we can't make the meeting that was set up for this coming Tuesday."

I was left trying to figure out how the hell he could have broken the display plate, but he just looked at me miserably; he said there was no way he was going. I couldn't believe it. I watched in shock as he went out the door.

I had some crazy idea that I could still save the deal, so I took the unit and went to Olympia and showed it. It was obvious they were still interested, so I faked it and told them I would be back with Ron the next week. They thought it was strange that the one side of the case was missing, but I used that opportunity to explain the innards to them, and they were fascinated. They assured me that they would be buying many more. I left, but the case remained at Rainiers. I knew it was dead, so I left the corpse behind.

Ron didn't call again. Finally I called Alice. She listened to me for some time and then asked me to come to the house later that evening. She met me at the door, invited me into the living room, shooed her eldest daughter out of the room, and broke out a bottle of scotch, pouring us each a half glass. I was on the verge of turning it down, when she silenced me with a finger and offered the opinion that I was never going to see Ron again: I was shocked. She picked up my glass and gave it to me.

"Would you like to go to bed with me?" Her voice was soft and defeated.

More shock. I automatically gulped down a large drag of the liquor.

She continued with harsh words, but in a gentle voice, "Of course you wouldn't, but that is the deal I made with Ron. He can have me when he wants … not that often, and he pays me $200 a week to help pay for this place and take care of my kids. In the meantime, he comes and goes as he wants. I don't try and change him and I probably don't know a hell of a lot more about him than you do. You and I are in the same bed, except for the screwing.

"He isn't going to ever see you again if he can help it. You are just another one of the faceless. He uses everybody. He is the con man, you and I are the conned: there is an army of us. The guys at Rainier, to whom he sold the idea of the sign, didn't see it as just another of Ron's cons;

however, the company that did the original sign work figured it out and pulled the plug. I had done enough of the questionable paper work to see what was coming. I have to tell you, he really did like you, but to him you are still one of the great unwashed who believes in Justice, Truth, and the American way. A fool, one of millions, and for Ron, your only purpose in life was to be his loser."

I realized after a few drinks and a lot of silence that I could go to bed with her if I wanted, but there was really nothing left for me but to go home, take a shower, and forget the whole damn thing.

Sometime later I saw Alice's oldest girl, Mary, on the #23 bus. She told me that she had just had her 21st birthday, had moved into her own apartment, and had a boyfriend. She said that Alice worked with Ron for another couple more months, and then he disappeared; she hadn't seen him since. Mary allowed that she had been lucky enough to avoid being raped by any of the boarders, but more than one had exposed himself to her. She felt sorry for Alice but was going to make sure she didn't end up the same way.

I listened to her as the bus wound downtown, and after she got off at her stop, I wondered how she would make sure she didn't end up like Alice. But somehow I believe Mary had seen enough of Ron Spear to be able to see through him a hell of a lot easier than I had.

Note: Despite its chapter number, this is the last chapter I have written for my second book. I had avoided writing it for many years, and now I know why. With this incident, it has become obvious to me that I have had a pattern with my work bosses and partners: I seem to pick those who will eventually victimize me. But, I now realize that "it is me drawing all those dirty pictures" as the psychiatrist's joke about the Rorschach test goes. I'm a student of life, but it is not a formal educational institution. So, I learn by being the apprentice until I outgrow the boss and am thrown out on my ear. A difficult way to pay my tuition for the vast education I have acquired over the years, but it has worked.

22 | Of Mice and Men and Healthcare Jobs

A fter I gave up on Allied Arts and Ron Speer, I found myself working the night shift as an orderly at Good Samaritan Hospital in Portland, on the 4th floor—I was very much single. This whole floor was my bailiwick; it was here that I found my 3rd wife, Jan. (More about this 3rd wife and her family in Chapter 24: Sweethome.) Jan and I ended up working together in a secluded and oversized "Railroad Ward" at the otherwise deserted end of the 4-West Back. While it may have been secluded from the main hospital wards, empty it was not. This one very large ward was arranged in two rows with twelve beds per side for a total of 24 patients when full, and I never remember it when it was not full. In the 1800s, there had been so many railroad workers maimed—with no insurance and no available hospital services—and because of numerous personal injury suits, the railroad tycoons found it necessary to contract with local hospitals to provide minimum care for their workers. Four West Back was 80% amputees.

The ward worked for two reasons: other patients in the hospital did not have to deal with these pitiful wrecks, whose lives were often living tragedies, and the railroad patients themselves were never aware of the limit on the services (cut rate) they were receiving in payment for spending the rest of their lives with missing limbs. But, the main advantage of this segregated ward was that the patients used "tough love" to help each other accept their conditions. It was hard to get much sympathy because you had lost a hand when the guy in the next bed had lost both legs. This whole ward was filled with jokers whose main job at this stage of their lives—in addition to helping each other—was to give the staff as bad a time as possible. If you did not understand this, your tenure in this ward would be very short!

The 3rd floor consisted of medical patients, with 3 South being the pediatric ward. I seldom was called to this area, but was kept more than busy with the 4th floor. When multiple car accident victims arrived, there was a whole array of equipment, like pipes and pulleys, rotary beds, and other hardware to be set up.

The rest of the 4th floor always had a number of quadriplegics and paraplegics—many were ex-loggers—who had a better union than the railroad workers. In general they were well taken care of and, for the most part, could survive with the combination of their attitudes and, most importantly, support from their families. Often these patients were young men at the beginning of what promised to be a full adult life: they were virile and cocky. Then suddenly, after having a forest adventure with a very large tree or logging equipment, found they were now less than half of what they had been.

Kubler-Ross &Kessler (2007) teach that there are five stages of loss that dying, severely injured, and permanently disabled people go through: denial, depression, anger, bargaining, and finally acceptance. Movement through these stages can take place in a few weeks or months or years or, in some cases, may never be resolved. I worked at Good Samaritan long enough to see hundreds of patients work their way through these phases. Some would give up early and inexplicably decide they would be better off dead; others soldiered through, preferring life to death, even if the change in that life would be substantial. And then there were those who couldn't manage to live but couldn't quite arrange the dying: they persisted as little more than unhealthy carrots, sometimes for years. They were the "un-living" patients who either needed nothing ... or needed everything, every minute, every day. They hated themselves and every human who came within their range.

Often it was easier for me to take care of the ones who decided to die. In a hospital or emergency setting, it does not take long for the staff to figure out who is smart enough—or maybe dumb enough—to be responsible for more and more work: it was not long before I was the "go-to-guy" for the patient's last "view" of Good Sam. I was the chosen one, designated to take them for that last ride to the 4 West Back elevator at the far NW corner of the huge building; its terminus was in the basement morgue. I found that I could give a final benediction to these folks without undue strain since I don't really believe in (soul) death. They did, of course, but I never had one of them argue the subject with me.

The night supervisor was Miss Giddings. I thought that she was the neatest package I had ever seen. She was petite but, as an ex-Navy nurse, could be tough as nails. I had no doubt that she knew that I would have liked to proposition her; I would have if I could have! However, we both knew I couldn't, so I just tried to impress her.

Taking patients, or rather ex-patients, down to the morgue had become pretty regular for me. The hospital was a huge brick affair—founded almost a hundred years earlier—and covered a full city block. Also in the complex was a building across the street on the north side that housed clinics and offices on the lower floors with a nurses' residence on the 3rd and 4th floors. There was a fracture ward directly across from the 4th floor student nurses' residence; it had been statistically proven that these patients got well faster than others on that floor. The student nurses were really smart but they couldn't get the curtains to close properly! The 4th floor was a lot of territory to cover: I was happy to do it. I was only one of three orderlies prepared and assigned to morgue duty at night.

Waltzing Hardy

At 3:00 A.M. when I stopped by the nurse's station, I saw Miss Giddings at the desk. She called me over and informed me that patient Hardy Smart had just died, gave me the room number, and handed me a tag and a paper shroud. The tag was for the patient's left toe, and the paper shroud was to cover the rest of him. This would necessitate removing his hospital gown in order to replace it with the paper shroud, normally a pretty straightforward kind of operation. When I got to the room, I found that Mr. Hardy Smart might have been hardy and might even have once been smart, but what was very much in evidence was that Mr. Smart was very, very large. At that time, I was just 29 years old, weighed 220 pounds at 5 feet 10 1/2 inches tall and was in pretty good shape. Mr. Smart was at least 300 pounds, over 6 feet 2, and had been downing more than his share of calories. He was, as a former football lineman, not obese but he was definitely overweight! This was a condition he was not destined to overcome anytime soon, but that made me realize that he was going to be a handful. I thought for a few seconds about calling for help, but my pride got the best of me; besides, it had been, and continued to be, one of those nights when the "ambuli" seem to think we were the only game in town. I would handle it myself.

I managed to wrestle him out of the hospital gown and into the shroud and tied the tag with his name, room number, and a tracking number. I never figured out what the tracking number was for. I was not aware of the hospital ever losing a deceased patient, but then, on occasion, we would take a limb or two to the morgue, so I guessed that perhaps tracking numbers would make sure that a patient who had say, lost a leg, would not get a wrong one from some other hapless leg-loser.

Needless to say, hospitals have been upgraded since I worked in them. The equipment we had to use then was barbaric by today's standards, but it was what was available: this included gurneys. These were very high off the ground—about 3 ½ feet—with two immense main wheels just behind of the center of gravity and two tiny (by comparison) steering wheels in front. These steering wheels—like those on super market carts—usually had an evil mind of their own. At any rate, though I should have asked for help, I got the late Mr. Smart out of the bed and onto the cart; I was feeling pretty good about having done it without help. Once this was done, I grabbed hold of the cart and pointed it down the long hallway—stretching almost half a block—to the NW corner of the hospital where there was the dedicated elevator that went down to the morgue.

While standing on the back wheel brace and ripping down the long hall, it was my habit to occasionally get up to highway speeds. There were just two problems with this operation on this particular night: the sheer "dead weight" of Mr. Smart and a gurney that had a flat spot on the left main wheel. I cursed myself for not checking everything before I put the cart into overdrive. At anything like a normal pace, the flat wheel would have been just a nuisance; however, when I took the vehicle to cruising speed, a rhythmic clicking and distinct tremor was produced each time the big wheels made a cycle. As though he was uncomfortable and needed to change positions, Mr. Smart's ample butt started heading for the edge of the cart. I have studied physics, and it came to me in a flash that in a relatively short period of time, Mr. Smart was going to egress the vehicle.

Now, the obvious solution was to hang onto the cart and dig my feet into the well-mopped and well-polished floor. However, if this was done too precipitately, the cart would stop but Mr. Smart would not: his momentum would continue. The coefficient of friction being what it is, there was a good chance that Mr. Smart would be sailing down the hall sans cart, with his shroud up around his neck displaying the full extent of his manhood. This was too demeaning an end to what should have been a calm, if not sober, trip to the quiet, cold boxes.

As luck would have it, Mr. Smart reached a point where both his heavy legs were off the gurney and his back was arching, ready to follow. The cart had nearly stopped, but Mr. Smart was in almost as bad a position as was his driver. I had steered the slowing cart against the left wall, and this had stopped his movement by pinning him against the wall. But, he was now off the cart, facing the pea-green tinted wall. It was obvious I had to do something to get back in control of this potential disaster.

Somehow I had to get myself around the gurney with said gurney turned out of the way so that I could get my body against his and lock his knees. Holding the cart with one hand, I managed to get the other hand on Mr. Smart's back. Kicking away the gurney, I artfully spun his hulk around on one locked leg so that I could press my bulk into his lower torso, stopping him from collapsing into a leaden heap on the floor. That maneuver was completed successfully. There we stood, face to face: Mr. Smart's cold and clammy body was pressed against mine, his head snuggled on my shoulder. I realized that I could finesse him back on the cart as long as I could keep him upright, but by now, the damned cart was just an inch further away than would have been convenient. I tried to keep his body upright while at the same time I was fishing the gurney back into position with my free leg. To someone coming upon the scene, it would have looked as if I were trying to dance with him. The sweat was pouring down my face, the back of my neck was drenched. I was in a location where nobody else was likely to come by. I was beginning to realize that, ultimately, I was going to have to let him slide down the wall and onto the floor, then call for help. This was unacceptable, but my strength was waning. I would have been cussing Mr. Hardy Smart if I had the breath left in me.

There is some kind of magic—clairvoyance or sixth sense—possessed by those who are given the position of night supervisor. It allows them to stop suddenly in the middle of doing something mundane, sniff the air, and respond as if they had received some sort of ethereal message of something wrong, as well as the exact location of the problem. I had seen this happen too often not to believe that it was real. It did, however, seem to me that Hardy—I felt that we had been together long enough to be on a first name basis—and I had been dancing for a long time.

Miss Giddings' voice, steely with just a touch of disbelief, rang out behind me. "What in the hell are you doing, Larry?"

I was so out of breath, that I could only gasp, "T-T-Trouble."

"Yes, well … " she responded and proceeded to help me get the vagabond body back on the recovered gurney.

When we had finished, she smoothed out the shroud and gave me with a quizzical look. She asked, in a not unfriendly voice, "Do you think that you can manage the rest?"

With my breath nearly back to normal, I looked at her sheepishly. "Yes, Miss Giddings, I'm sure I can."

And without further incident, I did.

Another embarrassing Miss Giddings' event occurred after I was given a penicillin injection at employee health for a sinus infection. Back on my ward, within about 15 minutes, I went from perfectly normal to anaphylaxis: my tongue had thickened and I had bumps where my arches should have been. I was in deep doo-doo. The ward nurse shuttled me off to employee health. After receiving a shot of epinephrine, I wandered into the empty central supply room and sat there, feeling no pain. Alerted, Miss Giddings found me there, totally irrational. In my "drunken" state, my true feelings came out. I leaned forward right into her face and, smiling stupidly, said the following: "Mzzz Giddings, you're the best damn old nurse this damn old hospital ever had."

"Larry, I think you better go home now." With an ironic smile, she continued, "I'll sign you out."

A hospital orderly doesn't speak to his supervisor like that!

Langston

While I had many interesting experiences during my tenure at Good Sam, one that stays with me is my time with the ex-logger, Tom Langston. He came in from a hospital on the Oregon coast. He was a man who had no right being alive after a catastrophic logging accident. His lungs had collapsed and he had stage IV decubiti 3 centimeters deep. He was brought to us to die. But that was not to be. The Good Sam community rallied around him; he received intensive treatment for all of his problems. But he remained a completed paraplegic: he had use of arms, hands, and his upper torso, but no useful legs.

I met him on 4 East, first in a two-bed ward and then later in a six bed specialized paraplegic ward. What was special about him was his dignity: he was a proud man. I had no idea what his personality was before his accident, but it probably was similar to Tom Hufford, my to-be brother-in-law. Langston was a tree-topper by occupation—one who goes clear to the top with a belt around him, his purpose to cut off the useless top of the tree so that it falls away from him, breaking clean. One time out of a thousand, this does not happen and the tree splits. Tom was that one one-thousandths; his safety belt nearly cut him in half.

When he reached the rehab stage, he was an inspiration to his fellow paras and to the staff. If any of the other paralyzed patients needed help adjusting to their new condition, Tom was there for them. Why was Tom one who not only decided to live and to live as fully as possible? His wife—unlike many other paralyzed loggers' wives—was there for him. She visited him regularly, bringing the kids. Whatever he had been before, his family knew he was not the same, but he was still a man and somehow, more so. His no-nonsense "let's get on with it" approach was transferable to others who found themselves in this horrible life-changing situation. He was a natural leader who never asked for or ever gave mercy. He had an innate common sense and an abiding joy for whatever life had in store for him.

One night he had chosen to go to the fracture ward where, with many traffic accident victims in various splints, slings, and other orthopedic paraphernalia, he would laugh and joke with these guys. Traveling in a wheelchair and pretty independent—sometimes downright frisky—he zoomed in and was planning on screeching to a stop, but he completely misjudged his distance and speed and was propelled out of his wheelchair onto the floor. It was my luck to have entered the room right behind him and, for a split-second, I had the idea of helping him back into his wheelchair. Fortunately for both of us, I discarded that idea. He knew where I was while the ward of patients knew where he was and, most importantly, he knew where he was: there … on the floor. I knew if I tried to help him, he would have knocked me into tomorrow with his powerful arms. A patient in a far bed, who had been talking raucously, stopped only for a second before he continued the story he had been telling. I didn't move. Everyone else continued their conversations while Langston, in the most extended and difficult position possible, started to inch his way back into the wheelchair. I was standing directly behind it so I cautiously, surreptitiously locked the wheels. Conversations that were started before his fall continued for a very long time as Langston struggled silently, sweat pouring off his face.

After 20 minutes he managed to pull himself into a wheelchair-sitting position. Everything you needed to know about Langston was made clear in those interminable minutes. When there was a lull in the conversation, Langston screwed his face back into some semblance of a smile and said, "Well, Guys, it's time for a nap." I could feel the tension in the room—and the false humor—suddenly disappear in a moment of grateful release. Langston wheeled himself back to his room. I was very moved by what I had seen and felt I had to let him know. I approached his bed and attempting some kind of sympathetic support, asked if he needed anything.

He gave me a tired smile, which contained an implicit warning, and said, "Yeah, you can get the hell out of here."

Langston seldom shared anything with staff; however, several months later he stopped me and, with a smile, asked if I knew he had gone home for a visit. Surprised, I told him I didn't; I waited for him to elaborate. Langston paused, took a deep breath, and continued, "Well, everything had been going pretty good at home," then he added—to make it sure I knew he wasn't talking about his wife—"except with the kids." He clarified, "Susan, my daughter, got pretty smart-alecky and said she didn't want to do what I told her to, and when I threatened to spank her, she said, 'I'll just run up stairs and you can't get me!'"

Langston looked off in the distance as though remembering and said, "So I told her, 'It may take me a long time, but when I get there I'll make it worth my trouble.'"

She shaped up.

Then he went silent. That conversation was the most personal thing Langston ever shared with me. I just nodded and went on with my orderly business. Then one day, Langston went home, and I never saw him again. But, I'm not likely to forget him.

Near Fatal Encounter with a Urine Jug

In those days, instead of neat plastic bedside urine bags, the drainage containers for Foley (indwelling) catheters were one gallon, heavy glass jars. These were to be emptied at the end of every shift, and on a ward with many paraplegics, this was a full-time job at 6 A.M.. This particular night had been one of those crazy ones that occur way too often in healthcare; also I was especially tired having spent many hours prior to my shift painting. So in my tired, staggering condition, I picked up a nearly full urine jug and promptly dropped it. But to me, the whole scenario was in slow motion: the bottle dropped an inch every three seconds. I knew if it hit the floor, it would wake everyone and the whole ward would spring into life and have needs instantly. So I deliberately caught it on my left great toe—just like a tag on a morgue-bound body. The pain was incredible! As I was trying to express my pain quietly so as not to awaken the whole twelve bed ward, I was hopping around on one foot, whispering, "Oh, God, Oh Jesus, O God!"

Langston woke up. "What are you doing, Larry?"

Now I was trying desperately not to laugh; I shushed Langston, and picking up the bottle, limped out of the room.

Saint Vincent's Hospital

Considering all the various jobs I have had, one might think that I was a poor worker, but nothing could be further from the truth; I worked my butt off on almost all of the jobs I had. The problem was I just couldn't get over not doing things my way … when I knew that my way was the right way! Sooner or later this always resulted in my coming up against a boss who felt that working for me was not in his job description. I mention this especially in relationship to working in hospitals. There, when staff is short-handed, and they know you are capable of doing more than your job requires, they will let you.

I have never been afraid of blood and guts. So, when a surgeon was short-handed in emergency and needed an extra finger to hold a cut artery, he was not bashful about letting me do it. This was especially true if the doctor knows that you know you have no business doing that and, afterwards, have no need to tell anyone about your extra-curricular activities. Such was my relationship with Don Adams at St. Vincent Hospital. He bent the rules often when it was obviously necessary and took my help for granted—as I expected him to.

Don was one of a group of St. Vincent interns who were to be the last brought there for rotation through the various services; the hospital staff no longer had the time or energy to manage them … and they did need managing! Don was known to be a hotshot, and though married with four children, got into more than his share of nurses' panties. My fourth-wife-to-be, Sherry, had little time for him, and others put up with him or stayed away, but no one could fault him as an intern. He was good and he was full on all the time and driven.

He was a man's man as well as an accomplished female heartthrob; I just loved the man. He treated me like a colleague and did his best to explain the various things he did for patients. He was a soft-talker—when it suited him—but could blister the paint off the walls if things were fouled up. On several occasions, his wife, with their children, came to pick him up after work, and it was clear that he was going out of his way to give her short shrift. This flew in the face of his general concern for people and his patients in particular.

At this time Sherry spent a lot of time with her best friend and fellow student nurse, Charlene. Charlene was going steady with her doctor boyfriend, Don Carlson—another one of the intern group. Carlson and Adams were close friends and shared everything including girl friends on occasion. That group of people was the closest thing to an intellectual rat pack you could imagine. They used to have a guy's-only poker game every fourth Wednesday of the month. One or more of them would lose their ass at these all night affairs.

One Wednesday night just after midnight, I got a frantic call from Charlene. She said that Don Carlson had called to tell her that Adams had had a massive heart attack; his fellow doctors had performed open heart massage on him right there on the card table. It was touch and go; they got him into an ambulance and to the hospital. However, though he got the best treatment of anyone who ever went through that hospital, he was declared dead at 3:00 A.M. A profound shock went through the hospital. He had looked like the healthiest man you would ever expect to see. His wife came and was totally out of it; she had no idea that he had even been sick.

We all felt as though we had been run over by a truck, but as the days somehow went by, we began to get the full story. In med school, Adams had, while learning cardiac auscultation (listening to the heart through a stethoscope), discovered a loud heart murmur; upon further diagnostic investigation, he learned that he had undiagnosed genetic cardiomyopathy, a disease for which there is no cure and which considerably decreases life expectancy. There was no question in his mind that he was going to die before middle age. Thus, he determined that he would keep his condition secret, graduate from medical school, get married, have children, and live life to the fullest for whatever time he had. And that is exactly what he did. Later it was discovered that he had taken out over five million dollars in life insurance and his family was covered for life.

At the funeral, his wife said that even though she understood why he had tried so hard to distance himself from her, she would rather have had the husband she fell in love with than the five million. And she was furious at him for making the decision without asking for her input. Would it have made a difference? There is no way to know, though if he had received supportive treatment, it was only about 10 years later that heart transplants (the only long-term treatment for cardiomyopathy) were coming into use. Sherry felt that Adam's reputation as a man was overblown, but he was definitely one of my heroes.

I actually routinely did more questionable activities at Good Samaritan than I did at St. Vincent's. I was on call for the fracture wards, and routinely turned patients every half hour after surgery for spinal fusions. This unbelievably rich, idiot doctor would fill a ward full after having done the same kind of mostly useless procedures in England. He was a thoroughly hated man, with the bedside manner of Attila the Hun. He would have as many as twenty patients on the floor after a marathon of very expensive operations.

These patients would be read the riot act if they complained of pain or expected any moral help from this butcher. But one patient got even. After a new batch of fusions had been done, I went into a four-bed ward and saw one of the patients leaping from bed to bed. I pulled the call bell and raced to the nurse's station for help. When we came back immediately, all four patients were awake, but were just lying there quietly. Nobody said anything but the nurse called the doctor, who, for a change, bent his schedule and came in. He looked in the ward and then came back out and called the charge nurse and me all sorts of nasty names for wasting his time.

Looking directly at me, he said, "Doctor ... ah, I mean Mr. Wahl ... is apparently unaware that a first post op day back-surgery patient has pain just opening an eye and none are quite ready for the circus—for at least two or three days!!"

For a change, I kept my mouth shut.

Twenty minutes after the wretched doctor had left, a nurse's aide came back, holding her head and saying that same patient was out of bed, looking out the window. He swore there was a ragged-looking man staring in the window at him. When she tried to get him back into bed, he hit her in the face and knocked her down. When we arrived at the ward, he was still standing at the window, cursing the man outside. Three orderlies and two interns later, we wrestled this confused man into his bed and into full restraints. We wrote out a complete report for the good doctor who we knew would not come back until the next day. Nobody had ever heard of a first night surgery patient pulling this kind of a stunt, either before or after.

How did the bouncing patient's surgery work out? Just fine! Two days later he was mentally alert, feeling fine, and no worse the wear for his antics. The man at the window, who would have had to be 40 feet tall to peer into the 4th story window, was also fine.

Ozbelli

Back at St. Vincent's: Dr. Ozbelli was a 46 year old intern from Turkey. He was allowed to enter the internship through a student exchange program between the sponsoring country and the United States. He was a very—make that very, very—large man, who had an arranged marriage with a 15 year old in his native country. It was questionable if the United States was ready for the likes of him; the hospital certainly wasn't. Outside of my current wife, Ozbelli was the only human being I had ever known with unlimited energy … 24/7.

In a very short time, he made himself known to everyone, both as a doctor and as an unusual human being. He was one of the doctors who endeared himself to me personally by telling me that on my off time I could sit-in on a post-mortem he was doing at 6:00 A.M. one Saturday morning. Since I had taken many bodies to the morgue, I was well aware of the place. What I was not nearly so familiar with was 6 A.M. On the appointed morning, I arrived at the door of the morgue, knocked, and was let in by Ozbelli; he looked terrible. He had been out drinking and dancing—he was capable of drinking, dancing, and talking all night long and often did. Apparently he had outdone himself on this occasion, and the man who greeted me at the door was in the midst of the most horrible hangover in his recent history.

I snuck into the room, afraid that he might rescind his offer, but he just looked at me with those bleary eyes and wordlessly suggested that I could stay and watch as long as I was very, very quiet. I wordlessly agreed to these conditions. I helped him move a body from the boxes to the transfer gurney and stripped off the gown; the ex-patient was a medium height, medium weight, lightly-muscled male. Without a word, Oz made the traditional Y-cut, starting at the right shoulder to the xiphoid process of the lower sternum, then a similar cut from the left, and straight down from the sternum to the pubes. He carefully removed the organs, one by one, and weighed them, all the while talking into a lapel mike in a toneless, gravelly voice that had little life in it. I was full of questions but did not ask any of them, and so the whole procedure took place in silence except for the slush of organs removed from the body and the splat of organs tossed onto the scales. When the cavities were mostly empty, about an hour into the post, he took the cut below the chin and tore the face off and pulled it over the back of the head, along with the scalp. He then went for the electric saw and cut off the top of the head, exposing the meninges and the brain. His examination, for reasons I was not privy to, was much slower and more exact as he sectioned the brain and looked for anomalies: there were none. I assumed that he may have had reason to believe that the patient had died as the result of a stroke; thus the careful, but non-revealing examination. Anyway, finally he was done. He put all the parts back where they belonged, including all the samples he had taken, let me help him put the body back in the box, and signaled me out the door; he stayed to write additional notes.

Later that night when I saw him again, he was his usual vibrant self. He looked at me quizzically and asked, "Did I do a post this morning … with you?"

I agreed that he had. He asked if I had assisted him, and I said no: I just watched.

"Funny," he said, with obvious lack of memory, "I don't remember a single thing you said."

I allowed that I had said very little. At this point, we were interrupted, and he went off with another one of his intern friends.

Possibly because he might have imagined that I had actually helped him with the post, he invited me—along with a couple of staff nurses, two student nurses, and a few other friends—to go with him to a restaurant just outside of downtown. The restaurant—I think it was called "The Country Kitchen"—offered a coupon for a free 72 ounce steak if you could eat one with all the trimmings: potatoes, veggies, etc. When Ozbelli took this challenge, only two other people in five years had downed the six-plus pounds of food.

After he had finished the meal, to much urging and applause, he proceeded to dance with every female in the party, and when they wore out, he snagged a few women coming into the restaurant, this to much uproarious good humor. About two in the morning, I gave up and drove home, while a handful of the rest were making plans for going to an all-night bar. When his rotation was finished, Oz left for Turkey. I'm sure that our loss was Turkey's gain!

JJ

One of my fellow orderlies at St. Vincent's Hospital used the name JJ. JJ was one of the happiest, most well adjusted young men I knew. He was tall, well built, and good-looking. In short order he found a dozen or so girl friends among staff and student nurses. He and I became very good friends, and along with Lyle Kester, the diminutive cousin of ex-roommate and longtime friend, Ron Kester. JJ was great to work with.

JJ, Lyle, and I were sometimes called upon to control psychiatric patients who either came in wild, or became that way. There was one such patient who, on an earlier shift, had become irrational, was given sedation, and put in full restraints. When the night staff came on, the floor charge nurse decided that he should be taken out of restraints. This accomplished, the patient immediately became fully out-of-control! JJ, Lyle, the charge nurse, and I wrestled him back into bed. About two hours later, another nurse took pity on this patient—whose history she had not bothered to check—and off he went again. We were called back, and this time there was no question about getting him secured. He fought off all of us, as well as a heavy dose of sedative; a half hour later, sweating and swearing we got him back in bed. The following day they wrote orders to transfer him to Oregon State Psychiatric Hospital, but it took five burly cops to get him there.

We met JJ's parents at a party at his home. He now had a steady girlfriend, and we danced and partied the night away. A few months later, as JJ was approaching his 21st birthday, his friends were invited to another party at his parent's house. Near the end of the evening, his parents asked for our attention: they led us outside where a little, brick red Ford coupe was parked. It had a rumble seat and its convertible top was down; we all drooled. JJ looked like he had died and gone to heaven.

After we all went back into the house and after JJ had received the keys to his car, JJ's parents quietly led him into a back bedroom. It was like a long time before they came out. Suddenly the party seemed to have had the oxygen sucked out. JJ, sober-faced, excused himself, and we heard him drive off in his birthday car. His parents were obviously very upset; one by one, we quickly made our "thank-you's" and left the house.

A couple of days later we learned that JJ had not come home that night or the next. His girlfriend was hysterical; the police had been notified. We searched his known haunts until one of us found the coupe with the red ribbon still tied around it and the keys in the ignition, but no JJ and no note. His disappearance became a police problem. Many weeks later, we learned that when JJ's parents called him into the back room, they had told him, for the very first time, that he had been adopted. In apparent crisis over this totally unexpected disclosure, he left and stayed gone. It seemed that his 21st birthday was his last day on earth, as far as any of us ever knew.

AAA Ambulance

I left Good Samaritan Hospital after marrying Jan, but our marriage never really went very well. While going to Portland State College, I went to work for AAA Ambulance Company as an attendant. It was there that I met Bill Ravelli who was the office manager. His mother, as he let slip from time to time, could have been the original model for "Auntie Mame." However, his mother was even more eccentric—or just vanilla crazy—along with her multi-million dollar English family fortune. According to Bill, his mother felt that she should have been royalty, but being only filthy rich, she needed to marry someone claiming royalty: this turned out to be an Italian count named Ravelli. When Bill and I became good friends, he told me his story in bits and pieces. The story was pretty unlikely, but I didn't call him a liar. More about Bill in the next chapter.

23 | Bill Ravelli

As mentioned in the previous chapter, I started to work at AAA Ambulance that was owned and run by a crazy Irishman named O'Conner, a heavy drinker and a not too responsible human being. He was a member of the "Foot-Printer's," a social club for former detectives. His wife was a nurse and pretty much let him do whatever he wanted to. I never found out how Bill Ravelli got the job but, when I hired on, he was the manager of the three ambulances and crews—24 hours on, 48 hours off—that drove the three vintage Cadillac ambulances. The office was in a very large, old house, with bedrooms upstairs and a recreation room with a pool table and a small television. Bill had a dispatcher's room of his own.

Bill was short, heavy, with anemic coloring, and more than his share of problems. But there was something about him I was drawn to. After a few intellectual battles, I came to the conclusion that he was one of the smartest people I had ever run into and, in a relatively short time, I also discovered he was well suited to the job. He had developed a system for keeping track of the radio calls, but more importantly, he had a special system for keeping track of us. Bill was good at handling the very crummy characters who would turn out for this low-paying, long-hours job; I suppose I came under that heading as well. Since the turnover was excessive, often people were trained right off the street. None of us had any real ambulance training—this was before the advent of the EMT (emergency medical technician)—but since I had worked in a hospital, I had more experience than anyone else.

It was a cutthroat job. The four or five ambulance companies in the Portland area were not above poaching on each other's territories. Theoretically, each company had a section of the city and the hospitals they would cover but, on quiet days, we enjoyed cruising in other companies' areas, looking to steal business. Bill had a very special way of billing that kept the drivers and attendants honest. There was never a call that he didn't know where we went and how much we received in outside payment for services. He was a genius at keeping the books straight; some of the old timers, especially Clarence—who was my driver for quite a while— would have stolen the pennies off a dead man's eyes.

By the time I had been working at AAA for three months, I began to realize that some of the outrageous comments Bill made, especially about women, indicated he had problems with the opposite sex. When I would ask, he would tell me things about himself that were, at best, very hard to believe. But the man had a battery of experiences, both work and travel, that helped me believe some of the things he only hinted at.

My own life was so rich in experience, and I was so practiced at seeing other people's naked realities, I usually expected to see life at its most evil. I began to realize that Bill Ravelli had led a very strange life as well. It was hard for me to conceive of evil as a separate commodity. Evil, I knew, was rooted in sex that thrust millions of human beings from "ejaculate conception" into great dysfunctional families.

Bill's biological mother was a natural fool. To be a natural fool, you have to be unbelievably, incredibly rich and privileged in order to even attempt to survive your foolishness, and—with pardons to the cultural group—being English didn't hurt either! Years later I was to see the comedy movie, Auntie Mame. Flora, Bill's mother, was the perfect model for Auntie Mame—more accurately "Auntie Maim." The play is performed for humor but there was little of that commodity in Bill's life. Bill was more a servant in his indecently wealthy mother's palatial digs than he would ever be as the supposed eldest child, soon to be master of this particular palace. The dozens of servants with whom Bill grew up while his beautiful mother was making the rounds of parties and multiple assignations, became various aunt/uncle/parents for the young man. His life had originally come about when his mother realized that all the money in the world would not make her an English Lady. To solve this problem, she married the Italian artist, Count Eugenio Ravelli.

As hot as Flora may have been to her English suitors, Count Ravelli turned out to be a properly handsome, but totally cool and inherently disinterested husband. He stuck around after Bill was born, painting hour upon hour, totally uninvolved in their marriage or in anything his wife was doing. His wife, with no interest in changing her pre-marriage social escapades now that she was a bona fide countess, soon found her count fleeing back to his native Italy. Flora did not miss him; however, Bill got little chance to bond with his handsome father. By a trick of genetics, Bill looked like a pasty, dumpling clone of his mother with not a single feature or any sign of the dark brilliance of his father.

The count, who had nothing in the way of real money, had wrenched a good deal out of the estate as his part of the bargain, and their friends with their parasitic living arrangements and lavish parties made sure that there was a steady drain on the estate's value. Later when the English courts found that granted dukedoms and great houses could be taxed, it became more and more difficult to maintain their consuming lifestyle. Bill's perceptions of the estate and life style were most likely accurate: there were hundreds of professional photographs, along with multiple descriptions of sales and shows that took place on the estate, and newspaper clippings documenting multiple parties. Most telling to me was the intimate knowledge I had of all the treasures that resided in the Ravelli Portland household.

The peculiar position that Bill held in this erstwhile hierarchy consistently deteriorated over the years that he remained the only son and "the-master-to-be" of the estate. By the time all of these rewards should have come under his control, his mother's excesses and England's demands had reduced his inheritance to ha'pence on the pound. The legal and financial considerations were explained to Bill by the family accountant, who also had kept the Ravelli Count and Countess out of court and out of penury, but the good days were gone.

Bill spent a good deal of time with that family accountant, and I assumed that it was in that office in the bowels of the estate where Bill learned what he now obviously knew about bookkeeping and "book-cooking." This accountant made the final arrangements for the sale of the estate, set up a large, if not lavish, trust for Bill to draw on, and assisted the Countess Flora to flee from England to the United States, where she set up housekeeping in the Roosevelt Hotel in Hollywood, with a handful of a few loyal factotums. In her new environment, as a still beautiful but aging countess, she could screw many foolish young men to her heart's content. She would continue to know no more about her son than when they had lived together; under no circumstances were they anything but ships that passed in numerous nights. In the meantime, if there was anything Bill wanted in the way of material goods, he got it. He showed me a 1/4th scale train, including a steam engine, three passenger cars with child-size seats, and a little caboose, which he could ride over three acres of track. Bill had told me once how many bedrooms, baths, and fireplaces were in the estate, but the numbers were so outrageous that I couldn't contend with them. Even my "Uncle Al's" domicile couldn't compare!

Late one incredible day, Bill called and asked if I would like some of the paintings his father had done. It did not take more than a second for me to agree and to get myself over to Bill's modest home. There I was astounded to see three 55-foot Bekins' Moving Vans parked at the curb. The truck Bill saved until last to show me contained Count Ravelli's art: more than three hundred paintings in the van, carefully packed and crated. These represented the count's entire life's work, from the age of six until he had predeceased Flora at about the age of 40.

The first truck was empty by the time I arrived. Bill's wife, Judy, told me it had been packed with enough furniture to equip their small house thirty times over. Judy had pulled the pieces out one by one and went over the supply of treasures with people who came to these impromptu estate sales. Judy could smell money like a hound dog can smell sweat; she had worked all through the morning helping customers buy and truck away provincial and "Louie the 14th" tables, chairs, and beds, as well as special furniture. I was especially dismayed when watching the Bekins' men unloading two large 14-foot columns, saved from some part of the estate. There was no ceiling in Ravioli's present "estate" large enough to entertain these two "white elephants." Bill apparently had absented himself from the furniture sale, which had started hours before Bill had contacted me.

The second truck was amazing: it held a very small sampling of the massive multiple libraries extant on the estate. Obviously Flora had chosen these books for their potential value, although I'm sure she had not read many. The selection included a complete set of Bibles, numerous first editions, dozens of folios of architectural drawings, and books on special auctions. Here Bill did take a hand. As I surmised, he had read many of them over the years and held a real love for them. He pulled out a few dozen special editions to keep but had the majority shipped to various storage sites. He would not let Judy near them, although she recognized that some of the illustrated, hand-written works by monks were worth thousands, and books in Latin, written for Flora's predecessors, were probably priceless. As it turned out, it would have been better if they had been left in her hands, for their fate was miserable: many of the precious volumes were damaged beyond repair when they were consigned to the leaky, damp basement of a duplex I later helped Bill move into. It was at this time that he let me pick a few of them including a 200 year old, illustrated edition of the King James Bible in 12 volumes. These I later donated to the Rosicrucian Library.

When it was time to deal with the truck containing the paintings, I became witness to one of the most savage attacks on valuable art—with the possible exception of the historically infamous "Bonfire of the Vanities." Bill was totally in charge of the activities, and his dealings with the hundreds of his father's paintings showed all the restraint, class, and sympathy of an inquisitor at that historical "marshmallow roast." The larger paintings, which I am sure hung in places of honor on the walls of the estate and had ornate frames that were valuable in and of themselves, were set in one pile on the grass, where Bill systematically cut the paintings from the frames and put the empty frames so they could be bid on by many of the collectors present. When Bill cut the first one from its frame and held the naked and helpless painting in his hands, I couldn't believe what he did next. He had started a large bonfire where he was burning the crates in which the paintings had been stored. Without a moment's hesitation, he threw the painting into the fire, turned quickly, went back to where he was triaging the collection pulled from the truck, and, with cool dispatch, sent painting after painting into the flaming exile. I have no idea how many paintings Count Ravelli had painted in his lifetime, but that Bekins' truck must have held a large percentage of them.

To say that I, as an artist, was in shock would be a vast understatement. The gathered participants for the sale/fire watched in silent horror, apparently having been given the rules of this roast long before I came upon the scene. By the cremation of the twentieth or so painting, I stepped in front of Bill and just looked at him. Bill knew exactly who I was and what I was capable of, and, after only a few seconds of face-to-face communication, I knew exactly who he was. I shrugged my shoulders and stepped out of his way.

Bill was actually getting tired from his chores, his face a mask of hatred, glistening with sweat and grime. I could see by the lights in the house that Judy was looking from the kitchen window, her face an inscrutable mask. I thought over and over that I had never seen anyone, much less a friend, who needed killing more than Bill Ravelli. Then I thought of Tony Scrano, my stepfather, and my hot hatred for him; I could do nothing but just stand there, watching the carnage continue.

At one point Bill stopped and looked around as though he had just come out of a particularly hideous nightmare. He looked at the crowd of bidders, truck drivers, and neighbors—all of whom had opinions long drawn on this strange man—and took several deep breaths. He then looked directly at me and walked over to where I was leaning against one of the trucks; he had that simple boyish look he got when he knew that he had done something bad or had told a particularly ugly joke. He reached out and I took his hand without a word. Apologetically he said, "Larry, if there is anything you want, go ahead and take it. I'm finished here."

He walked away, and I hurt so much for him. But I hurt even more for his father whose large and beautiful collection I had just seen go up in smoke. I found a small painting, a portrait, which I immediately identified as Bill at about six years old, and set it aside; I knew that it would definitely not have lived to see another day. One of the less than a dozen left was a large painting that I recognized as a real treasure: it was probably the worst painting that I have ever seen! It had all the cleverness that only a fine painter can provide, but every technical thing that could be wrong with it, was. It was on canvas, but represented a dozen different mediums that went from areas almost completely devoid of color to flowers strewn about an open window that looked for all the world like it had been done by the notorious Saturday Evening Retired Ladies Painting Club. Various sections of the painting wandered off into impossible tangents without really becoming abstract, and linear lines spewed off in all directions. I just loved it! It was obviously a joke: a bad painting performed by a very good artist. I imagined that he had held a class in which he had tried to show his students all of the mistakes an artist who is just starting out or hasn't been paying attention in class would make.

I took those two paintings home and showed them to Sherry. I didn't tell her about the rest of the terrible destruction I had witnessed, but instead enjoyed taking her through the funny painting, pointing out all the sly, subtle, and humorous "mistakes" that Count Ravelli had made. And the one of Bill, I could see how perhaps it was a painting that he had done to show off his only English child. I thought this because these two paintings were near the end of the slaughter, as though they would be the pièce de résistance. The funny weird painting, because some of it was over-painted in water colors, unfortunately met with the same fate as some of Bill's books, for it was stored in an attic space in our 74th street home where a roof leak finished it off.

The count's portrait of Bill, I still have, and though I was offered a good amount for its frame, I would not part with it. It is a picture that tells far more than either the artist or the sitter would like to admit. In the painting, the artist must have looked at the young boy, wondering, "Who in the hell is he, and where did he come from?"

You could see all of the beautiful technique that went into exposing the too blond, too bland model that stared back at the artist with a vaguely disappointed look. A painting is like a chess game in that it usually has three phases: (1) the lay-in, the quick fertile strokes to establish the basic forms and suggest the colors, local and reflected; (2) the pulling-together of anything in the painting that is not quite right; and then (3) the best and hardest work, during which the greatest payoff is supposed to occur. In Bill's portrait, you can feel a profound sense of disinterest arising in the artist, and it becomes clear that he is bored with the effort. A door is literally closed on the subject: the canvas is stopped before it is finished; the relationship between the artist and the model goes to hell; the job is just not worth finishing … and so it isn't!! That final payoff is never acquired.

The Webly

After the incident with the paintings, I lost track of Bill for a while. I was up to my neck in the affairs of a painter's life and my adventures at The Mansion (Chapter 27) before I was again conscious of Bill. I now had art studios that provided me with work, and work I did. Bill had been doing our bookkeeping and our income taxes. I remember his wicked dry sense of humor—British, you know—and how often Sherry was impaled on it. For a year or so she was totally unable to cope with him, but finally finding him in a desperate position and wishing to keep his expertise for our taxes, actually arranged for him to live next door to us in Tigard. Here, while I worked night shift at "The Building" (more about my studios and art career, as well as "The Building" in Book III), she and Bill would work side by side, he on multiple outside tax returns and she on her Master's thesis. They became comfortable with one another.

Bill and Judy had grown further apart; Judy had given up all appearances of "the good wife" and cheated on him with impunity. Bill became more and more strange and disconnected. Thus, while we were still living in Portland, Bill appeared at our door wearing a kind of apologetic smile. We were shocked at his appearance: He was bedraggled and every visible ounce of his skin appeared to have been pulverized into a purple "jump suit." He informed us that Judy had kicked him out of the house. When we asked about his impossible skin color, he told us that he had had it with one of Judy's live-in lovers and, in a fit of rage, had taken out his Italian father's Webly, break-action, 50 caliber pistol and emptied it into the fornicator's sports car. This turned out to be a mistake, for the interloper wrestled the heavy English military side arm from Bill and proceeded to beat him with it until he was literally black and blue.

Bill had been going downhill since his divorce from Judy, and although he couldn't passionately love her, the divorce and the loss of his children was devastating. In the process, Bill and I became very close—the painting incident was left in the distant past—so I helped move him into a duplex in southeast Portland. The building had enough room for the boxes containing the hundreds of books that had come off the Bekins van; they were piled up in the walk-through basement connecting the two duplexes. It was this same basement that flooded and destroyed many of those beautiful and valuable books.

With skills learned at the English accountant's side, Bill found a way into his trust fund and whittled away his supposedly lifetime fortune. During this time, Bill and I frequently worked nights for private security outfits to make up a livable salary—Bill, because he never lost his expensive habits and so was broke most of the time; me, because of a special project into which I had sunk all my time and energy. Thus we found ourselves on the Balaclava, one of the two Russian tankers tied up at a god-forsaken, deserted dock. Unloved and disputed, these two seagoing C-3 tankers, embroiled in legal actions, were parked for six months with only two security guards aboard day and night.

In order for anybody to stay on these stone cold ships—there is nothing colder than a ship dead in Oregon winter waters—it was necessary to provide heat in the ship's petty officers' mess-room. This ample room usually accommodates the ship's complement of junior officers, such as cooks, electricians, carpenters, and the like, and provides sports magazines and crime, sex, and mystery novels. An attached pantry was connected to a pass-through to the crew's galley. Normally this would be as cold as the rest of the ship, but shore-to-ship power was supplied. With a little imagination, a few blankets, and the built-in tables and chairs, it was passably comfortable. Every hour or so, one of us would go out and patrol the decks, crew quarters, and engine room. Basically, this was a fire watch for the two ships—rust-buckets they appeared to be, still they were obviously valuable to someone.

In these eight-hour shifts with absolutely nothing to do, we talked, and I learned much of the rest of his history. Bill never admitted openly that he was gay, but it was obvious, and he knew it was. At what precise time he fell in love with me I'm not sure, but that he did is not open to argument. Bill never made a pass at me; in his heart of hearts he must have known that I was constitutionally straight. But I knew that we were sharing secrets we would tell very few people.

"Druuunk!!!"

Bill's English-made Webly revolver was a standard side arm for English officers as they took over many countries in England's attempt to control the known world. The weapon was constructed to stop their enemies, some of whom would have been able to take a chest full of bullets and still finish off many an English officer. This was the same weapon that Judy's boyfriend had used to nearly beat Bill to death after Bill had emptied it into the boyfriend's car. It did not figure in my life until much later during my last "date" with Bill.

Bill was a professional at heavy duty boozing, but had never before challenged me to a drinking bout. We started at four on a Wednesday afternoon, and by the time we had closed out the fourth bar—at midnight—I realized that something was seriously wrong with Bill. In such situations, I become John Wayne. Knowing that I am in an unusual position that could be very dangerous, all the tricks of the spy's trade kick in: I match the amount of alcohol consumed with an equal amount of adrenalin. I know, however, that the alcohol is going to win in the end, but I can usually put off the more crippling effects until the situation is safe.

By midnight we had both put away a couple of fifths without being falling-down drunk. Think in the terms of how much liquor you could put away with $900 and you will be in the ballpark. Along the way, I realized that Bill wanted me defenseless; there was nothing friendly about this. Eventually we ended up at his apartment, and we talked, we talked, we talked …

At some point, the loaded Webly came out of a drawer, and we talked about weapons, murder, and sex. Stunned, I realized that part of the evening, from Bill's point of view, was to include intercourse, either willing or forced, and because the weapon was sitting on the table between us, a murder/suicide for Bill or me, or both. Both Bill and I alternately picked up and laid down the gun. Then while talking in a mock attitude of indifference, I managed to casually unload the weapon and put it back in the drawer, having palmed the bullets. I took my leave.

It was now three in the morning, and as I drove down the deserted Bertha Beaverton Highway, all the liquor took effect as the adrenalin settled back into a more normal range. The highway became a combination rollercoaster and Fun House. I was barely able to stay on the road—weaving from one lane to the opposite on the two-lane road—when I spotted an Oregon State Patrol car entering the highway behind me. If he stopped me with my blood alcohol level in the stratosphere, I would be in deep, deep shit thanks to Bill's idiocy. So once again I called upon the adrenalin as I waited to lose the cop, but he stayed at legal speed, just behind me; I realized that he was doing a running check for "wants and warrants." This process involves radioing in the driver's car license, and even at this time of the night, takes several minutes. Somewhere this side of my passing out, the patrolman got the data there were no "wants or warrants" and pulled off at the next side road. I went back to using the entire highway.

The next thing I remember is driving down our street to our "tile house." I realized that I needed to navigate the elevated driveway into the garage and I needed to do this without taking out a corner of the house. I managed this, but just parked in the driveway and staggered up to the front door where I rang the bell. Sherry answered, awake and alert, and asked if I was all right. I uttered a single word … " Druuunk!!!" and collapsed onto the tiled hallway.

Sherry tried to rouse me, but I was finally done for the night and most of the following day. She dragged me into the living room, but couldn't manage to get my bulk up on the davenport, so she threw a pillow under my head, wrapped me in a blanket, went to bed, and waited for a report the next day. When I did wake at three in the afternoon, I didn't have even a well-deserved hangover!

Bill got his revenge later when he failed to send in social security payments for my one employee. When we tried to contact him, he was gone without a trace and we never heard from him again. Whatever happened to the poor little rich boy is anyone's guess, but I imagine he went back to England. In my prayers for him, I ask that he find someone willing to share his life, but if that did not happen, I would guess that he finally might have his last date with the Webly, alone.

24 | Sweethome

I vaguely remember a movie named "Sweethome, Alabama." There used to be an imaginary, geographically fictitious line between the Northern and Southern United States—called the Mason-Dixon Line. I have been doing impressions of "good old boys" all my life based on the many I worked with, but had set foot in the Deep South only on merchant marine sailing trips. Being in the South, I think, has everything to do with temperature—"sooooo yaaa'll move slower down South." My Sweethome was not in Alabama, but that was about the only difference.

On my 11 to 7 night shift at Good Samaritan Hospital in Portland, the head nurse called me to the 4th floor orthopedic ward where I often was located and said, "Larry, I'm going to send you to 4 West Back. There's only you and one nurse on duty: you two are the staff." She went on to explain that 4 West Back was the old—read ancient—railroad contract ward.

A nurse and an orderly—namely me—would staff this ward for the night, having the responsibility for 24 patients in one huge, open ward where 80% of the beds held men with various job-related injuries. It was dark, of course, and no patient's lights were on, so the first thing to fill my eyes was the nurse. I had expected an old, very large woman with orange hair and a behind ample enough for two (I know, I was an MCP until Sherry straightened me out). However, what I found was a slim, but well-built, student nurse, 20 years old with honey-colored hair in a bun, blue eyes, good-looking legs, and a pert, smiling face; I had just met Jan Nothinger.

If it had been busy—which, given the patient load, it should have been—what happened in minutes wouldn't have happened in days, if at all. Between start of shift and 7 am, I only had to answer three lights, while Jan wrote nursing notes, and the two of us stared at each other with tentative looks. What was about to happen was as predictable as two trains on the same track loping along at 80 mph on a collision course. We both appeared to have little question that we were looking at an inevitable sexual and emotional crash that would shake up the neighborhood for miles. There was no thinking involved. She was housed in the student nurses' residence across the street, and I had a rented apartment two blocks from the hospital. She learned that I was an artist; by the end of the shift, she had a modeling "contract," and I had a model.

We played at modeling. I learned that she had a vision of her body being out of shape because one breast was a little bit higher than the other. I had little difficulty in persuading her that both would easily fit in my mouth, and, all in all, we found very little to complain about in each other's persons, personalities, or appetites. Almost without thought, she became my woman. My being ten years older was not a problem, and for two weeks we just screwed and screwed. We didn't work together after that first night, but eventually it became apparent that we were going to get married.

The First Trip

In the course of time-outs for conversation, she told me about her family living in Sweethome, a small rural town about 90 miles southeast of Portland. It turned out that four families lived together on one farm complex. There was Jan's family: a mother and father, a ten year old brother, and an older sister, Ardis, married to Tom Hufford (the 2nd family) who owned and operated a "Gyppo" logging business out of the house. Tom and Ardis (3rd family) had an eight-year-old daughter, Cheryl (whom I adored). Jan's grandfather and grandmother also lived on the extended farm (the 4th family), along with dozens of chickens, pigs, dogs, cats, horses, and cows. And there were Amos, his wife Sarah, and their teenage daughter. Amos worked for Hufford and their families were often together, but they did not live in the farm complex.

The families had grown up with the logging business, and Tom Hufford was as close to a CEO as anyone in that wild and rugged country. Feeding this extended family was tricky. Everyone contributed to the family bounty; the nature of this kind of logging venture is hand to mouth at best. The necessary logging equipment, on the average, cost about the same as a Greyhound bus. Given the way they worked—turning down nothing and picking up the work that the big boys would not touch—their days were funny, perilous, and occasionally deadly.

All of this information just sort of passed over my head; it was interesting but the day-to-day realities of a bunch of gyppo loggers had little to do with me. Though I was born on a farm, I was no farmer and, though having been around people who worked hard for a living, I was no worker—when I didn't want too be. I thought of myself, when I thought at all, as a huge brain on one end with a constantly available penis on the other. I had no concept that I would have to blend in with this group. But this was to change. I realized that in getting married to Jan, there was no way that I was not going to get to know her family. Jan told me that there was Tom Hufford, and then there was the rest of the family. I realized that I was going to visit a farm of some sort that had farm people. I assumed that they would readily see that I was a city person and a total washout as far as being able to exist in their particular milieu. Jan was college-educated and a sophisticated, brainy nurse, so I expected that I would go out to see the "family" dressed in my best clothes and sit around and visit. I didn't own any boots, did not have any appropriate clothes for logging or hunting, and had little in common with these … common folk.

I noticed that Jan, who had learned to deal with my self-centered, total immersion in art, was wearing a Mona Lisa smile as we got ready to go to the farm. I actually caught her laughing silently while I was adjusting my tie, dressed in my best casual suit. We drove for a couple of hours and sure enough, deep in forest and ranch country, we found the farm, a few miles out of downtown Sweethome. It was a nice-enough looking town, and I thought I had planned this trip just about perfectly.

When we drove into the yard, I was jolted by what appeared to be the whole cast of the Beverly Hillbillies. Leading the troop were Grandma and Grandpa, an assortment of children, a couple of guys out of a redneck movie, one giant of a man—whom I at first thought must be the brother-in-law Tom—and another giant, calloused and tanned, hulk of a younger man, who belonged somewhere on the family tree. After meeting the welcoming party, Tom came up to me as the rest of the crowd disappeared back into the various houses. I was left with just Tom, who turned out to be a surprisingly small but wiry character, totally underplayed. Jan had disappeared into the kitchen to help with the dinner for the engaged couple; Tom and I stood there sizing up each other.

Tom had deep, soft brown eyes and fair but tanned skin. He was probably a good mix of English, Scotch, Irish and maybe a little French. He asked me about what I did for a living, and I started to tell him all about the hospital. He seemed interested, but sometime during my narrative, he seemed to lose focus on me: a strange worried look crossed his face as he looked past me towards the underside of the porch. A very large skunk slunk from under the porch, and I lost interest in my hospital work history as quickly as Tom had.

Tom started to talk to me in a kind of monotonous whisper. "Larry, don't make any sudden moves."

I was not inclined to do so under any circumstances. I had gotten wind of skunks before, but never had been this close to one.

Tom continued in this soft, propitious voice, while the skunk just stared at the two of us as though trying to determine if it was worth his time to spray us. Tom appeared to be talking to the skunk, but it was an intended aside to me. "Didja know these things can be safed?"

I reached back in my memory and thought of the time a hypnotist had put a chicken to sleep by turning it upside down and gently rubbing its tummy. I had seen a movie where a jungle-smart white man had walked up to a rhino in the middle of the road and rubbed it fearlessly between its eyes, close to that deadly horn, until the huge animal had fallen over … asleep. But a skunk?

I was so totally involved that I didn't think about having to take a bath in tomato juice, which I had been told was the only way to get rid of the skunk smell. Then I noticed that Tom was bending over, lower and lower, as he slowly approached the "beast," and finally knelt down until he was almost eye-to-eye with it. It did look a lot like the skunk was completely out of it. I was totally impressed. Tom scooped up the beast, turned it over, rubbed its belly a couple of times, and then yelled, "Here, Larry. You work on him!"

In one fluid movement, he had deposited the fairly good-sized skunk in my arms. Suddenly everyone including Jan appeared, all laughing hysterically as the (denatured) pet skunk and I peered into each other's startled eyes. For the first, but not the last time, I had joined the army of people who had been flimflammed, fooled, conned, and generally snookered by Tom Hufford. I was to learn that he was the county's eminent practical joker, loved by all but trusted by none. These assorted victims had formed a club, all of whom would gladly set Tom up with new, unknowing victims. This day the fool was I. I laughed as heartily as the rest and shook Tom's hand after I had gently placed the pet skunk down, who bore the unimaginative name of "Le Phew," and joined the rest of the family for dinner. It was my first time being Tom's "bitch" but definitely not the last!

The Second Trip

Having learned my lesson, for the next trip I didn't bother wearing a suit, just wore slacks and a woolen shirt. When we got to the farm at an unnaturally early (for me) time, we sat down for a huge breakfast. I was introduced to my first taste of venison; it was not bad at all. I wondered why we had been invited for breakfast, considering that I had worked the night shift, but went along without comment.

After the meal, Tom walked up to me, professionally sized me up, and asked, "You're pretty good-sized, Larry. How tall are you?"

I admitted that I was 5 foot 10 and 1/2 inches tall. It was then that I noticed that Tom was motioning me towards a small room where I could see a whole array of rifles in a tall opened case. He reached in and pulled out a small carbine for himself. With the door still open, he looked at me contemplatively and repeated, "five ten, huh. Well, you're too large for this little rifle. I'll have to get something that fits you."

I had never been handy with rifles, long or otherwise, but was aware that they are not apportioned according to the height of the individual who is going to them, but, "what the hell, when in Rome … " He sorted around in the cabinet and finally came up with one of the largest, heaviest-looking rifles I had ever seen. This turned out to be a 30-40 Krag. If it would not have killed an elephant, it sure as hell would have slowed him down. He put this "cannon" into my hands, looked around for appropriate ammunition, and announced that we were all going deer hunting.

By the time our army had been recruited, there were six of us. I had, in my checkered past, dispatched living human beings for Uncle Sam, but had never harmed a single other creature. The people that I killed—I was told—needed it for King and Country, but they were usually armed. Since I was not dressed for this adventure, Tom saw to it that I was outfitted in old, very worn and torn bib-overalls from Jan's grandfather, into which both a twin brother and I could have fit. It was ridiculous, but of course that was the idea. I was still trying to get along with the family, and it seemed that the only way to accomplish that was to impress Tom.

We started out in two pick-ups: de rigueur transportation in this part of the woods. Amos, I noted carried a "Carlson's Raiders" rapid-fire, fully automatic, circa World War II rifle. Any buck coming within range would not simply be killed, but would be blasted out of the county by at least twelve high velocity rounds before Amos would be able to get his finger off the trigger. How many discernable cuts of meat would be left after that fusillade was questionable, but it sure cut down on the odds that Amos would wound anything that we would then have to track.

When the trucks came to a stop, and Amos and I piled out of Tom's pickup, the two of them exchanged knowing looks: this tenderfoot jackass looked like a refugee from a second-hand clothing store for former scarecrows! Tom put on a soft, gentle voice and, in a believable way, said, "Larry, off this road, the trail ahead gets pretty nasty. It is a little too rough for you, so the guys and I will walk up the hill through the heavy brush until we reach a clearing. This will take quite a while, so we decided to let you take the easy path down through the draw. You will probably get there ahead of us, so just wait by the big stump. You can't miss it. That way, we'll all get lucky."

I bought this empathy for the tenderfoot and started out with my "canon"—down the hill and through the draw. The draw was, in truth, kind of pretty with all sorts of fallen timber lying about. As I walked on, it became obvious that this was not going to be a brisk saunter for me. I crawled up on one large, fallen tree, expecting the ground to be just on the other side; I was startled to find that the "ground" was four feet down. The 30/40 Krag struck me alongside the head, as we dropped down, gently crashing into a large branch that then returned the favor by hitting me hard on the head.

To my credit, I stopped and surveyed the terrain littered with fallen stumps, a tangle of trees, and covered with nonstop, large, vicious vines, which tended to hide the sky from my view. This impossible landscape, if you could call it that, indicated to me that for Tom's approval, I was going to pay a heavy price in time and effort. The territory ahead gave every evidence of having been impassable to man from the first day of Earth's creation. I gave serious thought to retracing my steps, but decided that if I were going to play the fool, I would have to own the part.

After my fifth and sixth falls off slippery logs, with feet snared in heavy twisting vines, camouflaged by tall grass and ancient undergrowth, I stopped and unloaded the rifle. With all the noise I was making crashing through the draw, the only thing I was liable to shoot was my own foot. The gun that weighed in the neighborhood of nine pounds gained six ounces with every step and a full pound with every fall. I was not a happy hunter. In what seemed like an hour later, sweating and cursing, I found a small hill ahead of me, cleared of rubbish and underbrush and featuring a very large stump. Sitting around this stump were my other five "companions," all sporting shit-eating grins.

Amos was flushed with laughter since they had heard me crashing through the quarter mile of impossible trashed timber. What I was doing was driving every living creature, from field mice to whole families of large and small animals, ahead of me, up the draw, and into the locale of the hunters who had bagged three bucks and a small partridge, while lying about the comfortable campsite. They did have the decency to offer me a cup of coffee from the campfire they had arranged. I quickly noted the clear road that the two-parked vehicles had easily driven to the stump, probably three or four minutes after my first crushing drop.

As we loaded the fallen prey into the vehicles, I realized that I had arrived. I was not the first, and I certainly would not be the last, to be "Tom'ed." In later trips, meeting various people in the neighborhood, I would learn that nobody—absolutely nobody—would believe any story or information that came out of Tom Hufford's mouth. And yet he was the most loved character in the land. He was at the top of my list of friends, a list that was never that long, and I appreciated the hell out of his lying, deceiving ass!

This next Tom-event occurred during a different trip; it exemplifies the nonsense in which I found myself embedded on yet another hunting excursion. The time it was after dark, and the goal was to outsmart the forest ranger. Tom and his buddies called this hunting by strobe light. The idea was to catch an unwary buck in the bright spotlights that were mounted, in abundance, on the pick-up. Once the lights immobilized the buck, it was easy to pick him off at a fairly close range. Then the problem to be solved was how to get the buck home without attracting attention: it couldn't be tied to the hood or roof of the truck. In a stroke of genius, Tom decided that the rest of us would hide out in the flatbed while the buck would be seated upright in the front seat, clothed in a plaid shirt and red hunting cap, between Tom and me. While it was hilarious to see, we never knew if it would have worked or not, since the ranger must have been busy with other things that night.

The Third Trip

It had gotten to the point where, leading up to the wedding, Jan and I were spending more and more time in Sweethome. Watching Tom con some poor innocent was now a spectator sport for me, and I had learned many of his ways. When the party of the six of us parked on a country road somewhere—geography was not my native language—I noted that the two-lane road curved along what I later learned was the South Fork of the Santiam River. The river was about 20 yards wide at this point, and the current was moving at a pretty good clip. Three of us had packed in Tom's pickup, two of our group were in a crew cab vehicle, and Amos was some quarter mile behind, driving the D-7 tractor with a huge cable reel attached to the back.

We all piled out of the car, and Tom looked studiously up a hill, which from about 20 feet above the river, rose at a 45-degree angle. Tom went to the crew cab and came back dragging a quarter-inch steel cable with a heavy "choker" attached. He handed it to me and said in a causal voice, "Here Larry, run this up the hill to that fallen stump for me." The indicated stump was about 40 feet up.

Having gotten rid of some of my citified innocence, I immediately answered, "Yeah sure, me and what army?"

It was then that I noted Amos had driven the tractor up the road, parked a hundred feet behind the other two vehicles, and was paying out similar cable from the D-7 reel. Two of the guys went back to help him and Tom. Laughing, Tom removed the choker from the short line it was attached to and reconnected it to the longer line from the tractor. At this point, three of us grabbed hold of the line and choker and started to struggle up this serious hill. I did my part, but still the three of us had to inch our way. Our efforts finally resulted in 100 feet of cable linking the drum on the back of the tractor to the end of the line. We were red-faced and out of breath as Tom, the smallest of us, now struggled with the chocker—a kind of heavy metal noose—to get it under the fallen log. Amos grabbed the loose end, and with a little digging, they completed the cable circuit around the fallen, partially buried, but very substantial-looking log.

The mechanics of this endeavor were apparently simple enough. The job was to have Amos fire up the wench carrying the quarter-inch cable, gently and carefully pull it taut, and then pull the log down the hill. Pretty straightforward ... you would think. As we got off the hillside and came down to where the trucks were parked—considerably away from where the log would presumably slide effortlessly down the hill—we watched in dismay as the fallen log seemed unwilling to cooperate. At first, Amos gave the fallen soldier more and more pull. The sound of the tractor engine strained to remove the apparently all but free spar.

After a while Amos put the engine in neutral and came walking back to where the rest of us were standing. "Damn!" Amos said with a worried look, "That blasted thing looks as though it is planted there. I can't see what is holding it up."

Tom allowed that Amos should run the tractor a little further back up the road and see if a different angle wouldn't do the job. We all moved a little bit farther down the road; we were out of the way of any path the log itself could have taken. Amos got back on the D-7 and gave it gas. The engine went into a full deep-throated roar, and we could hear the engine gasping for additional horsepower. But the damn log just lay there, resolutely defying the second law of thermal dynamics, gravity, and a serious source of power.

As we waited, disbelieving, Amos lost patience with the reluctant wooden column and, while still keeping full tension on the cable, started moving the D-7 slowly down the road. We marveled as we watched the quarter-inch cable shrink to half that and start singing like a lovesick violin. None of us noticed that the cable, just flicking the surface of the hill and sending up a cloud of dust behind it, was headed toward the base of a tall stump about five feet in diameter. This "bad boy" had been left behind, probably for the same reasons that the log we were trying to coax to the road would be left. However, the dynamics of the situation were very much different than any us could possibly have conjured.

When the "singing" cable crossed the stump, it was like a magician's trick. The stump didn't seem aware of the cable, just sat there, but we could see that the cable, being pulled at an angle by the tractor, appeared on the other side of the stump: no effort or stress. It seemed as if the stump paid no visible attention to the cable that had just effortlessly passed through it. Then there were a few seconds while the stump finally acknowledged that it had just been freed completely from its mighty roots. It began rolling down the hill, slowly at first, and then faster and faster—toward where we were standing!

We all moved as though connected by a single mind. Amos, two hundred feet behind us, let off the gas and just watched in amazement as the stump—"God Almighty. Free at last"— started bouncing down the hill. Its jumps got longer and longer, as though it was trying for some varsity record. After seconds/minutes of falling, it caromed, with a crunching splat, onto the road equidistant between Amos on the tractor and our parked trucks. The severed stump sat on the road for what seemed like an age, and then, as though arranging with its agent for the second leg of its flight, took off in a grand parabola, sending its thousands of pounds of weight into the middle of the South Fork of the mighty Santiam River, creating a geyser of water and spray forty feet high.

There followed a long, reverential silence.

Before we had started our ill-fated logging attempt, Tom had pulled six loggers' helmets from the crew car and made sure that each of us had one. The National Forest Service warden was always trying to catch up with Tom and nail him and/or his crew for multiple infractions that the warden knew were constantly being perpetrated by these gyppo artists. The oversize log that we were originally trying to bag probably legally belonged to someone else. The operant word is legally: What was a necessary regulation was more like an extremely mild suggestion to Tom.

Thus no one was surprised when the warden came a few minutes after we had retrieved the slack cable and chocker and were just packing up. The warden parked his car right behind the tractor and slowly exited his vehicle. He was a smart man and knew of Tom's many antics. He looked at each of us, dutifully clad, shoed, and helmeted; he asked how we were. And looking carefully around and checking the equipment in the vehicles, he viewed with special interest the D-7 and the need thereof, though he didn't ask. He is a policeman looking at what he knows is the scene of a crime, but unfortunately for him, finding neither viable suspects nor evidence of a crime, cannot proclaim even a minor infraction of the regulations. He finally gave up. The nefarious stump in the rising waters looked totally at home. Finding nothing else out of place, he left.

It was a near escape. We had probably broken any number of safety and National Forestry rules, but Tom had emerged untouched. Well, at least this time. But as we stood there, Amos started to laugh and proceeded to tell a tale not for general consumption. Screwing up his ruddy, moon-face into a hideous smile and turning to me, he said, "Hey Tom, tell Larry 'bout how you loaded your first brand new pick-up."

For the first time I saw Tom flustered. He actually blushed, and turned away, saying,

"You go ahead, Amos, you tell it so much better than I do."

Amos warmed to the subject and, with the rest of the crew listening, he recounted how their company had finally paid off one of the major pieces of equipment and, for a change, had had a very good year. It seemed that Tom had set his heart on a perfect piece of inventory: a brand new, heavy duty, Ford pick-up.

As Amos closed in for the kill and built to the punch line, he said, "Well, Larry, picture a scene just like the one we had today: similar log, same cable, same problem, same results." Here he stopped for maximum effect, " … except that Tom's brand new Ford was parked a lot closer down the road than we are now. The truck was so new it didn't have insurance yet; Ol' Tom was so anxious to use it. The same kind of heavy load, traveling at the speed of a small airplane, loaded the truck in one shot before it rebounded off into the Santiam."

Tom spoke up. "Yeah, but give me credit. The next day I got the insurance. They paid off because we wrote up all the details, but dated them three days earlier!"

Tom continued the story, laughing with the rest of us, describing how all four wheels—not just the tires—had flattened out against the road on the same plane as their axels while the drive shaft had been buried in the roadbed; the whole thing was totaled in what had taken only about three seconds. Tom called for a friend's tow-truck; he had sworn the friend to secrecy. The car was towed (what was left of it) to the back yard of the house, covered in tarps, and kept secret for three days until the paper work was done. He then called the same friend, thoughtfully compensated, to drag it to a lot for inspection by the insurance company.

After Amos and Tom had shared this story with me, I knew I had indeed arrived and was now definitely part of the crew.

Tom had his own inimitable way of transferring bad news, especially to other suckers. When he had the insurance contract for the destroyed Ford pickup in hand, he waited a day, then had the wreck, sitting pitifully low on a flatbed truck, towed within a block of the insurance agent's office. This company insured all of the high-tech equipment that even a small gyppo outfit had to have to stay in business, so a damaged but new Ford pick-up was not too big a deal.

Tom shuffled into the small office and told the agent, a nice little man called Jack, his version of what had happened: "I had a little accident with my new Ford."

"Gosh Tom, I'm sorry to hear that. I know how you really loved that bright white pick-up and I remember you showed me the decal you wanted put on the side. Did you get that done?"

Tom adopted a stricken look. "No, I had the accident before I got a chance."

With a try at serious concern, Jack said, "I'm sorry. What happened? An accident?"

"Well, not actually. A wheel fell off."

Now, with a little more real concern and in a surprised voice, Jack asked, "It just fell off?"

"Yeah, flat on the ground." It was obvious that Jack had never been one of Tom's victims before, so it was like taking candy from a baby.

"Well, my God, that's an easy problem; the manufacturer is responsible, and we can bill them directly!"

Tom smiled wanly and then added, "Well, actually it was a little more complicated."

"How?"

"It was more than one wheel."

Jack exploded in spite of himself, "What do you mean more than one wheel? Two, three … ?

"All of them!"

At this point Jack lost all sense of reality. He tried to keep his voice even as he snorted, "I've never heard anything so ridiculous, Tom. Have you been drinking?"

Making sure he did not allow a smile to sneak onto his face, Tom answered as evenly as he could, "Well, it is still even more complicated so maybe I better just show you the truck."

"Yes, I think that that might be a very good idea!"

Tom waved toward the door, and the two of them left and headed down the block.

When they approached the flatbed truck, Jack saw that there was a small crowd, including the whole logging crew, smiling and looking at the wreck.

Jack just stood there looking like he was trying to figure out exactly what the hell he was looking at. Finally he looked at Tom and said over and over, "You son of a gun! You son of a gun!!"

Everyone broke out laughing, including Jack, who then let the logging crew give him the real story of what had happened to the truck, but of course they didn't bother to tell him exactly when it had happened. They all repaired to the nearest bar and saluted the very short existence of the brand new, white, Ford pick-up.

Tom knew that he had someone else to cover for him when next he had the opportunity to scam some luckless innocent who had the bad luck to meet … Tom Hufford.

After several months, Tom became more likely to let me in on some of his efforts, legal and otherwise, and I found the entire extended family more and more interesting as well. Tom's cute eight-year-old daughter, Sheryl, was my very favorite of the children; we forged a bond based on art. She was very clever and almost as full of good humor as her father. I could see her in light of what my child Kathy might have looked like at this same age.

Tom was not an indifferent husband, and I am sure that he loved his wife, Ardis, as much as she loved him, but Tom was really the father of the whole extended mess, not excluding the company itself—which was always hanging by a thread. The cost of some of the equipment and the various strains on the finances were always with him. Such was the case when Ardis came to him and complained about a strange noise in the family station wagon. This car was Ardis's lifeline to all the homemaking and community activities in which she was involved. Tom tried to find the time to take a good look at the wagon, but something always drew his attention away. Ardis gave up on nagging him. She had discovered that when it started banging and clanging, the noise would become less if she made the car go a little faster. This worked for a while, but gradually the noise got louder and louder while Ardis got faster and faster.

One day as she was tooling down the road, the noise got unbearably loud, so Ardis gave the car more gas. When she looked down at the speedometer, she found she was going over sixty miles an hour. This, she knew, was much too fast for this country road and she made the decision to stop, park, and wait for Tom to finally do something about the problem. As it turned out, the car came to its decision before she did. As she started to take her foot off the gas and check on Sheryl in the back seat, the car, at sixty miles an hour, suddenly locked up! All four wheels stopped completely, and Ardis fought to keep the slewing station wagon from hurtling off the gravel road. With wheels locked, it skidded fifty feet and finally stopped in the middle of the road, with the engine no longer running. Another car was right behind her and immediately stopped to render assistance, having noted that the car had gone through maneuvers no station wagon was ever created to perform. When she tried to restart the engine, she didn't even get the satisfaction of a click.

The neighbor—this included anybody living in the same county—had driven her to a phone, where she called Tom. I was with him when he answered and I noted the concern he had when he talked to Ardis, especially when he asked if anybody had been hurt. Tom signaled me to follow him as we went to the garage, climbed into a flatbed truck with a lift on it, and drove out of the yard. About twenty minutes later, we came upon the empty station wagon. The engine still had wisps of blue smoke coming out of it, but Tom didn't open the hood; instead, he directed me to help him load and chain it up. We carried it on the truck back to the house, picking up Ardis and Cheryl at the neighbor's. Ardis didn't say a word, but her expression spoke volumes. She simply described, tersely and without feathers, exactly what she had done, what the car had done, and then walked off to start dinner.

Tom got on the phone, and soon the rest of the gang appeared. The wagon was transferred to a garage where they were allowed to see the engine from underneath. From Ardis's quick but accurate description, Tom knew a new engine would have to be supplied, no question. We all took turns looking at the engine. The oil pan was intact, so Amos dropped the pan, and the oil flowed into a handy pan—except for that part of it that always flows directly into the mouth, beard, and face of the mechanic. Amos let out a small whistle, and said, "Tom, you just won't believe this … "

Tom answered, "Yeah, I bet I will."

We pulled over the big jack and lifted the car so we could get completely under it. What Amos had whistled about was apparent. The u-shaped, heavy, bolted, steel carriers that hold the retaining bearings, through which the crank-shaft turns, had had so much pressure applied that the threaded bolts had been stripped and were a couple of inches away from being seated—they were just barely hanging there! But far more startling was the fact that the six-cylinder crankshaft, built to be unbreakable, was separated into three pieces.

When we got the engine completely disassembled, Tom put the pieces of the crankshaft in a big shopping bag and signaled me to come with him. We drove to the Ford dealership in downtown Sweethome. I entered the office first and was given a cursory look, while Tom brought up the rear with the shopping bag.

The parts manager looked suspiciously at Tom and the bag and finally asked, "What you got in the bag, Tom? We don't fix any broken cats."

"It's just another example of shoddy service," Tom said with a straight face.

"Yeah, well there's a lot of that going around. You want repair or replacement?"

If you didn't know these two people and didn't know for a fact they had had dealings before, this might have sounded like a real conversation. Tom lifted the heavy bag up on the counter and rolled out the three pieces of the drive shaft.

To his credit, the parts' manager's face didn't change expression, but he handled the various pieces with workman-like precision, wiped off his hands, tipped his cap back on his head and said, with serious and thoroughly believable earnestness, "Yeah, Tom, we see this sort of thing all the time. There is no question that this was the result of shoddy workmanship." Here he carefully picked up the parts piece by piece and put them back in the sack. "I'll write this up, send a copy to your insurance company, and you should receive your check in … say … a couple of … centuries."

As we left, the parts' manager continued to smile, but was slowly shaking his head from side to side while the business manager appeared and again rolled the pieces out on the counter for the amazed crowd that had gathered as soon as Tom and I came in. He let them all take a long look at what would be another Tom Hufford story.

After two years married to Jan and spending much time with her family, I came to realize that I didn't have much of an idea of what something resembling a normal life would look like. The adventures with her family did nothing to help life make more sense to me in the long run. Tremendous personal differences between Jan and I came more and more to the surface, especially after we moved to a very large and complex building, which had, in the long past, been a U.S Army Regimental Headquarters in Portland. It was located in an older part of town, just south of downtown—now a rebuilt and integrated part of Portland State University, previously known as Vanport College.

This building—our new home—had a full print shop in the daylight basement and two stories above, with an outside stairway leading from street level to vacant rooms on the first and second floors. Steve Gann was the owner of the entire building; it was his printing shop in the basement. A room on the second floor was perfect for a studio, and I equipped it as such. The first floor apartment appeared ideal; there was even a small, closed-in yard in the back where our dog, Diggle-D-Diggle, could run.

While still working at Good Samaritan Hospital, I decided to start a pre-med course at Portland State University. I worked evenings at the hospital and took classes by day. Since I took on—attempted to take on—16 units of pre-med courses, I have no idea when I slept, if at all. Jan got the opportunity to work with the Portland Red Cross in a local training and disaster unit. With these schedules, we saw less of each other. The trips out of town for her became longer and longer, and the Portland Fire Fighters, who supplied support and transportation for the nurses, started to see more of her than I did.

Steve Gann hired me to do some sign work for him, and though he had promised that the shop, directly below our rooms, would not be operating through the night, that is exactly what he started to do. His wife was pregnant, and when Jan was back from out of town jobs and I was at school, he and Jan gradually struck up a friendship. When I complained that I could not sleep at night because of all the noise the presses were making, I got no relief from Gann. And Jan always seemed to be on his side …

Where our love life had been close to perfect, in the times when we could get together, Jan seemed to have more and more trouble with sex and extended the lovemaking into contests to see who could last the longest; I believed it was my fault that I was not satisfying her. With my heavy work and school schedules, our life became impossible. Eventually, trying to fit our agendas together became less of a consideration, and we drifted farther apart. I started to stray. It became apparent the she was having more than work relationships with the handy-randy firemen with whom she was thrown together on many overnight trips.

The Last Trip: Pick-up Sticks or Not

There was one more visit to Sweethome: the last time that we were all a "family." Tom and Ardis also had their problems: beloved Sheryl was diagnosed with leukemia. Her illness severely drained the family finances even though her health went downhill in a hurry. Almost as violent was a blow to Amos—and to Amos, unforgivable: his pretty teen-age daughter was pregnant. I was amazed by the reaction of this man I thought of as a friend. He literally threw her out of the house, with less concern than he might have had for one of the deer he decimated.

Tom's logging company was coming apart. Ardis started drinking heavily; she was a pathetic drunk. I made a point of going with them to the Children's Hospital where Sheryl lay dying. They had spent weeks watching her slowly disintegrate, and, on this day, I was insistent that they leave the unconscious child and take a few minutes to eat and rest. It was obvious that Sheryl was not going to make it to tomorrow. I stayed with her, to spell them. I talked to Sheryl about the journey she was about to take. Though unconscious, I knew that at some level she could hear my voice. In my mind, she merged into Kathy, and I was finally able to say good-bye to both Sheryl and Kathy. Mercifully, she died, and Tom and Ardis's nightmare was finally over, but unfortunately so was their marriage, the company, and their extended family. After this, I was not aware of anything getting better for my Sweethome family; the whole assembly became part of the past for me.

It was during this period of hardship, before Jan and I had our final breakup, that I went on one last adventure with Tom. He was under tremendous pressure, and there was little joy to be had. He asked me to come with him on a job. It was only later that I realized how strange and singular that job was, and it was dangerous to the point of insanity. What I saw was a grim Tom who, trying to put on a brave face, informed me that we … we had a special job. Since I had never been privy as to how the family business was legally set up or, in any real sense, how their contracts were found or how they were connected to the counties in which they were allowed to operate, I had no feeling for procedure. These were not the kinds of problems with which I was interested in anyway. I only wondered why it was to be just Tom and me on this particular mission.

Tom loaded the crew cab, and we drove for some distance before stopping. I could hear the river, the Santiam, but it was strangely hushed. We exited the truck. Tom opened the supply area and handed me a 12-inch chain saw, while he extracted a Triton, much, much larger. We walked down a small trail and stopped before one of the strangest scenes I have ever seen.

On jobs for the government, there were many times I knew my life was in jeopardy, but the jeopardy dealt with human parameters. There was human greed, cowardice, viciousness, arrogance, pathos, anger, madness, and murderous intent: any of these characteristics can be found in any human being under the right circumstances.

What faced us, as we stood on the swollen bank of the Santiam, was the largest logjam I had ever seen, outside of a movie screen. But this was no movie. A hundred large logs were heaped, helter-skelter, in the middle of the growing river, in one unbelievable array of disorganization and chaos. The top of this giant pile of "pick-up-sticks" was about thirty feet high; toward the banks on both sides, the log pile graduated to lesser spiky groups of more simple tangles. I watched Tom, waiting for some explanation … for the rest of the crew.

When Tom jumped up on the first two logs in his path and made his way to the center of this mess, I shrugged, thought a moment or two, and then followed him out on the pile, still thinking that he would say something, anything. But he didn't … until I caught up with him in the middle of the river. He looked surprised when he saw me, especially since I had no cork boots and he knew that I wasn't very nimble in forests or on logs. (Looking back on this incident, I think I was supposed to be the witness to his suicide, but I fouled that up because then he had to take care of me.)

After he had surveyed the gigantic arrangement of lumber on the hoof, he looked at me again, studying me seriously. For Tom, this was both unusual and off-putting. There was no humor here, this was not a joke, and it sure as hell didn't appear very funny.

"Larry," he said, shouting over the sound of the bloated river, "take your saw and start cutting over there to your left, on the far bank. See if you can find a log jammed into the bank and work on that. It will take you a little while, but just keep at it. When you finish, move across to the other side and just wait."

I looked thoroughly confused, so he said harshly, "Just do it! There won't be a second chance. What you are trying to do is crack that spot about twenty feet from that far edge. Nothing will happen, and everything will be fine. I will be right here, more or less at the bottom of the central pile. Nothing will happen for several minutes, but what you do is critical."

Critical was a hospital word, and I understood it well. But I had never heard the term coming out of Tom's mouth. It was not reassuring.

Almost casually, Tom started up the powerful Triton and made a couple of cuts. I was turning, getting ready to go to where he had directed me when I heard the Triton shut down.

He signaled me back over to him and with more reality and earnestness than I had ever heard from him—he enunciated every word—said, "When the right time comes, grab your saw and run like hell for the nearest bank." Looking sternly at me, he said no more.

"When the hell is the right time, and how am I supposed to know it?"

A grim smile traced its way across his face. Actually it was just a kind of flicker and then it was gone.

Tom fired up the Triton. Without cork boots or spikes, I gingerly made my way across a half dozen logs until I saw one that had its big butt high up in the air and its pointy end lodged solidly into the bank we had come from. With the noise of the river, the Triton, and my own chain saw, I couldn't have heard Tom if he were yelling at the top of his voice. I set about cutting my log about six feet from where it impaled the bank. I cut through, but nothing happened except that the log was cut.

Although the journey across the logs was treacherous because of the curved sides and the skewed arrangement, there was a definite solidity to this immense sculpture. It appeared rock solid and it looked and felt as though it had never moved and never would move: it had just grown there. Even in my mind's eye, I could not see the accidental forces that had built this structure as solid as if it had been modeled in concrete. And so, I wondered how long this would take and how I would know when it was time … the right time. With idling pauses from his Triton, I could hear Tom picking his way through the tangle, but still nothing was happening.

Then it happened!

There was a small, but inescapable shudder. That was it … just a small shudder. I looked up to see Tom literally dancing across the logs, coming towards me at full speed. If I had thought, I would have dropped the chain saw and run without it, but Tom and the Triton would be upon me in a split second. It had taken me a careful three minutes to gain my position at the edge of the logs, but it took less than three seconds to reach the bank and safety. At some point, I felt Tom's hand just barely touching my right shoulder. We were out of there that fast, though Tom had been thirty feet away from me.

During the last few steps, a heavy 40-foot spar had passed a safe four feet above my head, one that could have squashed me like a bug, but it had been only an unreal blur. Everything was in total motion. The sky was spinning, the logs were arcing in impossible directions, water was splashing, and huge waves were piling one upon another. The river was roaring with pent-up passion. We found ourselves standing safely by the side of the truck, while all the rest of nature went into paroxysms of crashing fury as truckload after truckload of timber was sent down the infuriated river.

As we stood shaking, fully adrenalized, laughing insanely, and banging on the truck, Tom yelled over the sound of logs and moving river, "Goddamn it, Larry, why were you in my way!"

"Screw you, Tom, I felt your fingers but you never got a friggin' chance to push!"

We both slid down to a sitting position, our legs having decided we had stood long enough, and cradling our chain saws, we laughed the hysterical laughter of the intentionally damned!!!

Later, when I might as well have been living alone and as I was unable to sleep or do art work, I took a room in a house in SE Portland with an attic in which I was allowed to paint. It was my relationship with an older woman working at the hospital that was the final straw for Jan. Without any discussion with me—I didn't care anyway—she had Gann, who was also an attorney, set her up with divorce proceedings; at the same time he helped her clear our rooms of our shared belongings and furniture, including many of my personal items. During this endeavor, one day I discovered Tom in the house helping ransack it. We just looked at each other with great sadness. I expected nothing different from him, since he was much more family to Jan than I was.

25 | The 4th Wife

I probably was the worst possible example of a boy-man to suffer marriage upon a trusting soul. But that had not stopped me from three former ones. They should have been called mirages, for they were things of fleeting whimsy: a driving sexual need and not much else. The years of sailing and drifting and the years of working as an undercover intelligence agent/assassin—kept mostly unconscious of the acts I was ordered to commit—did little to establish anything resembling a normal persona. The story of my improbable early years does much to explain, but little to excuse, the dark and disturbed tapestry of my life.

I recognized Sharon (Sherry) Johnson, student nurse, as a target for marriage number four, although I did not think of the situation in quite such cold terms. Sherry was and is the most remarkable person I have ever known. She was small, like my real mother, but all the similarities ended there. Sherry was one of those people who you know is going straight to the top. However, when her nursing student friends found out we were planning to get married, they ostracized both of us, and, as a consequence, where Sherry had always helped each of them with their wedding preparations, and later their baby showers, not a one of them the returned the favor. I had a hard time forgiving them for these slights. I know that they were not thrilled that, at 21, she was going to marry a man ten years her senior who had three failed marriages. Strangely enough, this shunning was at the same time impersonal, for there was never anyone at the hospital who questioned my reliability, courage, willingness, or ability to work. At question was my suitability as a husband, and then there was the Catholic thing: Sherry was still a practicing, converted Catholic. I offered to write for a papal dispensation, but she was already disillusioned by the intellectual restrictions laid on by her adopted religion, so rejected that idea!

My first view of my future 4th wife was as she walked away from me on one of the wards at St Vincent's hospital wearing a "sack" dress—she swears it was her student nurse's uniform, but I know otherwise. Since I was still married to Jan—not that this had stopped me before—I viewed her with much interest, but with a hands-off consideration. Besides, her protective friend, Char, would have made sure I didn't get near her, at least not yet. I didn't see Sherry again— she was away from the hospital on special rotations—until a fateful New Year's Eve party at Don Carlson's. Don was an intern at St. V's and going with Char at that time, so unbeknownst to me, Sherry was also invited to this party.

It was a dark and smoky room with lots of alcohol flowing. I was lounging against the wall opposite the apartment door when I noticed more guests arriving: among them was the girl in the sack dress! Some time passed with more booze consumed, and then I noticed her looking at me—"across the crowded room!" The next thing I knew, she crossed that room, walked up to me, kissed me profoundly, and casually walked back to her side of the room!

I was not to see Sherry for another six months. In the meantime, my relationship with Jan had become terminal, and I had asked her to file for divorce. I was an orderly at St. V's on the evening shift but also was working for AAA ambulance. And in my spare time I was improving my painting skills and was hired to do wall murals for local bars. I occasionally saw Sherry at St. Vs, but we were both so busy that no further connection was made. Until ... one evening Char came down to the cafeteria (always the matchmaker, that one) where several of us were having dinner and discretely told me that Sherry had just broken up with an unsuitable boyfriend and was feeling awful. Would I like to meet her? Of course I said "Yes."

At the end of our shift, we orderlies were again horsing around in the cafeteria when here she came, having been told by Char that I would be there and wanted to meet her. Despite our initial physical encounter (across that smoky, crowded room!), she seemed rather shy and quiet—not how I perceived her to be. Maybe it was because I was with the guys or because, as Char had said, she wasn't feeling too good about herself. At any rate, I asked her if she would like to go somewhere for coffee—never mind that the cafeteria had plenty of it. So off we went in my 1937 Chrysler to search for a coffee shop still open at midnight. I don't think we ever found one, but when we first started out, Sherry reached up and tuned the radio to a classical music station. At that point, I was had!

Probably one of the more minor mistakes of my life was taking Sherry to see a show starring Alex Guinness—as Gully Jimson—in an English movie called "The Horse's Mouth." I wanted to give her warning of what she might be getting into if she were to marry an artist. The hero of the movie was a dedicated muralist who squeezed whole tubes of paint in an impasto technique, much as a plasterer would use his "mud" on walls. This meant that the character would have to pay for hundreds of dollars more for expensive tubes of paints; it was also a fact that he seldom had the wherewithal to pay for his supplies. In addition, he and his artist buddies—in a very funny scene—totally destroyed a luxury apartment under the false pretenses of painting a small canvas for a couple on vacation. Jimson was a lecher, a thief, and survived by living on a houseboat on the Thames.

I was not quite the same bird as "Gully Jimson," but this was the image Sherry came away with. She later told me that she was embarrassed because all of her classmates were at the same movie; this would give them more fodder for rejecting our relationship. Nonetheless, Sherry and I got along immediately, and I was at pains to tell her of all of the things about my background that I had available at that time in the late 1950's. But it wasn't until almost 20 years later, that I found memories of the terrible things I had done as an assassin. I wasn't supposed to remember, but was supposed to commit suicide at some time, "for unknown reasons." As I told all the things that I could remember, mostly about my ragged childhood, I was amazed that nothing I said seemed to discourage her from marrying me. I was committed to the truth—rather The Truth, as I knew it. Sherry, on the other hand, told me the truth as she thought it would appear good to me. As I met and tried to become a member of her family, I realized why she was in almost as bad a shape psychologically as I was.

Through 50+ years of a very weird 4th but strangely exciting and productive marriage—full of rocks and pitfalls—we somehow managed not to lose each other. The marriage was a coupling of friends and partners—even parents, as the need arose—if not of lovers. Her problems with sexual behavior of any kind were, if not pathological, certainly fixed and untreatable. It took some time for me to come to grips with this. I was a fighter, but I was also a lover, although the word lover could easily and truly be substituted with the word, user.

After living together in a rented house (the "pink house") on N.E. 75th in Portland for about 3 months, we were married on April 10, 1960 in Crescent City, California with her high school friends as attendants and her parents footing the bill. After a brief honeymoon on the Oregon Coast, we came back to our pink house—Sherry made me take the "just married" signs off the car a few blocks from home—and settled into an uneasy domestic life. Sherry worked at St. Vs and I worked at AAA Ambulance as well as at my studio on 23rd street. But low and behold, three months later, Sherry discovered she was pregnant. Like Dorothy, Sherry had been told she would have difficulty getting pregnant; like Dorothy, there didn't seem to be a problem!

You will find little mentioned in this book about the two children I had with Sherry. Eric was born 9 months and 2 days after our formal marriage. He was a beautiful baby with long blond curls, fine features, and Sherry's lovely Norwegian skin, but by 2 years old he never slept, was taking apart the vacuum cleaner, but could not crawl—just belly-wiggled until he stood upright and walked at about almost 3. He was mostly withdrawn from interaction and resisted being held or cuddled. He didn't talk, just imitated environmental sounds, especially the sounds the car made when shifting gears. But, he also started reading street signs by the time he was three, even though he would not talk otherwise. Sherry's public health nurse aunties pronounced him autistic and strongly recommended that we institutionalize him. Of course that was not going to happen. Sherry had so much guilt that she was unable to cope with him—all of the "literature" of the 1960s pointed to the "cold mother syndrome" as the cause of autism. (Interestingly, later research noted that some autistic children seemed to have mildly autistic mothers who lack social skills; "Was the 'refrigerator mother' made famous by Bruno Bettelheim actually a woman with very mild autism?" (Raley and Johnson, 1997, p 118) Thus I took over his rearing and trained him into functionality, boot camp style, in much to same way I did Johnny Graham. Because of my unorthodox management of Eric's non-effective behaviors, he was able to attend school, graduate from college with a degree in theoretical mathematics, live on his own, and maintain a job, albeit it is low end janitorial work.

However, Eric didn't acknowledge my role in humanizing him and was angry for many years.

Current theories regarding autism have proposed cerebellar hypoplasia (abnormally small in 88% of autistic children)—Eric was not able to crawl, but often normal or higher level cortical functioning—he was able to walk and had fine motor control. Even with normal motor cortex control, cerebellar function is necessary for coordination and balance. Eric manifested this deficit by not being able to ride a bike or drive a car: to this day, he still walks everywhere. And while the boot camp treatment was frowned upon in the 1960s, " ... when it comes to autism, the most effective parenting style is highly invasive ... forcing eye contact, forcing response, forcing connection ... ." (Ratey & Johnson, 1997, 225).

If we had had the resources then that are available today, Eric's diagnosis and management might have been different. From today's literature, Eric would be more realistically diagnosed as having Asperger's—a high level autistic syndrome in which the individual lacks the social skills that most humans use to effectively interact with others, but also may have a high degree of intellectual functioning and may possess almost savant-level skills in one or more of Gardener's Intelligences (Gardener, 1999). Eric excels in the areas of linguistic intelligence, as witness his excellent use of words and his poetry. The poems quoted below are two of the hundreds he has written. They aren't all winners, but the majority are excellent: he has won recognition and awards through online poetry sites. And recently he has been trying his hand at drawing and painting having produced several primitive/abstract but close likenesses of himself.

The first poem was originally written in the late 80s, but recently revised to include some additional understanding of his disability and his relationship with me.

From the beginning, our marriage was just one rough patch after another; it would be another 30 years before we learned how to effectively share power. We did have a deep and abiding love, from the beginning, but because we were both damaged, it took time and a lot of humor to learn how to express it appropriately. And when that happened, we then learned the most sustaining quality of a viable relationship: to realize who needed the help/support most and to give it to the more needy one. That one concept is probably responsible for the enduring and growing qualities of our loving relationship—that and a stubborn persistence that we shared.

Eric's Poetry

WE'RE NO ANGELS

Have you seen my little boy?
My wound-up bound-up
Bundle of joy?
Sir, he's in here somewhere,
Playing in a plush, pigpen puddle
Of how-to manuals;
Up to his neck in ecstasy.
Look at him waving his hands
Like a turbo-driven band
Conductor!
Oh he's cute as the devil
But he's no angel!

I've got me a shoulder seat!
All's gay and festive;
The weather's neat!
Boy, I'm having fun
Watching seven-masted samurai
Salute us, sharp and stern,
Bow, turn, and perform their duty
High up among sheets and sails.
The chief bids us sayonara.
What a day!
Sometimes, we make quite a team,
Yet we're no angels!

Have you seen my little man?
Silent partner in
My Vee-Dub van.
Son, where did you go,
What did you see, and how do you feel?
His reply is constant
Through Fall, Winter, Summer, and Spring;
Nowhere, nothing, don't know, Dad.

Not one tear, giggle, or grin.
No one's home!
If he loves me, I can't tell.
Well, he's no angel!

Truth be told, I've done my best;
Sometimes you were fun,
Sometimes a pest!
Stephen, understand;
If my hand was too heavy and harsh
Or if my mouth spoke words
Out of turn, out of tune, yet know
'Twas to save for you a life
That's growing, flowing, glowing
Worth knowing.
You've become a Man, my Son,
Though you're no angel!

Our years are long since past.
My pools of wisdom
Are filling fast.
Dad, after fifty
Years minus one worth of distance won,
My image of you has
Somehow become kinder, gentler,
Gracefully wider in scope.
I've seen how will, mind, and might
Pulled me through.
I am your Son, you, my Dad,
And we're no angels!

A CARTESIAN REPENTANCE OF SORTS?

Mathematics; a romance gone stale, perhaps?
Her streamlined clock-working regularity
Once wound me up in knots of ecstasy,
But of late it's become a boring box
From which to seek blessed release.

Witness how I've toiled night and day
With much sweat, more ink, and many tears,
Yet never discovered the proper equations,
In terms of SIN and TANH and EXP and DET
Or Big S over f of t thru Small d of t,
To give my God-breathed soul its reason to be.
Her alphabet; too simple to spell M-A-N.

Nature; what nutshell formula, in Heaven's name,
Could begin to approximate her infinite charms?
We once thought her a clarified crystal cut
From perfectly polished platitudes,
Or a fine-tuned functional fugue
Of smilingly sybaritic symmetries;
Much better to think of her as
A frustratedly freakish flip-flop
Fly-by-night fractal
Built from odds no mere mortal
Could fathom in a billion years.
Her alphabet; legible only to God.

Love; with her I could never contend.
One half a demon Ogress,
One third a sultry Siren,
One fifth a simon-pure Fairy Queen.
Tell me the proportions don't make sense
And I'll tell you—neither does she!
A rose in one hand,
A thorn in the other,
And warts on the third.
She tears down my walls of loneliness
Only to hide herself in the debris.
Her alphabet; the twisted runes of witchcraft.

Reprinted with permission, Eric E. Wahl (1988/2011)

26 | The 74th Street House

We called the first house we lived in the Pink House ... because it was pink. It was architecturally proportioned to fit on a medium-sized stamp. Our second house, a block away on 74th street and, though no mansion, had a kitchen, a small dining room next to a small living room with a hall behind leading to the bathroom and bedroom. Sherry says that we had our bed in the dining room; initially Eric was in the bedroom. But soon after that, the incipient artist took over—as was his wont—and turned the dining room into a studio with a full 14 by 16 inch silkscreen setup on a table. Not to ignore the living room, I painted an ink mural on the wall. But Sherry had her kitchen—a big one—and we repainted it to her specifications: she had her territory; I had mine. There was a full basement and a fairly efficient heating system. But, given my perpetual creep, the most exciting spot, during the summer, was the open, brick-red, cement front porch.

A Gypsy Melody

The two things I most liked to do during the first summer we spent at the 74th street house were working in the home studio and, on especially pleasant days, spending restful hours sitting on that warm front porch: I am unnaturally distasteful of cold weather and do everything I can to avoid it. When I was going through one of my several guitar phases—during which I had the illusion I was playing fluently—I would sit on the open porch and play my three, then five, and finally ... count them ... eight chords! The instrument was capable of giving a great deal more than I was getting out of it in tonal purity and rapturous sounds, but it was giving me quite a thrill.

Sherry was in one of her home-making periods: she did the most amazing things in the kitchen like canning vegetables, baking all kinds of

335

goodies, and even making pickles for me. She was making her sporadic, self-induced effort at "providing everything a good wife is supposed to produce for her loving husband." According to which manual of the Completely-Properly-Trained-Housewife-Extraordinaire this "ordinum" was derived, I am not sure. Yet once into these manic phases, nothing would stop Sherry from the impossible escapades of highly capable, but not sustainable, long-haul sorties into professional homemaking.

On the good side of this bizarre behavior was her otherworldly, fantastically insightful analysis of anything I happened to be doing that caught her attention. I offer the following as illustration. There I was, on the front porch, playing my eight … count them … eight chords, when a dark, young neighbor came walking by and stopped to listen to me play. I paused to introduce myself; he informed me that he was new to the area and happened to live with an extended family of Gypsies. We talked pleasantly for a while. I noticed Sherry had opened the screen door and come out. I introduced her as my wife; she acknowledged him with a nod of her head, but said nothing—just listened. I should have recognized I was already in trouble.

By way of getting acquainted, he said his name was Peter and that he had just married an Anglo wife, fairly unusual in Gypsy families, but it was working out well. Sherry went back into the kitchen, and Peter asked if he could watch me play again. I was so proud as I showed him my eight … count them … eight chords. He asked if he might try out my guitar. Well, after my little performance there was hardly any way I could refuse him, so, smiling uneasily, I handed him my instrument, which suddenly appeared very comfortable in his grip. Then effortlessly—but without my express permission!!—he quickly changed all the peg settings on the strings and proceeded to provide a furious outpouring of complex melodies, in multiple octaves, with strange key changes, and a machine-gun like explosion of every melody that had ever been spawned at the smoky campfires around a thousand Gypsy camps in a hundred exotic countries! When he was done, he invited Sherry and me to a "moving in" party at his house down the block, gave me a not unsympathetic smile, and waved to the dozens of neighbors who had come out to hear the impromptu performance. He quickly walked down the block to his waiting family.

My unfaithful love is returned to my arms, still wet with illegal excitement and joy, showing a quite not-to-be-believed desire to be back in his arms. The gathered neighbors all kind of shrugged and went back into their houses, while I just sat there on my warm porch with my quiet sullied instrument and ruminated. I didn't look up as I heard the screen-door swing open. Sherry, smelling of sugar and spice, edged up behind me, took me by the hand, and as I rose, cupped my face in her hands. Smiling lovingly and shaking her head in mock sadness, she informed me of the obvious: "Larry Wahl, you are the only man I know who would try to teach a Gypsy how to play the guitar!"

Cats on the Front Porch

On another memorable day, after my Gypsy encounter, instead of giving lessons, I was in a mood to receive them. We had a tabby cat that became my best friend and loved to sit with me on the front porch, with or without guitar. We had traded the most useless dog ever born for the most amicable cat, whom we called Sophie. We were thrilled with her until we discovered she was already with family—five to be exact. After their births, we responsibly directed four of them to other homes, keeping the coal-black runt of the litter that was named Ralph, as it turned out. Now, I had two cats as companions on the porch: Sophie and Ralph. Obviously Sophie had not been spayed so she was a fertile attraction to all the Toms in the neighborhood. I kept an eye on these until we got her taken care of.

Both Sophie and Ralph were on the porch one evening when King Tom came swaggering by, full of masculine grace, and paused in front of our porch. The effect of the tomcat on Ralph brought forth all the usual testosterone in both the adult and the kitten. Sherry made a habit of opening the screen door every half hour or so to check on her "extended family." Since Ralph was never on the porch without Sophie and his full attention was centered on the interloper, he missed that Sophie had ducked back into the living room with Sherry. What followed was a kitten absolutely convinced he had "back-up" available a few inches away and so he continued the hissing Halloween stance of the vicious tiger. Tom just stood his ground, looking back and forth from the inhospitable kitten to my hospitable face, gave the equivalent of shrugged shoulders, and sauntered on. Ralph had prevailed as king of the mountain until he made the mistake of glancing behind him for the mom cat that wasn't there. The cry of the warrior died in his throat as he made a visible dash through the screen door Sherry had opened again, almost tripping over her. So ends victory: Sic transit Gloria.

This event became a metaphor for Sherry and me: Be sure your back-up is available before you let your mouth lead you someplace your body really doesn't want to go!!!

The Grahams

While we lived in the Pink House, I met the across-the-street neighbors, the Grahams: the very essence of the dysfunctional family. Tommy and Johnny robbed their first gas station—or rather broke in after it closed—when they were nine and ten, respectively. The family was Mormon, but there wasn't a shadow of anything resembling spirituality in the entire group. The husband had left somewhere along the line, and the mother—not a brain trust-—had remarried a facially-deformed janitor. To his credit, he ran his own janitorial business and seemed to be genuinely attached to the children, which included a teen-age girl, her younger sister, Theresa, and the two boys. Theresa had just turned four when we first saw her. I remember standing across the street, watching her play. I had asked Sherry, "How far away do you think Theresa is from us right now?"

Sherry answered, literally and accurately, "Oh, about thirty feet."

I remarked, thinking dimly of the family's psychic resources, "No, I think you'll find it's more like thirty years."

An example of the many difficulties the family endured: Tommy, the eldest son, had continued his career as a thief by means of multiple car thefts and break-ins, and when I last saw him, had spent 12 years incarcerated before he was 25. Johnny, on the other hand, was totally illiterate. The only criminal thing in which I was aware of him being involved—other than the gas station caper—was the silent observation of a gang rape of a pudgy little girl in high school who had the lack of imagination to think that Johnny was her friend.

Johnny's mother asked me to help him learn to read so he could enlist in the army. I took on the job, but told her that I had to "own" him, body and soul: he would sleep when I told him to, get up when I told him to, and take lessons from me six hours a day. He did follow this regimen—not happily—for six weeks before a girlfriend convinced him to jump ship. By this time he had learned enough to pass the Army GED tests; he was honorably discharged after two years of service. He was still a pretty poor excuse for a human being, but he could read. Tommy, crook and all, was twice the human being Johnny was ever going to be, though you wouldn't trust Tommy with your car or your wife. Tommy was brilliant. When he challenged me to chess, I insisted he give up his queen; he did and still beat me, as I told him he would!

Dean Buzan

Dean Buzan lived directly behind the 74th Street house, which put him right next door to the Grahams, with whom, to the best of my knowledge, he had no contact. I met him across the property line of our adjoining yards. We were very much alike although he was ten years older; it seemed that he had had a life somewhat like mine. He had been married, became a drunk, lost everything, got straightened out, and remarried another reformed drunk. We became good neighbors and would have continued as friends had we not moved.

Dean was an excellent insurance salesman, owned his own house, and was very handy with tools. He and I argued all the time about my buying and using inferior tools—at that time in the early 60s, Japanese manufacturers flooded the market with barely functional crap usually found in baskets of cheap tools at Fred Meyers. Dean contended that I was constitutionally incapable of passing by without buying at least three of those inferior "two dollar wonders." He had little idea of my talents as an artist or anything else; however, I learned a great deal from him while he was jibing and having fun at my expense. Unlike me, Dean was a craftsman but not an engineer; this was to later give me a chance to get some respect for what I do well.

Our back yard was full of large rocks that had been part of the original construction of the medium-sized house. I decided that I was going to put in a fence along the east property line. A few attempts with a pick and shovel informed me of why no fences had been put in before: it was impossible to form a straight line that would not end up on rocks submerged just under the surface. I puzzled over this for a while and then called on my memory to examine the operation of pile drivers. These are extremely simple to use but have hidden mechanics folded into their physics with unbelievable power.

Essentially a pile driver is a large, tall crane tower on which the "piles"—round or square wooden, concrete, or steel objects, 20 or 30 feet long—are inserted into a basically vertical position, and then hit on the top with steam (or other) powered hammers that drive them straight into the ground. I had watched for many hours and had never observed anything stopping the five or six foot vertical drops of these piles making their way through obstructions with obvious ease. The secret, of course, is that the relatively small surface of the pile at the top absorbs thousands of pounds of pressure per square inch that is promptly transferred to the tip, driving it through anything. With this in mind, I got some four-foot lengths of ¼-inch aluminum pipe, set them loosely into the ground, and hit them carefully on the head with a nine-pound hammer. My concern was that when the pipe hit, at an angle, any of the numerous rocks, the pipe would bend or collapse and be deflected. What actually happened was that the tremendous force on the thin-wall pipe rolled the top edge of the pipe into a neat smaller and smaller circle while the pipe slid into the ground.

While I was happily working on my second pipe, Buzan came into the yard and asked me what I was playing at. I took the time to explain. He then countered with, "You might think that was what was going on, but you are wrong. It just doesn't work like that."

I listened patiently and then, after he left, finished the fence line in twenty minutes of careful but easy work.

There were more little contests like that, and while Dean won most of them, his defeats were hard for him to take. Once he came over, looking totally defeated and explained that he was finding it impossible to cut a "kidney" shape out of a ¾-inch piece of plywood. I could see where he had tried to draw several examples, all obviously distorted. Even though he had sought me out, he looked at me, hoping and praying that I wouldn't be up to the job he had found impossible. After I found out how long he wanted it, I took a heavy carbon pencil and quickly drew the proper two circles, one smaller than the other, and connected them quickly with the appropriate curves to form a perfect kidney.

The worst defeat for Dean was probably the most disastrous. He came over, asking if I had worked in fiberglass—I knew that he had seen me working with the stuff. We went into his garage where he had a 12 foot wooden boat, sitting hull up on saw horses, with sheets of fiberglass, extender, and activator laid out alongside. He was dressed in his business suit, and was obviously late for some meeting. I was truly feeling sorry for him when I realized that he had already started to put on the liquid activator. It was obvious that he had laid out too much material and activator; it was warm, he was sweating, and the stuff was getting ready to set-up. He worked rapidly, asking me questions but paying no attention to the answers. He seemed to believe that if he worked fast enough, he could beat the material to set-up, but the material wasn't in the mood to assist him. His tie was wrapped around his neck—a beautiful red one as I remember—when a sudden move loosened the tie and dropped it directly into the bucket of extender. I quietly left, not wanting to see a grown man cry, and never did find out if he made his meeting. I only know he did not finish the boat that night.

A few days later Dean came over, kind of sheepish-like, and asked me if I wanted to give him a hand. He had stripped all the old material off the boat, sanded it, and had everything ready; he was wearing overhauls and proper shoes for the job. We set about working a little at a time, with some sense that it was going to take whatever time it took. We finished in a couple of hours and shook hands on the job. A week later, with a good outboard motor attached to the stern, he took me sailing on the Willamette River, stopping at a former, paddle-wheel floating restaurant and bought me lunch.

Casey

To the left side of us was a large two-story house in which a man, a woman, and three children lived. The man was a mean drunk who was almost never home, and his plain, but well-built wife, Cindy, was usually at home and was always in the back of my mind. Nothing ever happened, but the thought was there. Though our garages were separate, a common parallel set of driveways led to both garages. Our Volkswagen van, purchased from the Graham's janitor husband, was usually parked just outside of the garage, so that I would be able to set up and paint as many as five or six canvases at night in black-light. It was pretty strange, but worked beautifully.

Of her three children, Cindy's eldest was Casey, about a year older than Eric. Eric never learned to play, much less play fair, and one day I came out of the front door to see the slight-built Casey hauling Eric around in a broken down Red Flyer wagon, which had two flattened wheels. From the strain on Casey's face, I could tell that, on this hot summer day, Casey had been doing this for some time. Casey would have continued all day, and Eric would have let him. I stopped this activity, and made Eric pull Casey for a while. Casey was quietly grateful, but Eric was flushed with anger. I heard Casey's succinct remark, "Hard, ain't it!"

In all the years that I have known Eric he has never done anything for anybody on purpose, and the fact that he has Asperger's syndrome—a high-functioning form of Autism— just does not cut it for me. He was born angry and has been a pain in the neck most of his life. Life has a way of coming back on you—as a young, adopted child, my dad was never appreciated for what he gave me, and so it was with Eric!. Casey was so grateful for any of my attention that I did special things for him, like carve a wooden machine gun for him to play with. He thanked me, matter-of-factly, in his soft gentle way that would have done honor to a faithful friend. He looked as though he knew life had given him a lemon, but took it in stride. He always had a smile on his face and was seemingly interested in everything.

On this particular night, the black-light painting was set up in the open garage; I was working away on multiple canvases. It was warm, about two in the morning, and the painting was going very well. I have been known to work all night once I get started and was well into an abstract, a 4 by 8 foot nude, a portrait, and two seascapes when I realized that I was not alone. There was a little midget, dressed in his P J's that were producing a bright pattern of their own from the ultra-violet light. I had no idea how long Casey had been standing at the opening of the garage. I could make out the quizzical look on his face, and thought, "Well, he might make an honest critic."

As he stood there watching me jabbing intensely bright colored paint on the canvases in the otherwise darkened garage, I lifted one eyebrow and, in all seriousness, asked him, "Well, what do you think, Casey?"

Casey stood there for a few moments contemplating the scene and then said, in this serious, adult manner, "You do very good work, Mister Wahl."

There was a momentary desire to smile, but I didn't. Instead I remained quietly contemplative. That serious commentary was as important an art critique as I have ever taken notice of, and I take notice of very few! I thanked him as if he were a professional.

A few months after this night, Cindy who was working two jobs, while her husband, who was gone for months at a time, came home to take the three kids to his parents in Florida, "for a visit." Cindy had decided to raise the kids by herself, had started taking classes to become a licensed practical nurse, and welcomed the chance to work extra. The problem arose when her husband informed her he was keeping the kids with him and that she could join him in Florida, or not. She had little choice, and so Casey left the neighborhood. I have often wondered what ever happened to him. Somehow I like to believe that he grew up to be a man as well adjusted as he apparently had been as a child.

Scientology

During these early years of our marriage, we tried out several spiritual philosophies. I had been somewhat active in the Rosicrucian Order in the late 40s when I lived in San Jose, California—Sherry joined in 1970 and still ascribes to the mysticism of this ancient philosophy—but while we were living on 74th Avenue, we both first joined a Buddhist group called Nichiren Shoshu and then Scientology. While I still use the chant—nemyo ringe kyo—for its grounding effect, we found the formal practice of Nicheran Shoshu too militaristic, we being more inclined toward Zen.

Our introduction to Scientology came as the original theory, Dianetics, through a very special man called Charley Broaded. Like Nicheran Shoshu, we retained the use of the "pure" principles of Dianetics even after we were drummed out of the Scientology corps as "subversive people." But, despite my not wanting to be part of the corrupted, people-based organization, I found much value in the "mystical" theorems put forth by Hubbard. The following are some of the ideas that I still espouse.

As Scientology—or more accurately, Ron L. Hubbard—teaches, "A Thetan (soul) has no garbage dump."

I translate this in my own words: "The crap you throw over your shoulder will not allow for any distance, will not go away. As you move along, so does it."

This rule of life is very real for me. I know that it is true: Sister Ursula proved it beyond any question. I never buried her until we metaphorically did, many years later. The writer Mark Twain wrote that the bad things one did in life were easily forgotten, but the good deeds— the ones that really cost you—prey on you forever. Twain had had an opportunity to seduce a beautiful woman, but demurred. As he said, he forgot about most of the rotten things he had done, but this good behavior haunted him the rest of his life. He would wake up in a sweat after dreaming about it, in agony over his misguided decision. It follows the cynical rule, "No good deed goes unpunished."

The general thrust of the thetan, or soul, is that it MUST produce an effect. In Scientology this is thought of as the soul's one and only edict. We become screwed up when we do something we (the thetan) really did not want to do. The only other way a thetan is considered to acquire bad karma, or lasting somatics (trouble right here in River City) is to not do something it intended to do. Doing something is never a problem. This does not have anything to do with the physical or legal consequences: the thetan does not apparently have a back-up co-pilot, i.e., a conscience. The thetan creates the effect it desires, or it does not, and the consideration of success is limited, therefore, to the individual pretty much doing what he or she wants. The catch is, if you believe or subscribe to this theory, you are required to do EVERYTHING you decide is desirable. Since you cannot choose "not to choose," the consequences for others of what you have decided trail behind you, like an unrelenting and non-erasable wake. Whatever mess—if only in your own mind—you have created, at some point in this or future lifetimes, you will eventually have to face the consequences (karma?)

As some rabid Scientologists have discovered, this rule includes them: Scientologists! As an organization, they have accrued some pretty goofy and horrendous karma. Being able to understand a set of rules, no matter how logical, has ab-soul-utely nothing to do with being able or willing to follow those same rules. As has often been pointed out, no rule is simpler than the Golden One, "Love thy neighbor as thyself." But what happens to the hapless neighbor if you happen to loathe yourself????

I spent almost a half a century using the CIA to get even for what happened to me in the Ghetto and in Chicago ... because it SHOULDN'T HAVE HAPPENED! ... or so says my thetan. Given the Scientologists' rule of engagement, this meant that I must have planned on something else happening to me that had edges but did not include nearly being beaten or starved to death: all of this before I reached the so-called "age of reason." It seems that the "age of responsibility" is arrived at prior to the "age of reason."

I still think the Dianetic principles are logical and reasonable explanations of human existence, but as noted above, we did not agree to all of the Orgs rules and financial "donation" requirements, so we dropped out even as they called us subversive.

A lot of living occurred in the 74th street house, and we would have stayed there much longer except the owners decided to sell; the newcomers wanted to take possession of their home. We moved to an interesting house—we christened it the German House because cupboards and doors had, written in German, what we assumed were instructions, such as "oben." I loved that house. The daylight basement had huge windows overlooking the freeway 150 feet below. It was an ideal studio, and I painted and painted. Sherry entered many of my paintings in the county fairs, securing a number of blue and red ribbons for me. One painting that I called the (Viet) Cong, Sherry entered in a prestigious art show at the Space Needle Park in Seattle. She was so upset when it was politely juried out that we made a trip up there to see what was so much better than her favorite, Cong. She learned a lot about the Art World on that trip: our competition was Soup Can and Andy Warhol realism.

But all good things come to an end: Within 8 months, the German owner decided that he wanted his house back, and we were again out. Next stop? The "Mansion."

27 | The Mansion

I got a funny feeling in the pit of my stomach when I first saw "The Mansion." It was certainly a mansion, but that begs the definition of "mansion." When referring to boats and ships, there is a general rule that says anything a hundred feet or more in length is a ship, but that distinction is lost, for example, on submariners. The old tradition in the navy was that "pig boats," as submarines were called early on, were always "boats" no matter what size. In the modern Navy, with the advent of the "boomers," size does not seem to matter: modern nuclear subs are usually called boats despite the fact that they are much larger than destroyers, which are always called ships.

Just such is the nomenclature for mansions. There are monstrosities whose foundations would cover an acre or so; realtors of these would consider what I was looking at on the corner of 13th and Schuyler a small shack by comparison. But, in my opinion, the naming of a house as a mansion has more to do with intention than anything else. In the hills of Portland are very large complexes that would make our mansion look like an outhouse, but to me it was the most beautiful edifice I had ever seen. Though it dominated the corner of the block, it seemed so specifically designed for me that I felt a surprising ease and understanding of the place at first sight. Everything about it was just right … for an artist.

Its mysteries started with the so-called basement. Usually a basement is underground, but this was underground only in a manner of speaking. What made it different was that it had a door at ground level on the street. This took place because the whole mansion had been built into a bluff about 60 feet above the terrain that started in a small incline, sloping down to the middle of the block. When you entered that "Green Door," you would find yourself in a 60 by 60 foot basement, with a complete cement floor. In the center of this huge room was a large, old central heating system with vents leading to the rest of the structure. Off to one corner, near the washing machine faucets was what Sherry determined was Fells-Napha Soap; actually it was about $1000 dollars worth of "weed," which remained untouched for the duration of our tenure! Just to the right of that street-side green door was the base of a multiple stack of fireplace assemblies. There were two fireplaces in the room on the main floor, connected by the same flue, back to back. One of these was a small fireplace that faced the north wall of a cozy little study/library, off a very large kitchen. The one on the other side was facing south, making it the attractive center of attention in the relatively small living room.

An archway from this living room opened to the central grand hall, which led to a simple but gracious main staircase to the second floor. Continuing from the living room, past the stairs, you would enter the formal dining room. Alongside this stairway was a direct doorway from the dining room to the kitchen. Once in the kitchen, you could turn directly 180 degrees where you would find a pass-through for food to the dining room and another door from the kitchen would lead into the study/library.

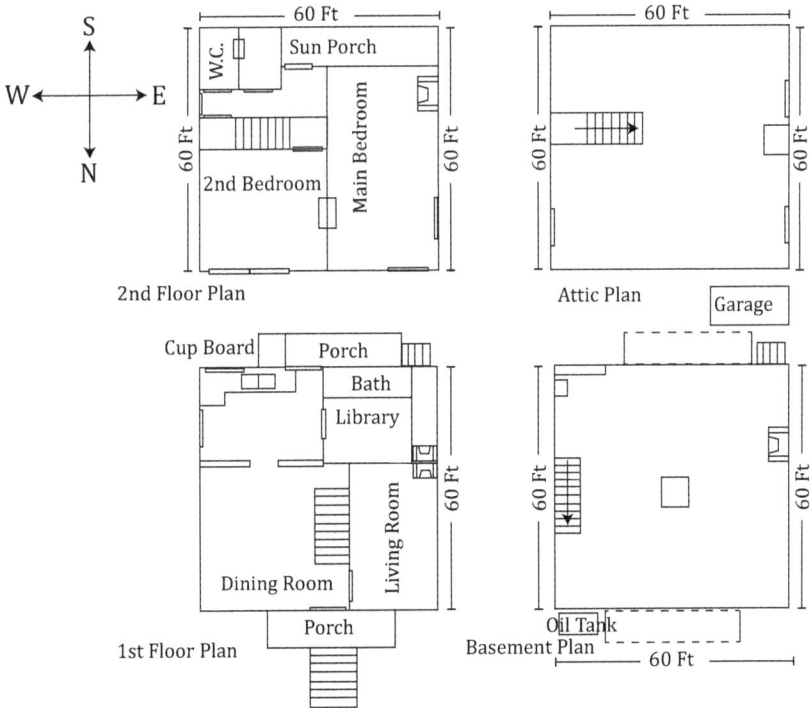

2nd Floor Plan

Attic Plan

1st Floor Plan

Basement Plan

The second floor (or the third if you were starting with the basement) was divided into a bedroom facing north and a huge master bedroom on the same side as the basement door. This room on the west side was 50 feet long from front to back and 20 feet wide with a full walk-in closet; the south end of the bedroom shared a wall with a fully windowed sunroom 10 feet wide and 30 feet long. A long hallway led from the door of the master bedroom to the other end of the house. The door to the other bedroom was on the left; across the hall was a room with just a bathtub, next to a room with only a toilet and a laundry chute to the basement. The door to the sunroom was on the right. A weird narrow stairway, left of the main bedroom, led from this second floor to a third, and perhaps strangest, floor in the building. This was a completely floored attic that ran the entire 60 by 60 feet of the building, had head-room all the way, with dormers on three sides. Everything in the building was on a grand scale.

It was clear from this rather strange layout that this building had been designed for entertaining many friends. It was a custom-built home and, by far, the largest on the block. But, it was the master bedroom with its third fireplace that caught my attention. It was massive. We put our queen-sized mattress on the floor with the head against the north wall, by the huge walk-in closet, and still had "acres" of space, so it seemed.

As we studied the strange layout of the building, we took stock of our new home. Our rent was $300 dollars a month, and though this seemed like a ridiculously small amount, we were to find out that heating the place would be very expensive. The heating oil tank took 73 gallons of fuel and had to be filled three times during the winter with additional fill-ups in fall and spring. Let's see … that meant that we were paying $3600 dollars a year rent, plus another approximately $3600 dollars a year in heating bills. Not quite the bargain we thought we had signed up for, but since my success as a painter was rapidly becoming established, I thought little of the long-range cost. Soon, I was eagerly engaged in completely redoing the kitchen.

Unfortunately, keeping such a house in good repair is a constant job. Through most of its life, it had been given tender loving care, but over the last few years when it had been rented out to a long list of people—including an ambulance service—who didn't give a damn for it or its history, it had been rapidly deteriorating. I completely worked over the kitchen, replacing sink and sideboards, work surfaces and floor covering. The roof still needed some work, especially over the sunroom where I expected to set up my studio. We planned to negotiate with the owners regarding a new roof.

We were both bringing in money, and it looked as though the Mr. Moon Show redo with Ed Lehey as Mr. Moon was going to be produced by KATU with me doing all the sets and remaking the original puppets (more about that later). Life looked very good. Certainly there was Eric, with all of his problems, but I was committed to do the very best for him that I could. Without anything else bearing down on us, this was do-able.

When I married Sherry, she was fully cognizant of my past marital status. Even though she became pregnant on our wedding night, it soon was clear to me that there was something terribly wrong with her sense of herself as a sexual human being. Any sex at all was tricky, like trying to make love while resting on a mattress made up of mine fields. It is my consideration that sex fitted someplace on her pleasure scale just below root canal work. This is not to say that she is not a loving person, far from it, but sex was just not a component in that mix.

While I did not have insight into the nature of my sexual addiction at this time (my mention of it in earlier chapters was retrospective), my perception was that I tried to give as much pleasure as I was taking—not always possible, for this is a tricky talent, and, in reality, sex has no more to do with loving a person than succotash has to do with engineering. So, after almost thirty years of living with and loving Sherry, I found it necessary one night to just roll over and say to her, "Oh, the hell with it, this is too much like work, so let's just give it up"!

We later had a long and caring discussion of the pros and cons of a non-sexual relationship and made a mutual decision that this was best. If she thought that this was going to be the end of our marriage, she was wrong. It is so obvious that we two misfits were meant for each other that I literally would have died if I had not been with her. That we were two very different, very powerful human beings was obvious, and there was and, for that matter always will be, a powerful tension between us as to who is in charge. She knows that it is either she or I, and suspects/ mostly believes that it is I. I know that it is either she or I, and suspect/ mostly believe that it is she ... depending, of course, on the month, the day of the week, the hour of the day, and probably the position of the stars, sun, and moon!

Eric was much too much for Sherry to handle, and so his communication and behavioral difficulties took a tremendous amount of my time. We were to discover from the pseudo-psychologist of Eric's day care center that he ate mashed potatoes with his hands (he had been eating with proper utensils since he was three)—"poor little guy"—and that he was severely retarded! As described in Chapter 25, Eric was not right, but intelligence and ability were not lacking: he was naming the streets of Portland and the gross national products of every state as soon as he began talking at four years old. We did take him out of the nursery school and entered him into a local kindergarten, which later proved also to be a disaster. While gifted with incredible, but narrow focused, intelligence, he had no ability to read people and his social skills were nil. He also seemed to have arrived on this planet with much internal anger.

At any rate, things seemed to be working out for me, and commissions were floating in; the mansion was going to be our home, and I WAS finally going to be able to make "one more dollar" than Sherry and be famous as a working artist. There was absolutely nothing that could happen that would upset the apple cart. But ... Sherry—given her six years of experience with Eric certainly should have known better—made a decision on her own, and with some kind of incredible timing, managed to get pregnant again. I met this fiat accompli with nothing resembling good grace and could see the studio work, which was the purpose for this monster of a house, slowly receding into a background of diapers and screaming infants. Sherry would be the first to tell you that she does not have "Mother of the Year" talent or interest, but her fear and antagonism for my artwork was palpable. She believed, as I did, that I was not going to survive much past 40 without croaking, so her answer was that she wanted to have a normal little piece of me. I needed another kid like a whale needs peanut butter.

My Side

28

By Sharon Wahl

L arry does not like to say negative things about me or guess at my motivations so he asked me to tell my side of the story about the disaster that was "The Mansion." Primarily, he wanted to know why I picked that particular time to get pregnant—and make no mistake, I did plan it since it meant not taking "the pill" for at least one month. Many times I had told him my reasons, giving him my best guess, and as the years have gone by, I have added information as it came to me. But, in writing this chapter, I spent much more internal energy on the task and was rewarded—if that is really the appropriate term—with some startling insights.

By way of explanation, I am a triple Scorpio. For those readers who are not familiar with these astrological labels, I tend to exemplify some very specific characteristics: I enjoy power and like having my own way—besides, I'm usually right; I am driven to use my talents to make a contribution, as globally as possible; and most significantly, I hold my thoughts and feelings very close. Indeed, I am prone to not share feelings with others—unless strongly provoked—and I often don't share them even with myself. So, as a child, when asked, "Why did you do this or that?" I usually formulated the response that I thought the questioner would like to hear and it was usually one that would put me in the best light. This behavior continued throughout most of my adulthood as well. Larry believes that frequently the truth is not in me, but more often than not, I don't know what the truth is!

So, at 70+ years of age, I finally wanted to delve into my unpleasant depths and answer his question as honestly as possible: "Why did you get pregnant at that particular time?" In order to find some answers—all of which I will outline for you presently—I had to put that situation into the context of me, him, the time, the events surrounding the time, the milieu

351

out of which we both arose, our hopes, fears, and plans (I'm beginning to sound like a tarot spread). You already know a lot about Larry from the earlier chapters, so I need to provide some more information about me.

In 1966, just before we moved into "The Mansion," I had been given the position at work that I really wanted, but was fearful that I was not competent to carry out successfully: I was appointed as head nurse of the Cardiac Recovery Room working with Dr. Al Starr (inventor of the original Starr-Edwards heart valve) where all the open heart surgery patients received their initial post-operative care. In those days, the responsibilities of the nurses in this small unit were tremendous, the technical support minimal. So, what I perceived as the ultimate professional honor had been bestowed on me. Unfortunately, I needed lots of support from Larry at a time when he had little to give. Even worse, he was launching his art career and needed much support from me. The makings of a disaster! But there is more to this insight.

I was a young woman in and of the 50s. For those who are too young to remember June Cleaver of Leave it to Beaver, my future role was to be the best housewife and mother I could, and June Cleaver was my role model. In high school, I had dreamed of being a journalist: I was editor of the school newspaper and co-editor of the Yearbook. I came in second statewide on the debate team, and was voted most likely to succeed. However, once out of high school, the dreams faded and I meekly prepared to go the nursing school in Portland, one of the three occupations approved for most women graduating in the 50s. I wish I could say I had more guts (balls?!) to have gone ahead and pursued a literary or newspaper career, but I didn't. The plan my parents and two nurse aunties had for me was I could (1) finish nursing school and then go home and take care of my parents for the rest of their lives—like my aunt Minnette had done—or (2) I could finish nursing school and work until I found a suitable mate to support me so I could be a nice wife/mother! When I met Larry during my senior year in college, I opted for the 2nd plan. And, I convinced myself I would just work until Larry was earning enough money to support a family. Of course, I'm sure that any of you who have read this far would have questioned my choice of this man to allow me to fulfill my wife/mother role. And so, six years and one disabled child later, we arrived at the "The Mansion!" As an aside, I reminded Larry that he had picked every house we had ever lived in, and all of them had used a good portion of the space for his studios. Until the 13th and Schuyler house, I don't remember being resentful about him taking that preemptory role, after all I was used to it; my father did the same thing: picking the cities and houses where we would live.

The insight that came full bore today as I prepared to write this also needs some context. For this I need to fast forward: I was attending the University of Oregon Health Sciences Center (as it was called in 1970) in the process of getting a Master's in Nursing Education. As several events unfolded, my fellow students and I noted a large number of our classmates got pregnant after starting the program and had to drop out. One of us, I'm not sure who, reported reading about a syndrome affecting women who were pursuing higher education. This syndrome was lovingly called the "anti-uppity woman syndrome" and, as the title implied, was the manner that women chose to keep their marriages intact and not out distance themselves from their mates. I even wrote a short paper on this, much to the amusement of my female professor, but as far as insight then, I came up dry.

So, with all of this background, let me iterate all of the possible answers to the question of what motivated me to get pregnant on that fateful day in late December in 1966. But, perhaps an even better question might have been, "Why didn't I want to live in 'The Mansion?'" Some extra explanatory notes may be necessary.

1. At that time, Larry gave little indication of a commitment to our marriage and often said he probably would not live past 40, which was less than a year away. Like many women, I made the mistake of thinking that another, normal child would keep him around and in the marriage. I don't know why I thought that since it hadn't worked in his first marriage.

2. Eric was such a difficult, angry, non-interactive child; I wanted to have a "normal" child, preferably a girl. What made me think, with both Larry's and my genetic backgrounds, that we could have a "normal" child … ?

3. I wanted, for once, a house that didn't have paint on the floor or a canvas stretched through from the living room to the dining room! As a child, we were the poor relatives and lived in some crummy places, the last being (while I still lived at home) a shack five miles out of

town with a long room that stood-in-for a kitchen, dining room, and living room. I remember my mother wailing that, before she died, she wanted to have a real living room where she could entertain guests. I undoubtedly brought that same need into my own marriage.

4. The house was too expensive. After our first fuel bill in January that surpassed the rent of this beautiful, but drafty house, I realized that there would be a considerable strain on our finances. Larry knew little about managing the money for a household (when I first met him, the closet in his one room apartment was littered with unpaid bills—also unwashed clothing, but that was to be expected of a bachelor! I convinced my parents to lend us enough to bail him out financially.) I earned little above the minimal wage at that time, and when Larry wanted or needed some piece of equipment, or in this case a house, that we could not afford, I was afraid to say no, that that might cause me to lose him sooner. So much for my self-esteem.

5. As Larry expressed—and I certainly agree—we have spent most of our married life in a gigantic power struggle for who was going to be in charge. He wanted that house as a studio, I wanted something homey, affordable, and not part of a business, i.e., I wanted a HOME. Part of my June Cleaver scenario was that we would have a place that was away from work, that we could relax in and just be together—that I could serve him wonderful dinners at 6pm every night. But at only six years into our marriage, I was not aware that we WERE our work, both of us!

6. Our careers were both blooming, but neither of us was that secure in what we were doing. We both demanded, of the other, support and full attention to our personal needs, but neither was able, or perhaps willing, to give it. It took us another 10 years to even begin to learn how to share attention and support, to know who had the greater need at any given time, and to be able to set aside, temporarily, our own need and give to the other.

7. I didn't want Larry to be an artist. There were several reasons for that: he didn't make enough money so that I could stay home and be a wife (that ubiquitous June Cleaver again); he became very distant when he was painting—I did not exist; the whole art culture was very frightening to me—out of control with too many lecherous women

lingering around; I was jealous of his talent and could not share in his work because of my lack of both interest and ability; I knew he was a writer and I could identify with and participate in that kind of work; my parents (I cared then) didn't approve of his occupation; and finally, if I had another baby, it would force him to get a "normal" job and we could have a "normal" life (what made me think with our genetic backgrounds we could have a "normal" life any more than a "normal" baby?)!

Now all of these sound like reasonably screwed-up human being rationales for having a baby and getting rid of "The Mansion," but the real reason just came to me as I examined my then career trajectory and Larry's supposed need to make one more dollar a year than I did. I fell err to the "anti-uppity woman syndrome": I tried to sabotage my own career by having a baby just as I was moving into a high-powered position. As I write this, I want to weep for the many other women of my generation who abandoned their talents because of this, as I want to berate myself for being so influenced by my 50s upbringing that I would even allow this to happen. But, as I told Larry, it is easier in retrospect for me to be angry at me for trying to damage my own career; it is much more painful to realize that I tried, and to a great extent, did damage his art career.

I loved Larry from the moment I first saw him "across the crowded room," and knew we were meant to be together. That we would wound each other as much as we did, I didn't take into consideration, but as Kahlil Gibran (1959) says, "When love beckons to you, follow him, though his ways are hard and steep. And when his wings enfold you, yield to him though the sword hidden among his pinions may wound you."

As tough as those years were, we are now at a place that is very special. He has, over the years, given me the self-esteem to "be all that I can be" so that I have been able to meet my unspoken goal of giving of my talents and meeting this lifetime's purpose. Because of his sacrifices for me, I have made a major commitment to give my full time, attention, and support to his career in whatever way he wishes to continue. Fortunately, it is never too late.

P.S. Regarding Larry's evaluation of my psychosexual nature, I'll discuss that more fully in my own book. Suffice it to say that I grew up with very poor role models, both male and female, and Larry's expectations didn't help.

Time Line for the Mansion

Although I can't verify the exact date, I believe that we moved from "The German House" sometime in late 1966, probably November or December. So many things happened in the approximately one year that we lived there, it would be easier to just list some of the events as was done in Chapter 1. As previously mentioned, I had just been given the position of head nurse in the mansion "Cardiac Recovery Room," a small 4 bed unit where patients who had major heart surgery came directly from the operating room and stayed until they were stable, about four to six days. This was a big jump in responsibility for me (and will be described more thoroughly when I get around to writing my own book!) and, as a result, I was blind and deaf to many of the things that were going on in both my husband's and son's lives. Hence, the need for the bulleted summary with several of the more critical events being elucidated by Larry in subsequent chapters. So, what follows includes estimated dates, but mainly is just a flow of consciousness:

- Larry working as a security guard early spring? Where?

- Eric to Fernwood Elementary, flunked out of 1st grade—to kindergarten, then back to 1st grade in Fall 67.

- Volkswagen bus that Larry painted a mural on side—got him a mural job

- Green used Pontiac for me—hole in the floorboard

- Del Chandaunet and Bridgton Road studio, probably April or May (see next chapter)

- June—met Ed Lehey and involved in Mr. Moon puppet show (see next chapter)

- Over summer, several acrylic painting demonstrations for J.K Gill in Lloyd Center and in several coastal towns in Oregon and California

- Hired by Ed Hardesty to paint mural for Grams Restaurant in Vancouver, WA-July, August—stretched across dining room and living room (Chapter 30)

- The Archerfish submarine arrives in Portland late August.

- The end of Part II of The Vallian Trilogy: An Inventive Life—to be continued in Part III The Vallian Trilogy: The Zen Connection.

So, now Larry continues his story in the next chapter about Ed Lehey, Del Chandaunet, the Gramms Restaurant Mural.

Demonstrating acrylic paint

29 | 535 Bridgeton Road and Mr. Moon

After spending most of the winter and early spring being a security guard for various agencies, I was anxious to get back to more painting. In the basement of the mansion—hardly an ideal studio—I had painted a large ship mural display for a local boat show. Our deal was based on my doing the mural for advertising their business with my payment being studio space on the upper floor of their floating shop and apartment at the Northeast Engine and Marine Company (NEMCO) moorage. I had done several murals in Portland, exhibited and won "ribbons" at juried fairs, and had been hired to give demonstrations of acrylic paints so I had good reason to expect more commissions to come my way. Thus, when the opportunity arrived to have a studio at the pier of the company for whom I had done the display, I took it without reservation. Unfortunately, I should have had reservations!

535 Bridgeton Road was located off a slough a few miles west of the Portland International Airport. The NEMCO float housed business offices next to a floating walkway and had a full four-room apartment above the offices. Besides the apartment, about half of the upstairs of the float was a wide-open area that was to be my new studio. The entire float contained a machine shop and supply area that took up most of the downstairs area. The moorage consisted of several floating buildings, some large enough to cover a good-sized boat, and some with apartments built at one end. NEMCO, a long standing marine engine sales and repair facility, had been at this same location since it had first been constructed by the original owner, twenty years earlier.

Del Chandaunet and his partner Louis, whose last name I have forgotten, were a couple of amateur businessmen; they currently leased the NEMCO space and had made the studio arrangement with me.

Chandaunet was now the legal owner of the marine engine sales and repair business and had never before been in the boat business. The business— before Chandaunet—had had a good reputation and had always paid its bills. This was a reputation Del and his partner were soon to put into past tense. It seemed that their main attraction to the building was its apartment that served as a picturesque place for assignations with all of the females the two of them dredged up from their non-stop parties in town.

After the Boat Show closed, when we were packing up the displays, including my seven foot panels, I got my first idea of just how irresponsible these two pups were. Into their large truck, along with their heavy engine displays, they threw the two panels of the background that supported the ship painting, promptly breaking off the extended bowsprit of the ship on the third panel. They did not have the grace to even accept responsibility for the damage, and since I was getting the upstairs space, I let it go. It was possible to repair the bowsprit and make it whole again, so I just moved into my new digs.

535 Bridgeton Road Studio with Ship Mural

As described, the two-bedroom apartment took up about half of that second floor, while the rest was entirely open except for a couple of support posts. There was also an overhead area above the apartment that had great headroom and storage space for material. In the remainder of that upper area, I had large double windows facing north towards the Columbia River and west with a clear view of the many houseboats. The nearest held two shapely stewardesses, both of whom Del and Company "boarded;" obviously they were "frequent fliers." The sales office had a constantly changing set of secretaries: women of all sizes, shapes, and professions.

If this sounds like "sour grapes," I suppose it was as these were some of the most beautiful women I had ever laid eyes on. But, they avoided me like the plague—probably from the press the guys gave me. It was clear to me from the first that Del and Louis were not going to stay in business too long, but I went ahead and advertised my space as NEMCO Wahl Galleries. My customers did not walk or drive in, they boated in. The entire moorage was the location for one long, never ending party.

A Portland dentist (called "Doc"), who advertised regularly on TV, had a 42-foot Chris Craft cruiser named The Enterprise. It was transferred from Doc's large boathouse (a barn-like floorless shelter in which a boat could be berthed and also contained enclosed living quarters) to its new moorage at the NEMCO floating pier, 200 feet away. The moorage apron ran around the outside 60-foot edge of our building. After it was moved, Doc commissioned Del to sell the Enterprise from our float. He gave Del a release that clearly said the Enterprise was to be sold "as is and where is" with the new owner taking full responsibility for care, repair, and upkeep. Into Doc's now empty moorage, there was installed a brand new Italian boat, with twice the engine power, half the crew capacity, and a top speed of 50 mph. Poor Enterprise looked as though she was going to be at our dock for a long time; Del now used her for parties. I saw the Enterprise leave the dock once for a short demonstration run up the adjoining Columbia River, but then it returned to the dock where it stayed moored. One fateful day, a couple from California stopped by when they saw the Enterprise, signed the papers, and took over ownership.

The following Friday, after their payment had cleared the bank, the middle-aged couple, with four friends aboard, cast off from our dock and cruised slowly out into the river. They had been gone all of about 15 minutes when we heard an explosion that resulted in a sick, sputtering, choking sound; great clouds of black smoke poured out of the port exhausts. The proposed shakedown cruise ended prematurely! Their lawyer explained sadly that the contract was very clear, and whatever shape the Enterprise was in, it definitely belonged to this couple from California.

Since they could not run the boat another five feet without inflicting more severe damage, the Californians contracted with Del to have the port engine overhauled. Business by this time was on such shaky ground that NEMCO had to go to the bank and pay cash for all shipped parts before the bank would release them. NEMCO was currently equipped to fix marine engines like turtles are equipped to run service stations, so Del had to pay a real marine diesel outfit to remove and repair the blown engine, cash first: NEMCO's new business reputation had preceded it.

I got to take a look at the bearings, pistons, and connecting rods as well as the piston cylinders when the two men working on the engine had removed all the innards. The cranks were bent, the cylinders split, and the connecting rods mangled. Fourteen thousand dollars later, she was ready to set sail.

I often worked on the weekends, but neither Del nor any staff was there. They did leave me a Portland number where they could be reached in an emergency. On a Saturday morning at about 11 o'clock, upon entering the float, I noticed that something was missing. It was the Enterprise, and I noted that the NEMCO line, secured with a NEMCO lock, had been severed.

Universally, vessels held by another's lines (mechanic's lien) are legally bound to the dock if the dock's lines are doubled or locked. There are legal maritime laws for "arresting" any vessel having destroyed another's lines with the intention of taking "French Leave." Obviously the California couple took the "lines" into their own hands!

Finally I was able to get Del on the phone—who probably had just gotten out of bed—and I asked if he had released the boat and, more importantly, had he gotten paid. The tone of his voice told me that the answer was no on both counts. I asked if he wanted me to have the Coast Guard arrest the new owners for clearly violating the mechanic's lien law. He agreed, and I started the procedure. The Coast Guard called back as Del and Louis came through the door: the boat had been spotted passing Warrenton, Oregon and was now in international waters, out of Coast Guard jurisdiction.

NEMCO was forced to hire a lawyer and a Los Angeles process server, at the cost of $1700, to have the boat "arrested" at the LA dock and the owners served with impound papers. NEMCO lost all of its profits on this little deal and was chagrined to see their dentist neighbor sailing off in his new Buggotá, loaded with guests, waving and saluting as he went by.

I had locked off the area I rented from Del after the float owner had served Del with a failure-to-pay-rent eviction notice. One day later, when I came up the stairs, I found my lock smashed open and my west window scored where a crane had been temporarily installed over the shop area below. The crane had been used to lift heavy bins onto a 20 by 20 foot raft docked alongside the shop; Del and Louis were clearing out their space. I decided to stay in the upstairs apartment, to watch the building for the owner, concerning fire and security. I borrowed a shotgun from a friend, replaced my lock, and invited Del up to talk things over. During the discussion, I "accidentally" dropped four shotgun cartridges on the floor. He got the message: Do not mess with my space!

While I was watching from my window, Del and crew continued to load the entire contents of the shop onto the raft. I was sure that what they were doing was illegal, but I didn't call the owner—I couldn't help appreciating their sheer guts.

The last thing that had been carefully placed onto the raft was the small forklift that had been used to move all the rest of the equipment. I thought sure that heavy forklift would sink the whole mess, or at least flip it into the slough. The 20-by-20 foot raft originally had a high, so-called freeboard, with large logs supporting its planked base a foot above the water. There was now less than three inches of freeboard.

Some months earlier, my other great friend, Ed Leahey, had left his outboard motor boat at the dock, where it still remained though Ed himself was "in the wind." Now completely loaded, Louis passed a single towline to Del on Ed's boat and they putted out into the Columbia channel dragging the entire 15-ton workshop, machinery, and supply bins. In my many adventurous years I have seen many things, but none as weird, or as insane, as the view of the slowly retreating barge!

They made the trip to Camas, about 20 miles up river, and I didn't hear from them ever again. I assumed that by the time Ed's motor boat had hauled two people and the entire machine shop the three hour, four knot trip against a calm but twelve knot moving river, the engine on the little boat probably was in its death throes. "The little engine that could," after avoiding a river full of dangerous wakes from passing boats, threatening every few minutes to dump everything, including it and its crew, to the bottom of the Mighty Columbia River, must have just made the Camas dock.

After all of this, the owner of the former NEMCO float moved the entire structure down river to another location; I had to leave as well.

Ed Lehey and Mr. Moon

But during my stay at NEMCO, a disaster was brewing in the person of Ed Lehey and his Mr. Moon show. With additional pressure and expenses, I could see the mansion, and all the dreams tied to it, slip-sliding away. During the installing of my 7-foot sailing ship mural at the Portland Boat Show, I had had the occasion to meet Ed Lehey, a radio announcer for KVAN. He was interviewing several of the shows' exhibitors, and because of my deal with NEMCO and my supposed studio located at 535 Bridgeton Road, he interviewed me as well. When Ed Lehey gave me the microphone, he damn near had to wrestle me to get it back: I was giving him and anyone listening to the station most of my painting history.

I learned a week or so after the boat show that Lehey had been the lead designer/performer in a very famous early children's television series called "The Mister Moon Show." Ed Lehey was Mister Moon, and being a tall, handsomely-built man, needed only a non-transparent plastic moon mask, fitted like a helmet, to complete the transformation into his character. He told me that the show was being revived and that the Portland television station, KATU, was interested in putting it on. He needed an artist/engineer to do the sets and build the dog hand-puppet that was Mr. Moon's dear friend.

I took on both of these jobs. The NEMCO Wahl Galleries—as I had named my float space—was the perfect place to build the sets. I was very eager for the opportunity to break into television on the ground floor with a new show, but I should have realized that the moon is a constantly changing and fickle object that can be full one minute and appear to have completely disappeared the next; this symbolism was wasted on me at the time. I should have noted that other than the advertising copy, he seemed to have none of the original equipment, including the moon mask. But I was not looking for problems.

It was an exciting time, but soon it became apparent that Mr. Moon had little of his own money to put into the operation. This meant that

I had to buy all my own materials and equipment. There were many times when I was just about to give up, but, being an infernal optimist, I soldiered on. In the three months that we were preparing for the show, Sherry and I helped move Ed into three different apartments. Yeah, I know, that should have been some kind of signal, but … this whirlwind activity was energizing, and, as I am such an adrenaline driven individual, learning all the ins and outs of the television world was truly fascinating.

The main difficulty I had with the show was that I had never seen it on TV. Ed told me that in the early days, besides the studio staff, he had a partner named Art Morey. Art was the brother of Ben Morey, who was the producer of a nature show about a live bear called "Big Ben." This show, which was very popular, was one with which I was familiar. As I toiled away at my studio, constructing the metal and wood set for the show, as well as the lighting board, I simultaneously built a miniature layout of the complete set in cardboard. It looked very good. The general idea of the set was that it was the inside of a space ship, looking through great crystal-clear windshields. The sets, both actual and miniature, were constructed so that the hand puppets could be handled from the left and the right of an apparent console that would hide the operators.

We went to a film production business that gave us a quote of five thousand dollars to film the first episode; KATU would pay the cost. At this point Ed had contributed nothing but historical information about the early show and had given me some direction on the dog puppet that he had operated—a puppet he apparently lost along the way. His description was of a Jack Russell-type terrier that talked and had, as Ed described it, a "gravely voice and a smart ass attitude." A large sponge was my choice for working material; it could be formed easily into a head and attached jaw using only large scissors as my tool. I dipped the formed head into a small vat of wax that gave a shiny, but curly look to the "fur." An operator's hand inside the head, using levers and wire attachments, could open and shut the mouth, open and close the eyes, and a thumb control would shift the eyes from side to side. I was going to add another control to work the eyebrows, but Ed said that we were running out of time, and the studio wanted to see a working model … the miniature set would do.

On the appointed day, Ed and I took the model to KATU where we met the station manager; I got my first look at a professional TV studio. I was introduced to everyone there including the floor director and the camera crew. All were anxious to see how the set actually looked on the screen. The crew "dressed" the set with a neutral background, and Ed and I, sitting in the glassed-in control room, finally saw my set appear in glorious color on a dozen TV monitors. It was a heady moment; there were congratulations all around.

I was so involved in observing everything going on that I barely took note when Ed took his bosom friend, the dog puppet, shoved his hand into it, and walked in front of one of the indicated cameras to do his thing, introducing the show. Up to that time, Rocky—the dog's given name—was just a puppet to me. I liked his looks and made sure that he could perform all the operations I had built in, but he was not very real. Ed took care of that problem, for me and for everyone around.

Rocky poked his head up, his eyes snapped open, and his gravely voice leapt out on the multiple speakers as he was viewed in all his glory from close up, medium, and long range camera angles. Ed's voice for Rocky was every bit as smart-assed as Ed had first described, and some of the comments that came out of Rocky's mouth were hilarious but definitely not for prime time listening. The entire set was speechless. Ed was Rocky and Rocky was Ed. The studio crew roared with laughter, and everyone involved knew that they had a winner! There were handshakes all around, and Ed gave me an accolade that made up for all the artistic appreciation I had ever been denied! I walked on air for a week as I played that scene over and over again in my mind.

But, at first gradually, then faster, things started to cool down. The original station manager became gravely ill, and I was no longer able to get anywhere near the studio. Something was definitely wrong! I even had a hard time finding Ed. I was just about ready to give up totally when Ed suddenly appeared at my studio, acting like everything was just fine, and told me that we were going to see Art Morey, who had written the show with Ed and operated two of the hand puppets: Miss Kitty (a cat of course) and Cecil, the Sea Sick Serpent.

As we entered the KWJJ radio studios—whose stock in trade was cowboy music—I noted the startled looks that we were getting from the staff. These looks were something between disbelief and simmering hatred. But we went up upstairs—unchallenged—stopping at a large office area with a long writers' table in the middle and a pleasant middle-aged man behind a desk. The two greeted each another heartily, and Ed asked Art Morey if he still had his "old friends." Art smiled, a little wistfully I thought, reached into a drawer, and came out with the two hand puppets. Ed said, mock seriously, "Larry I would like you to meet Miss Kitty and Cecil."

What happened next was truly amazing. Ed took the Miss Kitty puppet, Art put his hand into Cecil, and the two of them took off on a routine that seemed as though it had just been written; it had a strange reality to it. There was an undercurrent of insane rage in the puppet conversations, as Miss Kitty and Cecil—with an occasional aside from Ed as Mr. Moon—carried on like a couple of madmen.

I'm a good audience and occasionally have heard the best of the best do their thing on the stage, but never in my life have I literally thought that I was going to die because I couldn't get my breath from my retching, hysterical laughter. I was on the floor, gasping for breath, as the two of them flayed away in this three-character charade: x-rated is a masterpiece of understatement. However, it was obvious that they had gotten together to plan this to bring me back into the stalled project. But, shortly after this, the whole thing came to a screeching halt, and Ed permanently disappeared.

Some time later, I was modeling for a life class, when I met a very attractive middle-aged woman in the class and offered to give her art lessons. It turned out that she was the former wife of the owner of KWJJ and had been seduced by Ed, almost under his boss' nose. Of course Ed had been fired. The day that he took me into the KWJJ studio, some ten years after he had been fired for "nailing" everyone from the script girl to the owner's wife, he had not set foot in that studio. Our meeting was the first time in ten years he had seen Morey. Ed was very, very good at being very, very bad.

I was back in the Rent-a-cop business and had been working, with Bill Ravelli, on an almost deserted dock in Portland where two Russian C-3 tankers had been tied up for months. Bill and I stood the midnight to morning watch. When our relief arrived, I was startled to see Charlie LaFranchise who had had a risqué show on midnight TV in which he did "blue" enjoinder dialogue with the original Elvira, until the parent vigilantes had driven the program off the air. Here he was in a private security cop's uniform—like mine. I was unkind enough to say to him,

"Wow, how the mighty have fallen!"

He stopped on the gangway and looked me over, saying, "Yeah, well, what have you been fired from to bring you here?"

I answered evenly, "We were doing a remake of the Mr. Moon Show."

"The hell you were!" LaFranchise bellowed with some heat.

I told him about Ed Lehey, and he snorted derisively, "Off of what turnip truck did that ass-hole get you?"

Charlie went on to explain that Ed had been married and, since he had screwed his way out of every announcing job he had ever held, his wife had no difficulty getting a divorce. In the settlement, she got complete ownership of the Mr. Moon Show. Ed's wife was in the process of working with Charlie when she had a heart attack and died. We then agreed that what had happened to me and everyone else involved with the Mr. Moon fiasco was that Ed set up the complete show—fiat accompli—and then was going to his wife whom he believed he could talk into taking him back to run the show. He had taken me for about several thousand dollars, "killed" the manager of KATU (had a heart attack), and skipped out of town ahead of the crash. Really neat guy!

I continue to wonder about an emerging a life pattern!

30 | Gramms' Restaurant

One of the health spas I belonged to while we lived at the Mansion was a meeting place for local businessmen. Among them was a quiet, small, and unimposing man named Frank Beck. I had never talked to him before, but one day he introduced himself and asked if I knew who had painted the mural on the side of the Volkswagen panel truck parked outside. Surprised, I admitted that I had painted it. He asked me if I had ever done anything larger, and I said, "Yes, I have painted 20 and 30 foot wall murals for a couple of bars."

He seemed only mildly interested, but then gave me his card, which introduced him as the owner of a large downtown hotel supply company. Mr. Beck suggested I get in touch with his head designer, Ed Hardesty, and that he would give Mr. Hardesty my name. I thought at the time how perfectly this marvelous opportunity had fallen into my hands, virtually by accident. Anyone who knows me is totally aware that I have never believed in accidents. In my mind, I am a child of the Universe, and that Universe wants the best for me so, one way or another, the Cosmos or God or whatever He, She, or They is (are) will guide me through life, always giving me what I need. The codicil is that She (my preference) will always give me what I need, although often that does not necessarily look like what I want or arrive when I want it!

Armed with the idea that the to-be-contacted designer knew of me—the owner having smoothed the road ahead—I dropped in unannounced to Atlas Hotel Supply and confidently informed the secretary that I was here to meet Ed Hardesty about the proposed wall mural to which Mr. Beck had referred. Ed came loping around the edge of a cubical and looked at me quizzically, as I confidently explained my meeting with the owner. Ed Hardesty just noted my smiling and youthful (40) year old face and proceeded to lay out the back-bar plans for the new Gramms' bakery and restaurant, just across the Columbia River in Vancouver. Having spent my early years in Vancouver, I knew exactly where this was: it was a prime location for such an ambitious project.

Mr. Hardesty told me what the restaurant owner had in mind was a mural to be placed behind the service bar. I almost swallowed my confidence when I looked at the preliminary plans and realized that the proposed wall mural was to be 20 feet long and 8 feet high and would have to go in place before the back-bar could be installed. I also learned that the time for completion would be three weeks. When I asked what kind of painting he had in mind, Hardesty was distinctly non-specific. "Well," he said confidently, "I thought I would leave that up to you."

I almost lost it, but managed to ask what country the owner was from, since in looking at the restaurant and the bakery décor, I had noticed a kind of Heidi motif. Ed answered that the owner's original home had been in a small village located in a valley surrounded by tall mountains, in Switzerland. I took a long speculative look at the floor layout for the bar area and the back-bar where my mural was to go. I knew I had to get out of there before I wet myself, so I cut to the chase, and allowed as how I would have to have seven hundred dollars for initial expenses up front and would, in a week, deliver a black and white sketch of the proposed painting. He got up and immediately came back with a contract and a signed check for that amount.

Mountains, of which I had previously only done impressions, raced through my mind. I took my check to the bank to cash before this nice man came to his senses and cancelled it. I was still pathologically terrorized of being cold, so I had few pictures of mountains in my head. My paintings generally fell into two categories: the very old in sailing ships and late teens to obvious antiquity for female nudes. My reference books, however, included hundreds of mountain landscapes. I poured over these and started to pick and choose from among multiple peaks from a dozen different countries. The 8-foot tall, 20-foot long proposed painting meant that there was 20 feet divided by 8 feet, or almost a 3 to 1 ratio, so only a continuous sheet of paper two foot wide and over six foot in length would do for a base sketch: enough for the necessary detail.

To date, my wall murals have been exactly that, "paintings on a wall," so I ended up doing the sketch on common butcher paper. I had neither the time nor the patience with such a short production schedule to "canvas" art supply houses. I had thought of what in the trade is called "seamless": large sheets of colored background paper, designed for photographic settings, but too flimsy for skillfully worked over sketching. The common off-white butcher-paper, however, would give me some leeway in difficult areas, but would not take too much messing around. Butcher-paper has a water proof layer between two white sheets used for wrapping meat, but it deteriorates with excessive erasing. Get careless and you would tear the rough surface and end up with an unacceptable shiny waterproof area. If I had done 90 percent of the drawing and this tearing occurred, I would have to start all over. Given the time constraints, this would be a calamity. If on canvas of the given size of 8 by 20 feet, I would have to have the canvas professionally stretched on stretcher bar at a price that would eat up any profit, so canvas was out. I had already bought several ½-inch sections of aluminum pipe and some joint connectors. Without needing to use a wall and complex fastenings, I could use 4 by 8 foot hardboard that, when the unfinished side was gessoed, would produce a surface—once it was painted—that would be indistinguishable from real canvas.

Previously I had used these panels, avoiding all the vicissitudes of real canvas, to paint 4 by 4 and 4 by 8 foot paintings for Portland's Charlie's Broiler. Charlie's, "in its glory days," was a former whorehouse—warehouse if you insist on a more palatable name—and had a third floor consisting of twenty small rooms containing only a bed and a sink. I painted some very large paintings on the spacious ground floor; however, the owners wanted me to paint in situ while customers were still in the restaurant. Even with the kitchen and bar on the main floor, the main seating area was seldom full, so I did not impose on any customers. On the contrary, they would often plan to sit in locations where they could watch me paint. I was able to sell paintings and explain my art in the very act of doing it. Was I, and am I, a performer? You bet. I loved it!

As it happened, I affected profits enough when I was there, that I was given master keys for the restaurant complex so that I could work through the night if necessary. In painting murals—or any painting—there are house-keeping, lay-out, and background fill-ins that take painting time but are not too difficult and can be done while the artist is still acting as a raconteur. Other parts of the paintings call for intense concentration, and for this reason I liked working in the building alone at night. I had to go to the basement to turn necessary lights on and off. In the basement store rooms I found all the switch box markers and tags, supposedly describing what they were connected to, but poorly describing their functions. On Sunday, when the restaurant was closed, I thought I might have turned off the kitchen freezer boxes, but I was not positive. Over a two hour period, I called the two emergency numbers listed in the office but never got an answer, so I just had to leave and hope for the best. When I came back on Monday, I was greeted by an irate owner who told me that I had turned off the freezer boxes: he had 240 pounds of thawed beef. "The keys were all clearly marked!" he yelled.

When I got the chance I explained that rather than losing 240 pounds of beef, they could have lost the entire building to a fire, which they would have learned about in the following day's news. The boss was still very angry, but when we went to the basement, and he looked at the switches, he saw that he had no idea where the switches that control the freezer boxes were located.

We rode out the storm, and I continued to work there, but it is interesting that sixteen of the large paintings I had done there simply disappeared as I worked through four changes in ownership. As for that fateful night, to show that there were no hard feelings, the cooks were told to take the 240 pounds of beef, along with potatoes and other ingredients, and make what was listed on the menu as "Larry's Stew." That is Chef Larry, if you please!

Meanwhile, back at the Mansion, I connected the pipe standards, supports, and hardware to construct a back support, standing a couple of inches off the floor, but adjustable with special fittings so the bottom edge could be anywhere from two inches to eight inches up. I strung this contraption the long way across the basement, starting near the outside (green) door and extending to the interior steps leading to the kitchen. The back support had a lot of give to it so that the 20-foot array could be bent as much as was necessary. But it was also arranged so that, with the painting sitting on the bottom clamps, the panels could be pressed close enough to each other, making it possible to paint them as a single contiguous screen.

I started with a pale blue sky in the background, but dark enough to provide a good contrast to the eight major mountain peaks. But, even though I was well along with the layout, the lights in the basement—even augmented with several floodlights—were insufficient, and the area was much too cold, so I moved the whole affair upstairs. There, the painting started in the cozy living room, stretched across the entrance of the wide staircase, and ended partially into the formal dining room. It was, fortunately, a dining room in area, not in furnishings or use.

When I took the completed butcher-paper sketch to Hardesty, it was received with applause from the staff, although I had expected Mr. Beck to also make his appearance, but such was not the case. I gave Hardesty Polaroid photographs of the sections that I had completed. Both he and I were satisfied by the transitional hills that came out towards the viewer along the gently sloping valley. There, about in the middle of the painting, was a tiny village almost lost in the faint mist that surrounded it. This village was born of necessity: in the middle of the "canvas" was a manufacturing defect. Working in broad strokes, I had missed the defect, but if it were an actual canvas, it would represent an aberration in the weave. The center of the picture is the last thing the eye is drawn to; therefore, it is critical that the visual representation be homogenous with the distances it was supposed to signify. A good engineering friend once gave me the quote, "If you can't fix it, feature it … " The subtle but obvious glob became a picturesque village halfway between mountains and foreground. The point of view of the entire painting was from another set of mountains, inferred by the foreground to be much lower than the distant mountains, yet still three or four thousand feet from those in the background.

A week before it was to be delivered, I took Polaroids of this final stage. I was surprised when Hardesty asked me if it would be possible to put two more panels together at the edges of the completed painting, lapping over two feet at each end making it a full 24-foot painting. In effect, these were to be two more completed paintings added to the one contracted for. For once in my life, I acted like a true entrepreneur and told Hardesty I could do that but it would cost him a lot extra. I hoped the hell he would choke on the extra price, but he didn't. Having signed up for the job, I now had to figure out how to do it. The two 4 by 8 foot panels would have to fit in with the general form and style of the much larger master, but they would also have to be appropriate. There was less call for subtle touches in the left panel, which I decided to make very close for contrast to the faint, beautifully rendered village in the valley: a jut of land with a small thatched hut, drawn from about 30 visual feet away, with trees and foliage blending into the main painting—all easy to paint. I finished this panel and was satisfied that it fit in with the master. Then I saw an opportunity for contrasting the near view of the hut on the left with a visual effect on the right panel that would be the opposite in every way: in distance, in structure, in hue, in mechanics.

I drew several quick sketches and folded them over the butcher paper original, deciding on an area of sharp middle-distance crags, falling away and partially blocking the far distant valley on the right of the master painting. Now, however there was an obvious imbalance in the perceived mass between the left and the right sides. There had to be some huge structure, with supporting terrain, at a distance to balance the eye with the close-in thatched hut of the left. This object could be much smaller in comparison to the size of the latter (the hut), but it had to indicate an equivalent visual mass.

I thought that at the last minute, I was going to screw up the whole production. I felt flop-sweat and spent two days and nights thinking of nothing but that additional right panel; it was the only time in the process that I felt totally out of control. Finally I began to think in social terms: if Heidi lived in a thatched hut, what would be the opposite in social, economic, spiritual, and human terms? Then came the Epiphany! There had to be a filthy rich and utterly ruthless developer to build, on the right panel's craggy and presumably rock solid surfaces. . . what else . . . an enormous gambling casino, hotel, and spa. It would be ten virtual miles away from the hut, but a million miles from Heidi. That right panel clutched the granite foundations, blasted out of the crags, providing the best in living, entertaining, and gaming for the wealthy of a hundred different countries. This multi-storied monstrosity assumed it was put there by the gods and secured by heavy steel beams cantilevered over the rocks below. It was totally ridiculous in its petulant and overbearing claim to this pristine scenery, but was perfect in its insouciance for its casual but overwhelming comments on human greed.

Inevitably the day came when all of the components were placed in Hardesty's company truck. I followed in the Volkswagen. I was—as I had been from the beginning of the project—in a kind of single-minded stupor, so much so that I even forgot to take a picture of the completed painting. At its final destination, Gramms' Restaurant and Bakery, the whole painting was assembled a foot from the wall dividing the bar from the restaurant; not even the facade of fake wall with large glass windows was yet in place. The bar itself was pulled several feet from that wall, with its plush seats attached.

When I had finished putting everything together, and the entire 24 foot painting stood out in all its glory, I finally walked back to the disconnected bar and sat down beside Ed Hardesty. I noticed that he was sweating, and while I realized that I should have been the one sweating, Ed let me in on the reason that the time for the painting had been so constricted. As we sat drinking coffee from the kitchen, served by one of the staff still in the throes of completing all of the kitchen equipment installation, I heard the story of how three weeks into the construction, the Catholic Church had halted the work while they tried to get a stop order from the city, complaining that the bar was too close to the church … six blocks away! Unknown to me, the construction had been halted for over a week before Gramms was allowed to finish the job. Only now did I realize why things had been so tight and why Ed had looked as though he had aged a couple of years in the interim. I remember Ed had had this kind of sick smile on his face as though he had just missed being hit by lightning, but strangely he was still acting as if he were terrified. We sat there quietly, just waiting for something—I wasn't sure what—when a small, older, mustached man in white shirt, white pants, an apron, and work shoes dusted with flour came into the unfinished bar.

I took this fellow to be the dishwasher, obviously helping out setting up the kitchen. But, he took a seat on the other side of Ed and spent the next several minutes, without a sound, observing the painting from top to bottom and side to side. Ed's face looked, if anything, even greener than it had minutes before.

As the short-statured, middle-aged individual sat there, he finally started to talk, but it was apparent after a few seconds that he was not talking to Ed. Since we had not been introduced, I had the intense realization that he neither knew nor cared who the hell I was. At first his voice was barely audible above the noise of hammers and saws, but gradually the noise got less intense, and the "dishwasher's" voice got louder and more certain. "Yeah," he exclaimed, as he reeled off a series of names, "Dat's Mount 'bla' and dat's 'bla-bla', and der's Mount 'bla', and der is da far valley … "

I was a little dim at the time, but even I recognized—as the little man beamed absent-mindedly at Ed, who still looked ready to collapse, and got up and returned to his kitchen—that this was the owner, Mr. Gramms, and that both Ed and I had passed the test!

Of all the paintings I had done, it was the most complex and demanding. The process had been miraculously smooth, like a movie script, and it had all started at the spa when the owner of Atlas Hotel Supply had casually contacted me and set up everything that followed (or so I thought). Since I had been painting night and day, I had not gone to the spa for several weeks, but on a later visit, I again met Mr. Beck, who didn't seem to recognize me until I reintroduced myself. He looked at me for a second or two and started to leave. Then he stopped for a moment, looked at me tentatively, and asked, "By the way, did you and Hardesty ever get together?"

Full stop. Fade to black.

31 | Albina and the Summer of 1967

One of the more difficult things about living in the Mansion was that, originally, I deliberately had chosen it because of its location. I had, in line with my pro-minority stance, taken a position on the Model Cities Advisory Board in Portland; the Albina District had been chosen for the Model Cities Program. It was a mostly black neighborhood extending through parts of north and northeast Portland, across the Willamette River from downtown.

Our house was on the outskirts—N.E. 13th and Schuyler—but still considered a part of the Albina. Things had been in turmoil for months, and the situation was getting more and more out of hand as the summer of 1967 approached. The location for the Model Cities' office was further along the northeastern frontier of Albina; the "heat" was very definitely being felt there.

The fact that many of us on the Advisory Board were white produced tensions and rifts within the board itself, and being advisory only, we were a group without teeth to match our opinions. As the season advanced, marches, attacks, beatings, and fear increased in an ever-ascending crescendo. The Black Panthers had cars full of its members answering police calls heard over their scanners. They usually just stood by at the event location and kept an eye on the police. They were witnesses to the amount of police action and were always on the lookout for brutality.

There was good reason for their monitoring. When I had worked for AAA Ambulance and tuned into the police broadcasts, I was accustomed, early on the morning shift, to hear the informal "on duty" call of the district police car officer. This well-known bigot would call out in a thick parody of a Southern black voice … "UMGOWA." His call-out told anyone listening just exactly what he thought of any Albina resident. To this idiot, all citizens of the district were little removed from the native tribes living in deepest Africa; implicit was the concept that the whole place and all the people in it were somehow less than human. It was a dangerous and despicable joke to anyone expecting police even-handedness. After a while, there were slogans from the hard-core black organizations, including the slogan "burn baby burn" that was echoed by a large number of house fires, centering on white families living in Albina, but black families were victimized as well.

I took the threats seriously enough to water down the sides of our home each night. Rocks were thrown, neighboring windows broken, and unsolicited catcalls of "Honky" were leveled at us. I tried to engage the person or persons shouting at me, explaining that I was on their side and was a member of the Model Cities' Program that was working for their benefit. This seldom worked.

Years before, coming off a ship in Oakland, California, I found myself in the middle of a general strike being held in the downtown area: it was a sensationally electric experience. All the stores were closed and, if possible, shuttered. Thousands of angry people milled about in the streets, where driving a car was neither possible nor sensible; you had to try to make your way to your destination on foot. It was clear that you really should not be on the street for any reason. The people around you were like kegs of gun-powder: something you might say or do could be all that would be necessary to turn a mix of strangers into a mindless but single-goaled mob looking for somewhere to explode into vicious, incendiary, and violent action.

This was our city when we lived in The Mansion. We were located only a block off Broadway, and about three blocks from the Lloyd Center shopping mall, which was also under siege; it had its own daily criminal incidents. The police were out-numbered, fearful, and trigger-tempered. Thus, into this situation, for no discernable reason I could figure out, came the U. S. Navy submarine, Archerfish. It was anchored off First Street in the Willamette River and docked there for a week.

When Sherry was eight months pregnant, she had made an appointment with our loan company; however, she was unable to keep it on the appointed day. On that day, a single gunman came into the loan office with a loaded revolver to steal whatever was available. In the process, he shot and severely wounded the female manager, in the abdomen. The time of the robbery and the time of Sherry's missed appointment coincided.

I was on high alert as a consequence of the gathering tension and stayed close to home. The exception being that, when I went to the local bar—on the backside of our property—I took to wearing my 32-caliber revolver on my hip. I would usually have the company of at least two police officers, and there was always a car with three or more Black Panthers parked in front. Because of my security training, primarily at Westinghouse and North American, as well as stints as a special "rent-a cop," (and don't forget the CIA!) I was adamant about locking up anything for which I had responsibility. Sherry's take on these conditions was more than a little "loosey-goosey," surprising after the wounding of the loan officer. "That didn't have anything to do with me. I was smart enough to not be there" was her attitude.

On Aug 25, sometime after midnight, I had checked the front door before I went up to our bedroom. At the back of our kitchen was an adjoining porch with seven steps leading down to the street. Four of the seven steps were made of wood, like the porch itself; the other three were concrete. The only doors left to be checked were the door connecting the kitchen to the porch and the porch door itself. The porch door was a joke, but the kitchen lock was a heavy Schlage. Sherry continued puttering around in the kitchen: she was very hyperactive in this, the end of her ninth month. She could run me out energy without trying. Finally, she came upstairs and put on a robe and stated getting ready for bed.

I was still fully dressed when Sherry told me that Eric had called out, saying someone was outside, messing with the grape bushes. I grabbed the fully loaded 32 and proceeded downstairs, turning the lights off. It was now about 2 A.M. and the bar had just closed; I definitely heard someone on the back porch. I slipped out the front door, down the 15 steps, and quietly strode around the corner to the concrete porch steps. It was a new moon night and the local streetlight was out, but I could clearly see a black sedan loaded with four blacks, parked next to the curb directly behind me. I stared into the darkened porch. The porch door was open; I could see vague movement in the depths. The first thought that went through my mind was that there were four blacks looking at a white man with a gun at 2 A.M.: "I din't wanna hear no car doors clicking open!" So I saved my entire attention for the nut on the porch. I presumed he was a drunk from the bar so I challenged him. Even with a gun leveled at him, he came through the door in a very relaxed manner—way too relaxed! I ordered him to stop, asked who he was, and what he was doing. He appeared to be a white man with sandy-colored hair and seemed to be thinking about walking down the steps, nonchalantly. I fired a shot into the wooden step he was about to take. He looked at me with mock surprise and sat down on the step I had just ventilated. Just then, I heard Sherry call from the 2nd floor sun porch, "Are you all right, Larry?"

I immediately hollered back, "Call the police—tell them robbery in progress—and I've got the idiot at gunpoint."

I was still somewhat concerned about the four Black Panthers getting accidentally involved, but I thought they probably just saw one "honky" thinking about shooting another. As it turned out, they would just observe until the police got there. Police calls from Albina were not usually top priority, so the situation was not going to change for some time. I repeatedly ordered the "burglar" to identify himself, but he just sat there, silent, with an ironic smile on his face. Finally he said, "Fuck this shit!" got to his feet and started towards me.

By this time, I could see nothing resembling fear in his eyes and his swaggering ease told me he wasn't remotely close to being frightened … or drunk! I backed away because I realized that if he got within six feet, he could disarm me. By this time, he had cleared the steps, was on the sidewalk walking away from me. I hollered out the simple word, "Halt!" but he continued on. I fired a second shot at his feet; I had no intention of him ever reaching Broadway. The shot kicked up a flash just in front of his feet, missing both legs, but my intention was clear.

I said, "Unless you want to be thoroughly ventilated, come back and sit on the steps … now!"

He strolled back, climbed the stairs, sat in his original position, still smiling, and noted, "Shit Man, you missed me."

Now I was furious. I knew I was dealing with a trained combatant who somehow knew exactly who I was, but I wanted to make it perfectly clear that I was serious. I said, with clenched teeth, "You want to bet that at this range I'm going to miss you with the next four shots?"

He immediately corrected me, "You mean five."

The 32 looks like a 38 that holds six rounds. At a distance in the dark, he recognized the gun as a 32 holding seven rounds—not your average burglar! Completely out of patience, I growled, "Listen, asshole, I know you are something special and you've got me scared. If you as much as twitch, I'm going to drill you front and dead-fucking center!"

I sincerely hoped he believed me. This was the second time Sherry had been in potential danger—not to mention my curious son in the 2nd floor bedroom—my house was under siege, and four unpredictable Black Panthers were idling at the curb. Then a Portland Police car arrived, took in the scene, and parked directly in front of the Black Panthers. Pretty gutsy, I thought. A white sergeant and a patrolman stepped out; the patrolman took charge of the prisoner and marched him to the back of the car, while the sergeant and I checked the complete house with weapons drawn. Sherry was sure there was a second intruder still outside in the grape vines, but we didn't find one. The sergeant took our name and address, took a few notes, and left. The Black Panthers sat there for another 10 minutes, presumably waiting to see if anything else was going to happen, then drove off.

I had listened carefully, but I never heard the police give my intruder the customary, but new, Miranda law. (When I asked Sherry, while we were writing this, what had gone through her mind during this siege, she drew a complete blank. She noted that in the past, she hasn't seemed to perceive fear—just anger. Though she did remember that she went into labor the next day.) I do know we sat at the kitchen table and drank several cups of coffee. After this, I went out on the "prowled" porch and looked around and, to my surprise, I found a cigarette lighter decorated with the logo of the Archerfish submarine. It sure as hell hadn't been there before tonight.

I called the police station and asked when I should come down to press charges. I was told that the sergeant would come back to talk to me. I had, by this time, smelled a great load of spoiled fish! Sure enough, a half hour later, the same sergeant stopped by; I met him on the front porch. Before he could say anything, I asked, "What did you do with the sailor?"

He gave me a shocked look and answered, "Oh, we're taking care of him."

I accepted that no further action was expected of me—obviously I didn't admit to having found the lighter (which I have to this day!)—all the while being convinced, down to the bone, that "the asshole" was back on his ship—the Archerfish—having a good laugh … but he had failed to complete his assignment!

I now believed I was finally free of the CIA, and because of the Gramms' Restaurant painting, my art career would continue to flourish. Then, along came new daughter, Jill … and The Mansion would soon be a dream in the past. But, unbeknownst to me at this time, this was to be a major life transition: a new beginning for all of us.

To be continued …

Larry 1967

Epilogue to Part II

By Sharon Wahl

This book and the previous book of the Vallian Trilogy, Part I: The Engineer, has covered only the first half of the life of Larry E. Wahl, and while it gives the foundation for the person he is to become, it only lightly touches on the artist and not at all on the inventor. We have seen more of the engineer, which he seemed to have started being very early in life, and the beginnings of the designer and artist. The title of this epistle is The Vallian Trilogy: An Inventive Life, and when he started writing the autobiography back in the 70s, he fully intended to get right into his alter ego, Lewis X. Vallian, inventor and geometer. But, instead of just a preamble of him as inventor and a platform from which to launch his new geometry, it became a rare opportunity to revisit his past and put to rest many painful memories—this is what a good life review should do. Right now, at 84 years old, Larry has begun to like himself a little, to shed the self-hatred he has carried inside for way too many years.

When I asked Larry to write about his studios and the wonderful artwork he did from the 1950's on, he indicated that he would do that in the 3rd book. Now some of you readers may be flinching—already 84 years old and he will be doing another book? Yes, and probably several more if his editor can keep up. But, while the first two books have been a catharsis and, in straightforward terms, an explanation (he offers no excuses) for the life he lived for his first 40+ years, the third book will discuss the joys of his life: his art, his geometry (yes, math teacher Sister Ursula is turning in her grave), his patent work, and, amazingly, his 50+year 4th marriage. It will go a long way to give credence to all of the jobs and experiences he had by which he learned his trades.

After writing the Chapter on Ron Spear (and again after re-reading the 535 Bridgeton Road and Mr. Moon debacles), Larry abruptly came to the realization—and it was a distressing one—that he had a pattern of picking employers or partners who would mistreat him and/or betray him. But as we together explored this insight, it came out that if he stayed on a job very long, his skill and exceptional learning ability would launch him into administration, if he wanted the position—which he never did. So, at some level, he picked jobs where he could learn a discipline or field of endeavor—he tried the formal college education route only one time and it was a disaster—and bosses who were so threatened by his native abilities that they had to either demean him or dump him. But he got what he wanted: he was educated in most of the fields he needed to know to be where he is now—and he is still learning.

And what of the CIA experiences? I believe, and he concurs, that killing under the auspices of the United States flag—even if it did drag a little—gave vent to the rage that built up from his earliest childhood. Because he is, at the core, a basically good human (yes, he does argue about that, but I out-vote him every time!), he did not succumb to the horrors and destroyed life that he observed about fellow "agents." My point is that he is here, he is contributing by means of his geometry, art, and writing, and I am a vastly better person than I would have been without him.

And so, to conclude Part II of this Vallian Trilogy, the following will be an introduction to subsequent books. I wrote it originally just to provide "talking points" for Larry as he discussed his Vallian Coordinates with possible investors, to give him a time line to follow—you already know he thinks holistically and circularly, not linearly! This will also provide a basic outline for Book III, aptly titled, *The Zen Connection*. An elaboration of the outline was published in a monograph by the same name in 2010.

Talking Points: The Larry Wahl & V-GHOST Timeline

*   ~ 1930: Observed toy fish tank and identified difference between geometry of flat and 3-dimensional objects
*   ~ 1933: Observed the building of bridges on Oregon coast
*   ~ 1943: Sat on the bluff at Columbia Prep in Portland, OR and spent many hours watching the building of ships at the St. Johns shipyard (additional data in Part I of autobiography)
*   1951–1953: Westinghouse Electric—learning about various aspects of tools and geometric processes

- 1953–1955: North American Aviation—learning about and working with airplane design

- 1955–1956: Allied Arts—designer and stagecraft

- 1956–1957: Developing window displays using geometric designs with Ron Spear

- 1959–1960: Studio on N. W. 23rd Avenue--Commercial art and wall murals. Started Bau Haus Design

- 1960–1967: Studios at home and NEMCO River Gallery in Portland: Murals, design (Mr. Moon Show), working with geometric projects.

- 1968–1972: Rose City Art Center Bau Haus at 4010 N. E. Hancock in Portland: taught art/enginering classes and began work with cubes (1970) and spheres; developed the Ellipsesease. (RCAC Bau Haus incorporated in 1972)

- 1973–1980: Studio in Tigard, OR. Incorporated Unit One (1973) and worked on the production and marketing of Ellipsesease, and formalized cubic/spherical geometry as Vallian Coordinates.

- 1974: Developed and filed a Disclosure Document (DDA) re: the Ellipsesease with the patent office in July that was accepted in August after an intense telephone discussion with patent agent (changed patent law!)

- 1974–1978: Filed Ellipsesease Patent (pro se) in Sept 1974 and answered patent office objections while continuing to work on viable prototype. In Jan 1978, met with Bob Newton at Floating Point Corporation, and although this company did not do what was needed for the Ellipsesease, a tour of the premises provided a prophetic look at what Vallian would be involved with in the future. Abandoned ellipse patent in 1978 due to inability to continue to fund the project to build prototypes.

- 1975: Began work for Lawrence Security at the Ben Franklin Plaza in downtown Portland, protecting a new building as it was being built—analyzed the mechanical, electrical, structural, and security processes of this building in situ.

- 1975–1976: Taught engineering art and design at Oregon Polytechnic Institute in downtown Portland (CETA II program); given studio space to work on a variety of commercial design projects with Bill Stanley; as well as developing the cubisphere (Vallian Coordinates).

- 1978: Attended a Radio Shack Computer demo and workshop; heard Steve Jobs was a speaking against TRS-80.

- 1980: Moved to Menlo Park, CA. Worked with Gordon French (of Homebrew Club fame, Palo Alto, CA) learning computer graphics and writing a novel. Also worked on development of Vallian Coordinates.

- 1981: Established studio in home to write and work on the coordinates; did math and basic programming on a hand-held calculator/computer.

- 1981 June 1: Called Apple Computer Corporation to inquire about grants and to discuss his project

- 1981 June 29: Letter to M. Williams, V. P. Apple Computer, Inc. offering the company the rights to the Vallian System in exchange for equipment and help in programming the graphics application-no response.

- 1981 July 28: Letter to Steven Jops (sic) after being unable to make an appointment or have a telephone conference with Mr. Williams.

- 1981 August 10: Received phone call from Rod Holt of Apple Corp and Stanford University, discussed system for 20 minutes followed by Mr. Holt's comment; "How would you feel about my name being on it?" End of discussion!

- 1981 September 17: Received a rejection note from Tandy Corp (TRS) saying that the Vallian Coordinates were a hoax and refusing any involvement in the project. Original contact had been made by phone on June 21.

- 1981–1987: Throughout these years, continued to work on the coordinates in addition to writing science fiction novel IAMOT

- 1982 May: Purchased a CRTR Basic computer—the Osborn

- 1982 June: Hospitalized 9 days for removal of a gangrenous gallbladder and sepsis

- 1982 Sept: New studio born and named Lewis X. Vallian Associates—at 425 Cambridge in Palo Alto, CA.

- 1983 Feb to April: Hospitalized 4 times for coronary artery bypass grafts (CABG), dehydration and cardiac tamponade, venous clots and pulmonary emboli, and repair of sternal sutures.

- 1983 April: Bought TRS 80-12 computer and back to studio learning new computer and working on books and coordinates.

- 1984: Designed a prototype computer program in basic using hand-held computer

- 1985 October 15: Incorporated TOBI, Inc. (Transfer Operations by Image) to hold the copyrighted material from the Vallian Coordinates and the completed book, IAMOT.

- 1985 October 16: A fire destroyed a room in home at 1301 Mills St #4 Menlo Park and "killed" Osborn computer.

- 1985 November: First Apple Macintosh Classic Computer purchased and taken to Cambridge office; TRS 80-12 to wife's home office. From then on all computers purchased were upgrades of the original Macintosh (i.e., SE series, LC, iMac, MacBooks (laptops), MacBookPros)

- 1986 February: Hired Aldo Test patent attorney of Flehr, Hohbach, Test, Albritton, & Herbert, San Francisco. Paid $250 retainer to write patent for Vallian Coordinates. Explained concept to Ray, an associate, and another attorney who came down from SF

- 1987–1990: Due to a number of family emergencies, school (wife, Ed.D), and teaching trip to China in 1987, the coordinates were set aside temporarily but work on IAMOT and autobiography continued. While in China, had the unique opportunity to observe and question the architecture, building, engineering, sanitation, and business practices of the Mainland Chinese.

- 1990 January: Aldo Test stopped work on Vallian patent, too complex; indicated L would have to write his own. Picked up all of materials. Letter of explanation to associate Ray.

- 1990 September: Invitational meeting with Larry Smith and Jeff Hedrick re: development and patenting of Vallian Coordinates—letter of tentative agreement signed

- 1990 October: Dissolution of agreement with Smith & Hedrick due to irreconcilable differences

- 1990 November 20: Disclosure Document for Vallian Coordinate System filed with patent office

- 1991 January 7: Letter and package of Vallian material (1990 DDA) sent to Steve Jobs at Next, Inc. Returned unopened.

- 1991 September 16: Patent Application #7760513 Vallian Cubisphere System filed; extension filed 1992; withdrawn 4/4/1994 (too broad)

- 1991 December: Tentative agreement with Richard Tucker to work on programming of VCS

- 1992–1996: Richard Tucker does work-for-hire developing code for the graphics portion of the VCS

- 1992 January 6: Contract signed between Larry and Richard Tucker as work for hire

- 1992 January 23: Meeting of interested parties re: Vallian Cubisphere. Present were Larry and Sharon Wahl, Richard Tucker, George Cole, Naman Nichols, Eric Sonjeck

- 1992 January–August: Formal meetings continued—minutes available.

- 1992 August 11: Agreement signed by Richard, George, Larry, and Sharon

- 1992 September: Hospitalized for 2nd CABG

- 1992 December 29: Will written and signed/notarized giving Vallian Cubisphere System and rights to patent application to Richard tucker and George Cole should Sharon Wahl predecease Larry—replaced 2010.

- 1992 December–February 1993: Teaching trip to Guam and Saipan

- 1993 May 13: George Cole withdraws from VCS project

- 1993 July 13: Consultant's Work Agreement signed by Richard and Larry

- 1993 August 13: Letter to George Cole discussing the need for an "obvious, derivative, proven relationship between the code and the patent" and refusing to give release to George of materials, since he recused himself in May.

- 1993 December 13: Vallian Proposed Organization document by Richard Tucker

- 1993: Program Applications and Drivers Developed from the Vallian Cubisphere System patent document

- 1994 September 16 thru 26: Intense discussion with Richard Tucker regarding Vallian theory and Richard's contribution to the project

- 1994 October 7: Long discussion with Richard about latest version of Source Code (E)-- discussed necessary changes.

- 1994 October 7: Reviewed Mary Garman's resume with Richard; discussed her involvement with new start-up Ray Dream, Inc.

- 1994 October 27: Meeting at Borrones 1130 to 1300 with Hal Huntley, SRI Senior Systems Administrator; Dr. Julia Olkin, SRI mathematician, and Richard Tucker. Richard took over the meeting—gave impression he wrote the patent (see LW notes)

- 1994 November: Thank you letter to Hal Huntley and Dr. Olkin at SRI.

- 1994 November: Meeting with one of Richard's retired professor—nice but not his area of expertise (not interested) Dr. Royden, Stanford Professor Emeritus

- 1994 December: A 2nd meeting at Borrones with Hal Huntley and Julia Olkin, assigned by Huntley as intermediary. Shortly thereafter, Dr. Olkin got sick and then went on vacation.

- 1994 December 20: Package sent to Apple Corporation—signed for but never returned. Subsequent phone calls never found the same person twice

- 1995 January 8: At SRI with Dr. Oilken—no show. Met sometime after that at her office for 10 minutes; she indicated she was not interested.

- 1995–1996: Many conversation with people at Printer's Inc Café, e.g. Richard Walker of HP who toured the plant with Larry; Michael Nolan who brought a cover of the Ray Dream Program that stated "No floating-point needed" and use of triples, two main concepts of the Vallian system.

- Most of 1995: Continued working with Richard Tucker on Vallian code.

- 1996 February: Disclosure Document for VCS filed with patent office

- 1996 June: Richard resigned, stating that a patent was never going to be filed

- 1996 October 18: Code for VCS copyrighted as Vallian Virtual Articulated Super Tesseract

- 1997 April 30: Filed patent, Vallian Geometric Hexagon Opting Symbolic Tesseract

- 1996–to present: Continued to look for a reliable programmer

- 1998 May: Meeting with potential programmer Paul Clifford (recommended by Larry Smith) –not his area of expertise

- 1999 November 11: Patent # 5982374 granted; 3 maintenance fees paid since

- 1999: Copies of patent delivered to Aldo Test and Richard Tucker—"don't sell what you don't own."

- 2000–2003: Worked with Steffen Weber to program code for graphics and encryption application

- 2003–2005: Developed spherical coordinates contained in 1991 patent

- 2005 June 26: Filed Provisional Patent application for Vallian Spherical Tesseract (no more DDA!)

- 2005: Reopened negotiations with Larry Smith to assign patent—no agreement reached

- 2005: Continued writing autobiography—in edit 2008

- 2005–2009: Continued working on proof for new geometry

- 2006 May 22: Filed Pro se Application #11438781 Wahl Holographic Integrated Spherical Tesseract. Abandoned in 2008 after first patent office action due to possible conflict with granted V-GHOST patent

- 2007: Met with Chip Pertel and Dave Sederquist re: resources and programmers for V-GHOST. No agreements reached after several meetings.

- 2008–2009: Worked with programmer Manuel Gomez teaching him Vallian theory—he returned to Mexico in early 2009

- 2008 August: Article Elephant in the Room sent to Discovery Magazine UK—never received a response

- 2008: Set up Corporation, Lewis X. Vallian Associates, Inc. for Coordinate System and writing

- 2007–2009: Set up web pages: tesseraction.bz and wahl-y-ball.com for Vallian information and autobiography writing

- 2009 March: Letter and Elephant in the Room sent to Microsoft Research and Development Department—no response

- 2009: Conference with Tony Hodges re: need for programmers to convert original code to useable program—had met Tony several years previously at Borrones. No agreement reached after numerous meetings.
- 2009 April: Follow-up letter to Microsoft R & D--no response
- 2009 August: Conference with Newell Wagner re: Vallian Theory
- 2009: Continue writing and editing autobiography
- 2009 August: Writing Vallian History and Vallian theory for net and to be sent to Microsoft Macintosh Lab
- 2010 September: Conference with A. Newell Wagner re: Assignment of the Patent to Mr. Wagner
- 2010 October: Legal documents drawn up by Attorney Chilton Lee to assign patent to A. Newell Wagner but excluding future geometric work as may be performed by Larry.
- 2011: "Elephant in the Room" and "The History of the Vallian Coordinates" published and assigned an ISBN number

That's all folks!

Autobiography in Five Short Chapters

By Anonymous

I

I walk down the street.
There is a deep hole in the sidewalk.
> I fall in.
> I am lost ... I am helpless
>> It isn't my fault.
> It takes forever to find a way out.

II

I walk down the same street.
There is a deep hole in the sidewalk.
> I pretend I don't see it.
> I fall in again.
I can't believe I am in this same place.
>> But it isn't my fault.
It still takes a long time to get out.

III

I walk down the same street.
There is a deep hole in the sidewalk
> I see it is there.
> I still fall in ... it's a habit ... but,
>> My eyes are open.
> I know where I am.
It is my fault.
I get out immediately.

IV

I walk down the same street.
There is a deep hole in the sidewalk.
> I walk around it.

V

I walk down another street.

References

Front Matter

- Kurtz, E. and K. Ketcham (1992). The spirituality of imperfection. New York: Bantam Books.

Chapter 2

- Loomis, A. (1944). Figure drawing for all it's worth. New York: The Viking Press.

Chapter 3

- The 315th Bomb Wing Timeline: *http://www.315bw.org/timeline.html*

Chapter 12

- King, A. (1958). Mine enemy grows older. New York: Signet Books.
- King, A. (1959) . May this house be safe from tigers. New York: Signet Books.

Chapter 22

- Kübler-Ross, E. and D. Kessler (2007). On grief and grieving: Finding the meaning of grief through the five stages of loss. New York: Scribner.

Chapter 25

- Gardner, H. (1983). Frames of mind: The theory of multiple intelligences. New York: Basic Books.
- Ratey, J and C. Johnson (1997). Shadow syndromes. New York: Pantheon Books. pp. 214-78.
- Wahl, E. (1988, 2011). We're no angels; A Cartesian repentance of sorts?

Chapter 28

- Gibran, K. (1958). The prophet. New York: Knopf.

Back Matter

- Anonymous, Cited in Hollis, J. (1993). *The Middle Passage: From Misery to Meaning in Midlife.* Toronto, Canada: Inner City Books.

www.ingramcontent.com/pod-product-compliance
Lightning Source LLC
Chambersburg PA
CBHW060237100426
42742CB00011B/1556